Student Learning

Outcomes Assessment in

College Foreign

Language Programs

NFLRC Monographs is a refereed series sponsored by the National Foreign Language Resource Center at the University of Hawai'i, which presents the findings of recent work in applied linguistics that is of relevance to language teaching and learning, with a focus on the less commonly-taught languages of Asia and the Pacific.

Cultura-inspired intercultutral exchanges: Focus on Asian and Pacific languages
Dorothy M. Chun, (Editor), 2014
ISBN 978-0-9835816-7-3

Noticing and second language acquisition: Studies in honor of Richard Schmidt
Joara Martin Bergsleithner, Sylvia Nagem Frota, & Jim Kei Yoshioka, (Editors), 2013
ISBN 978-0-9835816-6-6

Practical assessment tools for college Japanese
Kimi Kondo-Brown, James Dean Brown, & Waka Tominaga (Editors), 2013
ISBN 978-0-9835816-5-9

New perspectives on Japanese language learning, linguistics, and culture
Kimi Kondo-Brown, Yoshiko Saito-Abbott, Shingo Satsutani, Michio Tsutsui, & Ann Wehmeyer (Editors), 2013
ISBN 978-0-9835816-3-5

Developing, using, and analyzing rubrics in language assessment with case studies in Asian and Pacific languages
James Dean Brown (Editor), 2012
ISBN 978-0-9835816-1-1

Research among learners of Chinese as a foreign language
Michael E. Everson & Helen H. Shen (Editors), 2010
ISBN 978-0-9800459-4-9

Toward useful program evaluation in college foreign language education
John M. Norris, John McE. Davis, Castle Sinicrope, & Yukiko Watanabe (Editors), 2009
ISBN 978-0-9800459-3-2

Second language teaching and learning in the Net Generation
Raquel Oxford & Jeffrey Oxford (Editors), 2009
ISBN 978-0-9800459-2-5

Case studies in foreign language placement: Practices and possibilities
Thom Hudson & Martyn Clark (Editors), 2008
ISBN 978-0-9800459-0-1

Chinese as a heritage language: Fostering rooted world citizenry
Agnes Weiyun He & Yun Xiao (Editors), 2008
ISBN 978-0-8248328-6-5

Perspectives on teaching connected speech to second language speakers
James Dean Brown & Kimi Kondo-Brown (Editors), 2006
ISBN 978-0-8248313-6-3

ordering information at nflrc.hawaii.edu

Student Learning Outcomes Assessment in College Foreign Language Programs

edited by
John M. Norris & John McE. Davis

© 2015 John M. Norris

Some rights reserved. See: http://creativecommons.org/licenses/by/4.0/

Manufactured in the United States of America.

The contents of this publication were developed in part under grants from the U.S. Department of Education (CFDA 84.229, P229A100001 and P229A140012). However, the contents do not necessarily represent the policy of the Department of Education, and one should not assume endorsement by the Federal Government.

ISBN: 978-1-943281-37-4

Library of Congress Control Number: 2015945930

book design by Deborah Masterson | cover photo ©2014 John Norris

distributed by
National Foreign Language Resource Center
University of Hawai'i
1859 East-West Road #106
Honolulu HI 96822-2322
nflrc.hawaii.edu

About the
National Foreign Language Resource Center

The National Foreign Language Resource Center, located in the College of Languages, Linguistics, & Literature at the University of Hawai'i at Mānoa, has conducted research, developed materials, and trained language professionals since 1990 under a series of grants from the U.S. Department of Education (Language Resource Centers Program). A national advisory board sets the general direction of the resource center. With the goal of improving foreign language instruction in the United States, the center publishes research reports and teaching materials that focus primarily on the languages of Asia and the Pacific. The center also sponsors summer intensive teacher training institutes and other professional development opportunities. For additional information about center programs, contact us.

Julio C Rodriguez, Director
National Foreign Language Resource Center
University of Hawai'i at Mānoa
1859 East-West Road #106
Honolulu, HI 96822–2322

email: nflrc@hawaii.edu
website: nflrc.hawaii.edu

NFLRC Advisory Board 2014–2018

Carl Blyth
University of Texas at Austin

Una Cunningham
University of Canterbury, New Zealand

Niki Davis
University of Canterbury, New Zealand

Janis Jensen
Kean University, New Jersey

Paul Sandrock
American Council on the Teaching of Foreign Languages

Julie Sykes
University of Oregon

Steven Thorne, Independent Evaluator
Portland State University, Oregon

Contents

Foreword ix

1. **The Usefulness of Accreditation-Mandated Outcomes Assessment: Trends in University Foreign Language Programs**
   John McE. Davis 1

2. **The Uses of Use-Focused Assessment: Two Chairs' Perspectives**
   Theodore J. Cachey, Jr. & Peter C. Pfeiffer 37

3. **"Centering" Collegiate Foreign Language Departments Around Useful Outcomes Assessment: Challenges and Opportunities**
   Lance R. Askildson & Hiram H. Maxim 57

4. **The Uses of Accountability**
   Amanda Randall & Janet Swaffar 71

5. **Formulating Effective Student Learning Outcomes Through Utilization-Focused Evaluation: A Case Study of a University Japanese Program**
   Shoko Sasayama 97

6. **Developing Learning Outcomes for First-Year Arabic at the University of Notre Dame**
   Ghada Bualuan & Amaya Martin 123

7. **Assessing the Intermediate Level: A Critical Juncture in German Outcomes Assessment**
   Hannelore Weber 143

8 **Journey Greater Than the Destination: A Department and Program Perspective on Utilization-Focused Assessment**
   Alessia Blad & Shauna Williams 173

9 **Assessing Student Perceptions of Writing and Culture in an Italian Curriculum**
   Anna De Fina & Donatella Melucci 199

10 **Foreign Language Curriculum as a Means of Achieving Humanities Learning Goals: Assessment of Materials, Pedagogy, and Learner Texts**
   Marianna Ryshina-Pankova 221

About the Contributors 247

Foreword

Student learning outcomes assessment (SLOA) presents college foreign language (FL) programs with both the opportunity and the challenge of not only stating and demonstrating their value, in terms of what and how well students learn, but also utilizing assessment information for illuminating and transforming their educational practices, effectiveness, and contributions to institutions and society. To date, common reactions by FL and other humanities educators to SLOA have ranged from perfunctory compliance, to ambivalence, to outright rejection, though there is also some evidence to suggest that in certain quarters, outcomes assessment has been embraced as a necessary and even welcome requirement for inspiring educational improvement. Indeed, at a point in time when rapid economic and socio-political changes may threaten the traditionally comfortable role for (and in some cases the very existence of) language and humanities programs in higher education, some have argued that it may be only through vigorous engagement with outcomes assessment and related processes that the contribution of FL education—language-proficiency-oriented and humanistic alike—will be perpetuated.

This edited collection explores something of the status quo of SLOA in FL higher education, with a particular focus on those actors and programs that have sought to take advantage of assessment as a medium for educational improvement. Couched under the broad cover term of "useful outcomes assessment," the common thread connecting all of these contributions is the idea that assessment should be an intentional process of inquiring into the valued results of what we do in FL education *and* acting upon empirical evidence to ensure (or at least endeavor) that such values are realized. In other words, we do not just *do* assessment; rather we have to *use* assessment to bring about educational good.

The book features two sections, covering (a) policy, research, and leadership perspectives on useful outcomes assessment, and (b) examples of outcomes assessment in practice in diverse language programs. The first section includes three chapters that help to situate SLOA as it is being realized in FL higher education in the US. In chapter 1, Davis introduces the accreditation-based mandate, policy climate, and practical expectations for outcomes assessment, and he then reports in-depth findings from a nationwide survey of college FL programs regarding their SLOA practices. His chapter presents current best knowledge regarding factors within institutional and department cultures that either contribute to or hinder FL educators' capacity to engage with, act upon, and learn from outcomes assessment. In chapters 2 and 3, the contributors provide unique insights based on their observations over sustained periods of working on SLOA projects, from two distinct perspectives. Chapter 2, by Cachey and Pfeiffer, offers reflections by two foreign language department chairs whose leadership efforts spearheaded exemplary assessment work over a number of years; their ideas here offer not only practical guidance but also perhaps a degree of inspiration for other program leaders faced with the challenge of initiating and sustaining useful assessment processes. Chapter 3, by Askildson and Maxim, explores the potential role of university language centers in providing a locus, impetus, resources, and expertise that can prove facilitative of useful outcomes assessment endeavors; their experiences as directors of such centers may prove particularly instructive as another avenue towards jumpstarting assessment that will make a lasting contribution.

The contributions in the second section report on multi-year projects that have implemented a use-driven approach to outcomes assessment, thus providing a handful of new examples of FL educators proactively engaging in assessment of their own will. Each chapter reflects a distinct purpose for working on assessment at different points in the assessment cycle, from initial clarification of program goals and values for student learning, to the development of learning outcomes statements, to the assessment of specific learning outcomes at distinct points within a curricular trajectory, and ultimately to the use of outcomes assessment as a means for awareness-raising, improved communication, and instructional transformation.

Chapters 4 through 6 reflect early stages in the outcomes assessment process, as the nature of student learning and its relation to curriculum and instruction is clarified and expressed. Chapter 4, by Randall and Swaffar, reports on the use of assessment as a means for encouraging faculty engagement in curricular thinking by beginning with the bottom-up inspection of the qualities of student work produced in German courses. An interesting theme introduced here (and addressed in other chapters) is the rejection of institutionally-mandated and accountability-driven assessment practices in favor of internally-oriented processes that encourage broad participation and reflection. In chapter 5, Sasayama describes how the formative evaluation of a Japanese program, incorporating perspectives from program administrators, instructors, and students, led to the realization of a need for change in the instructional focus of certain courses and to the development of a variety of teacher resources. In this case, the creation of student learning outcomes was a natural result of the evaluation, in that they provided much-needed guidance to instructors on the learning expectations for their courses. Chapter 6, by Bualuan and Martin, highlights the participatory process of generating consensus on student learning outcomes for first-year Arabic courses, followed by the initial collection of students' perspectives on their achievement of the newly stipulated outcomes. Of key interest here is the possibility of curricular improvement both on the basis of raising faculty awareness through the development of outcomes as well as through the initial collection of data focusing on perceived achievement.

Chapters 7 through 10 focus on the collection of various types of assessment data as the basis for on-going curricular monitoring and improvement. In chapter 7, Weber focuses on assessment of student learning outcomes in intermediate-level German courses, where critical development of student proficiency is expected as a gateway to more advanced learning. The use of multiple direct and indirect assessments in this case indicates how the complexities of student learning may call for a diversity of information to be adequately captured. Chapter 8, by Blad and Williams, describes how a program-wide assessment initiative was developed and sustained across a very large Romance Languages department, including the establishment of a committee, regularly scheduled meetings, and an annual focus on specific assessment targets (e.g., writing, speaking). Perhaps of most interest here is the extent to which communication and collaboration across distinct curricular levels, faculty groups, and languages were enabled through the on-going commitment to assessment. In chapter 9, De Fina and Melucci address the role of assessment in conjunction with a curricular innovation project in an Italian program, where a new emphasis on writing and culture was explored through student surveys. Key here are the insights into how the development of the assessment (a survey in this case) itself helped faculty come to a better understanding of the curriculum and learning outcomes, as well as the ways in which assessment findings pointed to both the positive impact of the curricular innovation and possible aspects of instruction in need of further adjustment. Finally, in chapter 10, Ryshina-Pankova reports on how a German program approached the challenge of assessing integrated humanities and language learning expectations as reflected in student writing at relatively advanced levels of instruction. Of critical interest here is how multiple factors (outcomes statements, pedagogic materials, instructional strategies) were evaluated simultaneously, by multiple instructors, as a basis for generating highly detailed expectations for exactly what writing should reveal about learners' development, and how those expectations were in turn assessed in collected student writing exemplars.

Much of the thought and work reported in this volume was supported by the U.S. Department of Education, in the form of an International Research and Studies grant ("Identifying and responding to program evaluation needs in college foreign language education," 2005–2008) as well as a Language Resource Centers grant at the National Foreign Language Resource Center at the University of Hawai'i at Mānoa (2006–2014). I am indebted in particular to the director of the NFLRC during much of that time, Professor Richard Schmidt, for his persistent belief in the value of this work and his intellectual, collegial, and financial support for the project. Many of the examples reported in this volume were also facilitated by Yukiko Watanabe, a PhD student at the University of Hawai'i at the time, and it is clear that the FL educators with whom she interacted benefited from her diligence, insights, and creativity in response to their diverse needs in pursuing useful outcomes assessment.

My co-editor on this volume, Dr. John McE. Davis, deserves substantial credit for his keen editorial eye, his efficiency, and his commitment to the core ideals reflected in this work. Indeed, it is primarily through discussions with John over a number of years now that my own thinking about the value of program evaluation and outcomes assessment has continued to develop. We have also embarked on a new, long-term project in this area with collaborators at the Center for Applied Linguistics, in the form of the Assessment and Evaluation Language Resource Center[1] (AELRC, also funded by the U.S. Department of Education). In the context of the AELRC, we will continue to research and disseminate ideas about useful student learning outcomes assessment and language program evaluation along the lines of the work reported here.

In the end, I believe that this collection—reflective as it is of distinct foreign languages in diverse program settings with unique assessment demands—suggests a positive iteration towards realizing the valuable contributions that outcomes assessment and program evaluation may make in FL education. Collectively, these FL educators have stepped away from the kind of thoughtless reactions and rejection that are typical of many others in the humanities, and they have also stepped away from mere compliance with external accountability demands and institutional mandates. Instead, they have moved proactively in the direction of deliberative, collaborative, empirical thought and action in support of educational effectiveness. By thinking about assessment in terms of how it might best be used in their own contexts and for their own purposes, they have demonstrated how we can harness powerful processes like assessment and evaluation in pursuit of the educational good that we all, I presume, hope to achieve. Ultimately, then, my hope is that this volume will serve as an impetus for foreign language programs and their related scholarly affiliates to rethink the potential of student learning outcomes assessment for playing an immediate, critical role in both supporting and, where needed, improving the value of what we do in FL education.

John M. Norris
February 21, 2015, Arlington, VA

---

[1] For more information, see https://aelrc.georgetown.edu.

The Usefulness of Accreditation-Mandated Outcomes Assessment: Trends in University Foreign Language Programs

John McE. Davis
Georgetown University

Student learning outcomes assessment is now an integral part of university accreditation and program review, a reform framework designed to improve teaching and learning throughout U.S. higher education. This study explores the impact of accreditation-mandated assessment on college foreign language (FL) programs. Impact is defined in terms of assessment "usefulness," or the degree to which educators in FL programs learn or act in productive ways as a result of assessment activity. FL faculty and staff from 100 post-secondary programs across the US were asked to report on their assessment practices in two areas: (a) the factors/conditions within their programs that help people to undertake assessment effectively (i.e., assessment capacity) and (b) the various ways in which assessment is used (i.e., the actions and instances of learning resulting from assessment activity). The study was generally focused on elucidating whether differences in assessment capacity (e.g., more or less effective leadership, assessment expertise) account for how faculty use or learn from assessment activity. Of special interest was whether the specific dimensions of assessment capacity leveraged on FL programs by accreditation review (e.g., institutional assessment requirements and support) are related to assessment usefulness. Findings suggest that while accreditation mandates have been successful in stimulating considerable assessment activity, programs with little assessment capacity beyond accreditation/institutional compliance lack the needed conditions for meaningful assessment use to occur. Rather, assessment usefulness—and important corollary consequences such as educational innovation and improvement—seems to issue from personnel-related factors originating within foreign language programs.

Davis, J. McE. (2015). The usefulness of accreditation-mandated outcomes assessment: Trends in university foreign language programs. In J. M. Norris & J. McE. Davis (Eds.), *Student learning outcomes assessment in college foreign language programs* (pp. 1–35). Honolulu: University of Hawai'i, National Foreign Language Resource Center.

Introduction: Outcomes assessment in U.S. higher education

Most if not all educators in U.S. college foreign language education will by now have experienced an increased institutional oversight over the educational processes happening within their departments and programs. On campuses across the US, language faculty and staff are now commonly tasked with the implementation of *student learning outcomes assessment*,[1] a required activity typically involving the articulation of student learning outcomes, gathering of information on student attainment of learning outcomes, use of that information toward some program improvement-oriented aim, and reporting of the entire exercise to the university administration. The impetus for these activities is largely the result of important changes in the traditional framework for assuring institutional integrity and quality in higher education: accreditation review. Yet, the influence of this pervasive new reality in post-secondary FL education has not been widely or systematically investigated such that there is an empirical understanding of how (or whether) accreditation-mandated assessment helps or hinders delivery of foreign language/literary education in U.S. colleges and universities.

Outcomes assessment, in fact, has had a long and largely separate history from its current association with institutional accreditation. Contemporary assessment practice derives (partly) from research traditions originating within the academy and a historical scholarly interest in undergraduate education (Ewell, 2002). Ewell (2009) describes assessment in this historical vein as motivated by an "improvement paradigm" (p. 8), and oriented in its methodology toward the use of assessment for improvement of university teaching and learning. Yet the more recent assessment injunctions experienced by university/college faculty arguably have more to do with ongoing concerns about the quality of U.S. public education (as well as tuition costs, time to degree, and cultural diversity of undergraduate student populations) and the use of assessment-based reform to redress perceived deficiencies. In response to discourses promulgating the view (over many years) that U.S. educational institutions are failing to supply a sufficiently skilled, globally competitive workforce (e.g., National Commission on Excellence in Education, 1983; National Governors' Association, 1986; Spellings Commission, 2006), state and federal governments have incrementally instantiated assessment-based reform systems—most notably via standardized testing in K–12 public schools—to hold educational institutions accountable for student achievement (Linn, 2005, 2008; Shepard, 2008).

Unlike K–12 public schools, however, in which legislation has instantiated assessment-based reform directly (i.e., via *No Child Left Behind* [NCLB] legislation in 2001), the federal government entrusts quality assurance in higher education to regional accreditation commissions, each holding member universities and colleges accountable for educational quality via accreditation review (Ewell, 2000). Accreditation review is the process by which universities/colleges reflect and report on how they are fulfilling their institutional mission and core educational purposes (Beno, 2004). Starting in the late 1980s, however—and under direct pressure from federal and state governments—accreditation commissions gradually incorporated

---

[1] Student learning outcomes assessment is "the processes that an institution or program uses to gather direct evidence about the attainment of student learning outcomes, engaged in for purposes of judging (and improving) overall instructional performance" (Ewell, 2001, p. 7). Note that this definition is distinct from the common denotation in applied linguistics of "testing" or assessment for the purposes of placement or grading in language programs.

outcomes assessment into review requirements, transforming how universities and colleges demonstrate they are attending to educational effectiveness (Ewell, 2000, 2009; Provezis, 2010; Wolff, 1992). Currently, all regional accreditation commissions require that institutions engage in outcomes assessment, as well as provide supporting structures and resources to aid faculty assessment efforts (e.g., a dedicated, auxiliary assessment unit with expert personnel; Provezis, 2010). The incorporation of assessment into accreditation review is thus regarded as the current tertiary educational accountability system in that it is meant to assure the public and other watchful stakeholders that institutions are "using ... resources appropriately to help students develop the knowledge, skills, competencies, and dispositions required to function effectively in the 21st century" (Kuh, 2009, p. 4).

The current, widespread adoption of assessment—or at least the expectation thereof—throughout U.S. higher education, then, can be attributed primarily to regional accreditation (Banta, 2002; Ewell, 2002; Kuh & Ikenberry, 2009). Moreover, despite the accountability dimensions of contemporary accreditation review, commissions have tried to frame assessment (via requirements and recommendations) as something resembling Ewell's delineation of the improvement paradigm. That is, most commissions advocate that assessment should function on campuses as something akin to a "culture" of continuous improvement, within which the institution supports a faculty-owned process of inquiry into teaching and learning. Inherent within assessment practice and methodology, then, are two (some would argue, conflicting) purposes: (a) educational improvement and (b) accountability to the public interest (Ewell, 2008, 2009; Provezis, 2010).

Given these purposes, the question has arisen, how well does the system achieve its aims? Research into the efficacy of accreditation-mandated assessment paints a mixed picture. A large-scale, national survey study from the National Institute on Learning Outcomes Assessment (NILOA) found that the single most frequent use of assessment in post-secondary institutions is to meet institutional accreditation requirements (Kuh & Ikenberry, 2009). On the one hand, then, assessment materializes effectively in college departments and programs to achieve (to some degree) accountability-oriented purposes. On the other hand, the extent to which assessment provokes meaningful educational improvement is less clear. The challenge for institutions and accreditation commissions is often characterized as an inability to "close the assessment loop," a phrase denoting an inability to complete the final step of the assessment cycle: concretely *using* information on student learning toward educational improvement (Kuh & Ikenberry, 2009). Thus, despite accreditation driving more assessment activity on U.S. campuses than ever before (Kuh & Ikenberry, 2009), the envisioned impact of accountability *and* continuous educational improvement does not seem to have occurred to the extent desired.

And yet, many examples attest to assessment's transformative potential. Numerous successfully useful, improvement-oriented instances of institutional assessment appear in the research literature (e.g., Banta, Jones, & Black, 2009; Banta, Lund, Black, & Oblander, 1996; Blaich & Wise, 2011; Bresciani, 2006; Mentowski & Associates, 2000; Driscoll & Cordero de Noriega, 2006). Moreover, researchers have identified key factors that seem most enabling of improvement-oriented assessment, such as committed institutional leadership, faculty incentives/rewards, financial/technical support, focus on use, incorporation of assessment into institutional decision-making, and faculty-ownership of assessment initiatives. Thus, while most would agree that universities and colleges have yet to engage in assessment to the extent hoped, there is a good deal of high-quality activity, as well as a deepened understanding of the factors—at the institutional-level at least—that seem facilitative of meaningful assessment usefulness.

Historically, the effects of accountability-driven assessment on U.S. foreign and English language education have been an area of interest in K–12 language education research. Research on accountability assessment in the US has most frequently focused on NCLB legislation and English language learners (ELLs) given the unique washback impacts ELLs' experience, but also (though to a lesser extent) on the debilitating effects of NCLB on foreign language education in K–12 public schools (Atkins, Supahan, & Lewis, 2008; Rhodes & Pufhal, 2010; Rosenbusch, 2005; Rosenbusch & Jensen, 2005; von Zastrow & Janc, 2004; Vuksanovich, 2009).

However, relatively limited research has focused on the washback influence of accreditation-mandated assessment on post-secondary language education, a state of affairs incommensurate with assessment's now ubiquitous national presence in college FL programs. Certainly, the encroaching influence of post-secondary mandated-assessment has been addressed to some extent in FL research discourses, most notably within periodic disciplinary commentary, as well as via a growing number of case studies from FL educators responding to new institutional assessment directives. Nevertheless, an arguably partial (though developing) understanding prevails as to how mandated assessment has impacted teaching and learning within college FL programs. FL educators appear to engage in assessment for a variety of purposes, spurred on by different impetuses and motivations, supplied with varying levels of support and expertise, working within different contexts and institutional/programmatic cultures, all of which result in quite different assessment actions and instances of learning (i.e., assessment uses). However, the educational usefulness of assessment across the spectrum of college FL programs is somewhat unclear, as is the helpfulness (or lack thereof) of new institutional assessment requirements. This study, then, had two broad goals: first, to redress the relative paucity of information about widespread assessment practice in U.S. college language education, and second, to deepen the inchoate understanding of how assessment succeeds or fails in college FL programs. That is, the study sought to understand the current usefulness of post-secondary student learning outcomes assessment, particularly in light of how much assessment appears to be driven by institutional accreditation review (Watanabe, Norris, & González-Lloret, 2009). Thus, the overarching question asked here was, How does institutionally-mandated assessment contribute to assessment usefulness in post-secondary foreign language programs?

Student learning outcomes assessment in post-secondary foreign language education: A brief review

Foreign language education has experienced its share of assessment-driven initiatives designed to effect widespread, even national-level, transformations in FL teaching and learning. A few notable examples include the development of the ACTFL (American Council on The Teaching of Foreign Languages) proficiency guidelines and Oral Proficiency Interview (Omaggio-Hadley, 2001), the *National Standards for Foreign Language Learning* (National Standards in Foreign Language

Education Project, 1996), and the Integrated Performance Assessment regime (Adair-Hauck, Glisan, Koda, Sandrock, & Swender, 2006). Accreditation-mandated assessment differs from these, of course, in that it is leveraged on FL educators by outside entities. Nevertheless, the accreditation initiative has the same basic goal as other FL assessment-driven reform efforts: to improve the quality of college FL educational practice. In the parlance of program evaluation theory, accreditation-mandated assessment aims to achieve this goal by instantiating in FL programs an enhanced *assessment capacity*[2]—that is, facilitative assessment structures, processes, tools, and so on—for the purpose of achieving particular *assessment uses* (e.g., improvement actions, increased pedagogical understanding, accountability). The recent history of how, and to what ends, accreditation mandates and other forces have stimulated productive assessment conditions and use in FL university programs to date has been (a) debated in FL disciplinary commentary and (b) demonstrated in a handful of case studies describing first-hand experiences with institutional assessment requirements.

Disciplinary commentary and recommended assessment approaches

The recent influence of accreditation-mandated assessment initiatives is reflected in the various instances of FL disciplinary discussion addressing assessment's role in contemporary post-secondary language education. A commonplace theme in this discourse, of course, is that assessment mandates have not been well received. Commentators draw attention to associations with government-driven accountability and the fundamental incompatibilities of (purportedly) political and economic motivations with language and literary education (Heiland & Rosenthal, 2011; Holquist, 2011). Moreover, anecdotal evidence indicates that the usefulness of assessment is very much in question. Common practice, rather, appears to be perfunctory compliance, or as Byrnes (2006) puts it, "pro forma external assessment rituals" (p. 575; see also Norris, 2006a; Watanabe, Norris, & González-Lloret, 2009). Various factors are suggested as to why accountability-driven assessment seems to thwart meaningful educational change within this milieu. Faculty lack the needed time and resources (Davis, Sinicrope, & Watanabe, 2009; Watanabe, Norris, & González-Lloret, 2009); assessment-driven scrutiny confronts educators with program weaknesses (Norris & Liskin-Gasparro, 2009); educators fear misuse of assessment findings (Norris & Liskin-Gasparro, 2009; Watanabe, Norris, & González-Lloret, 2009); and assessment methodology, itself, may have certain distorting curricular effects such as lowering learning standards, narrowing curricula, and overemphasizing "measurement" or quantification of learning (Norris & Liskin-Gasparro, 2009). Moreover, the general inefficacy resulting from these and other impediments has the additionally debilitating effect of alienating faculty and further entrenching the view that assessment is "fundamentally disconnected from the daily challenges of teaching and learning" (Heiland & Rosenthal, 2011, p. 10; see also Norris, 2006a).

Elsewhere, however, FL commentators have advocated for assessment as something worth undertaking in a serious way, to the extent that it should play a transformative role in the realization of important disciplinary goals. Key position

---

[2] Assessment capacity is defined here as the optimal infrastructures, practices, personnel characteristics, institutional context, and disciplinary support factors needed to undertake useful student learning outcomes assessment in college foreign language programs (Davis, 2012).

statements, for example, have recommended assessment as a way to address particular challenges in post-secondary language education (e.g., the "two-tiered" system) and to help redefine the national FL teaching agenda toward a more globally-minded multilingualism (MLA, 2008; MLA Ad Hoc Committee on Foreign Languages, 2007).

Moreover, a number of key expositions have advocated for specific assessment approaches to enhance FL educational quality, some conceived as alternatives to the reactive-type activity common in post-secondary FL education (Byrnes, 2006, 2008; Byrnes, Maxim, & Norris, 2010; Liskin-Gasparro, 1995; Norris 2006a, 2011; Ricardo-Osorio, 2010; Shohamy, 1992; Walvoord, 2010). In general terms, assessment experts/researchers extol the benefits of "assessment culture" (Ricardo-Osorio, 2011), "ownership" (Byrnes, 2008; Davis, Sinicrope, & Watanabe, 2009), and "spirit of inquiry" (Byrnes, Maxim, & Norris, 2010) to generally characterize desirably proactive mindsets and modes of activity. Within these broad notions, a number of more specific enabling factors are identified, such as "assessment literacy," supportive leadership, faculty "buy-in," inclusive participation, teamwork, and institutional support (Le Hir, 2005; Norris, 2006a, 2009b; Ricardo-Osorio, 2011).

A noteworthy assessment methodology comes from John Norris, who advocates a "use-focused" technique. Norris' approach is derived from Michael Quinn Patton's (1997, 2008) utilization-focused method of program evaluation. According to Patton (and Norris), focusing on and planning for evaluation use—and assessment use—at the outset of program development efforts strongly disposes evaluation projects toward concretely useful final outcomes that participants' desire and value (Norris, 2000, 2002, 2006a, 2006b, 2008, 2009a, 2009b). Within the use-focused assessment methodology, Norris further identifies a number of auxiliary factors that increase the potential for useful assessment practice. These include (a) methodological feasibility, (b) stakeholder participation, (c) cyclical, ongoing practice, (d) program-internal assessment motivation/impetuses, and (e) articulation of assessment tools to pre-specified assessment uses (Norris, 2006a, 2009a).

College foreign language assessment practice: Use and capacity

In support of these proposals, depictions of outcomes assessment experiences in FL programs suggest that assessment can indeed be a powerfully useful tool for educational reform. Instances of successful assessment practice/use are found in a handful of case studies describing productive responses to institutional assessment requirements, as well as capacity elements that seem to account for those successes (Carstens-Wickham, 2008; Le Hir, 2005; Liskin-Gasparro, 1995; Mathews & Hansen, 2004; McAlpine & Dhonau, 2007; Ramsay, 2009; Walther, 2009; Windham, 2008).[3]

What evidence of assessment use do we see in these studies? At the time of writing, most FL educators had yet to collect, analyze, and use evidence of student learning, though the implementation of assessment seemed to suggest a number of salutary impacts. For example, all participants in the assessment process generally benefited from an increased understanding of their educational purposes and

---

[3] Numerous studies address program-level outcomes assessment experiences. Studies reviewed here are those in which assessment experiences were explicitly responding to institutional/accreditation assessment requirements.

processes, many translating that understanding into plans for extensive program/curricular improvements (Carstens-Wickham, 2008; Le Hir, 2005; Mathews & Hansen, 2004; McAlpine & Dhonau, 2007; Ramsay, 2009; Walther, 2009; Windham, 2008). In addition, involvement in the assessment process had a number of incidentally positive impacts. For example, assessment collaboration enabled FL educators to share teaching experiences and materials, resulting in improved teaching skills (Walther, 2009). Moreover, the inclusion and participation of diverse program constituencies—and the increased communication and dialogue that ensued—brought together disciplinary factions (e.g., literature/language acquisition faculty) resulting in increased "collegiality" and "faculty unity" (Le Hir, 2005; Ramsay, 2009; Walther, 2009; Windham, 2008). Finally, some educators felt their quality assessment efforts demonstrated their professionalism to outside audiences, while others used assessment to generally communicate the value of foreign language learning in liberal arts education (Ramsay, 2009; Walther, 2009).

Gleaning from these depictions, the character and make-up of the programs (i.e., the dimensions of assessment capacity) are suggestive of factors that made assessment successful. At the broadest level, studies describe environments generally conducive to inquiry and reform, either at department or institutional levels (e.g., an extant "culture of experimentation" and "continuous improvement"; Walther, 2009, p. 121). Moreover, a conducive environment seems to include especially motivated staff (with "inquiring"-type mindsets) keenly interested in reform and innovation (see also Byrnes, Maxim, & Norris, 2010). Another important institutional factor is provision of financial support (Walther, 2009; see also Grau Sempere, Mohn, & Pieroni, 2009; Milleret, 2008; Milleret & Silveira, 2009). At the program-level, leadership seems to play an important ancillary role in helpfully shepherding the process along, marshalling needed support, empowering faculty, and facilitating participation and collaboration (Le Hir, 2005; Walther, 2009). Finally, assessment projects undertaken within the use-focused methodological paradigm evidence a number of additional helpful factors, such as inclusion of local stakeholders, use of multiple tools, trends toward ongoing and cyclical assessment activity, and, importantly, a commitment on the part of those leading assessment work (i.e., assessment "users") to concretely use assessment in meaningful ways (i.e., Ramsay, 2009; Walther, 2009: see also Byrnes, Maxim, & Norris, 2010; Grau Sempere, Mohn, & Pieroni, 2009; Milleret & Silveira, 2009). It would seem, then, that in the wake of increasing pressure to engage in outcomes assessment, at least some FL educators have been well-equipped with conceptual frameworks to carry out assessment in productive ways, and, that such frameworks have become part of on-the-ground assessment capacity in FL programs.

However, despite the usefulness of the various FL assessment capacity proposals and nascent supporting evidence, the current state of FL assessment research provides an arguably partial picture of the washback influence or impact of mandated assessment in college FL programs generally. If we conceive of the widespread influence/impact of accreditation-driven assessment in terms of its *usefulness* for educational reform, it is unclear the extent to which assessment in college FL programs is a concretely productive endeavor. Two elaborations on this claim demonstrate the impetus for the study. First, beyond anecdotal accounts and a handful of best-case assessment scenarios, it is unclear specifically how assessment is being used across the spectrum of post-secondary programs. Some educators are clearly using assessment toward educational improvement (among other uses), but what are the wider trends of assessment use in FL programs? Second, how does accreditation contribute to, or undermine, assessment success and usefulness in FL programs? Certainly, there is a developing sense of how and why such successes occur in a few cases, and a number of use-inducing capacity factors have been identified—ownership, leadership, and use-focused methods, among others. However, what role has accreditation played in these instances, as well as in the assessment efforts happening throughout U.S. college FL education? In some cases, institutional assessment mandates seem to thwart educational improvement; in other cases, assessment requirements spur on meaningful FL program reform. How, then, does accreditation review—via its requirements and recommendations for outcomes assessment activity and capacity-building—contribute to assessment usefulness?

Research questions

Reiterating, then, the above query, this study investigated how accreditation assessment mandates contribute to assessment usefulness in post-secondary FL programs. This overarching concern was addressed by posing four research questions (RQs):

1. What is the nature and extent of assessment capacity in college/university FL programs?
2. Which assessment uses are occurring in college/university FL programs?
3. What is the relationship between assessment capacity and assessment use in college/university FL programs?
4. What is the relationship between accreditation/institutionally-driven assessment capacity and assessment use in college/university FL programs?

Methods

The study used an online questionnaire to gather information about assessment usefulness in U.S. university FL programs.[4] One hundred programs reported on their assessment activity in terms of (a) extant assessment capacity and (b) how assessment is used. The following section describes the conceptualization and operationalization of *capacity* and *use* as a way to understand the impact of accreditation-mandated assessment in college FL programs.

Conceptualizing impact: Assessment capacity and use

Accreditation commissions seek to instantiate a formatively *useful* system of educational reform (i.e., assessment) in post-secondary institutions via requirements and recommendations associated with accreditation review. As such, this study judged the efficacy of this system in terms of its usefulness—or, the productive actions and instances of learning resulting from the implementation of required assessment activity. To do so, research methods and concepts were borrowed from program evaluation and organizational learning research. Program

---

[4] Participants provided information about assessment associated with *major* programs only so that data on assessment experiences would be comparable. Thus the term "program" is used here to denote a language major course sequence and/or BA language degree.

evaluation[5] and organizational learning research aims to understand the factors within organizations that contribute to evaluation usefulness: that is, the local conditions (e.g., extent of teamwork, risk-taking, resources, experimentation) that are predictive of productive decision-making, reform- or development-oriented actions, awareness-raising, and so on. Evaluation researchers have thus devised *capacity frameworks*, or lists and categorizations of environmental factors within government, private sector, and educational programs that predict evaluation usefulness.

Similar conceptualizations were used in this study to understand assessment usefulness in tertiary FL programs. To do so, assessment and program evaluation were regarded as broadly analogous processes in that both involve collection and analysis of information within a program for some ameliorative purpose or use. Moreover, assessment was similarly regarded as an activity that proceeds effectively—or usefully—given the existence of certain contextual, use-inducing factors (i.e., conducive assessment capacity). Thus, just as an organizations' evaluation capacity indicates the likelihood of evaluation use and learning, so too does a university FL program's *assessment capacity* indicate a potential for assessment usefulness.

Assessment capacity in a given college FL program is comprised of a complex set of local conditions, some of which will be the result of responding to institutional, accreditation-related requirements and some the result of other forces (e.g., proactively motivated faculty). Following techniques from program evaluation research, if one could establish a set of factors and conditions known to be conducive to using assessment in productive ways, determining the extent to which those factors exist within a FL program could be used as a measure to estimate the likelihood of assessment usefulness. One key aim of the study, then, was to perform an assessment "audit" of college-level FL programs, to get an overall sense of the assessment capacity environment in FL programs and thereby an indication of the potential within programs for assessment usefulness.

Importantly, the aspects of FL program assessment capacity of special interest in this study were those created via the specific assessment requirements and recommendations issuing from accreditation mandates, an important driver of assessment capacity building (e.g., "The institution implements and supports a systematic and broad-based approach to the assessment of student learning," New England Association of Schools and Colleges, 2005, pp. 12–13). During accreditation review, accreditation commissions will look for evidence that institutions are managing and supporting assessment in particular ways; for example, whether they are providing assessment expertise and funding, or requiring programs to report on assessment activity (among other things). Again, by exacting these requirements, accreditation commissions instantiate particular forms of assessment capacity, and this study investigated whether by developing capacity

---

[5] The term *evaluation* is used here following Norris (2006a), that is, "the gathering of information about any of the variety of elements that constitute educational programs, for a variety of purposes that primarily include understanding, demonstrating, improving, and judging program value" (p. 579). Ewell's (2001) definition of assessment describes a similar process of information gathering—on student learning—and use of that information toward certain uses (improvements in teaching and learning). Evaluation and assessment, then, are similarly modes of empirical self-research, though assessment is specifically focused on student learning.

in this manner FL faculty were enabled to use assessment in meaningful ways. In order to capture and analyze this dimension of assessment capacity, and others, in FL programs, a framework was needed identifying and listing the factors and conditions contributing to productive use of assessment in FL departments.

FL program assessment capacity

The following foreign language program assessment capacity framework was established to specify the various characteristics and conditions needed to achieve assessment usefulness in FL programs, particularly those factors most directly the result of accreditation mandates. The framework was created, initially, via a review of FL assessment, program evaluation/organizational learning, and accreditation literature, and then refined via focus group sessions with FL assessment/evaluation experts and interviews with five experienced FL assessment practitioners. The final framework was comprised of nine capacity categories. Taken together, the nine categories were thought to constitute the various structures, practices, personnel characteristics, and institutional context factors needed for productive assessment use in college FL programs (Davis, 2012). Those categories include

- **Institutional assessment support**—the various forms of assistance (e.g., funding, expertise, incentives, training) provided by an institution to aid assessment work and as specified by requirements/recommendations issuing from accreditation standards/literature;

- **Institutional assessment policies and governance**—specific assessment policies and governance patterns (e.g., integration of assessment into tenure/promotion review) that impact assessment activities and as specified by accreditation standards/literature;

- **Program assessment infrastructures**—particular assessment structures (e.g., outcomes statements, curricular maps, assessment plans) required by an institution, often the result of requirements/recommendations issuing from accreditation standards/literature[6];

- **Program-level assessment support**—financial, personnel, and material resources made available within the program that enable people to do and use assessment (e.g., incentives, technical expertise, funding, technology);

- **Assessment related leadership**—the ways in which program leaders (chairs, section heads, etc.) help assessment to be a productive endeavor (e.g., promoting, valuing, initiating, backing, and participating in assessment efforts);

- **Program ethos**—prevailing thinking/attitudes conducive to educational development and assessment (e.g., valuing of, and openness toward, educational innovation and development);

---

[6] The specific dimensions of institutional support, institutional assessment governance and policies, and assessment infrastructures were derived from accreditation commission literature, either in regional commission standards, outcomes assessment how-to literature, or from documentation produced by the Council for Regional Accreditation Commissions, which outlines expectations for all commissions for desired assessment-related practices in member institutions.

- **Assessment collaboration**—modes of collaboration that facilitate assessment work (e.g., willingness to work with others, stakeholder inclusiveness, a track record of collaborative accomplishment);
- **Assessment communication**—opportunities for, and/or channels of, assessment-related information flow and communication (e.g., knowledge sharing, consistent record-keeping); and
- **Additional high-quality assessment conditions and practices**—sundry additional conditions and activities hypothesized/observed to be conducive to assessment usefulness (e.g., use-focused methods, feasibility, effective assessment planning/reporting).

By establishing the above framework, the study created a set of hypothesized benchmarks for *useful* assessment capacity in post-secondary FL programs, or, seen another way, an optimal set of capacity elements that, if present in a program, would strongly dispose assessment efforts toward productive assessment usefulness.

Assessment use: A bellwether of useful capacity

In addition to reporting on aspects of the above framework, program informants were also asked to report on the various *uses* of assessment in their programs. *Assessment use* was defined as the actions taken or instances of learning in FL programs (e.g., course modifications, increased educational understanding, institutional assessment reporting) resulting from assessment activities, particularly those decisions or realizations resulting from findings on (i.e., information about) student achievement. A list of potential assessment uses in post-secondary FL programs was created via a review of FL assessment literature and suggestions from FL assessment experts and experienced practitioners. Table 1 lists the final types of uses presented to respondents in the questionnaire.

Table 1. Types of assessment use in FL programs

- develop/modify instruction/courses
- develop/modify significant components of your program (e.g., the language sequence, the sequence of upper-level courses)
- develop/create new programs
- compare the department/program with other departments/programs
- make requests for resources
- promote ongoing assessment efforts
- better understand curricula
- better understand teaching
- better understand outcomes assessment in the program (e.g., outcomes statements, tools)
- better understand the value or worth of the program

continued...

Table 1. Types of assessment use in FL programs *(cont.)*

- meet institutional assessment requirements (including accreditation or program review)
- create institutional assessment reports (including for accreditation or program review)
- justify/defend the program
- communicate department/program learning expectations to students, the institution, employers, the public
- showcase student knowledge, skills, and dispositions
- demonstrate the value of foreign language studies to students, the institution, the public

Evidence of assessment use was employed in the study as a type of dependent variable to analyze the usefulness of assessment capacity. That is, the level/amount of assessment use happening in a FL program was regarded as an indicator of the relative use-inducing potential of the assessment capacity extant within that program. To illustrate, if a program had high levels of assessment capacity (and thereby a greater potential to use assessment in various ways), then there should be evidence of proportionate (i.e., high) amounts of assessment use in the program. Conversely, a program with little assessment capacity should likewise demonstrate little assessment use.

Moreover, while all capacity categories were purported to contribute to assessment usefulness, the study was further interested in investigating whether any capacity categories are *more useful than others* in terms of more or less association with the occurrence of assessment use. That is, if amount of *use* is conceived as a bellwether or indicator of capacity usefulness, are some capacity types particularly necessary or helpful for successful use of assessment compared to others? Furthermore, and crucially, three capacity categories, and their relationships to assessment use, were of special interest: Institutional Support, Institutional Policies and Governance, and assessment Infrastructures (see Figure 1). Again, these constructs were thought to represent the specific dimensions of assessment capacity that accreditation commissions require or recommend institutions put in place.

Given these proposed variables and relationships, the study aimed to do two things: (a) collect information on assessment capacity and assessment use in FL programs and (b) subsequently look for *relationships* between assessment capacity and assessment use, particularly relationships between use and the institutionally-driven (i.e., accreditation) aspects of a program's assessment capacity. Structuring the study in this way was thought to shed light on those aspects of assessment capacity in a FL program most related to assessment use, and, especially, whether the institutionally mandated (and accreditation-driven) dimension of a program's assessment capacity is more or less related to FL educators using assessment toward improvement-oriented ends.

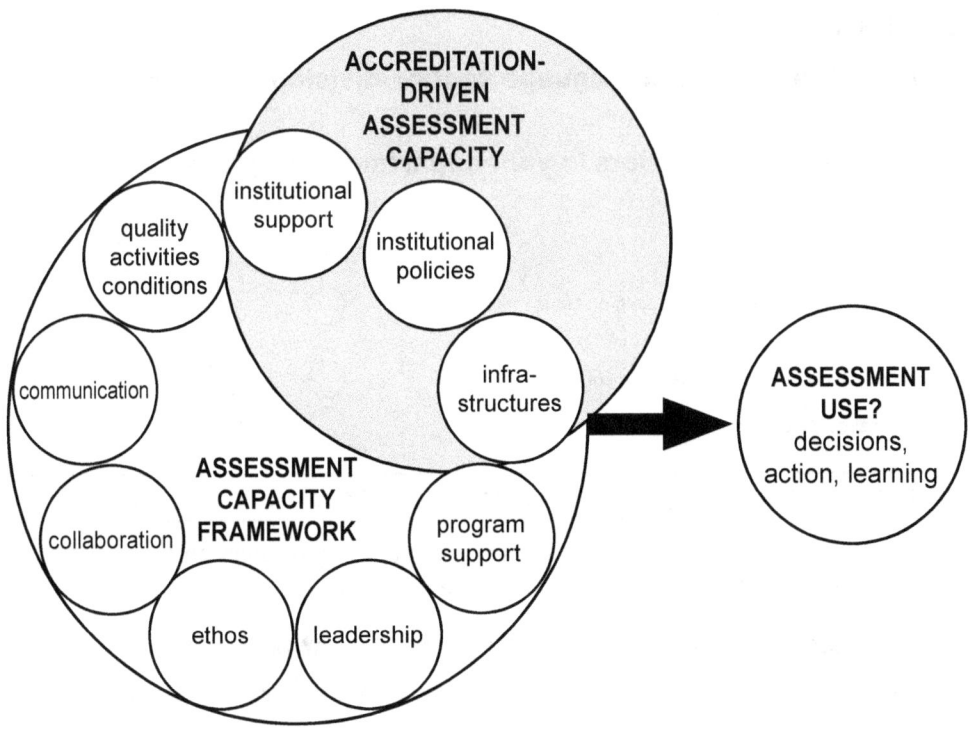

Figure 1. Relationship between assessment capacity and assessment use in college FL programs.

Questionnaire development and administration

An online questionnaire was used to gather information from FL educators on extant assessment capacity and use in college FL programs. The questionnaire was mainly comprised of rating scale response items. Rating items asked respondents to indicate the degree of capacity in each of the nine categories. Example capacity questionnaire items are provided in Figures 2 and 3.

INSTITUTIONAL SUPPORT FOR OUTCOMES ASSESSMENT

1. Does your university/college...?

	No	Developing	Yes	Don't know
a) provide training workshops for student learning outcomes assessment	○	○	○	○
b) provide technical assistance from outcomes assessment experts	○	○	○	○
c) provide technology support for outcomes assessment (e.g., data storage, data analysis, equipment)	○	○	○	○

Figure 2. Rating item asking about Institutional Support capacity in a FL program.

LEADERSHIP
(e.g., department chair or language section/division head, etc.)

1. To what extent do leaders in your department/program...?

	1 not at all	2	3	4 very much/ a lot
a) take the lead in initiating or coordinating outcomes assessment work	○	○	○	○
b) participate actively in outcomes assessment work	○	○	○	○
c) delegate assessment work effectively	○	○	○	○

Figure 3. Rating item asking about Institutional Support capacity in a FL program.

Rating scale items were also designed to capture information on the extent of assessment use in the program (see, e.g., Figure 4).

1. To what extent has anyone in your department/program <u>used</u> outcomes assessment FINDINGS (i.e., information about student performance) to ...?

	1 not at all	2	3	4 very much/ a lot
a) develop/modify instruction/courses	○	○	○	○
b) develop/modify significant components of your program (e.g., the language sequence, the sequence of upper-level courses)	○	○	○	○
c) develop/create new programs	○	○	○	○

Figure 4. Rating questionnaire item asking about assessment use in a FL program.

The questionnaire also elicited information on respondents' backgrounds, BA program size (in terms of major enrolments), the institutional setting of the program, the length of time people in the program had engaged in assessment, and tools used for assessment purposes.

A first draft of the questionnaire was reviewed by assessment and survey research experts, as well five experienced FL assessment practitioners. The questionnaire was piloted with six local FL educators (in similar departmental roles as targeted respondents) using a "think aloud" procedure.[7] Piloting and revision procedures resulted in a number of revisions, primarily having to do with reduction of items and the time needed to complete the questionnaire.

---

[7] The think aloud procedure involved asking the respondent to complete the questionnaire all the while verbalizing any thoughts or queries that come to mind. The procedure reveals problematic aspects of responding to the questionnaire, which the researcher notes and uses for revisions.

Respondents

Targeted respondents were individuals thought to be knowledgeable about assessment in FL departments and programs (e.g., chairs, section heads, assessment coordinators, undergraduate coordinators/advisors, heads of assessment committees). However, if a respondent was in a leadership position, it was thought that another respondent from the same program should supply information on leadership capacity (to avoid bias). Thus, collection of data on assessment capacity and use for a single FL program could happen in one of two ways:

(a) from a single respondent—someone knowledgeable about assessment, not in a position of leadership, and thus able to report on all aspects of assessment capacity and use; and

(b) from two respondents—a chair or section head reporting on assessment capacity and use, but not on leadership capacity, *and* a second respondent reporting on the role of leadership in assessment efforts.

A second questionnaire was constructed, with leadership items only, for respondents in scenario *b*. The leadership questionnaire underwent the same review and piloting procedures described prior.

Questionnaire administration

An email list was created of FL program informants at every U.S. university/college FL department with an identifiable webpage (*N* = 1,513; contact names and email addresses were collected from department websites). Respondents were invited to participate via an initial email, which contained a link to the relevant questionnaire (hosted at https://www.surveymonkey.com/). Two follow-up reminders were sent at one-week intervals. Respondents received a free book as compensation (provided by the National Foreign Language Resource Center). Again, a respondent in a leadership position received a questionnaire with *all* capacity items (including leadership). A respondent who is a chair or section head received a questionnaire with leadership items omitted, and a second individual was contacted to report on leadership capacity.

Data analysis

The variables and relationships the study sought to establish were (a) extent of assessment capacity in FL programs (addressing RQ1), (b) extent of assessment use (RQ2), (c) relationships between assessment capacity and use (RQ3), and (d) relationships between institutionally-driven capacity types, specifically, and assessment use (RQ4).

For RQ1 and RQ2, a mean capacity value was calculated for each program for each of the nine capacity categories (e.g., a mean score for each program for all item ratings in the *Institutional support* capacity category; a mean rating for each program for all *Infrastructure* item ratings, and so on). Likewise, a mean *use* score/value was calculated for each program (i.e., an average of all use item ratings).[8] Descriptive statistics for ratings in each of the capacity categories and assessment use (i.e., mean ratings, standard deviations, tallies of rating

---

[8] Cronbach alpha for capacity category and use means was calculated to ascertain consistency of ratings/reliability. All values were at .7 or above.

counts and percentages) were examined to reveal trends in extant assessment capacity and assessment use (addressing RQ1 and RQ2). Mean capacity and use values were also used in inferential procedures addressing RQ3 and RQ4. Inferential statistical procedures were utilized to reveal relationships between types of assessment capacity and assessment use, thereby shedding light on which capacity types seemed most (or least) important for assessment usefulness in FL programs (these included Pearson correlations, principal components analysis, and multiple linear regression). An additional, final procedure involved separating respondents into two groups—high and low assessment users—and performing a profile analysis (i.e., repeated measures ANOVA with two groups) to compare the assessment capacity of FL programs demonstrating greater or lesser assessment usefulness.

Results

Of the 1,513 programs contacted, complete data sets were collected from 100 programs ("complete data sets" refers to information from a single program on *all* assessment capacity categories and use, from either a single respondent or a pair of respondents). Thus, 6.6% of the population is represented in the study. Such a low response rate, of course, is well within the range of non-response error and potential bias (preventing generalization of results to a population; Dillman, 2007). Yet, the wide variability in the data suggests that results at least capture the *range* of capacity and use trends (and relationships) in the post-secondary FL program population, if not their precise proportions.

Respondents background information and program information

Respondents provided background information on themselves and their institutions and programs. As shown in Table 2, most respondents were professors at various ranks, though mostly at the associate rank (40%) and/or department chairs (33%). Furthermore, assessment was conducted in various institutional settings. Of programs, 52% were at private universities, 48% were at public universities. Fifty-six percent of programs were in graduate-degree-granting institutions (i.e., offering MA and/or PhD degrees), while 44% offered BA degrees only. Sixty-three percent of FL programs were a subsection of a language department, 34% were a dedicated department, and 7% were housed within a college or school (note that some respondents chose more than one answer option). Respondents also reported on program size, which was defined in terms of the number of major enrollments. The mean number of enrolments was 101.22 (SD = 304.31). The smallest program had two majors; the largest program had 2,500.

Table 2. Titles of respondents

title	n	%
associate professor	40	40%
chair	33	33%
professor	26	26%
assistant professor	15	15%
coordinator, [language] program	8	8%

director, undergraduate studies	6	6%
director, [language] program	5	5%
advisor, undergraduate	3	3%
section head	3	3%
coordinator	2	2%
senior lecturer	2	2%
other single titles	37	37%

Language degree programs represented in the study roughly resemble proportions in the original population (see Table 3). Unsurprisingly, Spanish (32%) was the most frequently indicated language major, followed by French (16%) and German (13%).

Table 3. Language majors

major*	n	%
Spanish	32	32%
French	16	16%
German	13	13%
Chinese	4	4%
Arabic	3	3%
Classics	3	3%
French & Francophone Studies	3	3%
German Studies	3	3%
Japanese	3	3%
Classical Languages	2	2%
Classical Studies	2	2%
Italian	2	2%
Norwegian	2	2%
Portuguese	2	2%
other single languages	24	24%

* Language major titles were self reported.

Respondents were also asked to indicate the length of time the program had been conducting assessment. The mean length of time was 5.68 years ($SD = 4.84$). The longest period was 25 years; the shortest was 3.6 months.

Research question 1: Extent of assessment capacity in FL programs

Respondents rated the extent of capacity in their programs/departments and institutions in the nine capacity categories noted above. Space limitations prevent reporting rating results for all individual items within each capacity category (see Davis, 2012, for complete results). Instead, Table 4 shows percentages of total ratings, for all items within a capacity category, at each point of the two rating scales. Note that two scale-types were used: (a) *1 = not at all, 2, 3, 4 = a lot / very much*; (b) *1 = no, 2 = developing, 3 = yes*.

Table 4. Total percentages of ratings in each capacity category

capacity construct	no	developing	yes	don't know, n/a
institutional assessment support	37.8%	11.8%	**42.8%**	7.6%
institutional policies & governance	23.6%	17.4%	**53.7%**	5.2%
assessment infrastructures	37.7%	22.3%	**40.0%**	
program-level support & resources	69.2%	10.7%	16.2%	3.9%
total	**43.5%**	15.7%	36.9%	3.9%
	1 *not at all*	**2**	**3**	**4** *a lot*
program-level assessment leadership*	**30.7%**	20.9%	24.0%	22.2%
program ethos	16.7%	**29.4%**	28.1%	25.9%
assessment-related collaboration	**32.7%**	30.8%	21.2%	15.3%
assessment-related communication	27.3%	**33.3%**	21.6%	17.8%
high-quality activities & conditions	**29.2%**	26.4%	25.3%	19.1%
total	**27.1%**	26.6%	24.7%	20.9%

* "Don't know" responses = 2.2%

Table 4 shows that assessment capacity appears to be highly variable in FL programs. On the one hand, all capacity types existed to some extent in FL programs; on the other, some programs reported no capacity in all categories. Moreover, some categories showed trends in the direction of more or less capacity. For example, capacity in the areas of Institutional Support (42.8%), Institutional Policies/Governance (53.7%), and Infrastructures (40%) was, on balance, marginally more present than absent in FL programs (or substantially more present if "developing" ratings are regarded as indicating extant, if nascent, capacity). Recall that these particular dimensions of capacity are claimed here to be the more institutionally-oriented (i.e., accreditation-driven) varieties. By contrast, the remaining capacity results, while largely split, tended marginally toward the "no" or 1–2 range, suggesting that capacity in these areas was marginally less developed. Program Ethos, however, was the exception with a greater proportion of ratings in the 3–4 range (28.1%; 25.9%). An initial interpretation of these results is that while there is wide variability in capacity levels, accreditation-driven, compliance-oriented capacity is marginally more present than other capacity types.

Research question 2: Extent of assessment use in FL Programs

RQ2 inquired into the degree of assessment use in FL programs, arguably a key initial indicator of the impact of the accreditation-driven assessment initiative.

Table 5. Assessment use in FL programs

To what extent have assessment findings been used to …?	M	SD	not at all 1	2	3	a lot 4
k) meet institutional assessment requirements	2.87	1.17	21.2% (21)	11.1% (11)	27.3% (27)	**40.4% (40)**
l) create institutional assessment reports	2.77	1.20	25.0% (25)	11.0% (11)	26.0% (26)	**38.0% (38)**
m) justify/defend the program	2.25	1.10	**33.0% (33)**	26.0% (26)	24.0% (24)	17.0% (17)
a) develop/modify instruction/courses	2.20	0.95	27.0% (27)	**36.0% (36)**	27.0% (27)	10.0% (10)
b) develop/modify significant components of your program	2.16	1.00	31.3% (31)	**32.3% (32)**	25.3% (25)	11.1% (11)
g) better understand curricula	2.15	1.02	**33.3% (33)**	30.3% (30)	24.2% (24)	12.1% (12)
h) better understand teaching	2.12	0.98	32.3% (32)	**33.3% (33)**	24.2% (24)	10.1% (10)
j) better understand the value or worth of the program	2.12	1.04	**35.4% (35)**	30.3% (30)	21.2% (21)	13.1% (13)
i) better understand outcomes assessment in the program	2.08	0.96	32.7% (32)	**35.7% (35)**	22.4% (22)	9.2% (9)
n) communicate learning expectations to students, the institution, employers, the public	2.06	1.01	**38.4% (38)**	26.3% (26)	26.3% (26)	9.1% (9)
f) promote ongoing assessment efforts	1.96	1.02	**44.4% (44)**	24.2% (24)	22.2% (22)	9.1% (9)
o) showcase student knowledge, skills, and dispositions	1.96	0.99	**41.0% (41)**	32.0% (32)	17.0% (17)	10.0% (10)
p) demonstrate the value of foreign language studies to students, the institution, the public	1.93	1.05	**46.0% (46)**	27.0% (27)	15.0% (15)	12.0% (12)
c) develop/create new programs	1.77	0.94	**50.0% (50)**	31.0% (31)	11.0% (11)	8.0% (8)
d) compare the department/program with other departments/programs	1.72	0.90	**54.5% (54)**	23.2% (23)	18.2% (18)	4.0% (4)
e) make requests for resources	1.72	0.90	**53.0% (53)**	27.0% (27)	15.0% (15)	5.0% (5)
total	2.12	1.01	37.4%	27.3%	21.6%	13.6%
			64.7%		35.3%	

note. Bolded values are the largest counts and percentages for a given item.

Results for assessment uses are shown in Table 5. The highest mean rating was for use of assessment to meet institutional assessment requirements ($M = 2.87$); the lowest mean rating was using assessment to request resources ($M = 1.72$). Turning to counts and percentages, aggregate use totals (at the bottom of Table 5) suggest that aggregate assessment use in FL programs was generally more absent or infrequent than common or frequent. Of use item ratings, 64.7% are in the 1–2 (i.e., low use) range, while 35.3% of ratings are in the 3–4 range (i.e., high use). The notable exceptions to this pattern, of course, are assessment use to meet institutional requirements (item k) and to construct assessment reports (l), the only use types in the 3–4, or frequent, ranges. Crucially, uses of assessment for various types of educational improvement and understanding (e.g., items a, b, f, g, h, i, j, m, n, and o) were less common than compliance-type uses. Note, however, that despite the overall trends, there were still numerous instances of assessment use for improvement and understanding. Some programs, then, do seem to be realizing the reform-oriented assessment goals envisioned by regional accreditors. Given the clear variability in these results regarding the uses of assessment, further analysis explored the types of assessment capacity that seem most related to, or that most account for, high amounts of assessment usefulness in FL degree programs.

Research questions 3 and 4: Relationships between assessment capacity and use

Again, four inferential procedures were conducted to explore the strength of relationship between amounts and types of capacity and assessment use: Pearson product-moment correlation, principal components analysis, multiple regression, and profile analysis. Each FL program's mean ratings for each capacity category (i.e., the average rating for all items in a given capacity category) and assessment use (i.e., the average rating for all items in the use category) were used in all four procedures.

Pearson product-moment correlation—pair-wise relationships between capacity categories and use

Table 6 indicates that all capacity variables correlated statistically significantly with assessment use ($p<.01$), a somewhat unsurprising outcome given the relatively large N size. Moreover, some correlations were stronger than others, particularly relationships between use and the more "personnel-oriented" capacity types having to do with how people think and act within programs. The strongest correlations were between assessment use and Quality Assessment Activities/Conditions ($r = .741$). Assessment-related Communication correlated next most strongly ($r = .695$), followed by assessment-related Collaboration ($r = .641$). Variables with coefficients in the .5 range indicated moderately strong effects (Cohen, 1992), including Ethos ($r = .565$), Leadership ($r = .543$), and Infrastructures (use: $r = .520$). The capacity construct with the weakest relationships was Institutional Support ($r = .354$); the next weakest were Institutional Governance/Policies ($r = .487$), and Program-Level Support ($r = .479$).

Table 6. Pearson Correlations: Assessment capacity and assessment use

	inst. support	inst. gov./pol.	infrastructures	program support	leadership	ethos	collaboration	communication	act. & cond.	use 1
inst. support	1	.453*	.458*	.585*	.364*	.396*	.464*	.473*	.367*	.354*
inst. gov./pol.		1	.622*	.429*	.505*	.351*	.448*	.499*	.541*	.487*
infra-structures			1	.606*	.463*	.372*	.512*	.597*	.672*	.520*
program support				1	.394*	.311*	.440*	.462*	.474*	.479*
leadership					1	.448*	.539*	.617*	.545*	.543*
ethos						1	.669*	.588*	.487*	.565*
collabo-ration							1	.758*	.709*	.641*
communi-cation								1	.761*	.695*
act. & cond.									1	.741*
use 1										1

* Correlation is significant at the 0.01 level (2-tailed).

Principal components analysis—underlying capacity variables

A noteworthy aspect of the Pearson correlation results was an apparent hierarchy of relationships between capacity categories and assessment use, with High-Quality Activities/Conditions demonstrating the strongest relationship and Institutional Support demonstrating the weakest. The remaining statistical procedures explore this hierarchy, as well as its implications for the ostensible usefulness of mandated assessment capacity in college FL programs.

To these ends, a principal components analysis was performed to explore which subsets of capacity variables correlated uniquely with one another (i.e., which factors seem to underlie assessment capacity and/or use) and what such groupings might imply about relationships between assessment capacity and assessment usefulness.[9] The analysis identified two factors accounting for 68% of the total variance in the sample (see Table 7). Component 1 was comprised of a number of variables at loadings of $r = .70$ or above: (a) use ($r = .836$), (b) Activities/Conditions ($r = .790$), (c) assessment-related Collaboration ($r = .799$), (d) Program Ethos ($r = .722$), and (e) assessment-related Communication ($r = .776$). Component 2, by

---

[9] Varimax rotation was selected since there was no empirical basis to expect components would correlate (Field, 2005). The analysis was set to retain factors with eigenvalues greater than 1.00.

contrast, was comprised of a different set of variables at loadings close to or above $r = .70$: (a) Program-Level Support ($r = .800$), (b) Institutional Assessment Support ($r = .773$), (c) Infrastructures ($r = .721$), (d) Institutional Assessment Governance/Policies ($r = .681$).

An initial observation at this stage of the discussion is that the PCA analysis seemed to isolate two distinct groups of co-varying capacity types. Component 1 reflects capacities less associated with institutional requirements and more, arguably, with factors and conditions realized by personnel within programs. Component 2, by contrast, is roughly opposite in composition. The group of loading variables for this factor did not include, crucially, Use, but rather a number of assessment capacity constructs associated with accreditation mandates and institutionally driven assessment capacity building.

Table 7. Principal components analysis: Factor loadings for capacity and use averages*

	component		
	1	2	h^2
institutional assessment support	.191	.773	.80
institutional policies & governance	.339	.681	.78
assessment infrastructures	.412	.721	.74
program-level support & resources	.231	.800	.77
program-level assessment leadership	.602	.383	.76
program ethos	.722	.172	.55
assessment-related collaboration	.799	.316	.51
assessment-related communication	.776	.398	.69
high-quality activities & conditions	.790	.383	.63
use 1	.836	.277	.69
use 2**	.861	.244	.58
proportion of variance	.41	.27	.68

Rotation method: Varimax with Kaiser Normalization.
* See footnote.[10]

Multiple regression #1—capacity categories that predict use

To further explore capacity variables that seemed most related to use, the study was interested in investigating specifically predictive relationships between capacity categories and use. Multiple regression procedures were performed for this purpose to see which of the capacity constructs (predictor variables) most strongly predicted assessment use (the criterion variable).

A stepwise multiple regression (beginning with all nine capacity variables) identified two statistically significant models for predicting assessment use based on a combination of two variables: Activities/Conditions and Program Ethos. As shown

---

[10] The original study was interested in *two* types of assessment use: actions resulting from findings on student performance (i.e., findings use, or "use 1"), and learning or other incidental benefits from involvement in the assessment process itself (i.e., process use, or "use 2" noted above). Given space limitations only results related to findings use are presented here.

in Table 8, Activities/Conditions alone predicted a large proportion of the variance in use, $R^2 = .55$. The addition of Ethos increased the prediction slightly, $R^2 = .60$. Unstandardized beta values (Table 9) indicated that an increase of one point in the Ethos and Activities/Conditions variables was related to an increase of between .27 and .61 score points on the assessment use variable.[11]

Table 8. Model summary: Use as criterion variable

model*	R	R^2	adjusted R^2	std. error of the estimate	change statistics				
					R^2 change	F change	$df1$	$df2$	sig. F change
1	.741	.550	.545	.6743157	.550	119.585	1	98	.000
2	.777	.604	.596	.6353846	.055	13.377	1	97	.000

* Model 1 predictors: (constant), activities/conditions; Model 2 predictors: (constant), activities conditions, ethos

Table 9. Coefficients: Use as criterion variable

model*	unstandardized coefficients		standardized coefficients	t	sig.	95.0% confidence interval for B		correlations			collinearity statistics	
	B	std. error	beta			lower bound	upper bound	zero-order	partial	part	toler-ance	VIF
1	−.006	.067		−.087	.931	−.140	.128					
	.741	.068	.741	10.936	.000	.606	.875	.741	.741	.741	1.000	1.000
2	−.006	.064		−.090	.929	−.132	.120					
	.611	.073	.611	8.358	.000	.466	.756	.741	.647	.534	.763	1.310
	.267	.073	.267	3.657	.000	.122	.412	.565	.348	.234	.763	1.310

* Model 1 predictors: (constant), activities/conditions; Model 2 predictors: (constant), activities/conditions, ethos

Multiple regression #2—the Activities/Conditions predictor variable removed

Since Activities/Conditions accounted for so much unique variation of the use criterion variable in the first regression, an additional analysis was conducted, though this time with the Activities/Conditions predictor variable omitted. This was done since the Activities/Conditions capacity construct captured especially high-quality assessment practices that would very much be expected to predict assessment use. Thus, a decision was made to omit this variable to see what other capacity variables might emerge as substantial predictors.

---

[11] Note that a key assumption was violated in this study having to do with the low cases-to-predictor variable ratio, in light of the low overall N of 100. Findings from the regression analysis must be interpreted cautiously given considerable unknown error associated with the large number of variables under analysis as compared with the small N-size.

The second regression identified three statistically significant models for predicting use, including combinations of one to three variables (Communication, Ethos, Program Support). Table 10 shows that without Activities/Conditions, Communication predicted the largest proportion of variance in use, $R^2 = .482$. Adding Ethos increased the prediction somewhat, $R^2 = .520$, and adding Program Support increased the prediction marginally, $R^2 = .548$. Unstandardized beta values (Table 11) indicated that an increase of one point in each of these three variables was related to an increase of between .19 to .47 score points on the use variable.

Table 10. Model summary: Use as criterion variable (activities & conditions omitted)

model*	R	R^2	adjusted R^2	std. error of the estimate	change statistics				
					R^2 change	F change	df1	df2	sig. F change
1	.695	.482	.477	.7228151	.482	91.366	1	98	.000
2	.721	.520	.510	.6996952	.038	7.583	1	97	.007
3	.740	.548	.534	.6823193	.028	6.003	1	96	.016

* Model 1 predictors: (constant), communication; Model 2 predictors: (constant), communication, ethos; Model 3 predictors: (constant), communication, ethos, program support

Table 11. Coefficients: Use as criterion variable (activities & conditions omitted)

model*	unstandardized coefficients		standardized coefficients	t	sig.	95.0% confidence interval for B		correlations			collinearity statistics	
	B	std. error	beta			lower bound	upper bound	zero-order	partial	part	tolerance	VIF
1	−.007	.072		−.096	.924	−.150	.137					
	.694	.073	.695	9.559	.000	.550	.839	.695	.695	.695	1.000	1.000
2	−.007	.070		−.093	.926	−.145	.132					
	.554	.087	.554	6.372	.000	.381	.726	.695	.543	.448	.655	1.527
	.239	.087	.239	2.754	.007	.067	.412	.565	.269	.194	.655	1.527
3	−.005	.068		−.068	.946	−.140	.131					
	.473	.091	.473	5.199	.000	.292	.653	.695	.469	.357	.569	1.759
	.228	.085	.228	2.685	.009	.059	.396	.565	.264	.184	.653	1.532
	.190	.077	.190	2.450	.016	.036	.344	.479	.243	.168	.785	1.275

* Model 1 predictors: (constant), communication; Model 2 predictors: (constant), communication, ethos; Model 3 predictors: (constant), communication, ethos, program support

Profile analysis

A final statistical procedure, profile analysis (using repeated-measures ANOVA), was performed to explore how programs with relatively high versus relatively low assessment use differed from one another with respect to type and amount of assessment capacity. Two groups were defined in terms of their average assessment use ratings (transformed into integers). Programs with a 3 or 4 mean use rating were grouped together forming the "high-use" group; programs with a 1 or 2 mean use rating were grouped together forming the "low-use" group. Of interest, then, was the question "For programs that tend to use (or not use) assessment, what does their capacity profile look like?" And furthermore, "What capacities do high versus low use programs have? What capacities do they lack?"

The key concern for profile analysis is whether groups differ from one another on a set of measures (Tabachnick & Fidell, 2001), or, in this case, whether high/low use groups differ from one another on their mean scores across different capacity categories. Three aspects of profile analysis indicate these differences: *level, flatness,* and *parallelism.*

Level refers to whether groups are statistically different from one another when the levels of the within-group factor (i.e., average capacity ratings) are collapsed. Put another way, with respect to capacity overall, do the groups differ from each other?

Flatness has to do with whether the entire sample (ignoring group differentiation) shows significant differences across the average ratings of the nine capacity constructs. That is to say, does the entire respondent group differ significantly in their mean ratings for each of the capacity constructs? Flatness exists when the within groups factor is not significant.

Parallelism refers to whether the groups along the levels of a within-subjects factor (capacity categories) are similar. The test for parallelism asks if, for example, the difference in mean ratings between Leadership and Ethos is the same for the high use group and the low use group. If so, the groups are parallel. The question of parallelism addresses the same question as the interaction effect in a two-way repeated-measures ANOVA.

Results of the two-way repeated-measures ANOVA procedure for use are shown in Table 13. Results indicated that only the level factor was statistically significant.

The first effect shown in Table 12 is the effect for flatness, indicating results did not deviate significantly from flatness ($F = .199$, $p = .980$, partial eta^2 = .002, power = .104). That is, the entire sample did not differ significantly across the average means of the nine capacity categories (i.e., the entire group FL programs in this study had similar levels of capacity in each of the nine categories).

The second effect shown in Table 12 is the interaction effect for parallelism. Results show no significant difference, indicating that the two groups did not differ in their patterns of highs and lows over the nine capacity categories ($F = 6.605$, $p = .115$, partial eta^2 = .017, power = .664).

The effect shown in Table 13 is the group effect for level, and it indicates significant differences between groups ($F = 68.624$, $p = .000$, partial eta^2 = .412, power = 1.000). Table 14 indicates that statistical differences for pair-wise comparisons existed between groups 1 and 2.

Table 12. Tests of within-groups effects (findings use)

source	sum of squares	df	mean square	F	p.	partial eta²	noncent. parameter	observed power*
capacity (flatness)	.775	6.292	.123	.199	.980	.002	1.254	.104
capacity x findings use (parallelism)	6.605	6.292	1.050	1.698	.115	.017	10.685	.664
error	381.141	616.590	.618					

* Computed using alpha = .05

Table 13. Tests of between-groups effects (findings use)

source	sum of squares	df	mean square	F	p.	partial eta²	noncent. parameter	observed power*
findings use (level)	207.316	1	207.316	68.624	.000	.412	68.624	1.000
error	296.061	98	3.021					

* Computed using alpha = .05

Table 14. Pair-wise comparisons (findings use)

(I) findings use	(J) findings use	mean difference* (I-J)	std. error	sig.	95% confidence interval	
					lower bound	upper bound
1	2	−1.013	0.128	0.000	−1.256	−0.770
2	1	1.013	0.128	0.000	0.770	1.256

note. Based on observed means. The error term is mean square (error) = . 280.
* The mean difference is significant at the .05 level.

Despite the lack of statistically significant differences for flatness and parallelism,[12] observations of Figure 5 suggest that trends can be identified (the implications to be developed in the next section). The two groups would appear to differ in key ways. First, the high-use group consistently demonstrated greater capacity values across all the capacity construct variables (supported by the significant *level* results). Further, the groups seemed to demonstrate opposite profiles or trends of assessment capacity. For the high-use group, the lowest capacity values/levels were in the categories of Institutional Support, Institutional Governance/Policies, Infrastructures, and Program Support. By contrast, the low-use group demonstrated the highest levels of capacity in these same areas. For the subsequent capacity constructs, there was a fanning out pattern such that the high the use group steadily climbed in mean capacity ratings, peaking at assessment Communication, while the low use group decreased in capacity ratings, the nadir also in the Communication

---

[12] Arguably, the number of Bonferroni adjustments required for the analysis made it difficult to achieve significant results.

category. For low-users of assessment, then, what little capacity they have was more of the institutionally-driven variety, with capacity progressively decreasing in the other areas; while for high-users of assessment, although on the whole they had higher capacities across the board, the highest were in the more program-internal assessment capacity dimensions.

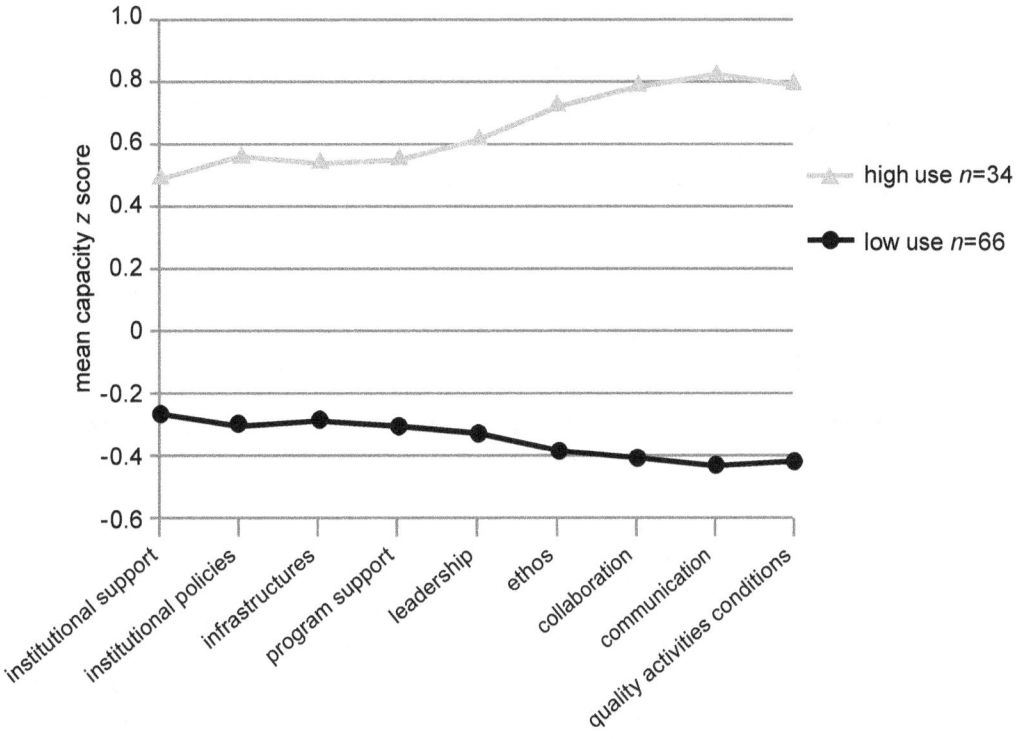

Figure 5. Profile analysis plot: Mean capacity scores for high and low use groups.

Discussion

Since the early 1990s, regional accreditation commissions have gradually incorporated assessment into accreditation review, aiming to drive educational innovation and improvement in U.S. post-secondary institutions. Despite a long history of using assessment toward various language education purposes, accreditation-mandated assessment figures to be one of the most pervasive and far reaching reform interventions in the history of university-level FL education. What has been the broad impact of this mandate in college FL education programs? This study has tried to understand this impact in terms of the types of assessment capacity in FL programs that seem most related to assessment usefulness. The specific concerns of the study were to gauge the amounts and types of assessment capacity in FL programs; to shed light on the nature and extent of assessment use in FL programs; and to ascertain relationships between capacity and use, particularly relationships between use and institutionally-driven capacity types.

Starting with the extant assessment capacity in university FL education, it would seem that many FL programs have established—or have begun to establish—the conditions, frameworks, and activities needed for productively useful outcomes assessment. Clearly, some programs have been energetic and industrious in their assessment efforts, developing robust capacity in all framework categories. Yet, if the optimal capacity profile in FL programs is development of capability across the board, not all programs have reached that mark. Capacity for many programs is either nascent or absent entirely in many areas. Thus, while some programs have forged ahead with assessment efforts, others lag behind. Moreover, evidence suggests that the (marginally) more developed capacity types are those associated with accreditation, or the various ways in which the institution manages, supports, or mandates assessment activity. The prominence of institutionally-driven capacity will be unsurprising in that it reflects the relatively recent phenomena of language educators reacting to new and pressing assessment requirements embedded within accreditation review. Assessment capacity building in FL programs, then, has been widespread, if uneven, and it is hard to imagine this considerable level of assessment activity without the widespread influence of institutional accreditation.

As with assessment capacity, the frequency of assessment use in FL programs is likewise a mixed picture. Overall, the trend of assessment use in FL programs is marginally more toward infrequency than frequency. However, imagining, for the moment, assessment activity in FL programs without the recent influence of accreditation, it seems fair to say that some assessment use in post-secondary FL education is at least apparent, an outcome for which the accountability movement and accreditation commissions can be credited. Tempering this positive view, of course, is the finding that FL educators most commonly use assessment to satisfy institutional requirements. Using assessment primarily toward institutional compliance, and less for improvement-oriented reform, is presumably not what accreditation commissions and other interested stakeholders have intended to accomplish. Such a finding mirrors a broad concern throughout higher education that many post-secondary educators and administrators—including FL faculty and staff, it would seem—are failing to "close the assessment loop" and use assessment toward improvement-oriented ends. Yet, these trends notwithstanding, a number of programs do appear to be using assessment frequently and in a variety of productive ways, including toward different types of educational understanding and innovation. The interest for this study, then, is how to account for these successes in some programs, and in particular, how (and whether) accreditation mandates influence these more promising instances of assessment use.

The various inferential procedures exploring relationships between assessment capacity and use start to shed light on these concerns (addressing RQ3 and RQ4). First, pair-wise correlations between use and capacity categories indicated that *all* capacity constructs have some relationship to use. Such a finding provides a certain validation of the assessment capacity framework generally, in that the overall construct was meant to be a comprehensive listing (to the extent possible) of factors that dispose a FL program toward productive assessment use.

However, crucially, correlations—and the other statistical procedures—also showed that some capacity types are more strongly related to use than others, a finding that would seem to have implications for the efficacy of accreditation assessment mandates. For example, the PCA analysis found two underlying variables, one with factor loadings on Leadership, Ethos, Communication, Collaboration, Quality Activities/Conditions *and Use,* and another with loadings on Institutional Support,

Institutional Governance/Policies, Infrastructures, and Program Support only. Crucially, use was not strongly associated with the second component. Moreover, the two multiple regression analyses further identified particular capacity constructs strongly related to use: in the first regression procedure, Quality Activities/Conditions (with Ethos increasing the prediction slightly); and in the second procedure, Communication (with Ethos and Program Support increasing the prediction slightly). Finally, the profile analysis procedure likewise delineated a number of key use-inducing capacity variables. High-use programs showed a trend of higher mean capacity ratings for Leadership, Ethos, Communication, Collaboration, and Quality Activities/Conditions, and lower ratings for Institutional Support, Institutional Governance/Policies, Infrastructures, and Program Support.

Taken together, results appear to isolate a key group of capacity constructs that, when present in a FL program, seem to strongly dispose assessment efforts toward meaningful use (a finding addressing RQ3). Specifically, this study has found that the productive use of assessment in FL programs is more likely to occur if there is (a) effective, productive collaboration on assessment work between program constituents, (b) skilled prosecution of assessment tasks (captured by the activities and conditions capacity construct), (c) facilitative communication between program constituents during assessment work, (d) a prevailing program ethos conducive to assessment-driven innovation, and (e) program or departmental leadership committed to assessment success. How might this group of capacity constructs be characterized relative to the other less useful capacity types? One interpretation, hinted at prior, is to regard these constructs as capturing specific aspects of assessment capacity related to the *agency of people within programs*—that is, the volition of individuals within FL departments that make assessment happen in particular ways.

A corollary finding, then (addressing RQ4), is that the institutionally-oriented dimensions of assessment capacity associated with accreditation review— again, Institutional Support, Institutional Governance/Policies, and assessment Infrastructures—*do not* contribute to use as powerfully as other capacity constructs in the assessment framework. The profile analysis reflected this finding perhaps most starkly. For those programs that rarely (or never) use assessment, the types of capacity in greatest supply were the accreditation-mandated, institutionally-driven varieties. More scarce, by contrast, were the program-internal, personnel-oriented capacity types proposed in this study to have the strongest relationships to assessment use.

Of course, it would be wrong to claim that accreditation-driven assessment is entirely unrelated to assessment usefulness. It stands to reason that effective institutional management and support from the institution aids FL educators in their assessment efforts. Recall that high-use FL programs enjoy more capacity in all categories, including the institutionally-driven varieties. Nevertheless, findings from this study suggest that more or less facilitative institutional support and governance is not strongly associated with a frequent and varied use of assessment in FL programs. That is to say (to be very explicit), the way in which the institution manages its accreditation-prescribed assessment responsibilities—the degree of technology support, technical assistance, funding, training, rewards/incentives, flexibility, monitoring, supportive institutional leadership, integration into university processes (tenure review, course proposals, etc.), provision of time, and so on—

these various aids and requirements do not have a strongly predictive relationship with assessment usefulness in FL programs. I thus interpret this finding as indicating that accreditation-mandated assessment as it is currently leveraged on university FL programs is handicapped in its ability to enhance foreign language educational effectiveness. The impact of accreditation-driven assessment, rather, has been to instantiate particular types of assessment practices that by themselves are insufficient for transformative assessment use.

Conclusion

The study has provided evidence suggesting that institutionally driven outcomes assessment capacity—in the best case scenario—is auxiliary to assessment efforts, but ultimately unable to cause the transformative, meaningful assessment experiences this particular system of assessment-driven accountability is tasked with creating. As such, there would seem to be empirical support for those who have claimed that the ultimate responsibility for making assessment a useful endeavor in post-secondary FL education lies with educators themselves. For the time being, mandated assessment functions as a bureaucratic, administrative add-on that succeeds mainly in satisfying accreditation review and fails (largely) in transforming educational processes. For such transformations to occur, some have argued for a sea change in FL educational practice toward a genuine valuing and pursuit of quality educational delivery—a realization of "assessment culture" in FL programs—within which assessment plays a primary role (Byrnes, 2008; Norris, 2006a, among others). What might a "culture of assessment" look like? Arguably, this study provides an initial conceptualization in terms of a framework for use-inducing assessment capacity. Of course, the framework proposed here does not capture the idiosyncratic, contextual elements needed to drive assessment use in all FL programs. Yet, there is now a more detailed conception of what might generally be required for productive assessment-driven inquiry in post-secondary FL education. Crucially, that mode of inquiry has less to do with the influence of institutional administrations and accreditation review, and more with the motivations of individuals within FL departments.

Acknowledgments

This study is based on a PhD dissertation research project undertaken at the University of Hawai'i at Mānoa. My thanks to Professor John Norris for his supervision, assistance, and surfing companionship.

References

Adair-Hauck, B., Glisan, E. W., Koda, K., Sandrock, S. P., & Swender, E. (2006). The integrated performance assessment (IPA): Connecting assessment to instruction and learning. *Foreign Language Annals, 39*(3), 359–382.

Atkins, M., Supahan, S., & Lewis, C. (2008). *Fighting for validation: California indigenous language teacher credentialing.* Workshop presented at the Language in Life Conference, Sausalito, CA. Retrieved from http://www.aicls.org/pdf/LILC08Teacher_Sum.pdf

Banta, T. W. (2002). Characteristics of effective outcomes assessment. In T. W. Banta (Ed.), *Building a scholarship of assessment* (pp. 261–283). San Francisco, CA: Jossey-Bass.

Banta, T. W., Jones, E. A., & Black, K. E. (2009). *Designing effective assessment: Principles and profiles of good practice.* San Francisco, CA: Jossey-Bass.

Banta, T. W., Lund, J. P., Black, K. E., & Oblander, F. W. (1996). Assessing student achievement in general education. In T. W. Banta & Associates, *Assessment in practice: Putting principles to work on college campuses* (pp. 153–230). San Francisco, CA: Jossey-Bass.

Beno, B. A. (2004). The role of student learning outcomes in accreditation quality review. *New Directions for Community Colleges, 126,* 65–72.

Blaich, C., & Wise, K. (2011). *The Wabash national study: The impact of teaching practices and institutional conditions on student growth.* Crawfordsville, IN: Center of Inquiry, Wabash College. Retrieved from http://static1.1.sqspcdn.com/static/f/333946/12586532/1307467024793/Wabash-Study-Student-Growth_Blaich-Wise_AERA-2011.pdf?token=riIB47543aeYy1ijRaafMJPVIMg%3D

Bresciani, M. J. (2006). *Outcomes-based academic and co-curricular program review: A compilation of institutional good practices.* Sterling, VA: Stylus.

Byrnes, H. (2006). The outcomes of collegiate FL programs: Specifications, assessment, evaluation. *Modern Language Journal, 90*(4), 574–576.

Byrnes, H. (2008). Owning up to ownership of foreign language program outcomes assessment. *ADFL Bulletin, 39*(2–3), 28–30.

Byrnes, H., Maxim, H., & Norris, J. M. (2010). Realizing advanced FL writing development in collegiate education: Curricular design, pedagogy, assessment. *Modern Language Journal*, Monograph. Cambridge, MA: Blackwell.

Carstens-Wickham, B. (2008). Assessment and foreign languages: A chair's perspective. *ADFL Bulletin, 39*(2–3), 36–43.

Cohen, J. (1992). A power primer. *Psychological Bulletin, 112*(1), 155–159.

Davis, J. McE. (2012). *The usefulness of accreditation-mandated outcomes assessment in college foreign language education* (Unpublished doctoral dissertation). University of Hawai'i at Mānoa, Honolulu.

Davis, J. McE., Sinicrope, C., & Watanabe, Y. (2009). College foreign language program evaluation: Current practice, future directions. In J. M. Norris, J. McE. Davis, C. Sinicrope, & Y. Watanabe (Eds.), *Toward useful program evaluation in college foreign language education* (pp. 209–226). Honolulu: University of Hawai'i, National Foreign Language Resource Center.

Dillman, D. A. (2007). *Mail and internet surveys: The tailored design method* (2nd ed.). New York, NY: John Wiley & Sons.

Driscoll, A., & Cordero de Noriega, D. (2006). *Taking ownership of accreditation: Assessment processes that promote institutional improvement and faculty engagement.* Sterling, VA: Stylus.

Ewell, P. T. (2000). Continuous improvement in the accreditation arena. *Assessment Update, 12*(4), 3, 13.

Ewell, P. T. (2001). *Accreditation and student learning outcomes: A proposed point of departure.* Washington, DC: Council for Higher Education Accreditation.

Ewell, P. T. (2002). An emerging scholarship: A brief history of assessment. In T. W. Banta (Ed.), *Building a scholarship of assessment* (pp. 3–25). San Francisco, CA: Jossey-Bass.

Ewell, P. T. (2008). Assessment and accountability in America today: Background and context. In V. M. H. Borden & G. Pike (Eds.), *Assessing and accounting for student learning: Beyond the Spellings Commission* (New Directions for Institutional Research, Assessment Supplement 2007, pp. 7–18). San Francisco, CA: Jossey-Bass.

Ewell, P. T. (2009). *Assessment, accountability, and improvement: Revisiting the tension. (NILOA Occasional Paper No.1)*. Urbana, IL: University of Illinois and Indiana University, National Institute of Learning Outcomes Assessment.

Field, A. (2005). *Discovering statistics using SPSS* (2nd ed.). London: Sage.

Grau Sempere, A., Mohn, M. C., & Pieroni, R. (2009). Improving educational effectiveness and promoting internal and external information-sharing through student learning outcomes assessment. In J. M. Norris, J. McE. Davis, C. Sinicrope, & Y. Watanabe (Eds.), *Toward Useful program evaluation in college foreign language education* (pp. 139–162). Honolulu: University of Hawai'i, National Foreign Language Resource Center.

Heiland, D., & Rosenthal, L. J. (Eds.). (2011). *Literary study, measurement, and the sublime: Disciplinary assessment*. New York, NY: The Teagle Foundation.

Holquist, M. (2010). Measuring the humanities: The slippery slope from assessment to standardization. In D. Heiland & L. J. Rosenthal (Eds.), *Literary study, measurement, and the sublime: Disciplinary assessment* (pp. 69–96). New York, NY: The Teagle Foundation.

Kuh, G. (2009). Foreword. In P. T. Ewell, *Assessment, accountability, and improvement: Revisiting the tension.* (NILOA Occasional Paper No.1). Urbana, IL: University of Illinois and Indiana University, National Institute of Learning Outcomes Assessment.

Kuh, G., & Ikenberry, S. (2009). *More than you think, less than we need: Learning outcomes assessment in American Higher Education*. Urbana, IL: University of Illinois and Indiana University, National Institute for Learning Outcomes Assessment (NILOA). Retrieved from http://carnegie.org/fileadmin/Media/Publications/PDF/niloafullreportfinal2.pdf

Le Hir, M. (2005). Advancing departmental objectives through assessment. *ADFL Bulletin, 36*(3), 28–39.

Linn, R. L. (2005). *Issues in the design of accountability systems (CSE technical report 650)*. Los Angeles: University of California, National Center for Research on Evaluation, Standards, and Student Testing (CRESST).

Linn, R. L. (2008). *Validation of uses and interpretations of state assessments*. Washington, DC: Council of Chief State School Officers.

Liskin-Gasparro, J. (1995). Practical approaches to outcomes assessment: The undergraduate major in foreign languages and literatures. *ADFL Bulletin, 26*(2), 21–27.

Mathews, T. J., & Hansen, C. M. (2004). Ongoing assessment of a university foreign language program. *Foreign Language Annals, 37*(4), 630–640.

McAlpine, D., & Dhonau, S. (2007). Creating a culture for the preparation of an ACTFL/NCATE Program Review. *Foreign Language Annals, 40*(2), 247–259.

Mentkowski, M., & Associates. (2000). *Learning that lasts: Integrating learning, development, and performance in college and beyond*. San Francisco, CA: Jossey Bass.

Milleret, M. (2008). The trials and tribulations of comprehensive program evaluation. *ADFL Bulletin, 39*(2–3), 44–48.

Milleret, M., & Silveira, A. S. (2009). The role of evaluation in curriculum development and growth of the UNM Portuguese program. In J. M. Norris, J. McE. Davis, C. Sinicrope, & Y. Watanabe (Eds.), *Toward useful program evaluation in college foreign language education* (pp. 57–82). Honolulu: University of Hawai'i, National Foreign Language Resource Center.

Modern Language Association. (2008). *Report to the Teagle Foundation on the undergraduate major in language and literature*. Retrieved from http://www.mla.org/pdf/2008_mla_whitepaper.pdf

Modern Language Association Ad Hoc Committee on Foreign Languages. (2007). Foreign languages and higher education: New structures for a changed world. *Profession 2007*, 234–245.

National Commission on Excellence in Education. (1983). *A nation at risk: The imperative for educational reform*. Retrieved from http://www2.ed.gov/pubs/NatAtRisk/index.html

National Governors' Association: Center for Public Policy Research and Analysis. (1986). *Time for results: The governors' 1991 report on education*. Washington, DC: The National Governors' Association.

National Standards in Foreign Language Education Project (1996). *Standards for foreign language learning: Preparing for the 21st century*. Yonkers, NY: Author.

New England Association of Schools and Colleges, Commission on Institutions of Higher Education. (2005). *Standards for accreditation*. Bedford, MA: Author. Retrieved from http://cihe.neasc.org/standards_policies/standards/standards_html_version

Norris, J. M. (2000). Purposeful language assessment. *English Teaching Forum, 38*(1), 18–23.

Norris, J. M. (2002). Interpretations, intended uses, and designs in task-based language assessment: Introduction to the special issue. *Language Testing, 19*(4), 337–346.

Norris, J. M. (2006a). The why (and how) of assessing student learning outcomes in college foreign language programs. *Modern Language Journal, 90*(4), 590–597.

Norris, J. M. (2006b). Assessing advanced foreign language learners: From measurement constructs to educational uses. In H. Byrnes, H. Weger-Guntharp, & K. Sprang (Eds.), *Educating for advanced FL capacities: Constructs, curriculum, instruction, assessment* (pp. 167–187). Washington, DC: Georgetown University Press.

Norris, J. M. (2008). *Validity evaluation in language assessment*. New York, NY: Peter Lang.

Norris, J. M. (Ed.). (2009a). Understanding and improving language education through program evaluation [Special issue]. *Language Teaching Research, 13*(7), 1–13.

Norris, J. M. (2009b). Introduction to the volume. In J. M. Norris, J. McE. Davis, C. Sinicrope, & Y. Watanabe (Eds.), *Toward useful program evaluation in college foreign language education* (pp. 1–4). Honolulu: University of Hawai'i, National Foreign Language Resource Center.

Norris, J. M., & Liskin-Gasparro, J. (2009, March). *The consequences of accreditation and outcomes assessment for college foreign language programs.* Paper presented at the invited colloquium Critical issues at the interface between assessment and U.S. language education policy at the annual conference of the American Association of Applied Linguistics, Denver, CO.

Omaggio-Hadley, A. (2001). *Teaching language in context* (3rd ed.). Boston, MA: Heinle & Heinle.

Patton, M. Q. (1997). *Utilization-focused evaluation: The new century text.* Thousand Oaks, CA: Sage.

Patton, M. Q. (2008). *Utilization-focused evaluation* (4th ed.). Thousand Oaks, CA: Sage.

Provezis, S. J. (2010). *Regional accreditation and learning outcomes assessment: Mapping the territory* (Doctoral dissertation, University of Illinois at Urbana-Champaign). Retrieved from https://www.ideals.illinois.edu/bitstream/handle/2142/16260/3_Provezis_Staci.pdf?sequence=6

Ramsay, V. (2009). Study abroad and evaluation: Critical changes to enhance linguistic and cultural growth. In J. M. Norris, J. McE. Davis, C. Sinicrope, & Y. Watanabe (Eds.), *Toward useful program evaluation in college foreign language education* (pp. 163–182). Honolulu: University of Hawai'i, National Foreign Language Resource Center.

Rhodes, N. C., & Pufahl, I. (2010). *Foreign language teaching in U.S. schools: Results of a national survey.* Washington, DC: Center for Applied Linguistics.

Ricardo-Osorio, J. G. (2011). The collaborative world languages department: A teamwork approach to assessing student learning outcomes. In D. Heiland & L. J. Rosenthal (Eds.), *Literary study, measurement, and the sublime: Disciplinary assessment* (pp. 321–334). New York, NY: The Teagle Foundation.

Rosenbusch, M. H. (2005). The No Child Left Behind Act and teaching and learning languages in U.S. schools. *Modern Language Journal, 89*(2), 250–261.

Rosenbusch, M. H., & Jensen, J. (2005). Status of foreign language programs in the NECTFL states. *NECTFL Review, 56,* 26–37.

Shepard, L. A. (2008). A brief history of accountability testing, 1965–2007. In K. E. Ryan & L. A. Shepard (Eds.), *The future of test-based educational accountability* (pp. 25–46). New York, NY: Routledge.

Shohamy, E. (1992). New modes of assessment. The connection between testing and learning. In E. Shohamy & R. A. Walton (Eds.), *Language assessment for feedback: Testing and other strategies* (pp. 7–28). Dubuque, IA: Kendall/Hunt.

Spellings Commission (2006). *A test of leadership: Charting the future of U.S. higher education.* Washington, DC: U.S. Department of Education.

Tabachnick, B. G., & Fidell, L. S. (2001). *Using multivariate statistics* (4th ed.). Boston, MA: Allyn and Bacon.

von Zastrow, C., & Janc, H. (2004) *Academic atrophy: The condition of the liberal arts in America's public schools.* Washington, DC: Council for Basic Education.

Vuksanovich, M. L. (2009). *The FLES teacher's voice: A case study examining the impact of the No Child Left Behind Act on elementary school foreign language teachers* (Doctoral dissertation). Retrieved from https://www.ideals.illinois.edu/handle/2142/16260

Walther, I. C. (2009). Developing and implementing an evaluation of the foreign language requirement at Duke University. In J. M. Norris, J. McE. Davis, C. Sinicrope, & Y. Watanabe (Eds.), *Toward useful program evaluation in college foreign language education* (pp. 117–138). Honolulu: University of Hawai'i, National Foreign Language Resource Center.

Walvoord, B. E. (2011). How to construct a simple, sensible, useful departmental assessment process. In D. Heiland & L. J. Rosenthal (Eds.), *Literary study, measurement, and the sublime: Disciplinary assessment* (pp. 335–352). New York, NY: The Teagle Foundation.

Watanabe, Y., Norris, J. M., & González-Lloret, M. (2009). Identifying and responding to evaluation needs in college foreign language programs. In J. M. Norris, J. McE. Davis, C. Sinicrope, & Y. Watanabe (Eds.), *Toward useful program evaluation in college foreign language education* (pp. 5–56). Honolulu: University of Hawai'i, National Foreign Language Resource Center.

Windham, S. (2008). Redesigning lower-level curricula for learning outcomes: A case study. *ADFL Bulletin, 39*(2–3), 31–35.

Wolff, R. A. (1992). Assessment and accreditation: A shotgun marriage? In Western Association of Schools and Colleges (Ed.), *Achieving institution effectiveness through assessment: A resource manual to support WASC institutions* (pp. 39–48). Oakland, CA: Western Association of Schools and Colleges Accrediting Commission for Senior Colleges and Universities.

The Uses of Use-Focused Assessment: Two Chairs' Perspectives

Theodore J. Cachey, Jr.
University of Notre Dame

Peter C. Pfeiffer
Georgetown University

The article offers examples of useful assessment practices of different scope from departments at Georgetown University and at the University of Notre Dame. The perspective taken is that of long-time chairpersons who lead the assessment initiatives in both institutions. The focus is on how academic administrators can fashion and conceptualize useful assessment projects in their own environments.

Introduction

In the following chapter, we want to present a "long view" of the value of our experiences with assessment projects as chairs of the Department of Romance Languages and Literatures at the University of Notre Dame University and the Department of German at Georgetown University, respectively. While there are considerable differences between our experiences with assessment as far as institutional and administrative contexts, scope of assessment projects, and specific assessment activities are concerned, there are also a number of significant and valuable experiences we share. First, we both view assessment activities as intellectually challenging and stimulating, a quality that supports the establishment of a discursive space where meaningful and structured conversations about the educational mission and practices of the department can occur as a *departmental* conversation. Second, we both view assessment projects as useful/beneficial in a variety of dimensions. In practical ways, such projects allow us insights into students' views about their learning experiences and into the effectiveness of our programs. They are equally useful in helping to communicate coherently and persuasively to internal and external audiences about the educational aims and values of our programs. Third, we share a sense of gratitude towards professional organizations, most importantly, the Association of Departments of Foreign Languages (ADFL) and the American Association of Teachers of German (AATG), which provided the contexts in which we first learned of assessment and could articulate and exchange our ideas on the value of assessment. In our experiences, assessment has offered a way out of the narrow institutional confines of a single department and provided a framework for addressing mutual intellectual and educational concerns across different languages and different institutions, thus creating a space for exchange that is complementary to that of disciplinary research. Finally, there is another similarity between us. We are both scholars trained in literary and cultural studies, not linguistics, with our individual research foci in Dante studies, and 19th and 20th century German literature and culture, respectively. Yet, as long-term academic administrators of our programs, we both found useful assessment afforded us an *intellectually* compelling and enriching framework for our and our colleagues' programmatic and departmental work. In the following, we will give a brief overview of the history of assessment projects and practices in our respective departments and then expand on a number of themes in the practice and usefulness of our assessment initiatives we feel were of particular relevance from our perspective as chairs, that is, as first-line academic administrators.

Histories of the assessment initiatives

Both authors are literary scholars who have engaged in assessment primarily in connection with their leadership responsibilities while serving multiple terms as department chairpersons. While one of the authors has developed over time significant expertise and a research profile in the assessment field, the other has largely depended upon the research and best practices developed by others as accessed through the secondary literature and through consultation with experts and practitioners in the field. Both authors have profited from participation in a consortium of schools engaged in assessment and have learned a lot from one another through collaboration in this context. This jointly authored essay is the result of our shared conviction that assessment represents a particularly fruitful way of engaging with an important dimension of our respective professional identities, and that our experiences with assessment, however diverse, might have some relevance for other colleagues including chairpersons who are considering developing their own assessment projects.

Georgetown

In the Georgetown University German Department (GUGD), the interest in assessment originated from a comprehensive curriculum renovation/reform. This project was initiated in February 1997, and first steps began to be implemented in the fall semester of the same year. As we specified learning goals, decided on pedagogical frameworks, developed teaching materials, and coordinated/articulated our four-year sequence of courses, it became clear we needed to know a lot more about students' learning and how our learning goals were, in fact, responsive to students' actual learning and educational goals. As it turned out, the development of a curriculum-specific placement test (Norris, 2006) proved to be an unplanned though almost ideal starting point for all common assessment initiatives over the years because it made us think comprehensively about every single stage of students' learning.[1] A number of aspects deserve special attention as they continue to influence how the GUGD and its members function and how we approach educational and curricular issues as they evolve. First, assessment helped us think *systematically* about course-level learning goals which ultimately lead to the understanding that learning objectives at the course level could most fruitfully be grasped when seen in a *curricular framework*. In this regard, assessment allowed us to truly understand and articulate the relationship between individual courses and the educational values that we, as a department, wanted to foster and as they are realized in the curriculum. Secondly, by ensuring all faculty members and graduate assistants were invited to participate in the conversations about learning goals and outcomes, appropriate assessment strategies, on-the-ground teaching experiences, and so forth, we created an *internal faculty development process*. This also modeled a departmental culture for and with our graduate students that socializes them into the profession and allows them to contribute substantively to educational issues pertinent to a program. Thirdly, assessment opened our eyes to a variety of *research opportunities* linked with assessment. These range from very practical action research to understand and address a particular issue within a course or course level to methodologically and theoretically more complex topics. I mention some of these further below. Fourthly, assessment has allowed the academic administrators of the department to understand the programs better and therefore also represent them better vis-à-vis other stakeholders and increase the legitimacy of the program's educational claims.

As we continue to work on assessment projects, a general *modus operandi* of how we approached assessment has evolved over the years. These practices ensure all the work that goes into a project provides useful wash-back into classroom pedagogies and curricular practices. This approach always runs through similar stages. The department, usually on the initiative of the chair and/or the Director of Curriculum, identifies current practices that would benefit from an assessment. The merits of the envisioned project are discussed among the full faculty. If there is agreement that the project is useful and buy-in by at least some faculty members is guaranteed, the chair sends out an invitation to participate in the project to all members of the department (tenure-line faculty; non-tenure-line faculty, graduate students, selected undergraduate students interested in language research or educational issues). At times, this has also included faculty members and graduate students from the Linguistics Department who are involved in assessment issues and who could benefit from the project and the data it generated – and from whose expertise the GUGD could benefit in return. Each project is run under the leadership of the faculty members most deeply involved. There are regular progress reports to the full department; progress and findings are discussed and consequences and follow-up projects are implemented with support by the department as appropriate. The chair has the responsibility to keep communication channels open and coordinate that all members of the department are, in fact, able to contribute to the projects.

---

[1] See some reflections on the administrative actions necessary to facilitate these processes in Pfeiffer (2002).

Following the development of the curriculum-specific placement test and the very positive experiences all members had with the discussions, workshops, and general conversations connected with it, the department continued with a variety of assessment initiatives of varying scope over the following years.[2] These initiatives were directed at both understanding how students' learning was impacted by the new curriculum and at gathering data to guide refinement of the curriculum. These included assessment of oral proficiency of students with external assessment criteria (Norris & Pfeiffer, 2003); various additional speaking and writing assessments (Byrnes, Maxim, & Norris, 2010); alumni questionnaires on professional and personal value of the major; and focus groups of graduating seniors on the value and identity of the major (Pfeiffer & Byrnes, 2009), on the program's contribution to humanities learning, and, to come full circle, on the development of a revised curriculum-specific placement test that will take into account current practices and a much more sophisticated understanding of our educational environment and our students' achievements. The different instruments used for assessing student learning and the effectiveness of our educational program provided a layered understanding of our specific learning environment and allowed us to speak with authority about our findings. Over the years, this more comprehensive understanding and data gathering, aided at times by conversations at the water cooler, led to numerous research initiatives and collaborations, including some with other departments and other institutions that would have been unlikely in other circumstances.

The resulting significant, and at times unusual, publications, often co-authored, are referenced in this article. Throughout these initiatives, participants developed a vocabulary and understanding that lets all members of the department talk with ease and without undue significance of traditional hierarchies about the intellectual substance of the curriculum, the theoretical frameworks and pedagogies we use, as well as materials and classroom implementation. While we did receive some financial support and technical advice from an office charged with helping develop new approaches to teaching and assessment (Center for New Designs in Learning and Scholarship, CNDLS), the most significant developments were all generated internally. They were driven by a wide range of questions from very practical concerns (e.g., What promises to be the most effective way to integrate teaching of language features with intellectually substantive humanities content?) to highly theoretical considerations (e.g., What theory of language can undergird what we have begun to understand about the teaching and learning process in our curriculum?).

Over the years, we have reached out to a number of constituencies to share the results of our various assessment and curriculum development projects. These workshops and presentations were sometimes coordinated at Georgetown with CNDLS and co-organized with professional organizations like the AATG and the ADFL.

Notre Dame

In the Department of Romance Languages and Literatures at the University of Notre Dame (NDROLL), engagement with assessment dates back to the chairperson's participation in the 2005 ADFL Seminar West (hosted by the

---

[2] See a detailed description of this process in Norris (2008).

University of Wisconsin, Madison) which featured a plenary panel, "Assessing Student Competencies, the Curriculum" in which John Norris presented a compelling overview of utilization-focused assessment.[3] NDROLL, comprised of between 40 and 50 regular faculty members, more or less evenly divided between research and lecturers distributed across multiple degree-granting programs, faced significant structural and curricular challenges at that time, and utilization-focused assessment appeared to offer an effective means of addressing them. From a structural point of view, NDROLL sought an alternative to the tenure-line language program director model, since it had a qualified and experienced cohort of lecturers in place, and an attempt to introduce three tenure-line assistant professor language program directors had recently collapsed. There was an urgent need to find a way to constructively engage the lecturer and research faculty together in a collective project to reform and upgrade the curricula of the undergraduate programs, as well as pedagogical methods. Assessment proved to be a means of addressing these challenges collectively.

Since the University of Notre Dame did not have in-house assessment specialists or assessment support infrastructure, NDROLL sought outside help, and John Norris was invited the following year to visit our university to speak about utilization-focused assessment. Having introduced the department to utilization-focused assessment, Norris subsequently led, together with Judith Liskin Gasparro of the University of Iowa, a very successful workshop that effectively launched NDROLL's utilization-focused assessment project, which continues today. NDROLL then obtained some modest funding from the University to support annual visits by John Norris and his then doctoral student Yukiko Watanabe, who has since joined the University of California Berkeley. Besides assistance from external consultants, the NDROLL assessment project has received support from the Center for the Study of Languages and Cultures (CSLC) at the University of Notre Dame, as well as from a consortium formed by institutions engaged in supporting assessment activities, including Emory University, Georgetown University, and Rice University, called the Consortium on Useful Assessment in Language and Humanities Education. While during the last seven or eight years, NDROLL has developed a strong cohort of assessment practitioners, the department continues to seek regular outside expertise for workshops and other professional development activities for its faculty in order to further enhance its assessment capacity. The University of Notre Dame has recently announced its intention to appoint assessment specialists in its Kaneb Center for Teaching and Learning to support assessment university-wide, and this additional support to NDROLL's continued engagement in utilization-focused assessment will be most welcome.

At the beginning stages of NDROLL's assessment initiative, more than a year was dedicated to developing learning goals for each of the undergraduate degree-granting programs. More time was spent on developing goals than was perhaps strictly necessary, but the benefits of establishing a constructive collegial conversation "across the curricula" for a relatively large multi-lingual department such as NDROLL's cannot be underestimated. Currently, ongoing assessment activity is annually carried forward in the department by a chairperson-appointed standing committee, the

---

[3] For further reflections on the Notre Dame experience with assessment from the perspective of the chairperson, see Cachey (2014).

Committee for the Study of Romance Languages and Cultures (CSRLC), which meets monthly, and is made up of both senior lecturers and tenure-line faculty representatives from each of the degree-granting programs. The committee organizes an annual retreat during which the entire faculty participates in a review and discussion of the results of the annual senior surveys for each degree-granting program, as well as the results of a direct measure assessment that has been the focus of the CSRLC's work during the year. The discussion of the senior surveys has led to significant changes in the programs, for example in the treatment of co-curricular activities, as well as in the areas of study abroad and advisement practices. Oral proficiency and writing in each of the degree-granting programs were respectively the focus of the first two cycles of the assessment project, which led to a variety of changes in the course design and in pedagogy. NDROLL found that the learning goals for writing in the lower division courses (based on ACTFL guidelines) were not ambitious enough, and that adjustments in the goals were in order.

Generally speaking, the assessment project found graduating seniors were achieving the goals the department had set out as regards oral proficiency. More importantly, curricular conversation growing out of the discussions of goals and student surveys helped foster an innovative interdepartmental collaboration with the Department of Economics, which led to the creation of a new joint major called "International Economics." The new major testifies to the extent to which assessment can help to enable curricular innovation, since the project, particularly indirect measures such as student surveys and enrollment data, had sensitized us to the needs of many students for a different kind of curriculum from the one we had been offering. NDROLL was thus in a better position to take up the invitation of the 2006 MLA report "Foreign Languages and Higher Education: New Structures for a Changed World." We were, in fact, beginning to look for ways of transforming our academic programs when the report appeared and were already seeking to move away from a rigid and hierarchical division between lower and upper divisions of the curriculum and from a narrowly literary curriculum in upper division courses.[4] In just two years of operation, the new degree program in International Economics has been successful in attracting more than 50 declared majors.

Direct measure assessments in the major skills areas have recently been focused on pilot blended or hybrid beginning language courses. NDROLL's ability to effectively assess student learning outcomes has made it possible for the department to expand the blended learning pilot and to initiate a new pilot on-line beginning language course. Again, our development of hybrid and on-line beginning language learning opportunities was stimulated by discussion within the context of the assessment project of indirect measures (i.e., surveys and enrollment data) that revealed we were failing to meet the needs of many students who are unable to take up the study of new languages language due to scheduling and other logistical challenges. NDROLL is currently focused on seeking ways to overcome these challenges and to make beginning language instruction more available by offering it in a greater variety of formats.

---

[4] See the 2007 MLA report, "Foreign Languages and Higher Education: New Structures for a Changed World," and for information on the International Economics major, see http://romancelanguages.nd.edu/joint-and-allied-programs/international-economics-major/.

Three aspects of assessment: Method, practice, advocacy

Useful assessment as a framework to address a variety of departmental challenges

As chairs, we found that useful assessment could provide a basis from which a number of departmental concerns could be addressed. Principled and sustained assessment initiatives can help balance the professional (non-institutional) attention required by disciplinary research communities, on the one hand, and the isolation of classroom instruction anchored in the institution, on the other. Assessment initiatives build a shared knowledge-base from which faculty members can fruitfully engage departmental and institutional priorities as a group and create, through that common effort, an intellectual community that fosters professional and personal growth. In addition, such an environment also supports professional mentoring for graduate and undergraduate students alike.

Georgetown

As stated above, the long history, variety, and scope of assessment projects in GUGD originated from a massive curriculum renewal undertaken by the department ("Developing Multiple Literacies," 1997–2000).[5] It is difficult to pinpoint the reasons why this project flourished while many other attempts at such departmental action across the country have been less successful. It may just have been a fortuitous constellation that brought together innovative linkages between second language learning research and curricular thinking, strong leadership, significant buy-in by senior faculty members, no deep divisions between faculty members or factions in the department, a great *esprit de corps* among the graduate students, and, probably most important of all, a strong shared commitment to undergraduate education on all levels and to graduate education. Whatever the reasons, the joint engagement in curricular conversations called for developing shared expertise in the best research on language learning and education, a clear articulation of our learning goals for the students, outlining steps on how we might achieve those goals, and mechanisms to find out whether or not we were achieving those goals and doing so effectively and efficiently.

It was clear we did not want to establish learning goals (the local Georgetown parlance for what might be more widely referred to as "student learning outcomes") in the abstract, but rather learning goals specific to our institution and based on our actual teaching experiences with our actual students. This required, above all, extensive conversations among experienced teachers. Teachers at all levels got together under the leadership of senior faculty members most involved in particular curricular levels. The teams then specified performance profiles for our students based on our collective experiences. These conversations in and of themselves created an environment that was highly unusual, as it brought together *all* teachers, regardless of rank, and thus initiated a virtuous cycle. It created a discursive practice which offered a space for actualizing the sense of academic community and focused on the institutional professional contexts (teaching; collaborations between faculty and between faculty and students; mentoring of junior faculty, graduate, and undergraduate students; scholarship grounded in program-specific

---

[5] See http://german.georgetown.edu/scholarship/curriculumproject/ for a detailed documentation of the project.

research questions). This institutional context then complemented the disciplinary contexts (disciplinary research, professional organizations) with which faculty members are usually most familiar.

Because curricular discussions and assessment activities went hand-in-hand, it is difficult to tease them apart and assign cause-and-effect-relationships to them. As stated above, it was a virtuous cycle that, once set in motion, continued to move along energized by the involvement and dedication of the department's members. In this context, *useful* assessment, that is, assessment that is put to use and has real consequences, might have its deepest impact and meaning not in the results of individual assessment projects but rather in the way it can fundamentally shift the operating principles of the academic unit. Instead of being an organization in which professors perform their teaching, research, and service duties mostly in monadic isolation, the department became the space where common goals could be articulated collaboratively, information gathering undertaken, implementation strategies developed, and all sorts of practical questions and problems discussed and solved. Assessment projects provided the substantive occasion for these conversations. Co-operations, both in the hands-on issues of materials development, pedagogies, curricular design, and so forth, and also in collaborative research projects, some of them between linguists and literature scholars, became common features of our departmental life.[6] This is where the chair has a pivotal role in planning, articulating, coordinating, and communicating the purposes of the assessment projects and assuring they have actionable (or deliberately non-actionable) results. Such leadership assures that faculty efforts and decisions have consequences that feed back into faculty actions and behavior, stimulating further conversations.

From another perspective, the value of assessment projects for the departmental culture can be described as building academic community and trust, a place of "concourse," as Cardinal Newman worded it when he described the university.[7] It was surprising to us how little we knew about the professional profiles of our departmental colleagues and how much of what we did know was focused exclusively on their disciplinary research and reputation, as opposed to their work as educators. As we engaged in the assessment work that included wide-ranging data gathering, it became clear we had to establish a deeper understanding of our work as it related to the department and its mission, and, importantly, to that of our colleagues. In stimulating a more self-reflexive approach to being a member of a department, we took the initial step towards creating a thorough and more substantive academic community than we had before. As chair, I initiated these conversations, was able to encourage and coordinate them, and provided material and immaterial incentives for colleagues to engage in these beneficial behaviors. The overall level of resources necessary was modest at best and often included such items as featuring someone's work on the web page or securing decanal support for a departmental retreat to consider the results of assessment initiatives and what steps to take next.

---

[6] In addition to the materials noted in Pfeiffer and Byrnes (2009), see Byrnes and Kord (2001) and Eigler (2001).

[7] "[A] University is a place of concourse, whither students come from every quarter for every kind of knowledge" Newman (2007, p. 15).

The overall shift in behavior among department members had a particularly important effect on how we, as a doctoral program as well, modeled being professors to our graduate students, many of whom go on to pursue academic careers. Rather than perpetuating a role of monadic scholarly existence that, by itself, can contribute little to a lively and productive departmental culture, our graduate students see there needs to be a balance between institutionally focused work and disciplinary scholarship/professional engagement. Again, it is the development of a common language that is essential for this mentoring to be successful, an insight I believe all our graduates have taken along as they took up positions elsewhere. Thus, we basically overcame the unfortunate practice of dissertation advisors who try to clone themselves in their doctoral students.

The role of the chair in all of this was first and foremost to assure all voices were heard and to channel the discussions towards actionable decisions. The chair surely cannot do this on his or her own, but without departmental leadership, very little is possible.

Reflecting on the long-term results of these various assessment activities, I believe useful assessment becomes useful to a large extent through careful and detailed organizational and administrative practices that can only be assured by the department chair. Good administrative practices yield results because they take the administrative process seriously as a meaningful process, as a way to define, identify, secure, and support opportunities for faculty members and students to learn, grow, and succeed. For a chair, the successful orchestration of these activities and the conscientious administrative follow-up in assessing their effectiveness are the essential aspects of his or her work. With this understanding, the administrative care a chair provides is the service that s/he contributes to the department's overall success. As chair, I led the planning, coordination, and implementation of the assessment activities while communicating the purposes of the department's actions consistently, both internally and externally. At times, straight-forward, sensible administrative practices had a direct effect on assessment activities. When we surveyed our alums, for example, the high response rate was surely influenced by the fact that I had instituted an annual personalized letter to these former students a few years before and thereby established a regular channel of communication with them. My active participation and in some instances leadership role in assessment projects also reinforced their importance as an academic pursuit valued by the department.

Notre Dame

Utilization-focused assessment can help a relatively large multi-lingual department to build bridges between its diverse programs and to establish a common language and conversation for addressing departmental challenges. This was the experience of NDROLL, beginning with the department-wide discussions that led to the articulation of learning goals for each of its programs. During the first cycles of assessment, we found that the programs had much more in common than we had previously recognized. We quickly learned it was easier and more efficient to address many curricular and pedagogical challenges across the groups and in coordinated manner, rather than independently as separate programs of French, Italian, and Iberian and Latin American studies. Before our assessment work began, each program had developed its own approach to curricular and pedagogical issues and had conducted its business more or less autonomously from a curricular and pedagogical point of view. By undertaking the assessment project jointly, faculty members in the respective programs came to the realization they were facing many of the same challenges and there were distinct advantages to establishing and maintaining a department-wide discussion of curricular issues, starting with sharing pedagogical "best practices" across the language groups. While developing the oral proficiency assessment project, for instance, it soon became clear that it was less efficient and effective for each faculty member to independently develop his or her own rubrics for rating and guiding oral practice and assessment. Indeed, rather than each program developing its own rubrics and practices for oral assessment, we found it more efficient to produce several basic models that were recommended at the department level and that were shared department-wide and later customized according to program and individual instructor needs.

Besides improving lines of communication and efficiencies horizontally across programs, utilization-focused assessment also improved integration vertically between the lower division and upper division curricula both within the individual programs and department-wide. To give just one example, we were surprised to learn, at the start of the writing assessment project, that most if not all the lecturer faculty had never seen any of the writing that was being produced in the upper division courses; nor had the teaching and research faculty any idea of what kind of writing was being done in the beginning and intermediate levels of the curriculum. We quickly realized that if we had any hope of bridging the gap between lower and upper division sectors of our curricula, the teaching and research faculty needed to understand where the students were coming from and the lecturer faculty needed to understand where they were supposed to be headed as far as the writing skill was concerned. Opening up vertical lines of communication and sharing faculty perspectives on the whole curriculum as regards all four skills was a gradual process that was started when we first articulated goals for the undergraduate degree programs. Over time, the project has led to a better integration of the lower division and upper division curricula.

In a department whose faculty composition is roughly split between lecturer and tenure line appointments, arguably the biggest advantage for NDROLL in developing use-focused assessment as an ongoing part of its culture has been the improved relations that it has fostered and the structural integration forged between the lecturer and teaching and research faculties. The teaching and research faculty has developed a stronger and more articulated appreciation for the vital role and contributions of the lecturers to the success of the programs and of the department as a whole, while the lecturer faculty has gained an enhanced appreciation for the commitment of the research faculty to the teaching mission of the department. Indeed, outstanding teachers are present in both cohorts, including several at both ranks whose teaching has been publicly recognized by various awards to be among the best in the college. Outstanding faculty in both the lecturer/teaching and research ranks are well distributed among the programs, and several of these emerged as department leaders in the process of developing the assessment project.

The composite make-up of NDROLL's standing assessment committee, the CSLRC, institutionalized the NDROLL's desire to capture the energies and leadership abilities of these faculty members, and includes leading lecturer faculty (including but not limited to program coordinators), together with teaching and research faculty representing each of the degree granting programs. The chairperson is an ex officio member of the CSRLC, which is chaired by the departments' Director of Undergraduate Studies, a senior lecturer. In effect, the assessment project actually helped us to mitigate some of the negative consequences of the two-tier faculty composition, which as the 2006 MLA report observed, has been so damaging for departments of language and literature nationally. Building and maintaining trust and respect both horizontally and vertically within the faculty are ongoing challenges for any department. NDROLL found that an important ancillary benefit of engaging in use-focused assessment was the extent to which the project provided a framework for addressing challenges on both these fronts.

The role of the chair in all of this was both rewarding and challenging. The chair needed to stress with the faculty, to begin with, that assessment was not about the evaluation of individual faculty member performance, and that program level assessment was designed to lead to meaningful improvements in curricular integration and student learning. Moreover, the chair needed to persuade the faculty of the enlightened self-interest of engaging in assessment as a means of demonstrating a commitment to undergraduate education. He did not miss any opportunity to point out how this activity was raising the department's standing in the college of arts and letters as measured by the dean's support of the department and its programs, especially among the language and culture programs.

Practice: Useful assessment as a regular departmental activity

"Assessment" is often viewed negatively by faculty members and chairs. It is taken as an imposition on their time and a "jumping-through-hoops" effort imposed by administrators eager to use corporate techniques to justify their actions. As chairs, we observed such misguided assessment initiatives many times. At the same time, we were intrigued by the opportunities well-designed, sustained, and useful assessment initiatives could offer. These would not be one-shot efforts with limited effects, but blended into the regular activities/practices of the department. Results were put to use by adjusting departmental and individual practices. These changes then led to new questions that would be taken on in new initiatives with a different focus but informed by the results of the previous effort. This cyclical aspect of useful assessment sustains the departmental conversation on issues of intellectual profile, pedagogy, linkages to institutional priorities, student learning, teaching materials, outreach, and so forth that stimulate academic community as outlined in the previous section.

Georgetown

Early on in my time as chair, I began a small assessment project of my own. I decided to write a brief report about the year's departmental activities and achievements to the dean, reflecting on what worked and what did not work, as well as outlining a few goals for the coming academic year. Mostly, I did this for myself to consider, in a disciplined manner, my work as chair and to clarify future plans. The few hours it took to think about and write this letter were some of the most productive in the year for me personally and as chair. One of the deans under whom I worked was baffled by the letter and had no response. Another dean was surprised and delighted to have the information, provided feedback, used the information with the college's Board of Visitors, and provided support for future goals whenever possible. Finally, the University, under pressure from our accrediting commission, required departments to develop what was termed "Departmental Assessment Plans" which on some level were a somewhat modified and formalized version of the humble letter I had written every year. Because I had found that exercise to be very helpful for me, I insisted that we took these "assessment plans" seriously and that they were the consensus result of a thorough departmental discussion. (In that, they were different from my letters, which had been strictly a communication between chair and dean.) I believe these conversations were helpful for the department in sustaining and reiterating common goals. The substance we gave the document internally made it worthwhile. Overall, the institutional administrative handling of this "assessment" was not helpful and proved useless because there was neither substantive feedback nor principled follow-up. As it were, these plans were written into an administrative black hole confirming all the negative prejudices many academics hold against assessment of any sort.

These examples demonstrate the full range of possibilities that lie in assessment projects. Assessment, even of the modest kind described above, was formational for me as chair and it was, arguably, a waste of time when it did not garner a response. Yet, from my experience, even when administrative responses from outside the department were lacking, engaging in carefully planned assessment projects was beneficial to the department itself. The benefits for the department were directly proportional to the effort and care put into determining the intended uses of the assessment, its design, and internal follow-up. (It was, in a way, the avoidance of the old "garbage in, garbage out" principle.) Of course, these benefits were greatly enhanced when there were substantive responses from outside, but the initial benefit, the departmental conversation about the substance of the assessment, what we expected from the outcomes, the collaboration in collecting and analyzing the data, the research projects linked to these data, and the departmental consideration of the results, easily outweighed any external administrative neglect. In some way, the looping back of the information through assessment substituted for the lack of responses from outside the department. Of course, this means that the chair (together with other senior faculty members) has to provide even more internal organizational and administrative attention and responsiveness.

Ultimately, department members found the intellectual stimulation of cyclical assessment projects building on one another compelling. I have outlined them in the previous sections. The on-going nature of the assessment projects with their different, yet often linked foci acknowledged the complexity of the phenomenon we wanted to assess, that is, the outcomes of us providing various learning opportunities based on our academic expertise for the formation of students into discerning adults. The multidirectional, layered understanding of student learning, of student attitudes, of teaching effectiveness, of subject-matter learning, and of long-term self-reported results (to name just a few) stands in sharp contrast to notions of one-dimensional assessment. Providing a substantive and principled model of assessment guided by the particular values of the program lends legitimacy to any discussion of the purposes of the program. Having observed and participated in both useful and not-so-useful assessment projects at all levels of the university's organization, I have found that on the departmental level, the usefulness and utility of assessment is directly related to the effort and care given by the faculty members, including the chair. The chair's unique role in this regard is that s/he has to determine and frame the project so that it can become useful in the most effective way. "Useful," here, means that it is directly linked to having meaningful consequences for those who put effort into the project. No one is better positioned to assure this outcome than the chair.

In conclusion of this section, I would like to address two frequent arguments against assessment as a regular departmental activity. The first is that a consistent focus on assessment will lead to a situation where learning and an overbearing departmental "community" lead to a stale and self-involved, provincial environment that is unresponsive to new ideas. The second contends that the energy spent on assessment is wasted time insofar as the time would have been used more productively on disciplinary research.

From my experiences, neither of these arguments has much purchase. One of the challenges of establishing a departmental culture of assessment that contributes to internal collaborative initiatives and supports a strong academic community is precisely that it maintains intellectual attractiveness. Not only the flexibility and curiosity of the faculty members, but equally important, the administrative acumen of the chair has to support this goal by assuring that different (internal and external) perspectives are voiced and considered. The chair also has to maintain an appropriate balance between incentivizing the disciplinary research profiles of the department and its teaching and service mission which is moored to the institution. This balance will take different shapes, depending on the mission of the institution and the department. The growing pressure to rebalance these missions by giving greater attention to student learning is largely due to the need to legitimize the costs and outcomes of higher education, especially in the humanities and social sciences. (By contrast, the so-called STEM disciplines are presumed to be self-evidently useful.) As a whole, graduate departments in my field and, I believe, in the humanities in general, have been woefully ineffective in preparing graduate students, that is, the future professoriate, to contribute thoughtfully, substantively, and confidently to this debate. They have largely ignored the needs of institutions other than those of their own ilk and tend to reproduce themselves without much reflection, dodging their responsibility towards the students and the profession at large. Departmental assessment initiatives can help anchor some of these debates in concrete conversations about the appropriate balance between these two facets of faculty engagement and model how to determine what this "balance" means in specific ways.

As to the argument that assessment impedes a faculty member's focus on research, I can only speak from my own and my department's experiences during an intense and sustained period of assessment work. Books and articles continued to be published, conference presentations made, and workshops organized. Their numbers did not decline. In fact, there was a marked increase of some of these activities, especially presentations at national and international conferences.[8] To be sure, the character of some of these publications shifted – there were articles in refereed journals on topics such as course design, oral proficiency achievements,

---

[8] Interestingly, our department was rated the second most research productive of all German departments in the United States by Academic Analytics during one year of the most intense assessment work.

development of writing competence, and so forth, authored by professors trained in literary/cultural studies and in linguistics. Some of these papers were co-authored with colleagues or graduate students. As chair, I made sure that the merit guidelines were reformed so that all research articles were treated equally in departmental merit evaluations. It was all peer-reviewed research with some of it of a different kind. This was a sign that we had moderately rebalanced our departmental view on research to include that which is located at the intersection of disciplinary research and its actualization in the departmental curriculum and learning environment. Historically, this is one of the roles that research is supposed to play in the American system of higher education, but it has been supplanted by an almost exclusive focus on disciplinary (and even sub-disciplinary) research. Assessment made it possible for us to recapture this dimension of research and put it to excellent use in our internal and external research profiles.

Notre Dame

It is a challenge to establish and maintain cohesiveness in any departmental setting, but the multilingual department presents its own set of challenges. In this respect, the challenges faced and the assessment approach used by NDROLL differed significantly from those of the GUGD. It would have been extremely difficult if not impossible given NDROLL's size and especially the diversity of its faculty cohorts, which are distributed across several distinct degree-granting programs, to undertake a coordinated curriculum renewal such as the one successfully undertaken by GUGD, "Developing Multiple Literacies." An admittedly less ambitious program of assessment has nonetheless served us well. We sometimes refer to our approach as "assessment light," given the fact that we have followed a simple and straightforward formula for assessment which normally calls upon NDROLL to assess one direct and one indirect measure of student learning in each cycle.[9] In planning for assessment we try to be cognizant of the fact that no one on the faculty has any time to waste and that at the end of the day assessment is an ancillary or support activity when considered in relation to research and teaching, which are the primary responsibilities of the faculty in the department. For these reasons, assessment activities have to be designed in such a way as to ensure that they will not be too cumbersome on faculty, and more importantly, that they will be useful.

It is fair to say that NDROLL has worn its assessment culture lightly. For example, when assessing the student writing samples that were collected from courses selected at key junctures of the curriculum, NDROLL did not develop elaborate rating systems and double grading of samples, but instead trusted the good judgment of subcommittees of experienced teachers who evaluated the samples using the same simple rubrics that had been developed for classroom implementation. The subcommittees reported back to the CSRLC on whether or not the quality of the samples corresponded to the goals established for the level, and made recommendations about how student performance could be improved, for example by more carefully fashioning prompts and by providing more effective feedback. The methodology that was used might not have satisfied the most rigorous standards of formal assessment practice, but the benefits of the focused conversation that NDROLL had about student writing were nonetheless extremely valuable and clear to all. These discussions led to the creation of a series

---

[9] For a synthetic version of this basic recipe, see Walvoord (2011).

of sensible and straightforward guidelines for the treatment of writing across the curriculum, including recommendations concerning the frequency and length of writing and the kinds of writing assignments appropriate at each level, as well as correction practices.

With respect to the correction of (i.e., feedback on) writing, NDROLL found that the practices of the faculty were "all over the map." There was, in fact, as we learned through a series of easily administered surveys, a great diversity of opinion among both the lecturer and teaching and research faculty about the most effective means of providing feedback on student writing. Little or none of this opinion was informed by current research about the question or anything much more than personal preference and/or long held prejudice about such matters. The solution the CSRLC recommended was to invite a researcher in the field to visit the campus and to lead a workshop on this topic. The presentation was exemplary in so far as it was consistent with the assessment culture NDROLL has tried to foster. The visiting scholar reviewed for faculty the diversity of opinion among experts in the field and modeled the manner in which individual faculty members might use current research to develop a principled and scientifically informed practice as regards error correction.[10] This was consistent with our assessment culture as far as pedagogical practices were concerned. The NDROLL assessment project has had from the beginning as one of its premises, respect for the professional capacities of the faculty and the right of the individual faculty member to use his or her discretion as regards teaching practice.

The aim of the NDROLL assessment project, then, has been, quite simply, to create an instrument or vehicle that would foster constructive communication about the curriculum across our language and culture programs. Simple and straightforward approaches to assessment might prove to be more effective in a larger department such as NDROLL where the capacity for assessment both in terms of faculty and logistical resources are relatively few. As we were fond of saying about the NDROLL assessment project, and it became something of a mantra among us, "the journey is more important than the destination." In other words, more important and more enduring than the results of any one direct or indirect assessment measure has been the enhancement of the quality of NDROLL conversation about the curriculum and pedagogical practices brought about by collective engagement in assessment activities. The fact we found the writing proficiency levels achieved by our students more or less corresponded to our expectations and that the same was true in terms of oral proficiency were only secondary outcomes of the project when compared to its more general cultural benefits. Similarly, we learned a lot about what is working and what is not working in our respective programs from the senior surveys that have been conducted over the last couple of years. But the most important result of the NDROLL assessment project has been the creation of a sustainable curricular conversation that is meaningful and that promises to continue to have a positive impact on our respective programs. From this perspective, even a minimalist approach to establish a meaningful program of assessment such as the one that was undertaken by NDROLL has potential for improving departmental

---

[10] The presentation, "'Journey to Ithaca' Best Practices for Error Correction and Feedback in Foreign Language Writing," by Lourdes Ortega of Georgetown University, is available at http://cslc.nd.edu/assets/96893/notredame_ortega_cfinwriting.pdf

culture and by extension student learning in multilingual departments of languages and literatures.

While the chair had an important role to play in launching the NDROLL assessment project, leading faculty in each of the programs and in both of the faculty cohorts, that is, both teaching and research and lecturer faculty, had to commit to the NDROLL project to make it successful. The development of learning outcomes for the undergraduate majors in each of the programs, for example, would have been impossible without the genuine commitment of faculty members and the respective programs and especially those faculty members who showed real leadership in undertaking the work. As the project developed, the department chair worked closely with the assistant chair of the department, who leads the CSRLC committee. Together the CSRLC, in consultation with the department chair, develop the year's agenda for the project. Specifically, during the spring term, the committee discusses and identifies a direct measure and an indirect measure to be assessed during the following year. The chair and the assistant chair include this plan in the annual report which they compile at the end of the academic year, which includes both the results of the previous year's work and plans for the next.

The role of the chairperson in the NDROLL assessment project as far as the running and implementation of the project has diminished as the project has developed. The first major step in the direction of a sustainable model for assessment in the department, given the fact that chairs change, was the establishment of the CSRLC on which the chair serves as an ex officio member. Over time, the committee, which is chaired by the assistant chair who is a member of the lecturer faculty, has proved to be very capable of carrying forward the agenda with the active support of the chair. For the future of the project according to the NDROLL model of assessment, it is important that the chair take a less prominent role and allow the standing committee to continue to develop the project. While there is no question that the commitment of future chairs will be vital for the continued viability of the project taking the form of advocacy for the project, and support of the faculty in terms of professional development opportunities, release time and salary consideration, colleagues in each of the degree granting programs will need to continue to appreciate the value and "usefulness" of the project for contributing to the success of the department and its students, and to commit to its continuation.

Advocacy: Useful assessment as a basis for internal and external advocacy

American higher education has come under increasing pressure to legitimize the costs associated with its operation and the effective, even efficient, utilization of increasingly scarcer resources. This is particularly true for disciplines in the humanities that seemingly do not have an immediate practical "usefulness" for students. As chairs, we found the results of our assessment initiatives particularly useful for understanding the multi-faceted outcomes of student learning and to use these data to communicate them internally to members of the department, current students, and the administration, as well as to external stakeholders such as alumni, donors, and professional associations.

Georgetown
As chair of the department, I was the public face and voice of our small unit both on campus and to the outside world. During that time, I utilized the results of

our departmental assessment projects regularly and to great effect because it showed that we took seriously our responsibility to explain what our educational and research efforts were to multiple and varied audiences. The administration on different levels was happy to have a department to showcase when issues of assessment were raised by external evaluators or models sought for internal emulation. Current and prospective students and parents appreciated getting a detailed account of what they could expect from our programs. Alumni welcomed the opportunity to provide feedback and receive information on the analyses of their responses. Donors were glad to be given dependable accounts of how their contributions helped students and faculty. Professional associations and colleagues in the field benefited from some models of assessment we had developed, and we in turn learned from them how to improve on our own efforts.

The assessment efforts provided a rich web of understanding the full range and contexts of our academic work. Useful assessment became a way to make real and give substance to a professional ethos of responsibility.[11] Surely, not everything we do and want to accomplish in liberal arts education is immediately assessable. But to my mind and from my experiences as chair, useful assessment in the ways we have detailed it in this contribution helps us to respond with substance to legitimate questions of how we as academics contribute to the public good of education.

Notre Dame

"Owning," as we like to say, our own use-focused assessment project has made us much more effective in articulating the value that we bring to the university and to the humanities and the College of Arts and Letters in particular. The faculty of NDROLL collectively, but also individually, have become much more effective advocates of an integrated vision of the study of languages and cultures other than English, and much better able to defend ourselves or counteract the reductive viewpoints of colleagues, including university administrators who often reveal themselves to have a severely reductive (e.g., it's just about language learning; let the language center handle it all) view of what teaching and research in the discipline and in our respective areas is really about. It has also allowed us at Notre Dame to resist and to preempt some of the negative aspects of top-down perfunctory accreditation driven assessment pressures.

While the assistant chair and members of the CSRLC committee provided leadership to the assessment effort in the department, the chairperson advocated on behalf of the department's assessment project to deans and other administrators of the University. The administration welcomed the initiative and provided support for our efforts to improve the quality of NDROLL programs in the form of modest grants in support of our activities, including the use of of external consultants, the costs of proficiency testing programs, and the expansion of professional development opportunities. The assessment project proved to be a very effective means of demonstrating to the Dean of the College of Arts and Letters the commitment of NDROLL to undergraduate education, and the project has improved considerably the department's standing in the College.

---

[11] The Consortium of Financing of Higher Education (COFHE) calls assessment "a fundamental responsibility" of higher education, see http://web.mit.edu/cofhe/assessment/statement/index_files/Page717.htm

NDROLL has a well-earned reputation for leadership in assessment in the languages and cultures other than English and in the Humanities, in general. This reputation translated into the strong support of the college for curricular innovations initiated by the department, including the new International Economics major, which had to be approved at the level of the Academic Council of the University, and the NDROLL's recent pilot programs in hybrid and online learning, an undertaking that had to overcome the objections of some in the college, including some other departments of language and literature. The Dean's support of NDROLL initiatives in blended and online learning can be credited in large measure to NDROLL's proven capacity for curricular coordination and assessment of student learning.

The chair's efforts to advocate for assessment, and in particular, for utilization-focused assessment, in the College of Arts and Letters and more broadly in the university were less successful. On more than one occasion, NDROLL arranged for John Norris and other assessment consultants to lecture to faculty groups and departments outside NDROLL and to meet with faculty leaders at the university including colleagues in the theology department, the vice president for undergraduate education, and the leadership of the Center for the Study of Languages and Cultures (CSLC). The mixed results of these initiatives were due to broader contextual situations, including a strong ambivalence, even resistance, to assessment among humanities scholars.[12] In general, there was little interest in assessment in the College of Arts and Letters except for grassroots initiatives in a few departments, for example, in the theology department, which has undertaken some important assessment projects. Useful assessment practices, in fact, might help programs to improve and the humanities in general to advance its position within higher education. Given the potential for useful assessment to facilitate the reframing of the goals of our programs and to help to bring about needed reform, it is regrettable that it has not yet played a greater role in addressing "the crisis of the humanities." In fact, as both NDROLL and GUGD have discovered, one of the primary benefits of engaging in useful assessment is the benefit of being able to more efficiently and effectively communicate to the wider community the value(s) that we express, starting with the skills, knowledge, and dispositions that we offer to students.

Conclusion

In closing then, for chairpersons who might want to consider undertaking an assessment project in their department, we recommend keeping in mind the following general considerations and practices:

- Program level assessment is not about the evaluation of individual faculty performance. It is about trying to understand how the department/program is achieving its educational mission.
- Useful assessment must be useful for improving student learning and not waste valuable faculty time and effort. This requires administrative attention and follow-up from the departmental leadership.
- The journey of assessment is more important than the destination. It is in the doing that most benefits will accrue.

---

[12] See Holquist (2011).

- When starting up an assessment project, seek support, expert help, and political allies both within one's institution and outside it.
- Identify and engage key faculty to work as a team to advocate for and develop the project.
- Start with articulating learning outcomes. Keep it simple and straightforward when assessing student learning outcomes in subsequent phases of the project. The goal is for assessment to become a regular, ongoing activity within a department.

Acknowlegments

The authors wish to thank their colleagues and collaborators for the work they have done. Only through the actual doing of it can one gain insights into what an assessment project can accomplish.

References

Byrnes, H., & Kord, S. (2001). Developing literacy and literary competence: Challenges for foreign language departments. In V. Scott & H. Tucker (Eds.), *SLA and the literature classroom: Fostering dialogues* (pp. 31–69). Boston, MA: Heinle and Heinle.

Byrnes, H., Maxim, H., & Norris, J. M. (2010). Realizing advanced foreign language writing development in collegiate education: Curricular design, pedagogy, assessment [Monograph]. *Modern Language Journal, 94* (supplement s1).

Cachey, T. J. (2014). Reframing assessment: Innovation and accountability between the global and the local. In N. Mills & J. Norris (Eds.), *Innovation and accountability in language program evaluation* (pp. 230–244). American Association of University Supervisors and Coordinators.

Eigler, F. (2001). Designing a third-year German course for a content-oriented, task-based curriculum. *Unterrichtspraxis, 34*(2), 107–118.

Holquist, M. (2011). Measuring the humanities: The slippery slope from assessment to standardization. In D. Heiland & L. J. Rosenthal (Eds.), *Literary study, measurement, and the sublime: Disciplinary assessment* (pp. 69–96). New York, NY: The Teagle Foundation.

Modern Language Association Ad Hoc Committee on Foreign Languages. (2007). Foreign languages and higher education: New structures for a changed world. Retrieved from http://www.mla.org/flreport

Newman, J. H. (2007). *Rise and progress of universities* (original 1872–73). Retrieved from http://www.newmanreader.org/works/historical/volume3/universities/chapter2.html

Norris, J. M. (2006). Development and evaluation of a curriculum-based German C-test for placement purposes. In R. Grotjahn (Ed.), *Der C-Test: Theoretische Grundlagen und praktische Anwendungen* (vol. 5; pp. 45–83). New York, NY: Peter Lang.

Norris, J. M. (2008). *Validity evaluation in language assessment.* New York, NY: Peter Lang.

Norris, J. M., & Pfeiffer, P. C. (2003). Exploring the use and usefulness of ACTFL oral proficiency ratings in college foreign language departments. *Foreign Language Annals, 36*, 572–581.

Lourdes Ortega, L. (2012). *Journey to Ithaca: Best practices for error correction and feedback in foreign language writing.* Retrieved from http://cslc.nd.edu/assets/96893/notredame_ortega_ cfinwriting.pdf

Pfeiffer, P. C. (2002). The future of German: An administrative perspective. In G. Peters (Ed.), *Teaching of German in America* (pp. 393–406). Cherry Hill, NJ: American Assocation of Teachers of German.

Pfeiffer, P. C., & Byrnes, H. (2009). Curriculum, learning, and the identity of majors: A case study of program outcomes evaluation. In J. M. Norris, J. McE. Davis, C. Sinicrope, & Y. Watanabe (Eds.), *Toward useful program evaluation in college foreign language education* (pp. 183–208). Honolulu: University of Hawai'i National Foreign Language Resource Center.

Walvoord, B. E. (2011). How to construct a simple, sensible, useful departmental assessment process. In D. Heiland & L. J. Rosenthal (Eds.), *Literary study, measurement, and the sublime: Disciplinary assessment* (pp. 335–352). New York, NY: The Teagle Foundation.

"Centering" Collegiate Foreign Language Departments Around Useful Outcomes Assessment: Challenges and Opportunities

Lance R. Askildson
Kennesaw State University

Hiram H. Maxim
Emory University

Due to the well-documented divisions within the curricula, personnel, and pedagogies of collegiate foreign language (FL) education, FL departments are often not structured in a way that facilitates collaborative approaches to programmatic issues. This structural deficit is particularly noticeable when departments embark on assessment-related work because of its inherently programmatic nature. To address this challenge to FL departments, this chapter discusses how language centers, because of their advisory and supra-departmental role on campus, can serve as vital partners to FL departments in approaching assessment from a useful and programmatic perspective. Specifically, and based on the experiences of the authors as language center directors at their respective institutions, the chapter presents four ways that language centers can provide leadership and support for useful assessment in collegiate FL education: (a) providing departments with expertise and guidance on useful assessment, an approach that is typically not well-understood among university faculty; (b) providing opportunities for assessment-related professional development through workshops, seminars, lectures; (c) providing a forum and location for collaboration and communication within and between departments; and (d) using the language center's prominent position on campus to disseminate and advocate for best practices in assessment.

Askildson, L. R., & Maxim, H. H. (2015). "Centering" collegiate foreign language departments around useful outcomes assessment: Challenges and opportunities. In J. M. Norris & J. McE. Davis (Eds.), *Student learning outcomes assessment in college foreign language programs* (pp. 57–69). Honolulu: University of Hawai'i, National Foreign Language Resource Center.

Introduction: Current climate and challenges in FL education

The predominant departmental structure in collegiate foreign language (FL) education in the United States presents a real conundrum for practitioners and administrators interested in conducting program-wide outcomes assessment. Marked by a division between so-called "language" courses at the lower level and so-called "content" courses at the upper level, most collegiate FL departments lack a coherent or unifying approach across the entire 4-year undergraduate program that would allow for investigations into programmatic learning outcomes. Such curricular inarticulation has received substantial attention in recent scholarship (Byrnes, 1998, 2006; James, 1996; Kern, 2002; Maxim, 2006; Swaffar, 2006) and was cited by the much-publicized MLA Report (2007) as a serious issue facing collegiate FL education. Yet, to date there have been very few departments that have undertaken full-scale curricular reforms to address this structural division.[1]

Typically, there have been several reasons for departments' inability to overcome curricular bifurcation. To begin with, curriculum construction has not been a focus typical of foreign language teacher education or the development of the professoriate. As a result, faculty are not socialized into thinking curricularly as they enter the profession. Also, professional development opportunities available to foreign language practitioners have rarely focused on curriculum construction or related concerns. Consequently, even when faculty have an interest in curricular issues, there are few opportunities to become educated in the principles and practices necessary to implement curricular reform. Last, there has not been a culture of collaboration within FL departments, which in most cases is a prerequisite for curricular innovation. The tendency has been for courses to be developed in relative isolation without significant or systematic attention to their relation to other courses or larger programmatic goals.

This lack of curricular thinking within collegiate FL education has significant consequences for outcomes assessment (never mind learning outcomes per se!) at the programmatic level. Without a coherent curricular framework in place, a department becomes hard-pressed to either articulate or measure its programmatic learning goals. Compounding this challenging scenario is the belief among many faculty members that the type of humanistic and dispositional learning that is often central to foreign language education cannot be measured or assessed (but see Norris, 2006). In light of this predicament and the aforementioned inability to overcome curricular bifurcation within the collegiate FL profession, the chances for successful and meaningful outcomes assessment would appear to be slim.

However, while not a substitute for substantive and systematic curricular reform, this chapter will present how a language center can serve to overcome some of the structural and professional obstacles to conducting useful outcomes assessment. Through their advisory and supra-departmental roles, the language centers at each institution—the Center for the Study of Languages & Cultures at the University of Notre Dame and the Emory College Language Center at Emory University—emerged as critical partners to their respective foreign language departments, and they presented a unique locus through which to promote both the practice and culture of assessment across departmental boundaries. Indeed, as we will discuss

---

[1] See Byrnes, Maxim, and Norris (2010) and Maxim, Höyng, Lancaster, Schaumann, & Aue (2013) for examples of two collegiate programs that have undergone curricular reform.

in the chapter, the unique nature of the language center (vis-à-vis foreign language departments) provides the opportunity to centralize outcomes assessment expertise while also coordinating and disseminating useful assessment practices in a manner that engages faculty and departments at every stage.

Language center as assessment facilitator

Through their experiences as directors of their respective institutions' language centers, the two authors participated first-hand in the implementation of FL outcomes assessment projects over several years and in interaction with multiple language programs. It is on the basis of these experiences that several important dimensions of the leadership potential of language centers vis-à-vis assessment became clear. Specifically, in each of the following four sections, this chapter will examine a unique leadership role that the language center can play in facilitating outcomes assessment within and across foreign language departments: (a) providing departments with expertise and guidance on useful assessment, an approach that is typically not well-understood among university faculty; (b) offering opportunities for assessment-related professional development through workshops, seminars, and lectures; (c) hosting a forum and location for collaboration and communication within and between departments; and (d) using the language center's prominent position on campus to disseminate and advocate for best practices in assessment. Prior to examining these leadership experiences in some detail, we first sketch in the essential point of departure for our assessment-related endeavors.

Guiding both language centers' assessment-related work was their fortuitous involvement with the Foreign Language Program Evaluation Project (FLPEP) at the National Foreign Language Resource Center, University of Hawai'i at Mānoa, and their subsequent affiliation with the Consortium on Useful Assessment in Language and Humanities Education, an organization consisting of individual foreign language departments from the participating institutions (Emory University, Georgetown University, Rice University, University of Notre Dame) that aimed to foster a "culture of responsible and useful assessment of student learning outcomes in the humanities" (Consortium on Useful Assessment in Language and Humanities Education, 2012). Through their participation in both initiatives, the language centers learned about and adopted a utilization-focused approach to assessment that then served as the basis for their subsequent work with individual departments. Utilization-focused outcomes assessment (derived from Patton's, 2008, *Utilization-focused evaluation* approach; see Norris, 2008) distinguishes itself from other varieties of assessment by placing the users and uses of the assessment process at the center of its implementation, focusing on learning outcomes specifically. Oftentimes, ill-considered assessment practices document learning in ways that are only modestly useful to students and faculty. Utilization-focused outcomes assessment asks faculty and staff to pose two fundamental questions in order to design assessment practice that is ultimately useful to its end users and purposes: (a) Who will be the users of assessment findings, and (b) How will these findings be used? By concretely specifying and articulating what assessment will be used to do, and by whom, in a language program, relevant assessment instruments will produce assessment data that are meaningful to their intended users and uses. In this way, assessment findings become inherently more useful and assessment becomes a productive means to a desired end. Ideally, this end results in the adjustment of teaching, curriculum, and/or testing content in order to improve student learning—the ultimate purpose of engaging in assessment in the first place.

Within a collegiate foreign language context specifically, utilization-focused outcomes assessment asks language departments and programs to articulate clearly defined learning outcomes for their students and then design assessments that capture student outcomes attainment in ways that departmental stakeholders value. This process then demonstrates gaps between intended learning and the actual learning outcomes that students display at the end of the program of study. Rather than simply stop the assessment process at this stage of documentation of learning, however, utilization-focused outcomes assessment demands departments then use these findings to improve their teaching, curricular structures, and testing instruments in order to improve learning outcomes in the future. Moreover, this process is intended to become regularized within the cycle of assessment in order to cultivate a culture of continuous improvement for the benefit of students, faculty, and departments (see Norris, 2006).

Providing expertise and guidance to departments

One of the most important ways for language centers to facilitate foreign language outcomes assessment is grounded in the opportunity to engage and educate their foreign language faculty colleagues on this topic. For most faculty members, outcomes assessment is synonymous with testing, generally, and quantitative measures, specifically. Developing both an understanding of and expertise in a utilization-focused approach to assessment requires some not insignificant initial (and ongoing) investment. While individual departmental structures are often ill-equipped or poorly incentivized to encourage development or mastery of new assessment methods and resources, the language center is often well situated and resourced to invest in such mastery for the benefit of the broader foreign language departmental ecosystem. Thus, language centers are an important vehicle by which to bring together the full cohort of foreign language departments and programs in order to provide local expertise and guidance on developing outcomes assessment practices within their curricula and according to institutional needs and culture.

At the University of Notre Dame, the language center played an instrumental role in helping to leverage and disseminate the work of one foreign language department—among a total of five foreign language departments within the institution—that had already made some investment and progress in developing its own utilization-focused outcomes assessment practices. Indeed, by drawing upon the nascent outcomes assessment work by Notre Dame's Romance Languages & Literatures Department, the language center was able to bring together the remaining four language departments and begin disseminating local examples of outcomes assessment as a means of engaging others in the relevant literature, ideas, and praxis. Essential to this process was an early and formalized partnership between the language center and expert consultants within the Foreign Language Program Evaluation Project (FLPEP) at the University of Hawai'i's National Foreign Language Resource Center. This external partnership allowed the language center to cultivate specific research-driven expertise within outcomes assessment—which necessarily continued throughout the initial 4-year period of Notre Dame's assessment project—so that the language center could, in turn, provide substantive expertise and guidance to its own foreign language departmental constituents. Developing local expertise in outcomes assessment through the FLPEP partnership required the language center and its faculty and staff to devote significant amounts of time and resources to the initial effort and then maintain this intellectual development throughout the endeavor. It was precisely the need for such immediate and sustained allocations of resources that made the language center an ideal vehicle by which to develop local expertise in outcomes assessment at Notre Dame, and then continually serve as a guiding resource for foreign language departments as they negotiated their own assessment praxis. Such investment would have been difficult and unattractive to most departments on their own, and would have likely limited impact to the invested department alone.

Concretely, the language center at Notre Dame began its efforts to engage departments in the assessment project through the creation of a learning community—facilitated by the Romance Languages & Literatures Department and in consultation with FLPEP consultants—that invited department chairs and their faculty to read a variety of outcomes assessment literature (which was placed on a common website). Following this phase of introducing departments to the relevant assessment literature, the language center organized a formal panel of assessment experts for a pan-departmental audience as a formal opening to Notre Dame's outcomes assessment initiative among the five participating departments of foreign language. Importantly, these initial efforts characterized the language center as a collegial resource and the assessment initiative itself as an intellectual and curricular phenomenon with which the departments and their faculty were encouraged (but not required) to engage. In fact, although departments clearly understood the extrinsic value of assessment for institutional and even accreditation purposes, the lack of an immediate mandate to participate—coupled with the knowledge that a proactive approach would allow them more autonomy and control over the likelihood of a future mandate to participate—offered an attractive incentive of self-interest for many. This tone and context allowed departments to see the value in accepting the offer of expertise and guidance from the language center and led to spontaneous invitations to meet with departmental leadership to begin interpreting the outcomes assessment literature within their local contexts.

As the language center's role in facilitating outcomes assessment work within individual departments began, a series of internal worksheets were developed to facilitate early discussions and processes. These customized worksheets allowed departments and faculty to see the relevance of the assessment initiative from within their respective programs and proceed accordingly as the language center provided expert guidance on how to achieve departmental aspirations within the outcomes assessment approach. As these discussions progressed, the Notre Dame language center moved beyond consultation with faculty and department chairs to providing direct technical assistance in the development of new assessment instruments, the interpretation of assessment findings, and the application of such findings to curricular adjustments.

For example, after one particular department worked with the language center over a period of a year to articulate new learning goals for their degree programs, they realized that they were unable to specify learning outcomes at intermediary levels of the curriculum (e.g., lower and upper-division coursework) because of a lack of any concrete assessment data at either tertiary or intermediate levels for these newly defined learning goals. In response, the language center provided technical guidance on the selection of an assessment instrument to gauge language acquisition outcomes and helped to develop a custom survey instrument to assess additional knowledge and dispositional learning outcomes that were assumed to result from the existing curriculum. The language center then helped administer assessment tools, gather data, and interpret results over the course of a semester, providing particular guidance to the department on issues of statistical analysis and qualitative data reduction and display in order to appropriately interpret findings. At the conclusion of this process, the language center provided additional guidance on specific pedagogical and curricular adjustments that could be made in order to address the demonstrated gap between the expected and actual learning outcomes within the program.

Such expertise and guidance allowed the language center to significantly facilitate assessment work across all foreign language departments while also allowing each department to drive and own its own assessment ends. More importantly, the focus on addressing articulated gaps within the curriculum via use-focused assessment lent itself directly to application of assessment findings to this end. Thus, when the language center developed an oral proficiency assessment to help one foreign language department better evaluate the outcomes of its curriculum, the assessment findings that indicated a significant drop in oral proficiency growth in second year coursework were immediately used to adjust course content to this end. This focus on assessment for use rather than assessment for documentation helped departmental faculty to see such use-focused assessment as a tool to advance their own needs rather than a top-down mandate for purposes of institutional research and accreditation.

Whereas the language center at Notre Dame was able to take a proactive approach to assessment in advance of any internal or external mandates, foreign language departments at Emory found themselves having to respond to a sudden institutional mandate to all departments to implement a programmatic assessment plan in order to comply with the guidelines of the university's accrediting agency, the Southern Association of Colleges and Schools (SACS). Coincidentally and fortunately, Emory was invited shortly thereafter in 2010 to join with the University of Notre Dame, Georgetown University, and Rice University to form the Consortium on Useful Assessment in Language and Humanities Education, an organization consisting of individual foreign language departments from the participating institutions that aimed to foster a "culture of responsible and useful assessment of student learning outcomes in the humanities" (Consortium on Useful Assessment in Language and Humanities Education, 2012). Because of its pan-departmental reach the language center became the logical facilitator and coordinator of Emory's participation in the consortium. Up until this point, however, the atmosphere surrounding assessment at Emory was far from ideal: Faculty were being required during the unprecedented economic downturn of 2009–2010 to respond with minimal internal guidance to an external mandate about a topic in which they had very little interest or expertise.

In short, the language center faced a tall order. Nevertheless, the language center reached out to each of the six foreign language departments, explained the purpose of the consortium, and sought their participation in a process of becoming versed in and ultimately implementing useful assessment practices at the programmatic level. As an early indication of the foreign language departments' interest in meaningful engagement with assessment, five of the six departments responded favorably and attended the first organizational meeting of the consortium at Georgetown University in October 2010. While the exposure to useful assessment practices and the exchange with departments from other participating universities helped each department to see the benefits of utilization-based approaches to assessment, there was also clear consensus among all participating Emory departments that they needed much more guidance and consultation on how to transform their fledgling assessment plans into a meaningful exercise that would ultimately improve learning and teaching in the department. To that end, the language center reached out to consultants from the FLPEP and invited them to campus twice in the following year to meet individually with each interested department to discuss specifics related to their assessment practices. In most cases, the consultations focused on relatively elementary principles of useful assessment, such as identifying intended users of assessment information, formulating student learning outcomes, prioritizing assessment-related needs, developing appropriate methodologies, and analyzing assessment data. Throughout the consultations, particularly when discussing the collection and analysis of assessment data, all participating departments were reminded of the need to use and act upon the data. In other words, constant emphasis was placed not only on *doing* assessment but also *using* the collected information to improve teaching and learning. This critical step in utilization-focused assessment allowed colleagues to begin to see that assessment has concrete and immediate benefits for their own programs and can be much more than an activity required for accreditation purposes.

Providing professional development and education for faculty

Faculty professional development and education is a natural and intended consequence of creating a utilization-focused outcomes assessment culture within foreign language departments. The systemic implication for regularized assessment of curricular outcomes is a departmental culture in which faculty understand that assessment of learning informs and oftentimes changes pedagogy and curriculum. Cultivating such a culture is significantly facilitated when entities such as language centers are available to devote dedicated attention and resources to individual faculty professional development and education. While curricular development is encouraged within departments, it is often subsumed in priority and support by other service, teaching, and research obligations. Meanwhile, the foreign language center is oftentimes tasked with both a professional development role and a pedagogical and curricular support capacity. Thus, the language center offers a means of supporting this important parallel goal for outcomes assessment: Professionalizing and educating individual faculty in order to cultivate a sustainable departmental culture in which outcomes assessment can continue and thrive.

At the University of Notre Dame, the language center had an explicit mandate for faculty professional development alongside pedagogical, curricular, and language technology support. Thus, in addition to providing guidance to departments in support of the outcomes assessment initiative, the language center worked to professionalize faculty within this endeavor as well. In practice, the language center worked with many individual faculty and language program coordinators to help them implement outcomes assessment practices at the course or section level. In several instances, faculty program coordinators for lower-division courses worked closely with the language center to learn how to incorporate new knowledge and dispositional content (e.g., exposure to literary movements, historical knowledge, appreciation for cultural values) into their first year language courses. In many cases, the need to incorporate such "new" content was a direct result of the articulation of learning goals for the purposes of outcomes assessment and the realization by instructors that many of the expectations for student learning were not reflected within their curricula. The language center thus provided individual training and resources alongside speakers and pan-departmental workshops in order to introduce faculty to alternative pedagogical approaches and/or technologies to address these needs. In one case, the language center sponsored an external faculty speaker and workshop to introduce a new model for integrating comparative cultural analysis into early language coursework through technology. In another, the language center provided speakers, workshops, and instructional resources to help individual faculty improve their assessment and feedback on written assignments. In all of these examples, the language center was able to combine its expertise in outcomes assessment with complementary strengths in pedagogical, curricular, and technological support in order to help educate faculty and support the broader outcomes assessment culture in their respective departments.

In addition to localized support for professional development for outcomes assessment, the Notre Dame language center also supported faculty professional development beyond campus. The language center frequently funded individual faculty participation in relevant conferences on themes directly related to our outcomes assessment efforts. Several faculty cohorts also received funding to participate in language center sponsored symposia focused exclusively on sharing best practices in outcomes assessment. These faculty were, in turn, then invited to share their findings with colleagues in their departments as well as within campus roundtables and panel events focused on outcomes assessment themes. Perhaps the most compelling example of faculty professional development and education, however, is the participation of several such faculty as contributors to the present edited volume. The language center actively encouraged faculty involvement in this volume and their contributions to a formal publication on foreign language outcomes assessment speaks forcefully to the profound degree to which they have developed in their professional approach to assessment.

At Emory, while the meetings with consultants from FLPEP were immensely beneficial to departments in their development of a useful assessment plan, it was clear to foreign language faculty that they needed more regular guidance and support than outside consultations were able to provide. To that end, the language center offered three sequentially organized language assessment workshops for foreign language faculty that aimed to walk them through the practical implementation of language-based outcomes assessment. Attendance and participation were high for each workshop with 10 different languages from all six departments represented. Organized and conducted by the language center director, the workshops relied heavily on the helpful resources provided by the FLPEP, which gave concrete instructions and activities on the entire process of useful outcomes assessment. Significant time was spent on formulating effective student learning outcomes statements as well as developing, adapting, or adopting appropriate methodologies for collecting student performances. Another major focus of the workshops was establishing a curriculum map that indicated at which points in the curriculum specific learning outcomes were targeted and assessed.

Although there remained a programmatic focus to these workshops, faculty who had immediate course-specific questions regarding assessment also participated. An added benefit of these workshops was the sharing of experiences and concerns regarding language assessment. What had started so negatively as a result of the university-wide mandate to respond to accreditation demands, had shifted to a much more constructive dialogue and interest in understanding—via assessment—the learning taking place in foreign language classes.

Facilitating collaboration and communication among stakeholders

While the language center can play an important role in cultivating expertise in outcomes assessment and then using this insight to both guide departments and educate individual faculty to great effect, the most natural contribution for the language center within such an assessment initiative is its ability to facilitate communication and collaboration across and beyond individual departments as a result of its supra-departmental position. Indeed, the language center is uniquely suited to these capacities because of its structural placement across all foreign language departments and its associated mandate to support foreign language programs broadly. The language center already serves, in most cases, as a trusted arbiter for foreign language departments in the interpretation of new pedagogical techniques, language learning technology, and curricular or testing innovations, and it provides expertise in these areas as well as encouraging their appropriate integration across all departments. Moreover, in pursuing these various aims, the language center is often positioned in a manner that incentivizes regular interaction with units external to foreign language departments, such as learning technology offices, university teaching and learning centers, institutional assessment offices, and a broad array of outside relationships with professional, scholarly, and educational vendor organizations. The language center is also well positioned to disseminate innovation and best practice within individual departments to the broader cohort of departments in order to facilitate collaboration and collective gains. Thus, the language center's structural placement—alongside its mandate to communicate and facilitate innovation and best practices across all departments—is particularly germane to supporting outcomes assessment as it allows individual gains to become collective gains through purposeful collaboration and sharing.

The University of Notre Dame language center made communication and purposeful collaboration across departments a centerpiece in its efforts to support outcomes assessment within the foreign languages. Whether new technologies, testing formats, or curricular models were sought from the outside or created inside a department, the Notre Dame language center served as a clearinghouse and share-point for examples of best practice and innovation. One of the most important mechanisms for supporting collaboration and communication across departments was the language center's bi-annual roundtable event. During these roundtables, representatives from each department were invited to speak about their outcomes assessment work to a broader pan-departmental audience. Speakers brought and shared examples of process documents outlining their staged approach to assessing a particular language skill, knowledge set, or disposition, as well as new assessment instruments and teaching technologies. A moderated discussion then followed in order to focus attention on areas of priority for the broader outcomes assessment initiative, such as completing a full cycle of assessment and assessment evaluation (i.e., review and improvement of the assessments per se).

Importantly, an expert from the FLPEP partnership and/or the language center also participated as a speaker and moderator for these events in order to ensure that the conversation was focused and well informed, as some discussions quickly became bound-up in questions of process and approach. These roundtable activities and the broader assessment efforts were also documented and shared on the language center website and, later, transitioned into a standalone website for the foreign language outcomes assessment initiative itself.

Beyond these roundtable events—which were also supplemented by invited speakers and workshops focused on introducing and sharing new assessment resources—the Notre Dame language center was able to provide significant "behind the scenes" support by encouraging sharing and collaboration through individual meetings with departmental chairpersons and key faculty. For example, when one language program began to struggle with a linguistic versus literary/humanities focus in the assessment of its students' learning outcomes, the language center was able to directly solicit an example solution from another department that had worked with the language center to address similar issues. In other instances, the language center connected individual faculty responsible for developing or implementing assessment instruments or new curricular integrations to colleagues in other departments who were trying to achieve similar assessment or curriculum development aims. Such facilitation of communication and collaboration—possibly by virtue of the language center serving as the common assessment-related touch-point for all departments—was a helpful auxiliary to the many explicit and public attempts to share information and promote collaboration. In addition to these achievements, the language center also facilitated the introduction, training, and migration of new language learning technologies to other departments from those that had already found success implementing them. The most striking example of this phenomenon occurred when the language center worked with the Department of Romance Languages & Literatures to facilitate wider adoption of their use of the Wimba Voice Board technology for oral practice assignments outside of class. Through formal workshops, individual trainings, and custom-made instructional materials, the language center helped Romance Languages expand training and adoption of Wimba within its own programs while also introducing and training faculty in other departments who had never had any experience with this technology.

At Emory, amidst the aforementioned negative view of assessment, the language center saw an essential need to bring foreign language faculty together to share their experiences and concerns. Fortunately, the combination of the consortium gatherings, the second of which took place at Emory over three days, and the language assessment workshops provided opportunities for faculty to not only talk with each other but also to share materials, methodologies, and ideas regarding useful assessment. Of particular interest and assistance to faculty was the sharing of their respective programmatic assessment plans. Surprisingly, up to this point, there had been very little discussion across languages and departments about commonly held goals and beliefs about foreign language education at Emory. Being able to see what other departments had identified as programmatic goals was an extremely helpful process for identifying areas of commonality as well as areas of difference. To a large degree, seeing overlap in the goals of different programs served to relieve any anxiety among faculty or departments about the appropriateness of their stated outcomes. To build on this growing sense of commonality among the different foreign languages, the language center organized a series of meetings to discuss the larger mission of foreign language learning at Emory. Out of these meetings came a more unified sense of the priorities of language education at Emory, which was no small feat considering the longtime division between lower-level and upper-level instruction.

Another initiative that the language center sponsored to engender more collaboration and communication among foreign language professionals was a working group on assessment that met monthly for two semesters following the second meeting of the consortium in the spring of 2011. The purpose of this group was to maintain dialogue about assessment-related matters and to focus on specific issues that concerned all members of the group. Five different languages from five different departments were represented at these meetings, and one topic that received particular attention over several months was the collective analysis of assessment measures in each of the languages to determine the degree to which they elicited performances that showcased targeted learning outcomes. In several instances, the group helped colleagues see that existing measures were not providing sufficient data to determine if certain learning outcomes were being met. Without the collaborative and collective attention to these measures it is unlikely that such discoveries would have been made.

Disseminating and advocating for best practices in assessment

The language center can also play an important role in disseminating and advocating for best practices in outcomes assessment because of its prominent role on campus generally and among the foreign language departments specifically. This dissemination and advocacy is, of course, critical for local stakeholders, but it also offers an opportunity for the language center to communicate and articulate best practices to a wider external audience within the field of foreign languages and literatures and beyond. Indeed, the present volume and chapter is a striking instantiation of this additional role for language centers to play.

At the University of Notre Dame, the language center played an important role publicizing the outcomes assessment work of the foreign language departments on campus as well as within external bodies. By so doing, the language center successfully advocated for annual outcomes assessment support funding from the Notre Dame Provost's Office. In addition, the Notre Dame language center, in collaboration with individual faculty and departments, supported and participated in several major talks at various conferences and symposia outside of the institution. These public disseminations provided important opportunities to showcase the efforts of faculty and advocate for the value and importance of that work to a broader audience of their national and international peers. Later, the language center also served as a primary institutional instigator for direct inter-institutional collaboration with outcomes assessment projects at other institutions in the consortium. The expression of this advocacy role for the consortium came about when the Modern Language Association's Association of Departments of Foreign Languages devoted a session at one of its 2012 summer seminars to a panel of representatives from the consortium—three of which were language center directors—to share and advocate for their collective work on outcomes assessment in the foreign languages.

In addition to these external efforts to disseminate and advocate for best practices in assessment, the assessment-related activity among foreign language professionals at Emory resulted in foreign language faculty being selected to lead university-wide initiatives and discussions on assessment. For instance, the language center director was asked to chair the university's learning outcomes assessment committee, a provost-level body that was charged with reviewing assessment plans from all nine schools and colleges at Emory, sharing best practices, and helping shape a culture of assessment across the university. In addition, foreign language faculty played an instrumental role in a university-wide academic learning community organized around the topic of assessment. Ironically, a group of faculty who in 2010 felt woefully unprepared to implement useful assessment practices in their respective programs was now, thanks in large part to their collaboration and organization through the language center, already seen on campus as assessment leaders.

Conclusions and future directions

The present chapter offers a preliminary yet compelling case for the leadership role that language centers can play in initiating, supporting, and disseminating utilization-focused outcomes assessment within and beyond their institutions. While it is necessarily true that foreign language departments remain the primary locus and stakeholders for these assessment efforts, their colleagues in the language center can contribute in important ways that individual departments cannot. "Centering" foreign language departments around useful outcomes assessment is a new and timely manner in which foreign language centers and departments can collaborate to significant and mutual benefit. A commonality to the four thematic areas where language centers can demonstrate targeted support and impact in support of the assessment process is the independence and supra-departmental position that language centers enjoy. From that vantage point, language centers have a flexibility and autonomy that allows them to reach out to departments and bypass internal departmental boundaries that have potentially impeded constructive assessment-related work. To be sure, each institution has to determine the role that its language center can play vis-à-vis its work with departments and faculty, but it offers a compelling approach for accomplishing the type of programmatic thinking and enhancement that has long been a challenge to collegiate foreign language professionals.

Acknowledgments

Dr. Askildson would like to thank Dr. John T. McGreevy, Dean of the College of Arts & Letters at the University of Notre Dame, for his strong support for the utilization-focused outcomes assessment project and the Center for the Study of Language & Cultures. He would also like to recognize the indispensable guidance provided by Dr. John Norris and Yukiko Watanabe of the Foreign Language Program Evaluation Project at the National Foreign Language Resource Center, University of Hawai'i at Mānoa.

Dr. Maxim would like to thank the Dean of Emory College of Arts and Sciences and the Provost of Emory University for their support of the different assessment-based projects initiated in the Emory College Language Center.

References

Byrnes, H. (1998). Constructing curricula in collegiate foreign language departments. In H. Byrnes (Ed.), *Learning foreign and second languages: Perspectives in research and scholarship* (pp. 262–295). New York, NY: MLA.

Byrnes, H. (2006). What kind of resource is language and why does it matter for advanced language learning? An introduction. In H. Byrnes (Ed.), *Advanced language learning: The contribution of Halliday and Vygotsky* (pp. 1–28). New York, NY: Continuum.

Byrnes, H., Maxim, H. H., & Norris, J. M. (2010). Realizing advanced foreign language writing development in collegiate education: Curricular design, pedagogy, assessment [Monograph]. *Modern Language Journal, 94* (supplement s1).

Consortium on Useful Assessment in Language and Humanities Education. (2012). Retrieved from https://blogs.commons.georgetown.edu/humanitiesassessment/

James, D. (1996). Bypassing the traditional leadership: Who's minding the store? *ADFL Bulletin, 28*(3), 5–11.

Kern, R. (2002). Reconciling the language-literature split through literacy. *ADFL Bulletin, 33*(3), 20–24.

Maxim, H. H. (2006). Integrating textual thinking into the introductory college-level foreign language classroom. *Modern Language Journal, 90*(1), 19–32.

Maxim, H. H., Höyng, P., Lancaster, M., Schaumann, C., & Aue, M. (2013). Overcoming curricular bifurcation: A departmental approach to curricular reform. *Die Unterrichtspraxis, 46*(1), 1–26.

MLA Ad Hoc Committee on Foreign Languages. (2007). Foreign languages and higher education: New structures for a changed world. *Profession*, 234–245.

Norris, J. M. (2006). The why (and how) of assessing student learning outcomes in college foreign language programs. *Modern Language Journal, 90*(4), 590–597.

Norris, J. M. (2008). *Validity evaluation in language assessment.* New York, NY: Peter Lang.

Patton, M. Q. (2008). *Utilization-focused evaluation* (4th ed.). Thousand Oaks, CA: Sage.

Swaffar, J. (2006). Terminology and its discontents: Some caveats about communicative competence. *Modern Language Journal, 90*, 246–249.

The Uses of Accountability

Amanda Randall & Janet Swaffar
The University of Texas at Austin

This chapter examines the initial assessment experiences of a research university's German language program with 10 tenure-track faculty members and undergraduate and graduate PhD programs. The authors frame their case study by exploring why the administrative charge of engaging in assessment of those programs challenges traditions of academic autonomy and gives rise to faculty members' concerns about bureaucratic make-work and the imposition of evaluative criteria that do not reflect the content and knowledge applications they teach. To involve all faculty members in articulating their specialist understanding of teaching, the department used a process contrary to that proposed in the university's institutional focus on outcomes per se. Instead, the department looked first for concrete examples of what students have learned at different levels, and then asked faculty members to reflect about what teaching practices that learning suggests. The authors conclude by describing the essential component in the upper-division undergraduate program's assessment: engaging faculty in a shared effort to identify practices that enable specific learning objectives within a curriculum.

Introduction

The institutionalization and standardization of performance assessment began in American grade and high schools with the Elementary and Secondary Education Act of 1965. In subsequent years leading up to and beyond the 2001 initiative, "No Child Left Behind," the assessment effort in public schools has focused on various standardized tests as measures of achievement and created a legacy of controversy about their value, the frequency of their use, and their impact on school curricula and teaching practices (see Davis, this volume; Norris, Davis, Sinicrope, & Watanabe, 2009). Until the 1990s, postsecondary institutions were, however, not subject to broader assessment pressures (Courts & McInerney, 1993). Instead, both private and state colleges and universities maintained a level of academic independence that left them largely unaffected by the national movement toward assessment.

Changing status of accountability for universities in the United States

With shifts in public views about, and changes in the demographic reality of wealth distribution and remunerative, relatively stable employment opportunities, attitudes about the privileged status of higher education in the United States have shifted as well. Tenure is no longer sacrosanct (Gordon, 1998). Tenure reviews at five- to six-year intervals are now a regular practice in most institutions with criteria relating to the quality of teaching and research, and continuation or renewal contingent on administrative approval with respect to these criteria (Mignon & Langsam, 1999; Miller, 1999; Tierney, 1997).

These developments, commencing in the 1990s and thereafter acerbated in the mortgage collapse of 2008 with its subsequent impact on the U.S. economy, call attention to the increasingly costly price of higher education that is leaving many graduates unable to find work while at the same time burdened with formidable student loans (Thornton, 2010). Coupled with these realities is the advent of online degrees and of comparatively less costly (but nonetheless often expensive) vocational training programs, particularly short courses in information technology (Lewin, 2014; United States Congress, Senate, & Committee on Health, Education, Labor, and Pensions, 2012). Those options called into serious question, and offered real-world alternatives to, the concept that higher education in postsecondary schools paved the road to lifetime success. Was a college education worth the price?

To address this question, major universities, often in response to regional accreditation bodies, have begun to explore assessment options. Regional accreditation agencies like the Southern Association of Colleges and Schools, Commission on Colleges (SACSCOC) are not governmental, but are, rather, recognized by the U.S. Secretary of Education as "reliable authorities concerning the quality of education or training offered by the institutions of higher education or higher education programs they accredit."[1] Their oversight involves asking universities to identify and evaluate markers of both bureaucratic and educational quality. To assess student learning, universities typically outline what students are expected to learn in a particular major and then point to practices fostering successful learning within the confines of particular disciplines and adapting that learning for students' lives beyond graduation (Abbott, Cothrun, Kosta, Höyng, & Swender, 2015). In the case of universities overseen by SACSCOC, for example, postsecondary school departments are charged with specifying and reporting on learning outcomes, actions undertaken to achieve these outcomes, and the methods employed to assess student progress.

Consequently, this charge would seem to allow the professorate considerable leeway to define the research or teaching they are engaged in and to determine

---

[1] See http://www2.ed.gov/admins/finaid/accred/index.html for an overview of institutional accreditation bodies working with the U.S. Department of Education (U.S. Department of Education, 2014).

how teaching, learning, and research interact—a necessary contingency for an educational establishment with colleges that offer subjects ranging from medicine and engineering to education, science, and liberal arts. Many of these disciplines have licensing or certification tests or bodies, or close alignment of their work with federal grants (and hence also with intense and detailed peer review). The liberal arts and humanities, however, are left in the situation of needing to establish not only assessment criteria for their teaching and majors, but also the validity of these criteria as measures of student learning success.

Key problems for assessment of humanities programs

The question of validity and assessment is, in fact, urgent, and clarity about how to pursue this process is critical for success. Unfortunately, guidance on how to undertake and report on an assessment program in the humanities is often assumed rather than adequately articulated by home institutions. Ironically, understaffing of assessment programs occurs at a time when administrative staffing is proliferating in most universities to the extent of inciting debates about "administrative bloat" (Archibald & Feldman, 2009; Rogers, 2012). Moreover, increasing staffing dedicated exclusively to assessment implementation seems especially urgent when one considers the expanded scope of administrative work in setting and implementing the agenda in large research institutions.

The implications for departments, and the administrative assessment staff that is supposed to assist those units, are that, on the one hand, assessment initiatives and their impact on curricula development are recognized as influential for student enrollment, as well as for administrative support and regional accreditation. Yet, on the other hand, a frequent subverting message to the contrary is that institutional assessment administrators charged with implementing and validating assessment policies are often seriously overextended.

This issue emerges when a university's assessment units are headed by only one or two full-time directors who must address a wide diversity of programs. For example, The University of Texas at Austin—an institution of approximately 50,000 students, 3,000 faculty members, and 21,000 staff persons (The University of Texas at Austin, n.d.; The University of Texas at Austin & Office of Information Management and Analysis, n.d.)—has had only one assessment director, under the Office of the Executive Vice President and Provost. With the help of temporary or part-time staff or graduate research assistants, that director must orient and train faculty and staff in assembling and submitting standardized assessment reports for hundreds of departments and programs. Often the director is asked to consult with whole departments as well as with the person or persons charged with leading a department's assessment.

Contributing to their oversight responsibilities, such institutional assessment directors are serving two masters: on the one hand, the administration and its targets for assessment results to use in accreditation, and on the other hand, the departments themselves to which directors deliver instruction. Given the broad scope of the assessment charge, understaffing ultimately becomes a departmental issue. The department's faculty members must interpret and assess their program in terms of their individual instructional practices. Yet, often lack of funding or release time for staff and faculty asked to develop, design, implement, and analyze those practices and appropriate assessments thwarts the initiative.

As a result of inadequate administrative resources, for academic programs in the humanities, assessment can appear to be yet another set of unfunded mandates overseen by an often-isolated departmental assessment coordinator. Effective assessment is not a one or two person job. Moreover, it frequently involves changing the dynamics of intradepartmental relationships so that faculty members can rethink together how their programs could evaluate and demonstrate their units' and majors' features and strengths (Abbott et al., 2015).

In a time when business terms such as "quality" and "management" frequently appear in campaigns meant to help implement institutional assessment on university campuses, it is not surprising to find that a gap has opened between administrative and scholarly ideas about the purpose and practices of assessment (see, for instance, Brennan & Shah, 2000; Dew & Nearing, 2004; Gates, 2002; Sherr & Teeter, 1991; Vroeijenstijn, 1995). Discursively, this gap is addressed in terms of a "cultural" or "mental shift" in the perceptions and practice of assessment in higher education. First, as noted above, there must be a shift toward fuller faculty engagement, making it a collaborative departmental effort. Second, in engaging the faculty more fully, a perceptual shift is required—from viewing assessment as a burdensome mandate for accountability to a useful tool for ongoing curriculum improvement. Third, a shift is needed toward thinking about assessment as a student-centered process, as opposed to a self-referential administrative or disciplinary exercise (Abbott et al., 2015; Angelo, 1999).

That these shifts are talked about by administrative and faculty assessment directors alike does not change the fact, however, that the work of assessment still falls to the academic departments and programs; if anything, it reinforces it. In practical terms, then, this new dynamic tasks all faculty members in a department with two undertakings, often little understood because they are seemingly so alien to academics: The first charge is to actually understand how their individual courses contribute to the overall curriculum's objectives; and the second involves developing strategies for scaffolding those contributions as objectives ("outcomes") in curricular practice. These are not minor policy shifts. To be sure, the faculty members in most programs agree on general principles, such as fostering critical thinking. But few liberal arts departments approach their programs with the goal of identifying specific (and assessable) manifestations of objectives for the major—the learning outcomes that might be expected over the span of a course sequence.

Establishing criteria for measuring such features has usually been the purview of individual instructors' grading policies. Professors in the humanities assessing such features as critical thinking or rhetorical cogency in student essays are often willing to consider rubric categories to parse the elements to be the focus of grading, but resist applying numbers to those categories. In other words, consensus-building around quantifiable evaluation of student performance often runs afoul of humanists' perceptions regarding quantifiable, data-driven grading as opposed to their academic traditions that reward educated insights or other intellectual work that seems only to be assessable in a qualitative, intuitive, or global way.

As a result, although each course in a major tends to be understood by its faculty as relating to other courses in that curriculum, this relationship is rarely articulated in performance expectations. For most professors, course assignments represent primarily differences in content and catalogue "sequencing" rather than specifics about how to scaffold preparedness to undertake particular assignments at students' presumed learning level. In contrast, program assessment requires attention to how the components of a course build upon each other and bridge to further courses in the major. Hence, assessment in this mode requires faculty to articulate what students actually learn in each course in terms of *a developmental sequence*.

One means of raising faculty members' awareness of and interest in their program's curricular practices is to provide concrete activities that ask them to specify what their department's individual courses do. Only once the faculty has shared awareness about what individual learning tasks they use to enhance their students' knowledge acquisition can they articulate how they work together toward a common set of learning objectives across the courses in their program. Only with such awareness can the assessment director's charges *make sense* to the faculty as anything other than busywork. The reality is, however, that most humanities programs and departments lack this kind of experience in mapping their curriculum and identifying the specific outcomes in student performance that faculty members anticipate and desire.

Once assessment has been adopted as an institutional priority, the faculty will need time and resources to acquire and see the value of these insights that seem so removed from their own scholarly pursuits and time management heretofore. The fact that many graduate programs in the language and other humanities domains do not explicitly teach future professors how to teach and assess in their fields is also a major factor stymieing faculty-designed program assessment. But the scene is changing. At recent conventions and in professional journals, the topic of assessment is often presented in terms of teacher as well as student education (Brooks & Darhower, 2014). The inadequate integration of teaching practices into graduate programs in FL instruction at most universities has become a significant focus of attention in publications as well (Allen, 2014; Arens, 2012, 2014; Donato, 2009; Glisan, Swender, & Surface, 2013; Pfeiffer, 2008).

As noted above, the problems posed by understaffing of assessment support at the administrative and departmental levels confound the process. Ultimately, program assessment is perceived as adding time-consuming work to *current* faculty and staffing obligations. In consequence, departmental commitment to instituting a new articulation of their curriculum and to designing viable instruments and processes to assess it transparently seems extremely burdensome and promising little in the way of reward for teachers and learners. Yet without these steps, assessment programs cannot fulfill their most important objective: motivating major changes and improvement in teaching (Courts & McInerney, 1993; Graff, 2008; Norris, 2006).

Heteroglossia problem: Getting lost in translation

To compound these problems in implementation, those trained in assessment who are tasked with representing the institutions themselves often do not have the communicative tools that would help the faculty: The general guidebooks about university assessment that are available rarely speak to most specialists in academic fields outside of education and scholarship on assessment itself. Their semantics are foreign and often alienating for many faculty members because they are written largely by and for administrators (see, for example, Bloxham & Boyd, 2007; Middaugh, 2010; Palomba & Banta, 1999; Ruben & National Association of College and University Business Officers, 2007; Secolsky & Denison, 2012; Vroeijenstijn, 1995).

Efforts to address the need for field-specific guidance and examples are appearing in print and online (Anderson & Krathwohl, 2001; Norris et al., 2009). For the FL community, university department and project websites provide readily accessible suggestions.[2] Professional organizations also are beginning to offer fee-based consulting services and to recognize best practices for program assessment.[3] Too often still lacking in institutional assessment initiatives, however, is explicit reference to such field-specific examples—presenting tasks familiar to particular academic fields—for establishing what constitutes excellent, good, minimal, or unsatisfactory assessment practices and progress toward a program's stated learning "outcomes." That is, while scholars in the humanities are working on developing professional standards for program assessment in specific disciplines, the communicative gap between faculty members who design and implement assessment according to their profession's practices and standards, and administrators who speak in their own specialized terms, remains unaddressed.

This gap is further exacerbated by the frameworks used for regional accreditation reporting. One concrete site where administrative and faculty understandings of assessment effectively has gotten lost in translation is TracDat®, a web-based institutional assessment platform used by many American universities, including The University of Texas at Austin. The mutual misrecognition is both terminological and structural. While the system's "Key Terms" might be defined in a university-designed user's manual (sometimes in separate administrative and faculty editions), the academic department faculty and staff members tasked with developing, administering, evaluating, and interpreting assessment tools still must interpret bureaucratic terminology such as "Outcomes," "Criterion," "Method," "Results and Analysis," and "Actions" in terms of the pedagogical standards and nomenclature of *their* field.[4] Moreover, the structure of computerized assessment platforms implies a strict linear sequencing—from identifying a learning outcome, to assessing it with a specific method, to analyzing results, to taking concrete action in response to those results. To meet the narrative demands of the reporting system, then, departments must either design their assessments according to that sequence, or find creative ways to reframe their department—and discipline-specific assessment methods and goals—to fit the TracDat® terminology and workflow.

Implementing an assessment process that leads to accountability on the program or department level, then, requires a translation process, because assessment's technical metalanguage used in reports and planning on the regional and national

---

[2] See, for instance, the websites of the Stanford Language Center (Stanford University, n.d.; http://stanford.edu/dept/lc/language/index.html), Georgetown University's Department of German (2011; http://german.georgetown.edu/page/1242716536825.html), the University of Minnesota Center for Advanced Research on Language Acquisition (n.d.; http://carla.umn.edu/), and the University of Hawai'i at Mānoa Foreign Language Program Evaluation Project (2011; http://nflrc.hawaii.edu/evaluation/).

[3] See, for instance, the American Association of Teachers of German (AATG) Centers of Excellence (2015; http://www.aatg.org/?page=CoE).

[4] A description of the TracDat® system, as well as the user guides (academic and administrative versions) can be accessed by the public at http://www.utexas.edu/provost/iae/tracdat.html (The University of Texas at Austin & Office of Institutional Accreditation and Effectiveness, 2014c).

levels is not field-specific. Recognizing the urgency of this problem, the Assessment Director and staff at The University of Texas at Austin initiated a series of meetings with departmental chairs and their designated assessment coordinators to provide additional explicit "how to" definitions and illustrations of such critical TracDat® features as "student learning outcomes," "process outcomes," and "setting criteria for success" (The University of Texas at Austin & Office of Institutional Accreditation and Effectiveness, 2014a, 2014b).

In facing the general translation problem in institutional assessment, the humanities are at a particular disadvantage. While all academic fields value as the outcome of teaching their students' increase in knowledge about their respective subjects, some disciplines place greater emphasis on vocational successes, often measured in scores on standardized tests (boards, licensing examinations) that document learners' preparation for career trajectories. Medical and engineering schools, for example, have national competency or certification tests students must pass to qualify to enter their professions. In fields where the body of knowledge is identified in terms of a general consensus about what a professional needs to be able to do, performance on such, often objective, tests is acknowledged as validly indicating the relative odds for success for future professionals.

But for many other fields—those typically housed in colleges of liberal arts and humanities, for example—testing and other forms of course-level assessment often have remained in the hands of individual instructors, with little or no reference to institutional, local, regional, or national "standards" for what students actually can do if they "read books" and "write papers" successfully. Instead, more stress is placed on individual responses to test and assignment options that provide indicators of creative thinking and various forms of critical writing or speaking engagement. That is, humanities faculty have focused on what students do in a qualitative sense, rather than on what our particular fields might suggest they need to do or know in more technical senses. The humanities disciplines have not helped faculty, because since World War II, most fields have drifted toward an acceptance of methodological pluralism without necessarily specifying what basic skills in research and argumentation make the work valid in new and revitalized traditional methodologies (Bourns & Melin, 2014).

Increasingly, the call is being made for assessing performance in humanities course sequences with instruments designed to reflect the goals, knowledge, skills, and values of particular disciplines (Liskin-Gasparro, 1995; Norris, 2006; Palomba & Banta,1999; Pfeiffer, 2008). Nationally recommended test instruments for FL instruction exist. Potential resources for the development of nationally accredited program assessment instruments include the American Council on the Teaching of Foreign Languages (ACTFL) 2003-released "Integrated Performance Assessment" (IPA), a prototype for assessing students' developing language proficiency in line with its *Performance Guidelines for K–12 Learners* (1998) and the *Standards for Foreign Language Learning in the Twenty-first Century* (National Standards in Foreign Language Education Project [U.S.], 2006), both of which are proposed to apply to levels K–16 (Adair-Hauck, Glisan, & Troyan, 2013; American Council on the Teaching of Foreign Languages, 2003). Unfortunately, most postsecondary professors in language programs, particularly those who teach undergraduate and graduate courses, are unfamiliar with these documents and the ACTFL Standards' curricular proposals (Magnan, Murphy, & Sahakyan, 2014).

To be sure, a number of college foreign language departments have developed their own tests reflecting learning broader foci proposed by ACTFL (Arens, 2012; Liskin-Gasparro, 1995). But while the ACTFL Oral Proficiency Interview (OPI) has been adopted for language teaching programs at state universities (Brooks & Darhower, 2014), the ACTFL Standards' ramifications for undergraduate and graduate programs focusing on reading, writing, and listening comprehension are only beginning to be addressed beyond individual FL departments.

Rethinking assessment implementation

To show what is at stake when FL departments take up the project of assessment, and to exemplify one relatively encouraging approach to the task, this chapter describes how the Department of Germanic Studies at The University of Texas at Austin confronted the problem by looking first at student performance rather than asking faculty to agree at the outset on desired program outcomes and practices to assess. This case study describes a process of implementation aimed at circumventing and resolving the issues outlined in the above sections. As such, it presents a brief history of steps taken to address the following model of institutional assessment established by the university for the purpose of regional accreditation reporting (The University of Texas at Austin & Office of the Executive Vice President and Provost, 2014). This model came into effect in 2006 and underwent revision in 2015. To substantiate the "institutional effectiveness" of the university's educational programs in their TracDat® reports, all academic departments and programs had been asked to (a) identify at least three desired student "outcomes" for the department's upper-division undergraduate program, (b) design at least three methods per outcome to assess student performance and progress in that area (nine methods total), and (c) take at least one action in response to the results of each assessment method administered of the three methods (nine actions total; The University of Texas at Austin & Office of Institutional Accreditation and Effectiveness, 2014a).

After preliminary efforts to initiate discussions of student outcomes in faculty committee meetings in 2010 foundered on the rocks of individual testing practices and assumptions about outcomes in the major, several Germanic Studies faculty members volunteered to engage in assessment exploring a different path: Instead of discussing abstract premises and values, we decided to take a more empirical route—to test first and generalize later. We wanted to look at concrete results of upper-division students' learning in the course of our program to see what students currently do well and what they do less adequately.[5] Despite the initial difficulties in determining a plan of action, it was clear to everyone that in a period of downsizing and amalgamation of disciplinary fields under a variety of umbrellas, often in administrative efforts to ameliorate economic pressures, the study of program goals and outcomes would serve the survival of the department's identity and its role within its institution.

The department's chair delegated the assessment responsibility to its undergraduate course committee, which traditionally defines the various courses in the major and upholds these definitions in practice. As such, this was a group

---

[5] Initially, this group consisted of Peter Hess, chair of the department; Hans Boas, chair of the departmental course committee; Per Urlaub, then sole undergraduate coordinator; and emerita professor Janet Swaffar. We were joined by Corinne Crane in 2012.

that had some sort of overview of "what the major does" and each course's place in it. After agreement could not be found about which three major emphases of the program should be the initial target of assessment, the course committee agreed on a twofold strategy to set objectives for the program as a whole. Because our German major curriculum spans three different subfields (literature, linguistics, and cultural studies), our challenge was to, first, identify a starting point that would reflect students' work regardless of their particular subfield. Once we had a shared perception about a common performance site, we could then develop assessment instruments to be applied across course sequences in ways that would be relevant and informative to faculty members, whatever the subfield being taught (Grau-Sempere, Mohn, & Pieroni, 2009).

The choice of that approach reflects the character of larger departments in terms of their faculty and student make-up. The Department of Germanic Studies at The University of Texas at Austin currently has eight tenured and two tenure-track professors, one visiting DAAD professor, and two lecturers who teach graduate and undergraduate courses in German as well as interdisciplinary offerings. Typically, five upper-division undergraduate German courses are offered each semester. These courses cover advanced grammar, speaking and composition, literature, linguistics, and cultural studies, with class sizes averaging between 13 and 22 students, and total semester course enrollment between 80 and 100 students. The categorization of these courses as "major courses" must be qualified, however, because, even though they fulfill the catalogue requirements for the major, the students who take them are often double-majors or minors from fields across campus who have cast an eye toward future employment or graduate study involving diverse types of German language ability.

The diversity of our student enrollment and course offerings is just one dimension of the problems facing a department exploring curricular objectives without the clear national benchmark of licensing or bar examinations. We cannot simply construct major courses out of material that a national accreditation agency decided students need to be successful as pharmacists or psychologists or actuaries. Instead, lacking such national norms, each individual program has to define what students learn in courses that we teach and which ones seem to work for them. In the case of Germanic Studies at The University of Texas, the faculty consistently teaches five different courses per semester that are designed with well-established practices and offered mainly on the basis of historical appeal to students. Initiatives to change the articulation of the curriculum are met with understandable resistance. Also typical of larger departments, we have more tenured colleagues than younger assistant professors and lecturers, a characteristic that tends to reinforce curricular expectations from the senior faculty's point of view. The configuration of the undergraduate major has undergone some shifts in content, sequencing, and specifications in the course catalogue and syllabus requirements, but not with respect to reexamining our mission within the university and responsiveness to our student body.

Difficulties in developing shared perceptions about how to assess students' learning-outcomes also arise in part because of the professional reward system in the humanities. Especially in large departments, faculty members identify their roles in teaching as representing diverse fields, based on their established reputations as specialists—as those who, in the humanities particularly, have engaged in individual achievement rather than collaborative research, teaching, and publication. This tendency is reinforced by the tradition at research-intensive and research-extensive universities to promote faculty members in Liberal Arts colleges primarily for their independent publications in specialized fields. Teamwork and joint publication, unlike in fields such as the social and physical sciences, are frequently viewed in the humanities as conveying unclear evidence of a professor's capacity to engage in independent thinking (Modern Language Association of America & Task Force on Evaluating Scholarship for Tenure and Promotion, 2007).

As a result, educational values in departments such as history, philosophy, and language are anchored in this special status awarded to individual achievement, a status that influences academic thinking. Small wonder then, that humanities faculty often discount suggestions for assessing learning as an exercise in group-think. The established courses and procedures of humanities departments resist curricular and pedagogical changes because they appear to undermine autonomy and integrity in intellectual practice. In that case, though incremental changes are more difficult and time-consuming to address democratically, they are nonetheless often preferable to debating the big "outcome" issues. Thus, instead of starting with a list of desired outcomes—a discussion necessarily anchored in shared perceptions about teacher practices—the Germanic Studies assessment coordinator proposed the department focus on student achievement to find out about particular types of learning. Then we would be in a position to decide how to enhance that learning.

Exploring students' performance to uncover variation

Under the auspices of its undergraduate course committee, the Department of Germanic Studies took this alternative approach to engaging initially in rethinking curricular and pedagogical practices linked to accountability and assessment. Instead of asking, "What do we want our teachers to do?" or "What do we want our students to be able to do?" we reframed the question of student outcomes as the more intuitive, "What can our students do?" That focus shifted the discussion away from faculty "roles" in the abstract and into a more productive course of action that allowed the department to create an agenda for developing an assessment plan. The authors discovered that this new decision-making process has proven beneficial for the faculty from several vantage points. Not only has it fostered communication about what program outcomes they value with some linguistics courses offered in English, it has promoted reflection and conversation about options for teaching and testing that faculty members use and how they assess them in their courses at particular levels.

The department's Undergraduate Course and Program Committee decided that we needed to start with assessment that reflected the diverse emphases of our upper-division program. Hence, we would have to design, evaluate, and administer these instruments ourselves. One option would be to assess common types of assignments, such as student writing samples or cumulative tasks in portfolios, across the upper-division curriculum. But given the very diversity of upper-division course offerings—literature, culture, and linguistics, taught in both English and German—this approach might not be as useful for identifying global department outcomes as a more standardized test instrument might be. Also contributing to the design decision process was the fact that institutional expectations for assessment formats were left unspecified. For these reasons, we chose to take a hybrid approach.

After considering writing and oral proficiency options, the committee decided to begin by looking at students' reading comprehension because that option afforded the broadest coverage of departmental subject matter. Faculty members participated in selecting three short reading texts that reflected the content covered in the capstone seminars in linguistics, literature, or culture, from which seniors could choose to complete their major (Appendix A). The test instrument designed around the readings was *standardized* in the sense that it could be administered in any one of the upper-division courses. Professor Janet Swaffar proposed that a test could be both *qualitative and quantitative* if the faculty would use numeric rubric grading with two independent raters. Engaging multiple faculty members in the grading process each semester could thus serve as a segue into gleaning and sharing insights stemming from the assessment process.

Swaffar further suggested four simple tasks sequenced to reflect different types of comprehension. Thus, the test encompassed a breadth of elements that comprise not only evidence of reading proficiency, but of the extension thereof into different cognitive processes. She developed an initial model together with Professor Katherine Arens (Appendix C), with tasks targeting distinct cognitive stages, as illustrated in recent iterations of Bloom's taxonomy (Anderson & Krathwohl, 2001; Swaffar, 2014; Swaffar & Arens, 2005). The goal was to reflect the difficulties confronted by the learners as they progressed from receptive to active mental interaction with course information—a reflection of what is described generally in Bloom's taxonomy of cognitive complexity (Bloom, 1956).

Established measures such as recall protocols assess student performance in remembering a text's content by measuring the number of idea units from the text that they reproduced from memory (Bernhardt, 1983). In contrast, the assessment tool that the department developed aims to access and document not only students' memories or perceptions about textual information, but also to pinpoint different cognitive processes—to see how students were dealing with the materials presented in various tasks. An additional intention in constructing an instrument in this way was to encourage the faculty graders to think about how reading and working with readings engages these stages of learning.

To foster all faculty members' eventual involvement with the evaluation process, Arens and Swaffar chose a format that would be relatively efficient to administer and assess. Testing under time constraints (2 minutes to fulfill each of the last three tasks) served to encourage students to record their initial impressions immediately and efficiently after reading the text. As a consequence, it would enable any faculty member to engage in rubric assessment based on succinct student answers. In reducing redundancies common to more elaborate articulation, faculty members would need to devote no more than an hour or at most two hours to grading the performance results of 15 to 25 students (see Appendices C and D).

If the simplicity of the task and assessment rubrics developed could allow for relatively rapid qualitative grading, the time spent in the assessment process could be reduced for the faculty as a whole. Two faculty members who completed the initial round of independent grading would then provide the basis for determining the reliability of test results. Equally important, learning about patterns revealed in scoring might provoke ideas for new ways to present classroom materials.

Rather than administering the test only in a particular, recurring course or outside of regular classroom time, the committee decided to assess one entry-level course each fall and one of a rotating variety of advanced or senior courses in the spring. The advanced courses taking the test would necessarily differ, but that was considered desirable as repeated testing would reveal whether particular advanced courses yielded differences in performance. Over a period of several years, averaged performance on these tests would establish a baseline for expected performance and learning needs of beginners as well remaining problems of advanced majors and ways to address them.

In the second week of each fall semester, the test was administered in an initial course for majors in German conversation and composition. The same test was given in an advanced or senior course during the 13th week of each subsequent spring semester. For all classes, the assessment proceeded as follows: The test administrator comes in the last 25 minutes of a class hour. Students are told that the test is to assess our performance as teachers of our program and that scores will not be available to the instructor of the course until course grades have been submitted (Appendix B).

All readers in both the initial and the advanced upper-division courses shared the same time constraints. Students had 3 minutes to read and underline key words and phrases in each of the three German texts on the front of the page, and 2 minutes to answer the English language questions in English on the reverse side of each passage (see Appendix C for an example). These are the four tasks that students complete for each of the three readings. The cognitive reasoning sought in each task is provided in square brackets:

- underline phrases and words in sentences in a short German-language passage that convey its major idea or subject matter [recognition],
- articulate (in English) the main idea or topic of the text [content reproduction],
- provide (in English) a brief exemplification of the text's topic [analysis of part to whole],
- briefly link (in English) the text to the broader framework of German history, linguistics, or literature [synthesis of text understanding into a broader knowledge framework].

All students were provided with a description of the four tasks with the requirement that "all expression is to be IN ENGLISH," reiterated in all-capitalized letters in the directions. All passages to be read and underlined were titled, with sources identified but unglossed. As noted above, instructions were presented before handing out the readings and those instructions were reiterated on all three pages.

Despite the fact that the instrument was to be used to assess student learning within a German major in which virtually all the classes were taught in German, English was selected as the appropriate language to use in the assessment, for several reasons. First, it encourages students to think about and articulate textual meaning in their native language, an assessment strategy that studies have shown is especially important for both upper- and lower-division FL students (Kern, 1994;

Lee, 1985, 1986; Scott, 2010; Scott & de la Fuente, 2008). Second, it focuses on on evaluation of performance in a larger pattern of student comprehension. The pattern commences with indicators about their *recognition* of key content indicators in task one, which asks readers to underline language that conveys to them the main ideas of the text. The tasks that follow (exemplification and synthesis) are of increasing complexity following the principles of Bloom's taxonomy.

Another reason for using English was to minimize questions about whether a given term or sentence was accurately understood, that is, whether a German word or phrase was a semantic guess in German or an accurate translation in English. Misreadings and mistakes in comprehension were thus much more unambiguously evident than they would have been in German. Finally, research studies indicate that the use of English facilitates comprehension. Richard Kern (1994) and Virginia Scott (2010), in particular, discovered that thinking about a passage in a foreign language in English as well as the foreign language enhances students' understanding of what they read. Thus, native language articulation not only makes rater assessment less ambiguous; it apparently also enhances students' comprehension and recall of the messages in a text.

The preliminary underlining task, to be undertaken during a 3-minute period while reading a passage of 150 to 250 words, was also designed to prepare students for the second task. When they turn the reading page over to the reverse side, students are asked to *articulate in English* what they had comprehended as the text's topic, presumably based on the underlining done in completing the first task on the other side of the test.

The third task asks students to articulate information that *exemplified* the gist or main idea of a text. By having students demonstrate comprehension of a particular textual subset of information that supported the superordinate concept around which text messages were built, the test designers sought to identify whether these readers encountered difficulties in distinguishing this difference between major and minor premises in readings. The presumption was that such ability would be an indicator of *analytical* thinking that represented a distinct level of cognitive processing beyond recognition or recapitulation of more general information students perceived about a text's main idea.

The fourth and final task with reference to the test's reading passage asks students to reflect briefly about its relationship to one of the three major areas emphasized in the department's program for its majors: German linguistics, literature, or culture. To do so, these readers would have to draw on prior knowledge, absorbed at least in part from their major coursework in German Studies, and relate it to the information in the selection. For example, in considering a news story about the European Union, a student might identify the text as relating to German culture because it speaks to the country's historical and present international relations. In other words, students must position the implications of textual content within the realm of their preexisting knowledge, using synthetic reasoning to compare this example to a larger context.

To come up with a quantitative summary of these qualitative tasks, Swaffar and Arens developed a rubric scale with four options for grading: if adequately addressed, 3 points; partially addressed, 2; incorrectly addressed, 1; no response, 0 (see Appendix D for illustrations). These categories were not intended to assess global performance in the way that letter grades are awarded, for multiple and often different types of effort. Rather, the assessment goal was to differentiate between degrees of success students experienced when they engaged in specific modes of language comprehension.

The assessment coordinator trained a faculty member as a second rater by selecting five of the tests at random and grading them separately but immediately, comparing scores and agreeing on ways to distinguish between the four rubric scoring levels. Often that process involved explaining that an answer could be wrong in reference to the text content but still receive a minimal credit. For example, in Bertolt Brecht's short rumination, "If Sharks Were People," references such as "it's about people fishing" reflect a partial but inadequate understanding of the text and deserves a score of 1, whereas "the text compares big fish that eat little fish to people" fully grasps the main idea and should be scored a 3 or at least a 2. It was stressed in this training session that not all of the four task scores would be graded in comparable ways. As long as the raters' interpreted the rubric in the same way, there would probably be no more than a 1-point discrepancy between the raters' scores when ratings of all four questions were added up. This experience exemplified for the participating faculty members a way of conducting qualitative grading reliably.

Departmental responses to initial test findings

After administering three annual sets of the reading tests using different text samples, we had feedback on the relative reliability of our instrument. Consultation with university statisticians led to the decision not to report more than arithmetic percentages in initial administrations of the test. When we focused only on percentage ratings and inter-rater reliability in independent grading, we found that performance indicators in our first year of testing were confirmed in the instrument's subsequent four years of administration. Consistently, tests displayed a 50 to 60% increase in scores between results obtained from an upper-division beginner class in the second week of the fall semester and a senior-level class in the 13th or 14th week in the following spring semester. When test passages were changed in Spring 2012, scores remained consistently between 50 and 60% higher overall for readings of students in the advanced classes. Although average scores on some passages improved or worsened, overall results at 2–3% levels suggested that neither passage content nor genre per se influenced these differences significantly. Also consistent was underperformance on the fourth task, yielding the weakest average scores in the both iterations of readings.

These results served a twofold purpose for changing departmental attitudes toward the assessment process: (a) the fact that the test results were positive led to acceptance of and increased faculty interest and participation in these efforts, and (b) the faculty members in the program, aware that we had to expand our assessment goals, were more willing to use class time to allow for assessment administration. When Per Urlaub, a faculty member with a background in questionnaire development, offered to create a questionnaire for assessing student perceptions of the Germanic Studies program for strengths and weaknesses, that offer was, in contrast to reactions two years previously, enthusiastically embraced by the course committee. The goal of such a questionnaire would be to help us identify whether specific learning practices or background influences such as study abroad were related to test performance or to general performance in our program.

Curriculum mapping to assess current features of our program

To look at further benefits stemming from the assessment effort, the authors had a series of consultations with the then Director of the Office of Institutional Accreditation and Effectiveness, Dr. Linda Dickens. We were seeking guidance about how to build a broader consensus among faculty members about which teaching practices promote desired assessment outcomes. She agreed that a useful next step would be to have faculty members map their curricular practices in courses at the three major stages in our upper-division program: beginning, intermediate, and senior seminar courses. That way, the faculty could communally assess what was actually consistent and inconsistent in our program, thus identifying baselines for discussion about performance in our program. Concomitantly, participants might wish to adopt other colleagues' particular teaching practices, thereby increasing coherence within the upper-division program.

In our capacities as assessment director (Swaffar) and graduate research assistant (Randall), the authors arranged a 2-hour workshop held at the end of the spring semester 2014 to identify what was frequently and what was rarely done in the spectrum of classes representing the department's program. Worksheets completed by the seven attending faculty members, working in groups of two and three, revealed, for example, that German was consistently reported as the exclusive language of instruction with only occasional translation of individual words. Percentages in ratios of teacher-talk to student-talk varied with the size and level of classes, ranging between 70% teacher-talk to the reverse, that is, a 30% consistent estimate of teacher-talk for smaller intermediate and senior courses, all of which reported using more extensive group projects and student presentations.

After identifying similar patterns in pedagogical practices, the authors examined several areas of striking difference. Only two of the seven faculty members had reported the use of mixed media and technology in assignments and in class, and only two reported in-class reading or introduction of assignments as consistent practices. Evaluation of assigned writing also appeared to lack specific directions about features the instructors valued. Consequently, we solicited additional viewpoints regarding teachers' assessment of written essays and, in order to align teacher and student expectations, we segued this discussion into the use of rubrics for essay grading in the context of introducing assignments.

Introducing rubrics to assess writing outcomes

Professor Corinne Crane reported using rubrics in her work with the lower-division classes taught mainly by graduate students under her and Professor Urlaub's supervision as undergraduate coordinators. Professor Kit Belgum, an award-winning teacher of upper-division courses, volunteered that she used rubrics when grading essays. Thus encouraged, the workshop attendees agreed to a subsequent session in the fall to explore ways to specify desired outcomes in grading as a practical tool for evaluating written work and possibly applicable to inter-rater evaluation, as well. Swaffar volunteered distributing rubrics from ACTFL and Belgum agreed to illustrate her application of rubrics in introducing writing assignments and evaluating student performance. Implicitly, she would be making the case for encouraging the wider use of rubrics in the upper-division program and suggesting specific performance standards to be assessed. After the next workshop in fall of 2014, several teachers adopted rubrics in their essay grading, thereby preparing a broader base for pinpointing with some precision the type and desired writing performance outcomes in language use, critical thinking, and content references in assigned reading or media viewing.

Resequencing department assessment procedures to serve departments

The sequence of actions taken described here represents a modification of our University's assessment charge by taking actions (the reading test) to identify outcomes (performance on four different tasks), before having faculty members identify program outcomes to assess. That reversal served several purposes. First, test results overall demonstrated to faculty members that our instructionally shared program produced consistent improvement on one type of proficiency—reading. Second, the results also identified a particular weakness to be addressed, in this case the ability of students to link one particular reading to their broader spectrum of available information in one of our program's three emphases: linguistics, literature, or the cultural history of German-speaking countries. For future assessment purposes, that finding suggested a need to introduce classroom practices or assignments (actions) to address this issue. If systematically conducted, it allows assessment of the student performance that can be attributed to different classroom interventions (actions taken).

A portfolio assignment asking students to find two different points of view about immigration problems in German at the beginning and end of the semester, for example, could yield new data points for assessment: appropriateness of students' selections, accuracy in describing their content, and critical comparison of their viewpoints. This pedagogical assessment [method] would look for levels of improvement to validate the pedagogical "actions" the professor used to improve learning in conjunction with this assignment.

After several instructors teaching beginning, intermediate, and advanced courses have undertaken such assessments with their classes, these efforts can be examined to establish types of performance difference at beginning, intermediate, and senior levels. In this way, the outcomes identified could provide feedback to instructors about where to focus their students' attention and learning effort at various junctures in their German language development. Whether using rubrics for independent assessment or working together to establish shared standards during an joint evaluation session, such agreement would provide a point of reference and a tangible basis for deciding about desired outcomes for our program.

Conclusion

Those of us working most directly with the assessment process will be among the first to acknowledge that a great deal of work remains in tailoring practices for assessing specified learning outcomes. A number of conditions do, however, augur for success. First, the project has the strong support of senior members of the department. Under our chair, Peter Hess, exploring more assessment options is emerging as a departmental activity addressed in regular faculty meetings and an upcoming departmental retreat. We also plan to continue holding workshops to become informed about, and to communicate about, how newly initiated assessment actions and instructional methods are being implemented in individual classes. A second indicator is that departmental awareness of and commitment to assessment is expanding at a steady pace. Six regular faculty members and three graduate students have already generated and analyzed data for participation in preparing the annual TracDat® report. Plans for assessment expansion will eventually involve all the teachers in our program in stages projected in a three- to four-year timeline. Third, and by no means least of all, our institution has responded to the articulatory gap between administration and humanities faculty members concerning ways academic departments and programs can take charge of and present our assessment practices and results.

Instead of the relative isolation often reported by an individual staff person or a single faculty member designated to conduct assessments, the authors find that a constellation of procedures to involve the department as a whole has fostered the idea of assessment as a worthwhile community enterprise. Focusing on ways to involve the entire faculty and staff has prompted conversations about how wider use of assessment practices in-house can benefit students and encouraged faculty members to reexamine together the relationship between student performance and curriculum.

Acknowledgments

The authors have worked together for over a year on the assessment project described here. For this chapter, Janet Swaffar wrote a rough draft summarizing that experience to which Amanda Randall made extensive elaborations, doubling the size of the original and gathering the vital documentation for in-house and research substantiations. In addition, both authors wish to acknowledge Katherine Arens' and Linda Dickens' insights and editorial suggestions.

References

Abbott, M., Cothrun, K., Kosta, B., Höyng, P., & Swender, E. (2015). Restructuring foreign language departments brings national recognition. Presented at the Modern Language Association, Vancouver, CA. Retrieved from http://www.mla.org/program_details?prog_id=405&year=2015

Adair-Hauck, B., Glisan, E. W., & Troyan, F. J. (2013). *Implementing integrated performance assessment*. Alexandria, VA: American Council on the Teaching of Foreign Languages.

Allen, H. W. (2014). Foreign language teaching assistant professional development: Challenges and strategies in meeting the 2007 MLA report's calls for change. In J. K. Swaffar & P. Urlaub (Eds.), *Transforming postsecondary foreign language teaching in the United States* (pp. 177–193). Dordrecht, Netherlands: Springer.

American Association of Teachers of German. (2015). AATG Centers of Excellence. Retrieved from http://www.aatg.org/?page=CoE

American Council on the Teaching of Foreign Languages. (1998). *ACTFL performance guidelines for K–12 learners*. Yonkers, NY: American Council on the Teaching of Foreign Languages.

American Council on the Teaching of Foreign Languages. (2003). *ACTFL integrated performance assessment*. Yonkers, NY: American Council on the Teaching of Foreign Languages.

Anderson, L. W., & Krathwohl, D. R. (2001). *A taxonomy for learning, teaching, and assessing: A revision of Bloom's taxonomy of educational objectives.* New York, NY: Longman.

Angelo, T. A. (1999). Doing assessment as if learning matters most. *AAHE Bulletin, May.* Retrieved from http://www.aahea.org/aahea/articles/angelomay99.htm

Archibald, R. B., & Feldman, D. H. (2009, August 10). College administrations are too bloated? Compared with what? *The Chronicle of Higher Education.* Retrieved from http://chronicle.com.ezproxy.lib.utexas.edu/article/Colleges-Are-Too-Bloated-/47958/

Arens, K. (2012). After the MLA report: Rethinking the links between literature and literacy, research, and teaching in foreign language departments. In G. S. Levine & A. M. Phipps (Eds.), *Critical and intercultural theory and language pedagogy* (pp. 216–228). Boston, MA: Heinle Cengage Learning.

Arens, K. (2014). Discipline, institution, and assessment: The graduate curriculum, credibility, and accountability. In J. K. Swaffar & P. Urlaub (Eds.), *Transforming postsecondary foreign language teaching in the United States* (pp. 194–225). Dordrecht, Netherlands: Springer.

Bernhardt, E. B. (1983). Testing foreign language reading comprehension: The immediate recall protocol. *Die Unterrichtspraxis / Teaching German, 16*(1), 27–33.

Bloom, B. S. (1956). *Taxonomy of educational objectives: The classification of educational goals Handbook I.* New York, NY: McKay.

Bloxham, S., & Boyd, P. (2007). *Developing effective assessment in higher education: A practical guide.* New York, NY: Open University Press. Retrieved from http://public.eblib.com/choice/publicfullrecord.aspx?p=332673

Bourns, S. K., & Melin, C. (2014). The foreign language methodology seminar: Benchmarks, perceptions, and initiatives. *ADFL Bulletin, 43*(1), 91–100.

Brennan, J., & Shah, T. (2000). *Managing quality in higher education: An international perspective on institutional assessment and change.* Philadelphia, PA: Organisation for Economic Co-operation and Development, Society for Research into Higher Education & Open University Press.

Brooks, F. B., & Darhower, M. A. (2014). It takes a department! A study of the culture of proficiency in three successful foreign language teacher education programs. *Foreign Language Annals, 47*(4), 592–613.

Courts, P. L., & McInerney, K. H. (1993). *Assessment in higher education: Politics, pedagogy, and portfolios.* Westport, CT: Praeger.

Dew, J. R., & Nearing, M. M. (2004). *Continuous quality improvement in higher education.* Westport, CT: Praeger.

Donato, R. (2009). Teacher education in the age of standards of professional practice. *The Modern Language Journal, 93*(2), 267–270.

Gates, S. M. (2002). *Ensuring quality and productivity in higher education: An analysis of assessment practices.* San Francisco, CA: Jossey-Bass.

Georgetown University, Department of German. (2011, July). Assessment. Retrieved from http://german.georgetown.edu/page/1242716536825.html

Glisan, E. W., Swender, E., & Surface, E. A. (2013). Oral proficiency standards and foreign language teacher candidates: Current findings and future research directions. *Foreign Language Annals, 46*(2), 264–289.

Gordon, L. (1998, September/October). Tenure on trial. *Stanford Today Online.* Retrieved from http://news.stanford.edu/stanfordtoday/ed/9809/9809fea201.shtml

Graff, G. (2008). Assessment changes everything. *MLA Newsletter, Spring.* Retrieved from http://www.mla.org/blog&topic=121

Grau-Sempere, A., Mohn, M. C., & Pieroni, R. (2009). Improving educational effectiveness and promoting internal and external information-sharing through student learning outcomes assessment. In J. M. Norris, J. McE. Davis, C. Sinicrope, & Y. Watanabe (Eds.), *Toward useful program evaluation in college foreign language education* (pp. 139–162). Honolulu: University of Hawai'i, National Foreign Language Resource Center.

Kern, R. (1994). The role of mental translation in second language reading. *Studies in Second Language Acquisition, 16*(4), 441–461.

Lee, J. F. (1985). The effect of research design on free written recall as a measure of reading comprehension in a second language. *TESOL Quarterly, 19*(4), 792–793.

Lee, J. F. (1986). Background knowledge & L2 reading. *The Modern Language Journal, 70*(4), 350–354.

Lewin, T. (2014, October 13). Web-era trade schools, feeding a need for code. *The New York Times.* Retrieved from http://www.nytimes.com/2014/10/14/us/web-era-trade-schools-feeding-a-need-for-code.html

Liskin-Gasparro, J. E. (1995). Practical approaches to outcomes assessment: The undergraduate major in foreign languages and literatures. *ADFL Bulletin, 26*(2), 21–27.

Magnan, S. S., Murphy, D., & Sahakyan, N. (2014). Considering the standards for foreign language learning in postsecondary instruction. *The Modern Language Journal, 98*(S1), 12–39.

Middaugh, M. F. (2010). *Planning and assessment in higher education: Demonstrating institutional effectiveness.* San Francisco, CA: Jossey-Bass.

Mignon, C., & Langsam, D. (1999). Peer review and post-tenure review. *Innovative Higher Education, 24*(1), 49–59.

Miller, M. A. (1999). State-level post-tenure review policies. *Innovative Higher Education, 24*(1), 17–24.

Modern Language Association of America, & Task Force on Evaluating Scholarship for Tenure and Promotion. (2007). *Report of the MLA Task Force on Evaluating Scholarship for Tenure and Promotion.* New York, NY: Modern Language Association. Retrieved from http://www.mla.org/tenure_promotion

National Standards in Foreign Language Education Project (US). (2006). *Standards for foreign language learning in the 21st century: Including Arabic, Chinese, classical languages, French, German, Italian, Japanese, Portuguese, Russian, and Spanish* (3rd ed.). Lawrence, KS: National Standards in Foreign Language Education Project.

Norris, J. M. (2006). The why (and how) of assessing student learning outcomes in college foreign language programs. *The Modern Language Journal, 90*(4), 576–583.

Norris, J. M., Davis, J. McE., Sinicrope, C., & Watanabe, Y. (Eds.). (2009). *Toward useful program evaluation in college foreign language education.* Honolulu: University of Hawai'i National Foreign Language Resource Center.

Palomba, C. A., & Banta, T. W. (1999). *Assessment essentials: Planning, implementing, and improving assessment in higher education.* San Francisco, CA: Jossey-Bass.

Pfeiffer, P. C. (2008). The commentaries: The discipline of foreign language studies and reforming foreign language education. *The Modern Language Journal, 92*(2), 296–298.

Rogers, J. (2012, November 1). 3 to 1: That's the best ratio of tenure-track faculty to administrators, a study concludes. *The Chronicle of Higher Education.* Retrieved from http://chronicle.com.ezproxy.lib.utexas.edu/article/Administrative-Bloat-How-Much/135500/

Ruben, B. D., & National Association of College and University Business Officers. (2007). *Excellence in higher education guide: An integrated approach to assessment, planning, and improvement in colleges and universities.* Washington, DC: NACUBO.

Scott, V. M. (2010). *Double talk: Deconstructing monolingualism in classroom second language learning.* Boston, MA: Prentice Hall.

Scott, V. M., & de la Fuente, M. J. (2008). What's the problem? L2 learners' use of the L1 during consciousness-raising, form-focused tasks. *Modern Language Journal, 92*(1), 100–113.

Secolsky, C., & Denison, D. B. (2012). *Handbook on measurement, assessment, and evaluation in higher education.* New York, NY: Routledge.

Sherr, L. A., & Teeter, D. J. (1991). *Total quality management in higher education.* San Francisco, CA: Jossey-Bass.

Stanford University. (n.d.). Stanford Language Center [web page]. Retrieved from http://stanford.edu/dept/lc/language/index.html

Swaffar, J. K. (2014). From language to literacy: The evolving concepts of foreign language teaching at American colleges and universities since 1945. In J. K. Swaffar & P. Urlaub (Eds.), *Transforming postsecondary foreign language teaching in the United States* (pp. 19–54). Dordrecht, Netherlands: Springer.

Swaffar, J. K., & Arens, K. (2005). *Remapping the foreign language curriculum: An approach through multiple literacies.* New York, NY: Modern Language Association of America.

Thornton, S. (2010). No refuge: The annual report on the economic status of the profession, 2009–2010. *Academe, 96*(2), 3–80.

Tierney, W. G. (1997). Academic community and post-tenure review. *Academe, 83*(3), 23–25.

United States Congress, Senate, & Committee on Health, Education, Labor, and Pensions. (2012). *For profit higher education the failure to safeguard the federal investment and ensure student success.* Washington, DC: U.S. Government

Publishing Office. Retrieved from http://help.senate.gov/imo/media/for_profit_report/PartI-PartIII-SelectedAppendixes.pdf

United States Department of Education. (2014, December 1). Accreditation in the United States. Retrieved from http://www2.ed.gov/admins/finaid/accred/index.html

University of Hawai'i at Mānoa. (2011, January 24). FL Program Evaluation Project [webpage]. Retrieved from http://nflrc.hawaii.edu/evaluation/

The University of Texas at Austin. (n.d.). Campus profile. Retrieved from http://www.utexas.edu/about-ut/campus-profile

The University of Texas at Austin, & Office of Information Management and Analysis. (n.d.). *2012–2013 Statistical handbook quick reference guide.* Austin, TX. Retrieved from http://www.utexas.edu/sites/default/files/files/IMA_Pub_QuickReference_2012_Fall.pdf

The University of Texas at Austin, & Office of Institutional Accreditation and Effectiveness. (2014a, October 6). Assessment resources. Retrieved from http://www.utexas.edu/provost/iae/resources/

The University of Texas at Austin, & Office of Institutional Accreditation and Effectiveness. (2014b, October 6). Institutional accreditation and effectiveness. Retrieved from http://www.utexas.edu/provost/iae/

The University of Texas at Austin, & Office of Institutional Accreditation and Effectiveness. (2014c, October 20). Tracking assessment activity with TracDat. Retrieved from http://www.utexas.edu/provost/iae/tracdat.html

The University of Texas at Austin, & Office of the Executive Vice President and Provost. (2014, October 6). Institutional effectiveness. Retrieved from http://www.utexas.edu/provost/sacs/effectiveness.html

Vroeijenstijn, A. I. (1995). *Improvement and accountability: Navigating between Scylla and Charybdis: Guide for external quality assessment in higher education.* Bristol, PA: J. Kingsley.

Appendix A. Parameters for faculty text selection
Janet Swaffar & Corinne Crane

CRITERIA FOR TEXT SELECTION
(2 samples per submitter pairs)

GENERAL CRITERIA

Targeted Instructional Level:

Look for texts that you believe students at the <u>endpoint</u> of your advanced-level German course (e.g., GER 331L) **should be able to comprehend**, with limited scaffolded support from you, as the instructor.

> For your reference, the 4 tasks we are asking students to complete in the reading test (all in English) for each text are the following:
>
> 1. Underlining key words and phrases in the text
> 2. Identifying the primary topic of the text
> 3. Finding text examples that support/illustrate the main topic/subject
> 4. Linking the text's contents to students' knowledge of German culture, literature, and/or language

SPECIFIC CRITERIA

Texts should:

- be approximately **150-250 words** in length.
- represent **genres used in class or assigned readings** (e.g., narratives, newspaper excerpts, commentaries, letters, etc.). EXCEPTION: Avoid encyclopedic or textbook excerpts, since such texts often lack a clear authorial voice or point of view.
- contain **subject matter** that reflects **topics assigned and discussed in your course**
- represent **vocabulary** often used in your course
- represent **syntactic complexity** of **texts read in your course**. NB: Consider the type of language that students at the end of the course can read on their own. Texts should therefore: contain limited extended adjectival constructions; have sentences longer than three lines; avoid experimental language or stream-of-consciousness style.
- contain **discourse patterns to support textual coherence and cohesion** appropriate for the genre (e.g., historical excerpts used to identify events and their outcomes, diary entries or letters combine reflections with sufficient context for reader reference, scholarly or reporter excerpt specifies topic and mode of analysis). Texts **may contain explicit discourse connectors** (i.e., adverbial phrases, prepositions, conjunctions) to contribute to textual coherence (e.g., temporal/causal markers in historical excerpts).

Appendix B. Instructions for assessment administrators
Janet Swaffar & Corinne Crane

The University of Texas at Austin is asking all departments to assess progress students make as majors or minors in their program. To see whether or not we are succeeding in achieving our program's objectives, we are asking you to read three short passages without the aid of dictionaries or computers. Our goal is to compare the performance of relative beginners in our program with those about to graduate. *Your answers will be anonymous and not seen by your instructor or affect your course grade.*

You will have three minutes to read each text. As you read each individual passage, please underline 3-4 nouns ("who" or "what" words) and related phrases that suggest the main idea and its recurrence or development in the passage [TASK 1].

When the allotted three minutes are up turn the page over. You will then have two minutes to respond to the directions on the reverse side. You are asked to WRITE ONLY IN ENGLISH to a) state the subject or topic of the text [TASK 2], b) describe an example that *illustrates* the text's topic [TASK 3], and c) comment on ONLY ONE of the following topics: 1) German history and culture, OR 2) literature, OR 3) language – *bullets and phrases suffice*. When you are told the time is up, please go immediately on to the next page and begin reading (and underlining key segments of) the new passage.

Appendix C. Reading test sample
Janet Swaffar

Reading 3

YOU WILL HAVE THREE MINUTES TO READ EACH TEXT.
Task 1: *as you read*, underline 3-4 key words and phrases that you think reflect the passage's topic (its main subject and idea).

When the three minutes are up, you will be asked to turn the text page over and respond to the following tasks 2, 3 and 4 in English. You have 2 minutes (bullets and phrases are fine) to complete the 3 tasks.

Das kunstseidene Mädchen, Irmgard Keun, List Taschenbuch, Berlin, 2005 [1932]. S. 27.

Ich habe meiner Mutter alles erzählt, aber nur gesagt von 60 Mark und davon 20 für mich behalten und also im ganzen 80, denn man muss Geld schätzen, und wer arbeitet, lernt das. Und ich muss meine Mutter anerkennen als feines Weib, sie hat immer noch so was Gewisses von früher her, wenn sie auch heute Garderobiere im Schauspielhaus ist. Und sie ist wohl ein bisschen dick, aber nicht schlimm und hat die Hüte so etwas altmodisch oben auf dem Kopf – so wie's Tüpfchen auf dem i – aber momentan ist das ja wieder modern. Jedenfalls hat sie eine Haltung in den Schultern wie eine wirklich teure Dame, und das kommt, weil sie früher ein Leben gehabt hat. Leider hat sie meinen Vater geheiratet, was ich für einen Fehler halte, denn er ist ein vollkommen ungebildeter Mensch und faul wie eine jahrelange Leiche und brüllt nur manchmal von wegen männliches Organ zeigen – man kennt das. Nur außer dem Haus gibt er sich ein Benehmen mit elegantem Armgeschenke und Augenbrauengezieh und Schweißwischen – besonders bei jeder Frau, die über zwei Zentner wiegt und nicht mit ihm verheiratet ist.

Also ich halte nichts von dem Mann und hab nur mächtig Angst, weil meine Nerven es nicht vertragen, wenn er donnert – und wenn er mir von Moral spricht, kann ich nichts Richtiges gegen ihn unternehmen, weil er mein Vater ist.

Task 2: IN ENGLISH: What do you think is the text's topic or main idea?

Task 3: IN ENGLISH: Describe an example that illustrates a specific development of the text's topics.

Task 4: IN ENGLISH: How you see this text relating to what you know about ONLY ONE of the following topics:

    a) German history and culture

    OR

    b) German literature

    OR

    c) German language

Appendix D. Assessment scoring rubric
Janet Swaffar & Katherine Arens

SCORING RUBRICS: Each task assigned to the student will be assessed according to one or more rubrics, each of which has its own scoring scale, running from 3 (high) to 0 (not completed at all; completely erroneous). Use the rubrics below to fill out the score sheet for each student.

TASK 1: Underlining words and phrases that pertain to the main idea of the text and the question posed about it.

3 points: very specific OR explicit identification of the text's propositions through a strategic choice of words/ passages underlined	2 points: words/phrases underlined show partial comprehension of the text's main propositions	1 point: words/phrases underlined point only to general comprehension of some aspects of the text, not its overall main idea	0 points: nothing underlined; single words only underlined that do not cohere as an answer

TASK 2: English-language recapitulation of the text subject

3 points: reflects key ideas with relative accuracy—literal or implied	2 points: reflects key language about the topic, but only with partial accuracy; some misreadings or omissions	1 point: words/phrases from the texts are used, but their combination does not reflect how the text's handling of the topic; serious misreadings	0 points: no answer; complete misreading of text with few if any words or references from the text used as correct representations of text topics or redundant vis-à-vis other tasks noted

TASK 3: Exemplification of text message/author's point of view

3 points: explicitly and correctly links up example to the text's topic, goes beyond a redundant statement or draws inference	2 points: implicit or partially correct link of example to the text's topic	1 point: Relation to topic implied but example incomplete, missing, or non-illustrative of text's main topic	0 points: no answer; complete misreading of text; example with no relation to text or redundant vis-à-vis other tasks

TASK 4: Fit of text with prior knowledge: student answers evaluated according to one of the following three sets of rubrics:

A: Rubrics for Background Knowledge of German History and Culture

3 points: explicitly links text to a historical event or historically specific cultural phenomenon;	2 points: implicit link of text to a historical event, with few or inaccurate details; weak, general link to culture, often with historical errors/ stereotypes	1 point: misidentification of cultural-historical site, but some attempt to make link	0 points: no answer; complete misreading of text or ignoring specificity; redundant vis-à-vis other tasks

B: Rubrics for Background Knowledge in German Literature

3 points: explicitly assigns text to a genre, literary period, or text type (story, historical account, newspaper article); explicitly compares text with an equivalent	2 points: implicit identification of text type by analogy or example	1 point: misidentification of category to which text belongs, but some attempt to categorize	0 points: no answer; complete misreading of text or ignoring of need to assign text to a larger category

C: Rubrics for Background Knowledge in German Language

3 points: explicitly comments on some aspect of the text's language, with appropriate technical description or comparison	2 points: implicit or general commentary on the text's language; lacking technical precision or explicit/correct comparison	1 point: misidentification of language issue in text, but some legitimate (but unsuccessful) attempt to comment	0 points: no answer; complete misreading of text or ignoring of need to assign text to a larger category

Formulating Effective Student Learning Outcomes Through Utilization-Focused Evaluation: A Case Study of a University Japanese Program

Shoko Sasayama
Georgetown University

This chapter reports on a program evaluation conducted in a Japanese program at a U.S. university, with the ultimate goal of formulating effective student learning outcomes that are compatible with program goals, students' needs, and instructors' expectations. The evaluation was conducted over two years and consisted of three phases. In Phase I, student and instructor needs, program implementation, and possible ways to improve the program were explored, and suggestions for improvement were made to this end. Phase II, then, focused on monitoring whether and how these evaluation findings were put into use and what impact, if any, program changes had on student learning and program effectiveness. Upon confirmation of successful implementation of changes and their effectiveness, in Phase III, further innovations were implemented, including, in particular, the development of a clearly articulated set of student learning outcomes that consolidated what was learned in the evaluation findings thus far. The program evaluation not only achieved the ultimate goal of formulation of outcomes statements (known as findings use), but also improved communication among instructors (known as process use). It is my hope that the Japanese program will continue to thrive and contribute to students' learning of the Japanese language, based on this program evaluation.

Introduction

Outcomes assessment has come into recent prominence fundamentally as a result of a reform effort initiated by higher education accreditation bodies in the United States. Within the outcomes assessment "movement," institutions are required to demonstrate whether students have learned what they are supposed to learn, in other words, whether they have achieved expected learning outcomes, and to use that assessment information to understand, maintain, and where necessary improve program effectiveness (The Higher Learning Commission, 2003). The idea of outcomes assessment as a broadly formative endeavor, however, has gone missing in much of the recent rhetoric about assessment, especially within the humanities. Instead, outcomes assessment has come to be quite narrowly associated with quantifiable indicators, typified by quizzes, exams, and tests, that help institutions "prove" their educational effectiveness. This interpretation of outcomes assessment has, in turn, prevented institutions, academic programs, and college educators from reflecting on program implementation and effectiveness and/or considering ways to further improve their educational efforts; instead, it has often resulted in the fruitless expenditure of time, resources, and efforts, as well as potentially negative washback on what is to be taught in the classroom (Norris, 2006).

What we really need, it seems, is a reorientation in how we think about outcomes assessment. Accordingly, in this chapter I adopt a program evaluation approach to assessment, which helps us clarify from the outset the intended uses of assessment (e.g., How will the assessment results be used by whom to do what?) and facilitates collection of necessary and meaningful feedback, largely for the purposes of program improvement (Davis, Sinicrope, & Watanabe, 2009; Norris, 2006). Outcomes assessment in this view should ultimately inform what is working within a program as well as how the program can be further improved, which really is the heart of what program evaluation is all about.

Stepping back a little, then, this chapter addresses the fundamental question of "How should student learning outcomes (SLOs) be formulated to begin with?" Norris (2006) argued that SLOs are integral to any (language) program because they give us an opportunity "to state who we are, why we exist, what our value is to learners, institutions, and society" (p. 577). Building upon this idea, Watanabe, Davis, and Norris (2012) then suggested that learning expectations and values of a program should be made clear first, in order to establish a foundation for formulating effective and locally meaningful SLOs. In the current evaluation, in order to achieve these initial goals, I followed Patton's (2008) approach of utilization-focused evaluation in pursuit of a basis for understanding and reforming educational practices within a Japanese program housed in a U.S. university. In collaboration with colleagues in that program, I embarked on a journey first to explore learning expectations and values of the program from various stakeholders' perspectives, with the ultimate goal of formulating effective SLOs that helped to capture the intended contribution of the program and served to guide its instructors and learners in their efforts.

Program context and evaluation impetus

From Spring 2013 to Fall 2014, a Japanese program housed in a U.S. university engaged in a program evaluation endeavor, facilitated by the author, with the purposes of (a) increasing understanding of the goals for and contributions of certain classes in the undergraduate curriculum and (b) making suggestions for their further improvement. The class sessions in focus here are supplementary to the primary courses that make up the Japanese undergraduate curriculum, and they are required for students enrolled in the first and second levels of Japanese (i.e., roughly the first two years of instruction) at the university. Outside of main Japanese classes (which meet 5 hours a week), the supplementary program classes meet once a week for 50 minutes. The supplementary classes are taught by Japanese-L1 graduate students in close consultation with the faculty members who teach the main classes. These supplementary program instructors are frequently master's degree students who are enrolled in a variety of 2-year programs at the university, which in turn creates a constant need for identifying and developing new instructors. Generally speaking, since the program's inception, it has been the case that the classes were used as review sessions to cover materials from the main Japanese classes (e.g., grammar, vocabulary, kanji). For this reason, what has been addressed in these classes has been determined largely by the main class instructors, rather than the supplementary program instructors themselves.

At the time of the evaluation, I was one of the supplementary program instructors, and I had been teaching the first level supplementary classes for one semester. My own experience as a program instructor to that point, and informal communications with other instructors, had highlighted a few issues in the supplementary program that needed evaluation attention, including unclear purposes of the program, a seeming mismatch between students' expectations of the sessions and what we actually did within them, a lack of preparation for new instructors, and a lack of any evaluation of the sessions to date. To seek solutions to these issues, we decided to initiate a systematic evaluation of the supplementary program, following Patton's (2008) utilization-focused evaluation approach. The impetus for the evaluation, then, was internal, and the conduct and use of the evaluation was also internal to the program. Ultimately, however, the evaluation had implications for how the program was conceived, portrayed, and perceived, hence certain external dimensions of the program were also considered by the end of the evaluation cycle, including in particular the development of student learning outcomes.

Primary intended users and intended uses

Intended users and uses play a crucial role in utilization-focused evaluations (Patton, 2008); they are the key components that guide the entire evaluation process and enable decisions and actions on the basis of evaluation findings. Accordingly, as a first step of this evaluation, intended users were identified through a meeting with the coordinator of the Japanese undergraduate program, and intended uses were determined through subsequent meetings with identified intended users.

In the meeting with the coordinator, the following three groups of stakeholders were identified as likely intended users of the evaluation: the coordinator herself, the two main instructors who directly supervise the supplementary instructors and plan most of the activities in the supplementary program classes, and the three supplementary program instructors who are responsible for the actual teaching of the sessions. To maximize the possibility of making the use of evaluation findings happen, the evaluation was conducted collaboratively by involving these primary intended users from the early stages of evaluation. Additionally, the involvement of the primary intended users in the evaluation process aimed to give them ownership over the evaluation rather than implying that it was something they were obligated to participate in (Patton, 2008).

Accordingly, the evaluator conducted informal meetings with each primary intended user group in February 2013 to identify issues that required evaluation attention and discuss intended uses of the evaluation. These meetings revealed that (a) there were no pre-determined lesson plans for the program, and the content of the sessions was decided on a weekly basis; (b) there was no orientation for new (or experienced) instructors; (c) there had been no formal evaluation of the supplementary program; and lastly, (d) there were no expected student learning outcomes (SLOs) specifically articulated to the supplementary program. Additionally, in these meetings, the primary intended users expressed their interests in finding out about (a) learners' as well as instructors' needs and expectations of the program, (b) effectiveness of program implementation (i.e., actual delivery of the supplementary classes), and (c) purposes of the program and goals for each year (i.e., the first two years of the supplementary program). Based on these needs, the intended uses of the evaluation were articulated as follows: (a) to understand the reality of the program (e.g., instructors' and students' needs, program implementation), (b) to consider potential program changes on the basis of evaluation findings, and (c) to use the results as a resource to develop program goals and learning outcomes as well as a program instructor orientation and/or instructor manual.

Getting to outcomes: Evaluation process

The present program evaluation consisted of three phases: (a) needs identification (Phase I), (b) implementation of evaluation findings and resulting curriculum change (Phase II), and (c) further innovations and on-going monitoring of evaluation use (Phase III). In what follows, I will outline evaluation activities in each phase of evaluation.

Phase I

The first phase of this evaluation took place in Spring 2013. During this phase, learner and instructor needs, program implementation, and possible ways to improve the program were explored through various data collection methods to reflect the voices of multiple stakeholders (see Milleret & Silveira, 2009, for a similar endeavor of needs analysis for curriculum development and growth in a Portuguese Program).

Evaluation questions and methods

During the initial meetings, the primary intended users were asked by the evaluator what they would like to find out about the supplementary program classes for their further improvement. In the first phase, evaluation questions were formulated based on their responses to the following:

- What are the needs of the instructors regarding the supplementary program?
- What are the needs of the students in general and what do they expect from the supplementary program?

- What are the purposes of the supplementary program?
- How are the supplementary classes actually implemented?

To answer these evaluation questions, multiple data collection methods were utilized for data triangulation purposes, including an online survey with students, interviews with the primary intended users, and class observations. In the initial meetings with the primary intended user groups, information was elicited not only regarding issues that required evaluation attention but also information regarding various aspects of the program, including their ideas about the purposes of the supplementary program, questions to be included in the student survey, and how the supplementary classes were designed, prepared for, and conducted. These pieces of information provided valuable data to answer the evaluation questions, as well as informing the subsequent collection of additional data sources.

Student survey

At the outset, survey questions were formulated based on the initial meetings with the primary intended users. Feedback on these questions was received from two primary intended user groups (i.e., the coordinator and the main program instructors), and the survey was revised accordingly. Then, the survey was piloted with two supplementary program instructors and was revised based on their responses and feedback. In April 2013, the student survey was administered online through Qualtrics (www.qualtrics.com) to the students enrolled in the first and second levels of Japanese at that time. The survey questions were all open-ended and consisted of two major categories: (a) general questions about the students' Japanese learning and (b) specific questions about the supplementary classes. Within the first category, the questions asked about the students' general goals in and their motivation for learning Japanese. Questions about the supplementary classes ranged from (a) students' expectations and (b) perceptions of beneficial classroom activities to (c) recommendations for change. In analyzing students' open-ended responses, the evaluator categorized patterns by identifying recurring themes within each survey question.

Class observations

In April 2013 (towards the end of the spring semester), one Level 1 and Level 2 supplementary class were observed. During the observation, notes were taken to record activities about the conduct of the sessions and, in particular, the distribution of activities over the available class time. My own experience as a supplementary program instructor of Level 1 was also included as part of the observation data in an effort to account for how the supplementary classes were being delivered.

Interviews with intended users

In addition to the initial meetings conducted with each primary intended user group, where major information needed to answer most of the evaluation questions was elicited incidentally, the main instructor group and the supplementary program instructor group also participated in individual interviews via email. Email messages with the following intentionally broad, open-ended questions were sent out to each interview participant individually in May 2013. Both groups were asked what they thought the purpose(s) of the supplementary program should be from their perspectives. Note that all interviews were conducted in Japanese, the L1 of all of the instructors.

Timeline

Overall, Phase 1 of the program evaluation started with the initial meeting with the coordinator of the Program, followed by meetings with the main instructors and the supplementary program instructors. Based on the information gathered in these meetings, the over-arching evaluation questions were formulated, which then were sent back to the coordinator for further feedback. Subsequently, to answer the questions, data were collected through the student survey, classroom observations, and e-interviews with the instructors. The first phase was concluded in May 2014, with a reporting of the evaluation findings and suggestions for improvement.

Findings

In this section, I will report detailed findings from Phase I of the evaluation in the order of the four evaluation questions above. Findings are based on patterns in the data combined from the different sources and methods outlined above.

Needs of the instructors

Through the initial meeting with the supplementary program instructors, it became clear that they were concerned about the purposes and/or goals of the program and yet were unsure what they might be. Both supplementary program instructors expressed their concerns as follows:

> "Knowing the purposes would make it easier for us to prepare for the sessions... We'd know what's expected of us."[1]

> "If I knew the purposes of the program, I would feel more at ease. I wasn't sure what to do at first."

To this end, they suggested that a new instructor orientation or an instructor's manual that discusses purposes/ goals of the supplementary program and other information (e.g., what is expected of the supplementary program instructors; who the students are, including their needs and motivation for learning Japanese; whether they are simply supposed to follow the main class instructors' suggestions or whether it is okay to incorporate their own teaching ideas and materials) would be beneficial, especially upon beginning as teachers in the program.

Additionally, they expressed their interests in administering an end-of-term evaluation for the supplementary program. Traditionally, it has been left up to the supplementary program instructors whether or how to administer an evaluation at the end of the semester, and often times they were not informed about such an opportunity. The instructors felt that an end-of-term evaluation would be a great resource to reflect on their teaching and improve their classes. Lastly, the supplementary program instructor who was in charge of the Level 2 sessions expressed his concern about how best to use the assigned video materials, *Erin ga chosen: Nihongo dekimasu* (Japan Foundation, 2010) in the sessions. He had simply been told to use them in class and received no further instructions.

Goals and needs of the students

In order to investigate the students' overall goals in learning Japanese and their expectations of the supplementary program, the Level 1 and 2 students were invited to participate in an online survey. The response rates were 85% (17 students) for

---

[1] All instructor responses were originally given in Japanese. All translations are by the author.

Level 1 and 82.60% (19 students) for Level 2. Below, students' responses to each survey question on learning goals and needs are summarized, focusing specifically on the most frequent answers for each program level.

Goals of Japanese learning in general

In response to the open-ended question, "What would you like to achieve in your Japanese course?" the students mentioned a variety of individual goals, but a clear majority of the students at both Level 1 and Level 2 wished to improve their oral communication skills in the Japanese courses in general (see Figures 1 and 2). Some students (at both levels) also expressed their desire to develop their general Japanese proficiency and their interests in learning Japanese culture in their Japanese classes. In addition, a handful of Level 2 students exhibited their desire to improve not only their oral communication skills, but also their reading and writing skills and to engage in the further learning of grammar, vocabulary, and kanji.

Secondly, responses to the next open-ended question, "In what ways does knowledge of Japanese help you achieve your academic/ professional/ personal goals?" varied to a great extent among the Level 1 students, whereas the responses of the Level 2 students were more consistent. Three relatively popular responses of the Level 1 students were that the knowledge of Japanese would help them (a) achieve their Japan-related professional goals; (b) live in, study in, or travel to/within Japan; and (c) fulfill their personal desires of learning the Japanese language and culture. More consistently, over half of the Level 2 respondents expressed that their knowledge of Japanese would help them achieve their Japan-related professional goals (e.g., translating, banking, professor, international business). A handful of Level 2 students also mentioned achieving academic goals and fulfilling their personal interests as their primary motivation for learning Japanese (see Figures 3 and 4).

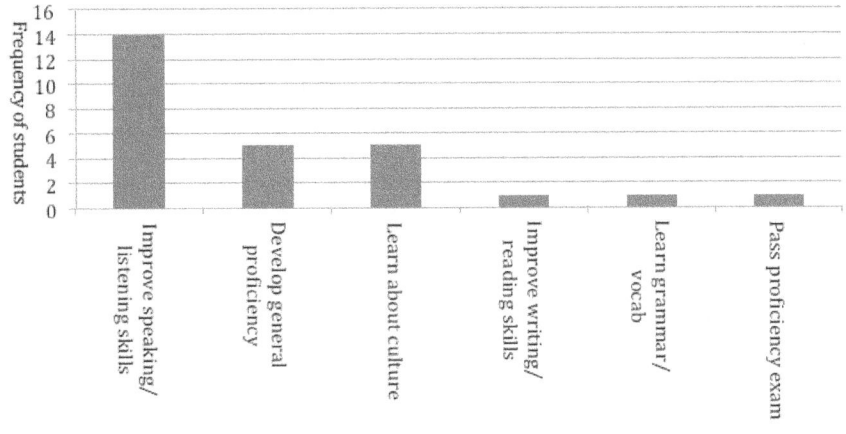

Figure 1. Students' goals in the first level Japanese course.

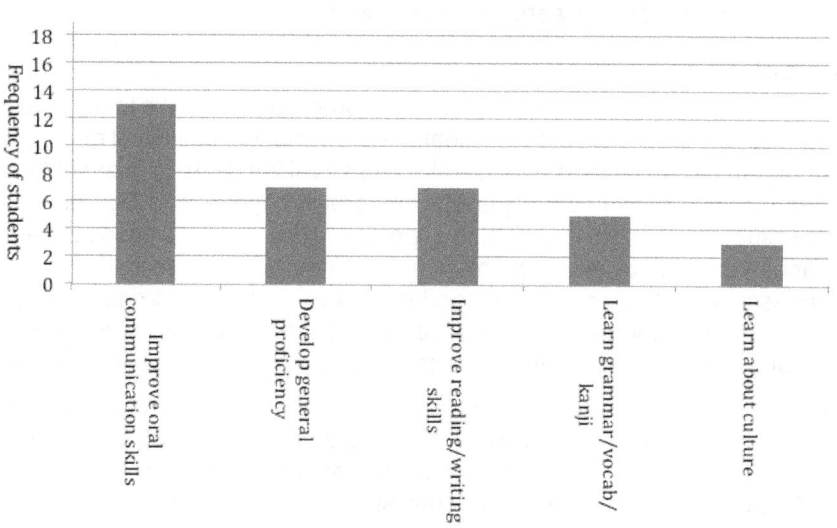

Figure 2. Students' goals in the second level Japanese course.

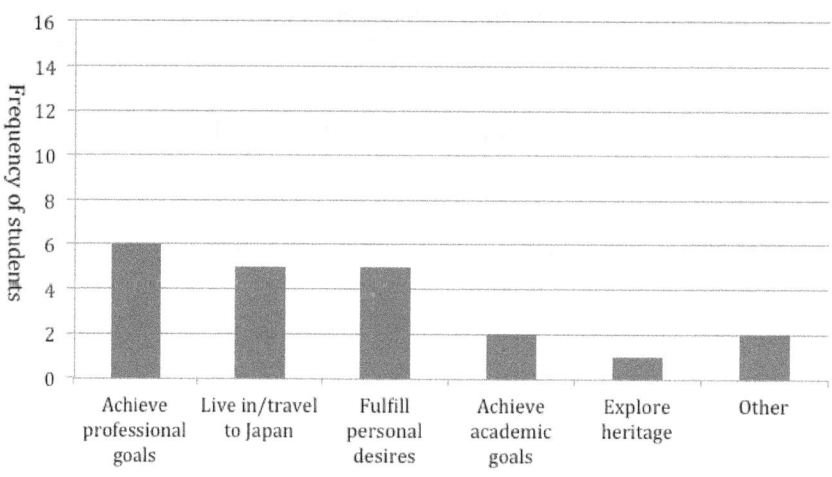

Figure 3. Level 1 students' motivation for learning Japanese.

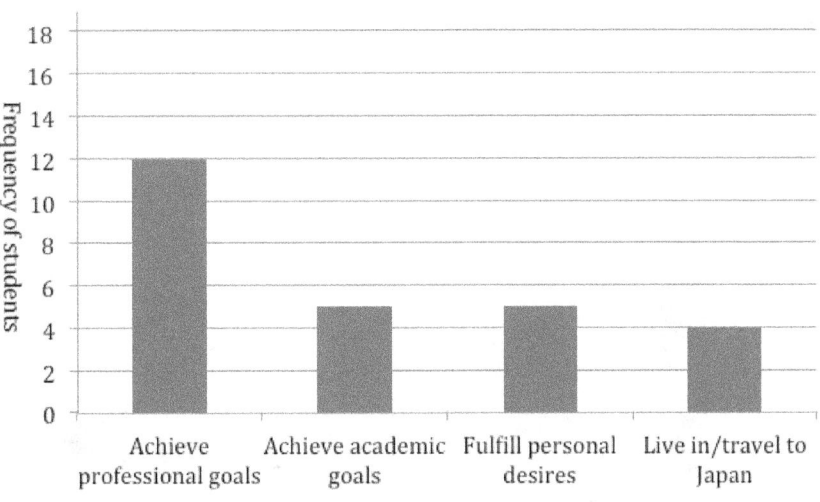

Figure 4. Level 2 students' motivation for learning Japanese.

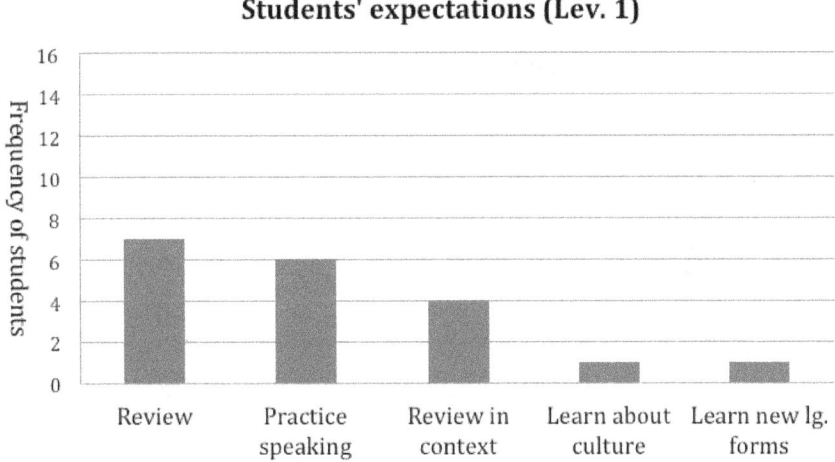

Figure 5. Level 1 students' expectations of the supplementary program.

Needs in the supplementary program

To get at the students' needs in the supplementary program specifically, they were asked the following open-ended question: "What do you expect to learn in the supplementary program?" Figure 5 shows that almost half of the Level 1 students expected to review materials from the main class. A handful of Level 1 students also expressed that in the supplementary program sessions, they wanted to practice their speaking skills and review what they had learned in the main class (mainly grammar and vocabulary) in context. At Level 2, the majority of the students (13 out of 19) mentioned "speaking skills" as a desired focus of the supplementary program sessions (see Figure 6). Other popular responses among the Level 2 students include (a) reviewing materials from the main class, (b) deepening their understandings of Japanese culture, and (c) reviewing in context.

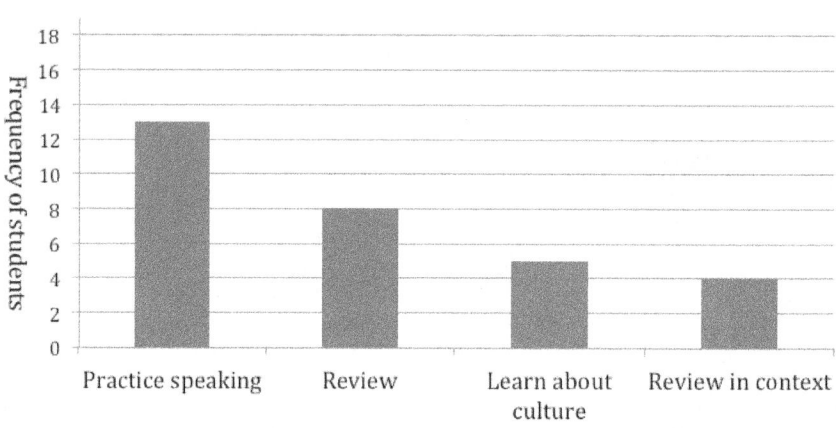

Figure 6. Level 2 students' expectations of the supplementary program.

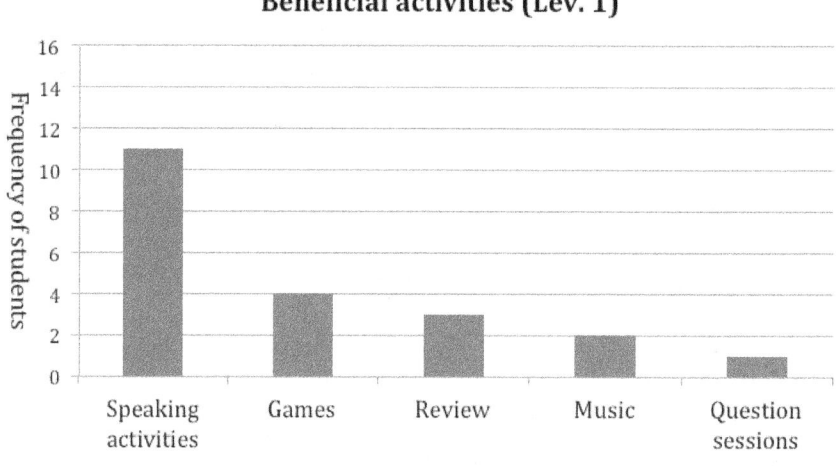

Figure 7. Beneficial activities for Level 1 students.

The next question, "Which supplementary class activities do you think are beneficial?" was included to deepen our understandings of classroom activities that meet and fulfill the students' needs. The most popular answer among the Level 1 students to this question was spontaneous speaking activities, such as practicing small talk, mini-discussions, and interactive games (see Figure 7). In their comments, they explained that these activities were beneficial for helping them develop fluency, improve their speaking skills, use grammar and vocabulary in context, and realize the gap between what they already knew and what they did not yet know. Similarly, at Level 2, *all* respondents mentioned speaking activities, such as story-telling activities, role-plays, and discussions, as the most beneficial activities in the supplementary program classes (see Figure 8). The common reasons were that these activities allowed them to practice communication skills, including speaking and listening skills, and to use and learn grammar in context. Review activities were also somewhat popular at both program levels. It is important to note here that none of the students at Level 2 mentioned the required video materials and their associated activities as beneficial.

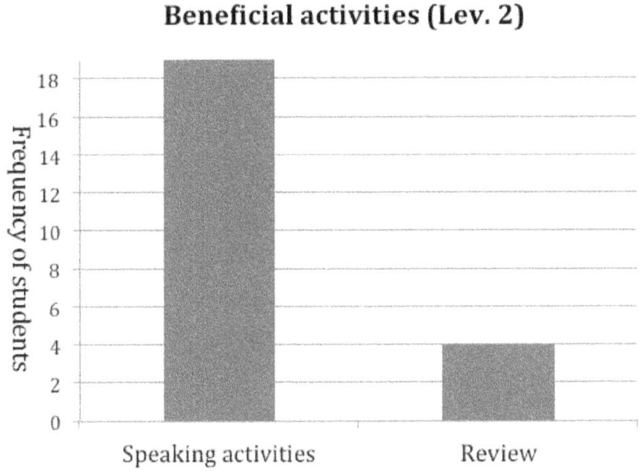

Beneficial activities (Lev. 2)

[Bar chart showing Speaking activities at approximately 19 and Review at 4, with y-axis labeled "Frequency of students" ranging from 0 to 18]

Figure 8. Beneficial activities for Level 2 students.

When the students were asked what aspects of the supplementary class sessions they would recommend to be changed, aligning with their primary goal in learning Japanese and expectation of the supplementary program, both Level 1 and Level 2 students expressed the desire to have more speaking activities in the sessions, especially instead of grammar and kanji reviews that were often accompanied by mechanical drills (See Figures 9 and 10). Below are indicative quotes from four students (two from each program level).

"Because the class size is so much smaller, there should be a larger emphasis on speaking more candidly, rather than on review of the grammar rules. I think we should get more practice in speaking with an emphasis on just getting our message across in any way we know how, rather than constant drilling on using the grammar rules correctly." (Level 1)

"I think the kanji reviews could be removed to give more speaking time." (Level 1)

"I feel that the ... sessions would be of more help if they involved more speaking activities." (Level 2)

"Instead of going over the [grammar] homework, more time should be spent doing conversation drills." (Level 2)

Additionally, regarding the video materials, one of the Level 2 students expressed that "simply just watching the Erin videos without really discussing the context I think is not as helpful." She also felt that "talking about our own experiences and forcing us to use our Japanese is really helpful."

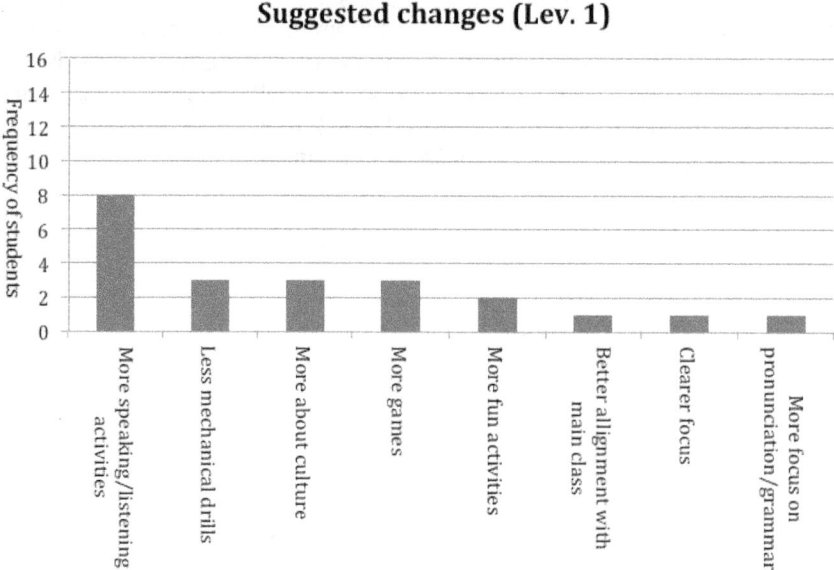

Figure 9. Suggested changes (Level 1).

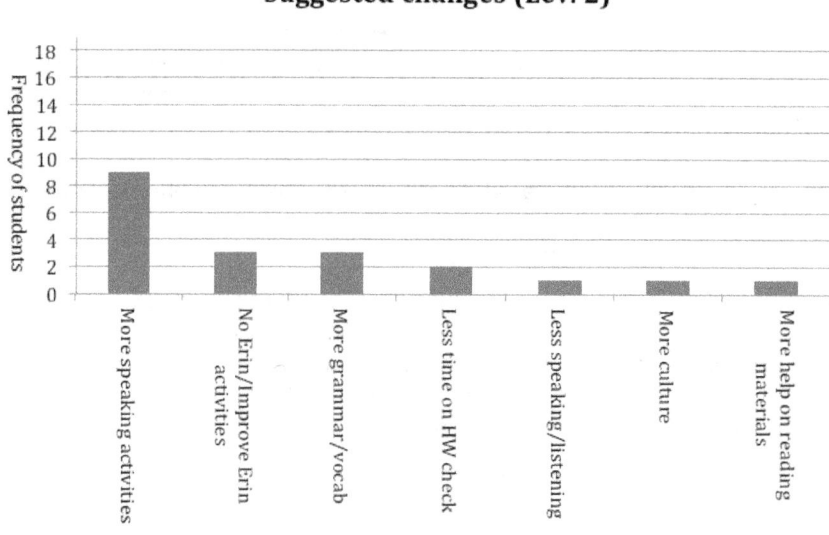

Figure 10. Suggested changes (Level 2).

In summary, it became very clear from their perspectives that the students at both levels (but more prominently at the second level) were hoping to improve their speaking skills; and to achieve this goal, they wished to engage in more speaking activities in the small-sized supplementary classes.

Purposes of the supplementary program

In the initial meeting with the supplementary program instructors, one much-discussed issue concerned the purposes of the program. The supplementary program instructors were not sure about the purposes and/or goals of the supplementary program and expressed their desire to know them, so they could better prepare themselves for the sessions and adjust their teaching styles accordingly. As a result of the meetings and interviews with the primary intended users, it turned out that they all had somewhat different purposes of the program in mind. According to the coordinator, the purposes of the program were to provide the students with opportunities to practice their speaking skills and to review main class materials. The main program instructors expressed that the purposes should be to give students opportunities to prepare for quizzes and exams, to practice the main class materials (e.g., grammar, kanji, vocabulary, expressions), and to give them opportunities for conversation practice. The supplementary program instructors expressed their initial confusion (i.e., upon beginning as teachers in the program) about what to expect or focus on in the sessions. However, as they gained more experience teaching and interacting with their students, they started to believe that the main purposes of the program should be to (a) give the students ample opportunities to use Japanese, (b) help them improve their speaking and communication skills, (c) give them an opportunity to practice the main class materials in context, and (d) give them a chance to ask questions that they could not ask in the main class.

Taken together with the students' major expectation towards the supplementary class sessions (i.e., practice speaking), the primary purpose of the supplementary program was suggested to be to give the students ample opportunities to practice their speaking and communication skills. Additional purposes could also include (a) to review and practice main class materials (in context), (b) to prepare for quizzes and exams, and (c) to introduce some aspects of the Japanese culture.

Actual implementation of the program

How the 50-minute class sessions were typically used was investigated through class observations, meetings with the supplementary program instructors, and the evaluator's own experience teaching the sessions. At Level 1, the content of the sessions varied from session to session, determined by the amount of kanji and/or grammar review needed for each session (as requested by the main instructors). The class typically spent the first five minutes practicing small talk, with the instructor asking the students about their weekend, exams, holidays, or whatever was a "hot topic" on that day. The second activity of the day was typically to listen to Japanese music that somebody in class had nominated earlier in the semester. The class spent 5 to 10 minutes listening to the music, filling in some missing words in the lyrics, and talking about the song or the singer in Japanese. These were the two consistent activities across the Level 1 sessions. During the time remaining (i.e., 35–40 minutes), the class sometimes managed to spend half an hour practicing spontaneous oral conversations, for example by playing *20-Questions* and *Guessing the Occupation* (where a student describes what s/he does as a part of his/her hypothetical job duties in Japanese, and the partner guesses what job it is) after reviewing kanji for 10 minutes. Other times, the class spent 15 minutes reviewing kanji (especially right before a kanji quiz in the main class), 10 minutes doing a listening activity, and 15 minutes practicing ready-made dialogues in the textbook.

By contrast, the content of the Level 2 sessions appeared to be relatively fixed (judged based on the class observation and interviews with the supplementary program instructor). The class typically spent the first 15 minutes practicing storytelling in Japanese. For example, the instructor would ask "*Ima taihen na koto ha nandesuka*? (What are you having trouble with?)," and the students would answer the question one by one as if they were telling a personal story. The next 20 minutes were devoted to checking the grammar exercises that the students had done as homework. The rest of the session time (i.e., 15 minutes) then was spent on the video materials, *Erin ga Chosen: Nihongo Dekimasu*. The class would watch a video clip, and then the instructor would talk about something related to the video. For example, on the day of the observation, they watched a video that described a school festival at a Japanese high school, and the instructor followed up with his own experience.

The class observations, meetings with the program instructors, and the evaluator's own experience of teaching the supplementary sessions also revealed that the program instructors had worked to expose their students to the language, give them opportunities to practice their speaking skills, and expose them to the Japanese culture to the extent possible within the curricular expectations at that time. For example, in one observed Level 2 session, the supplementary program instructor spoke in Japanese most of the time, elicited oral responses from the students whenever possible, and introduced some cultural aspects. In Level 1 sessions, the supplementary program instructors also used Japanese most of the time (despite the students' relatively low language proficiency), often utilized YouTube, for example to teach *hiragana* or to have the students listen to Japanese songs with the intention of introducing the Japanese culture, and sought to provide ample opportunities to practice their speaking and conversation skills. It is important to point out here that, as can be seen in the results of the student survey, these efforts of individual instructors had not been enough to thoroughly meet the students' perceived needs, in particular to improve their oral communication skills. Based on these findings, it was suggested that a larger-scale, more fundamental curriculum change may be needed to this end.

To sum up the findings from Phase I, the supplemental program instructors expressed their desire to be told explicitly what the goals and purposes of the program are, their interests in administering an official end-of-term evaluation, and their wish to learn how best to use the video materials (in the Level 2 sessions). The students who were enrolled in the first and second level Japanese courses in Spring 2013 wished to improve their speaking skills and expected to focus especially on speaking activities (see similar findings in Iwai, Kondo, Lim, Ray, Shimizu, & Brown, 1999), but also on review of the main class materials (in context), and on Japanese culture in the supplemental program sessions. Regarding the purposes of the program, it turned out that different primary intended users had somewhat different ideas about what the purposes of the program should be. One aspect that they had in common, however, was to give students ample opportunities to practice their speaking skills, which also coincided with the students' primary expectation of the program. In the main, everyday classroom, especially at the first level, how many speaking activities the students could do largely depended on the amount of kanji/or grammar review needed for each session (as determined primarily by the adopted textbook). At Level 2, almost half of the supplementary session time was devoted to grammar review (i.e., correction of grammar-based homework that the students had done prior to the session). The rest of the class time, however, was spent at the discretion of the supplementary class instructors on speaking activities at both program levels, most of the time.

Bringing the evaluation findings to use

Based on the evaluation findings outlined above, suggestions were made to help bring the evaluation findings to use. These suggestions are sketched out below.

1. Change the curriculum to include more speaking activities

   Naturally, the top priority for change was to develop a new curriculum that included more speaking activities. Especially at Level 2, it seemed to be an urgent task to develop speaking activities that built on the video materials in order to make the most of them. To this end, it was also suggested that the amount of time devoted to reviewing should be reduced (although not completely eliminated) to create more time for additional speaking activities. This global change in the curriculum was thought to play an integral role in further improvement of the supplementary program.

2. Organize an orientation for all instructors

   What became especially clear in the evaluation was a lack of communication among the instructors in the Japanese Program. Evaluation questions elicited by the primary intended users, in particular, pointed to the need for more rigorous communication among the instructors. To facilitate communication among them, it was suggested that an instructor orientation should be organized on a regular basis. This instructor orientation would help all instructors to exchange information about the students and share any concerns that they might have. It would also serve as a perfect venue to disseminate the evaluation findings to the new instructors. In particular, the purposes of the program, students' needs, and kinds of activities used in the past would be of interest to and useful for them. The program instructors' needs to find out about the purposes of the program and effective activities to improve their sessions highlighted the importance of sharing the evaluation findings with new supplementary program instructors.

3. Develop an official end-of-term evaluation for the supplementary program

   As a way of making program evaluation a consistent part of the program, it was suggested that an official end-of-term evaluation be developed for the supplementary program. It would help the program understand the effectiveness of new classroom activities, monitor students' needs and learning progress, and accordingly consider ways to further improve the program on a semester-to-semester basis.

4. Formulate student learning outcomes for the supplementary program

   In order to emphasize the purposes and goals of the supplementary program to both the instructors and the students, and to provide a point of reference for future evaluation of the effectiveness and value of the program, it was suggested that student learning outcomes (SLOs) particularly articulated to the supplementary program should be formulated. SLOs would help the instructors and the students alike understand what they should be working towards in weekly sessions, which in turn would encourage them not to deviate from the new curriculum and to develop and work with pedagogic activities appropriate to the achievement of agreed upon outcomes that were based on students' needs.

Phase II

Following the first phase of evaluation data collection, findings, and uses, we then proceeded to monitor the impact of changes implemented to the program for another year. Given the evaluation findings of Phase I, it was decided that we should focus primarily on the second level of the supplementary program, where a refocusing of activities seemed most necessary. Students at Level 2 had expressed consistent needs to engage in more communication-based activities so as to improve their speaking skills, and there was an urgent requirement to figure out an effective way to better incorporate the video materials into class sessions. Hence, the second level of the program was chosen as the primary focus of Phase II. Note that the primary intended users expressed their desire to first monitor students' reactions to the changes made to the curriculum as well as program effectiveness resulting from these changes; hence, the focus on developing student learning outcomes was delayed until the third phase.

Evaluation questions and methods

For the second phase, intended users posed the following evaluation questions:

- How were the evaluation findings put into use at Level 2 of the program?
- What impacts, if any, did program changes have on student learning and program effectiveness at Level 2, from the students' perspective?

In order to answer these questions, a careful record of changes to the curriculum and implementation of these changes was kept. Additionally, the student survey used during the first phase was administered repeatedly to the Level 2 students in Fall 2013 and Spring 2014. On both occasions, the survey was administered on paper at the end of each semester. As was the case in the first phase, students' responses were categorized into patterns according to recurring themes identified within each survey question.

Findings

Here, evaluation findings in Phase II will be summarized, in the order of the above-mentioned evaluation questions.

Changes implemented

Following the suggestions made at the end of Phase I, at Level 2, the curriculum was revised to include more speaking activities. To create time for these activities, it was decided that grammar homework correction that had been done in class was to be done outside of the class time. In class, the instructor only went over common grammar mistakes found in the students' homework, instead of checking each answer with them, for a much shorter duration of class time. New speaking activities were developed by the supplementary program instructors as well, and these activities included (a) a regular 5-minute conversation where the students engage in small talk with their classmate(s) and do their best to keep the conversation going for 5 minutes on various topics (see Appendix A for example topics) and (b) speaking activities built upon the video materials *Erin ga chosen: Nihongo dekimasu*. The latter activities took various forms, such as skills-integrated tasks, information exchange tasks, and opinion exchange tasks, among others. Some examples of the skills-integrated tasks were to (a) discuss what questions they want to ask their Japanese instructors and/or their seniors based on their biographies, and e-interview them; and (b) watch a video where a Japanese pop singer was interviewed about her part-time job experience, answer comprehension questions, and discuss their own experiences of work (see Appendix B). Information and opinion exchange tasks asked the students to share their knowledge, experiences, and opinions with the class (e.g., What's the college entrance examination like? If you were to go to Japan, where would you like to go?). These communication-based activities gave the students ample opportunities to practice their communication skills, use newly learned grammar and vocabulary in context, and be familiar with some aspects of the Japanese culture.

Evaluation impacts from the students' perspective

To understand the impacts of evaluation from their perspective, the students who were enrolled in the Level 2 Japanese course in Fall 2013 and Spring 2014 were invited to participate in the student survey. The response rates to the survey were 76.19% (16 students) in Fall 2013 and 93.75% (15 students) in Spring 2014. The Level 2 students in Fall 2013 and Spring 2014 expressed similar desires and needs in the Japanese Program overall and the supplementary program as had the previous group of Level 2 students in Phase I. The majority of the new group of Level 2 students wished to improve their overall language competency, but in particular their oral communication skills, in the Japanese Program in general (See Figure 11). Additionally, a handful of students also wished to deepen their understandings of the Japanese culture and history. The other desires included better learning of vocabulary, grammar, and kanji, and simply to enjoy learning the language.

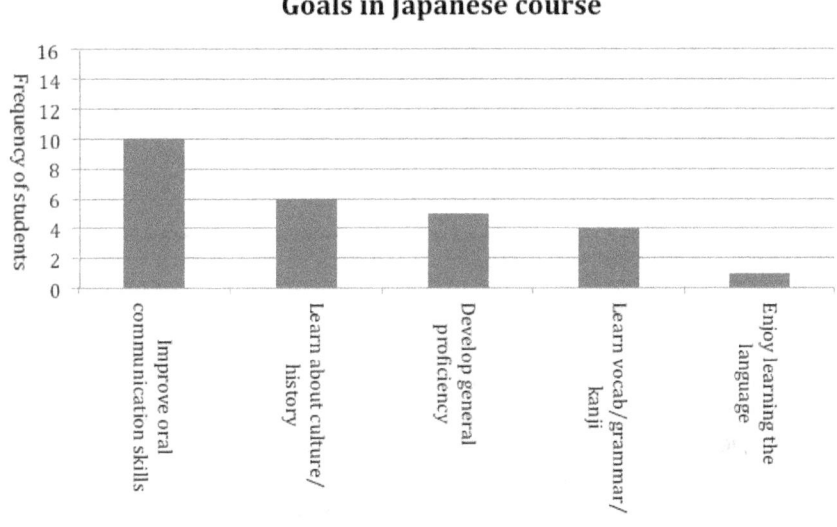

Figure 11. Students' goals in the Japanese course.

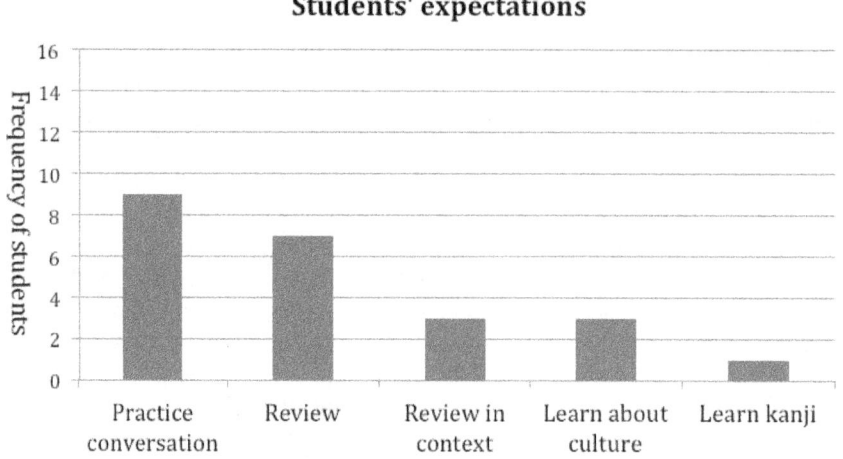

Figure 12. Students' expectations of the supplementary program.

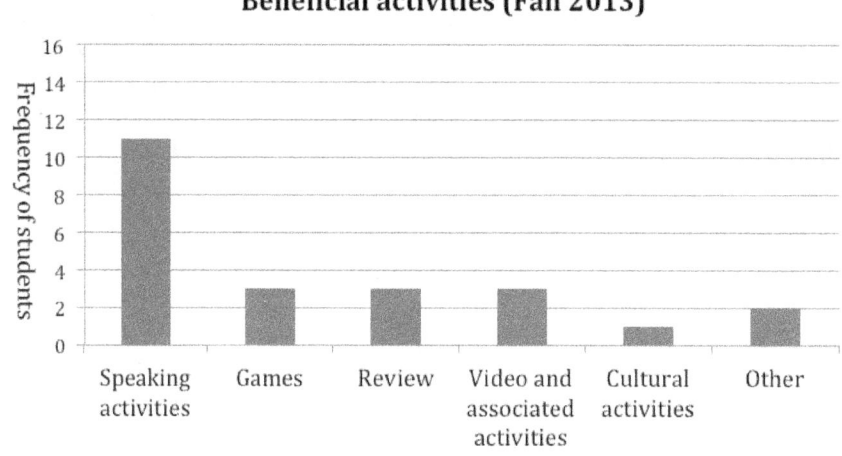

Figure 13. Beneficial activities (Fall 2013).

Similarly, in terms of their specific needs in the supplementary program, the majority of the students (nine, to be precise) expressed their desire to improve their conversation skills in the supplementary sessions (see Figure 12). Seven of them also wished to review materials from the main Japanese classes, and three wished to review these materials in conversational contexts. Three of them also expected to learn about culture, and one expected to review kanji in the supplementary sessions. In Spring 2014, all of the students, except for five, were enrolled in the second semester Level 2 Japanese course; hence, the trends observed in Fall 2013 of the students' general and specific needs of the program stayed almost identical in Spring 2014. When the students were asked what activities had been beneficial to their Japanese learning, in Fall 2013, 11 out of 16 students chose speaking activities, 3 chose games, 3 chose review, and 3 chose the Erin video and associated activities, among others (see Figure 13).

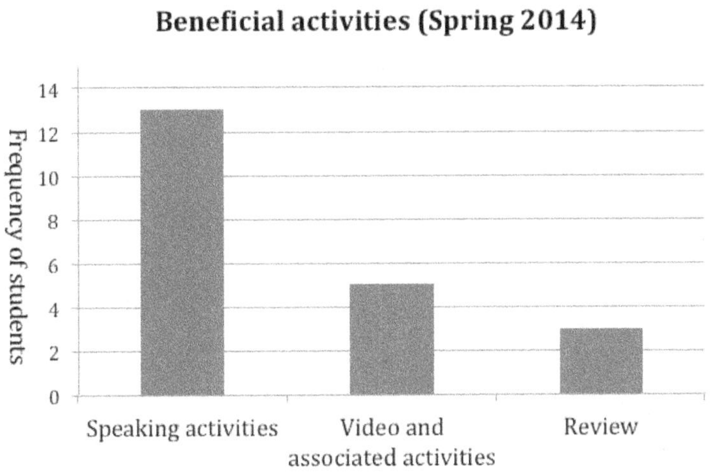

Beneficial activities (Spring 2014)

[Bar chart showing frequency of students: Speaking activities ≈13, Video and associated activities ≈5, Review ≈3]

Figure 14. Beneficial activities (Spring 2014).

Similarly, in Spring 2014, 13 students out of 15 expressed that various speaking activities, especially the 5-minute conversation (that was newly introduced in Spring 2014), had been beneficial for them. Five of them also chose the Erin video and associated materials as beneficial activities, and three chose review of the main class materials (see Figure 14). About the benefit of the 5-minute conversation, the students commented as follows:

> "The 5 minutes where we spend talking to one another in any Japanese. It allows us to talk casually and practice our speaking skills."

> "I think the conversations in the beginning are very useful because they force us to apply our knowledge of the language without prior preparation."

What is noteworthy here is that some students nominated the video and its associated activities, which were introduced as a result of the evaluation, as beneficial activities in the supplementary sessions. This trend is something that we did not see before the evaluation results were put into practice. To this end, the students provided the following comments:

> "Erin is also great because it is fun … and helpful."

> "The Erin listening comprehension activities are beneficial because they engage the class completely while offering follow up questions to test our comprehension."

> "I liked the Erin exercises a lot and the videos helped with my listening skills."

Additionally, the students described their overall experiences in the supplementary program as follows:

> "I think the [supplementary program] sessions are very helpful, because of the impromptu conversations, as well as adding another person to speak to, in addition to *** sensei [the main class instructor]."
>
> "It [the supplementary program] helps to review what we've learned in class. Also, Erin videos show us culture, which I think is important."
>
> "The cultural activities were fun and I learned a lot from them. Because I spoke more in [the supplementary program], I think my speaking skills improved."
>
> "We are constantly challenging our speaking skills [in the supplementary program]."
>
> "There is more speaking and conversation practice in the [supplementary program] sessions than in the main class, which is helpful."

These comments from many of the students highlight their positive attitudes towards the changes implemented to the supplementary program as a result of the evaluation.

Phase III

Given the successful implementation of the curriculum changes at Level 2 of the supplementary program, further innovations were implemented to the overall program in Fall 2014, including an instructor orientation, development of an official end-of-term evaluation, creation of an online materials back, and most importantly, development of student learning outcomes for both program levels. First of all, an orientation was held for all supplementary program instructors (of both Level 1 and Level 2) at the beginning of the semester in Fall 2014, in order to disseminate the evaluation findings and to facilitate communication among the instructors. We thought this opportunity would be important, especially given the fact that both Level 1 instructors were brand new and had very little idea about the supplementary program. During the orientation, the purposes of the supplementary program, learner needs, and activity ideas were discussed and shared. Additionally, the experienced instructors gave advice on successful class sessions. These included (a) use speaking activities where possible, (b) use Japanese as much as possible, and (c) it is okay to introduce our own materials as long as we consult with the main instructor, among others. Additionally, a debriefing was organized voluntarily at the end of the Fall 2014 semester by one of the Level 1 instructors. In this meeting, instructors discussed their overall experiences of the semester, what worked and what did not work, and ways to further improve the sessions. Secondly, the supplementary program instructors collaborated to create an end-of-term evaluation to monitor students' needs and reflect on and improve teaching practices. The draft evaluation form was reviewed by the main class instructors and the program coordinator, and their feedback was incorporated into the finalized version. Thirdly, an online materials bank, where all instructors could share teaching ideas and materials, was created to facilitate communication and collaboration among the instructors.

Lastly and most importantly, at the conclusion of Phase II evaluation activities, intended users agreed that the Japanese Program as a whole should create student learning outcomes (SLOs) for the supplementary program, based on the evaluation findings and subsequent implementation of changes. The process for creating outcomes statements was as follows. First, SLOs were drafted by the supplementary program instructors at each level, based on their experiences and observations of the changes that had been implemented from the evaluation findings. Second, the draft SLOs were reviewed and revised by the main instructors and finally by the Japanese Program coordinator. Accordingly, drawing on the empirical basis of two years of evaluation cycles, the intended user group felt confident in formulating the following SLOs for each level, incorporating all three purposes of the supplementary program identified during the evaluation process.

Level 1

Improving oral communication abilities

- Students will be able to ask simple questions and give simple responses, using what they have learned in the main Japanese classes.
- Students will be able to complete simple tasks, such as making a phone call to stores and making an order in a restaurant, using what they have learned in the main Japanese classes.
- Students will be able to achieve a variety of goals in Japanese, including talking about the past and future, asking simple questions, making comments on and giving acknowledgment (e.g., by means of *aizuchi*) to other students' remarks, based on their knowledge of Japanese they have acquired through the main Japanese classes.
- Students will be able to use grammar and vocabulary that they have learned in the main Japanese classes somewhat accurately in their spoken Japanese.
- Students will develop confidence in using what they have learned in the main Japanese classes in their spoken Japanese.

Culture

- Students will deepen their understandings of Japanese culture and everyday life.
- Students will be able to show their understandings about cultural aspects of their own country in relation with Japan.

Review

- Students will strengthen their understandings of the materials (e.g., grammar/ reading/ kanji) introduced in the main Japanese classes.
- Students will be well prepared for quizzes and exams in the main Japanese classes.

Level 2

Improving oral communication abilities

- Students will be able to keep a conversation going in Japanese with their classmate for at least 5 minutes, using what they have learned in the main Japanese classes.
- Students will be able to talk about various topics in Japanese, including some complex topics, such as dreams and goals, using what they have learned in the main Japanese classes.

- Students will be able to achieve a variety of goals in Japanese, including talking about the past and future, making recommendations, asking relevant questions, and making comments on other students' remarks, based on their knowledge of Japanese they have acquired through the main Japanese classes.
- Students will be able to use grammar, vocabulary, and pragmatics that they have learned in the main Japanese classes somewhat accurately in their spoken Japanese.
- Students will develop confidence in using what they have learned in the main Japanese classes in their spoken Japanese.

Culture
- Students will deepen their understandings of Japanese culture, including some complex topics, such as schooling and work in Japan.
- Students will be able to talk about cultural aspects of their own country in relation with Japan to a greater extent.

Review
- Students will strengthen their understandings of the materials (e.g., grammar/ reading/ kanji) introduced in the main Japanese classes.
- Students will be well prepared for quizzes and exams in the main Japanese classes.

The plan for utilizing these SLOs was that they would be passed down every semester to new instructors in the new instructor orientation. On the last day of instruction in each semester, instructors as well as students would also spend a moment to reflect on what they had engaged in that semester and what they had achieved as a result, referring to the SLOs. These SLOs have also been incorporated into the new end-of-term evaluation and were suggested to be included in a syllabus of the supplementary program.

Evaluation impacts from the instructors' perspective

At the end of Fall 2014, the two main instructors and one supplementary program instructor, who were involved in the majority of (if not the entire) 2-year program evaluation, were interviewed about the overall experience of participating in the program evaluation. Their impressions were quite positive, and their comments revolved around the two main uses of the evaluation: (a) new speaking activities to better meet the students' needs and (b) the instructor orientation.

Regarding the 5-minute conversation and other speaking activities that became a part of the new curriculum as a result of the program evaluation, the Level 2 main instructor expressed her appreciation as follows:

> "The students really like the five-minute conversations. I myself wasn't sure how we could use the video materials, but it's wonderful that the students can practice their oral skills while engaging in activities associated with the video materials." [author's translation]

Furthermore, about the instructor orientation, the Level 1 instructors attested to its effectiveness as follows:

> "New supplementary program instructors could learn what the sessions are like in the orientation, so the semester started smoothly this time."
>
> "The orientation strengthened communication among program instructors. They exchange materials and activity ideas."
>
> "The use of Japanese in the sessions must have been emphasized in the orientation. They seem to be using Japanese quite a lot in the sessions."

Similarly, the Level 2 main instructor expressed,

> "New instructors are more clear about what should be done in the sessions, and there is a stronger bond among the instructors."

Lastly, one supplementary program instructor expressed her appreciation towards the orientation as follows:

> "It was helpful to discuss how we can improve the sessions during the orientation. I feel that it's really important to be able to exchange ideas, suggestions, and experiences with the other instructors."

Thus, as can be seen in these comments along with other evaluation findings, the present program evaluation achieved not only *findings use* (Patton, 2008), such as implementation of the new speaking activities, the instructor orientation, and the clearly articulated set of student learning outcomes, but also *process use* (Patton, 2008), including in particular improved communication among instructors and sharing of teaching ideas and materials.

Conclusion

The present program evaluation was initiated to (a) deepen program insiders' understandings of the reality of the supplementary program (e.g., instructors' and students' needs, program implementation), (b) consider potential program changes on the basis of evaluation findings, and (c) use the results as a resource to develop program goals and learning outcomes as well as a program instructor orientation and/or instructor manual. The evaluation process required a lot of time and effort on the part of many primary intended users. However, the results seem to have been rewarding. Indeed, in the end, the evaluation achieved more than expected and contributed to the improvement of the supplementary program, as expressed by the intended users above. As a result of the evaluation, (a) new speaking activities were introduced to better meet the students' needs and the program goals, (b) an instructor orientation was organized to help disseminate the evaluation findings and to facilitate communication and collaboration among the instructors, (c) an official evaluation form was created to monitor students' needs and improve the sessions as required, (d) an online materials bank was created for easy sharing of teaching ideas and materials among the instructors, and finally, (e) student learning outcomes were formulated to consolidate what was learned in the evaluation findings and to maintain all of these impacts even after the conclusion of the evaluation. It is my strong hope that the supplementary program will continue to strive for, improve, and facilitate students' learning of the Japanese language and culture on the basis of the present evaluation.

Acknowledgments

I would like to extend my sincere appreciation to all the participants in the evaluation for making this program evaluation successful. I would also like to thank Dr. John Norris for opening my eyes to the field of program evaluation, for giving me guidance from the onset to the ending of this evaluation, and for valuable feedback on this manuscript. Thank you all.

References

Davis, J. McE., Sinicrope, C., & Watanabe, Y. (2009). College foreign language program evaluation: Current practices, further directions. In J. M. Norris, J. McE. Davis, C. Sinicrope, & Y. Watanabe (Eds.), *Toward useful program evaluation in college foreign language education* (pp. 209–225). Honolulu: University of Hawai'i National Foreign Language Resource Center.

The Higher Learning Commission. (2003). *Handbook of accreditation* (3rd ed.). Chicago, IL: The Higher Learning Commission of the North Central Association.

Iwai, T., Kondo, K., Lim, D. S. J., Ray, G., Shimizu, H., & Brown, J. D. (1999). *Japanese language needs assessment 1998–1999* (NFLRC NetWork 13). Honolulu: University of Hawai'i National Foreign Language Resource Center. Retrieved from http://nflrc.hawaii.edu/publications/view/NW13/

Japan Foundation. (2010). *Erin ga chosen: Nihongo dekimasu* [Erin's challenge: I can speak Japanese]. Urawa, Japan: Japan Foundation Japanese-Language Institute. Retrieved from http://www.erin.ne.jp

Milleret, M., & Silveira, A. S. (2009). The role of evaluation in curriculum development and growth of the UNM Portuguese Program. In J. M. Norris, J. McE. Davis, C. Sinicrope, & Y. Watanabe (Eds.), *Toward useful program evaluation in college foreign language education* (pp. 57–82). Honolulu: University of Hawai'i National Foreign Language Resource Center.

Norris, J. M. (2006). The why (and how) of assessing student learning outcomes in college foreign language programs. *The Modern Language Journal, 90*(4), 576–583.

Patton, M. Q. (2008). *Utilization-focused evaluation.* Thousand Oaks, CA: SAGE publications.

Watanabe, Y., Davis, J. McE., & Norris, J. M. (2012). *A utilization-focused approach to developing, mapping, and assessing student learning outcomes in college foreign language programs.* Honolulu: University of Hawai'i National Foreign Language Resource Center. Retrieved from http://archives.lll.hawaii.edu/evaluation/files/Module2.pdf

Appendix A. Example topics for the 5-minute conversation activity (translated into English)

What did you do during the winter holiday?
What's your new year's resolution?
What classes are you taking this semester?
Have you been following the Sochi Olympic games? What are your favorite sports?
Which country would you like to go to?
What movies do you recommend?
What are you having troubles with lately?
What's your plan for the spring break?
What did you do during the spring break?
Which season do you like the best?
Why are you studying Japanese?
What have you become able to do in Japanese this semester?

Appendix B. Sample skills-integrated activity

⁺エリン　第19課

- きゃりーぱみゅぱみゅ
- http://www.youtube.com/watch?v=teMdjJ3w9iM
- インタビュー (2:35-)
- http://www.youtube.com/watch?v=5dHwxKmcGG8
- きゃりーぱみゅぱみゅさんはどんなバイトについて話していますか？
- どんな経験をしましたか？
- してみたいバイトは何ですか？
- 彼女にとって、バイトをするときに大切なことは何ですか？

⁺エリン　第19課

- アルバイトをしていますか（したことがありますか）？
- どうしてアルバイトを始めましたか？
- どうしてそのアルバイトをえらびましたか？
- （アルバイトをしたことがない人）自由時間はどうしてすごすのが好きですか？

Developing Learning Outcomes for First-Year Arabic at the University of Notre Dame

Ghada Bualuan & Amaya Martin
University of Notre Dame

This chapter addresses the initiation of student learning outcomes assessment in the Program of Arabic Language and Culture (PALC) at the University of Notre Dame. It describes how assessment was used by Arabic faculty to modify the first-year Arabic language course sequence. Initially, the PALC assessment committee undertook the development of student learning outcomes for two first-year language courses in the Arabic major. The committee also implemented an assessment project to better understand how well the new student learning outcomes (SLOs) matched instruction and content in Arabic courses. Student feedback (via focus groups and an online questionnaire) was used to analyze which aspects of the curriculum encompassed the learning benchmarks articulated in the new SLOs (and which SLOs were unaddressed). In general, the committee found that current first-year courses did not provide sufficient instruction toward new listening and inter-cultural competence learning outcomes. The chapter also reports on lessons learned via the assessment process (e.g., assessment needs and challenges), as well as planned assessment work for the future. The chapter concludes by discussing how assessment greatly benefitted student learning and language teaching in the PALC—that is, we highlight the effectiveness of high-quality student learning outcomes and their positive impact on curriculum planning and the trajectory of student progress.

Bualuan, G., & Martin, A. (2015) Developing learning outcomes for first-year Arabic at the University of Notre Dame. In J. M. Norris & J. McE. Davis (Eds.), *Student learning outcomes assessment in college foreign language programs* (pp. 123–141). Honolulu: University of Hawai'i, National Foreign Language Resource Center.

Introduction

In the spring of 2011, the Program of Arabic Language and Culture at the University of Notre Dame (UND) became part of the "Utilization-Focused Outcomes Assessment Project" initiated by the UND Center for the Study of Languages and Cultures (CSLC). The project was an inter-institutional research collaboration investigating utilization-focused outcomes assessment in university foreign language programs, undertaken with support and assistance from the National Foreign Language Resource Center (NFLRC) at the University of Hawai'i at Mānoa. The participation of PALC faculty in the project was intended to help achieve an important CSLC goal: to foster assessment literacy among UND language programs, as well as within the UND administration, and more fundamentally to improve language learning.

Since the beginnings of PALC, faculty involvement in the CSLC project and interest in and engagement with assessment has steadily grown. In spring of 2011, a three-member committee was appointed to oversee curriculum development and assessment efforts. The overarching goals of this group were to review the curriculum of the Arabic program (in consultation with Arabic faculty), evaluate the effectiveness of the language courses, and identify program developments needed to ensure and enhance the program's academic excellence. In addition, the committee was to oversee the development of student learning outcomes assessment as a means of achieving these goals. The specific assessment-related responsibilities of the committee were to (a) identify and communicate any immediate needs or challenges related to assessment design, data collection, interpretation, or use; (b) outline an assessment plan for the remainder of 2011 and 2012 in terms of what was to be accomplished via the outcomes assessment project; and (c) periodically report to program faculty on ongoing assessment work.

The initial goal of the committee was to develop new student learning outcomes for first-year Arabic courses (entitled MEAR 10001 and MEAR 10002). Moreover, the committee also wanted a sense of how well the new SLOs would function within the current Arabic curriculum. That is to say, the committee wanted to know the degree to which first-year courses in their current state (at the time) would address the new language learning benchmarks. Were first-year courses providing instruction and learning opportunities that encompassed all the new SLOs? And if not, where was course development needed such that first-year instruction would fully address the newly developed learning outcomes?

Again, the committee's first assessment project was to engage in an iterative process of student learning outcomes development for first-year Arabic language courses. Once outcomes were developed, a second iteration in the assessment project was undertaken to shed light on the degree to which first-year courses addressed the new SLOs. The committee endeavored to gain this understanding via student feedback. Student feedback was targeted for two purposes. First, the committee wanted students' general perceptions of the new outcomes to ensure they found them clear, understandable, and meaningful. Second, the committee was interested in ascertaining students' self-rated outcomes performance—that is to say, the committee wanted a sense of the degree to which students felt they had attained the new first-year learning outcome targets upon completion of MEAR 10001 or MEAR 10002 (even though the outcomes had yet to be formally integrated into the curriculum). Information on students perceptions of their learning, relative to the new learning outcomes, was used as a diagnostic tool to reflect how well first-year courses in their current form provided (or failed to provide) instruction encompassing the new SLOs. In this way, the committee used assessment to better understand and improve its first-year Arabic course sequence. The remainder of the chapter describes how these aims were achieved, as well as the decision-making and actions that ensued as a result of the committee's assessment efforts.

Program in Arabic language and culture

The PALC is part of the Program in Arabic and Middle East Studies within the Department of Classics at UND. The department offers a range of courses on the history and culture of the Middle East, including Arabic literature, history, civilization, culture, and religion. The department also offers a major in Arabic. The Arabic major builds on fundamentals acquired in Arabic language courses over a three-year language course sequence, starting with MEAR 10001 and MEAR 10002 in the first year. Students are also required to take an additional three courses (in translation) in Islamic culture, Arabic literature, and Arabic history, as well as an elective of their choice offered within the program.

All students are also highly encouraged to do an intensive study abroad program in the Arab World, ideally in the summer of their junior year. Another opportunity to strengthen Arabic language skills and cultural competency is to take fourth-year Arabic courses, directed readings in Arabic at the fifth-year level, as well as enroll in *Language Across the Curriculum* courses, which are offered in English but also provide an Arabic language component.

In addition to coursework and study abroad opportunities, students can learn more about Arab culture through the Arabic Club. The Arabic Club frequently organizes a variety of events (now department traditions) including an annual Arabic culture night, a bi-annual Arabic newsletter, an annual Arab film festival, and other extra-curricular activities. Faculty and students take great pride in the Arabic Club in that it has provided a sense community within the program, as well as common experiences across generations of alumni.

Formulating learning outcomes for first-year Arabic courses

In early fall of 2011 the PALC assessment committee met to develop the student learning outcomes (SLOs) for first-year Arabic courses. The committee decided to develop the SLOs for first-year courses instead of focusing only on the Arabic major because of one main reason: Most students in first-year Arabic have not decided their major or majors yet. Focusing on first-year Arabic students as a whole guaranteed that potential Arabic majors would receive the appropriate instruction required for the major. Committee members were primarily responsible for drafting and revising SLOs statements, though advice and input were sought from individuals outside the PALC, including Stew Markel, the Assistant Director for Assessment & Testing at the CSLC at Notre Dame, and two assessment consultants from the NFLRC, Professor John Norris and Yukiko Watanabe. The Assistant Director participated regularly throughout the process by attending most of the committee's meetings and by providing feedback and guidance during the writing process. In addition, he helped extensively to format the survey for the self-assessment ratings, facilitated the focus groups meetings, and presented the focus group results. The external assessment consultants supported assessment development and practice through advising, feedback, and provision of resources for the duration of the project; they met regularly with the committee members twice a year for a period of 2 years and were available by email to answer questions and offer suggestions.

Initially, the committee drafted SLOs statements using the existing course outcomes as a starting point, though a number of additional goals informed SLOs development (see Walsh & Webb, 2009). First, outcome statements were to be expressed in terms of specific knowledge, skills, and attitudes/values to be developed by students upon completion of first year Arabic courses. In addition, all faculty members agreed on incorporating a cultural component of Arabic language use into the outcomes statements since faculty viewed language and culture as inseparable. SLOs statements were also informed by the American Council on the Teaching of Foreign Languages (ACTFL) language proficiency guidelines; ACTFL guidelines provide important descriptions of how students' performance can be demonstrated. That is to say, SLOs statements were influenced by ACTFL performance criteria for speaking, writing, listening, and reading in real-world situations and contexts (all SLOs are listed in Appendix A).

Developing the SLOs statements presented the committee with a number of challenges. The first was limiting the number of outcomes. The committee realized that too many outcomes would be overwhelming, not only to students but instructors as well. The second issue had to do with level of outcome expectation (or perceived difficulty). The committee wanted outcomes to be challenging without appearing unreasonably difficult.

A number of additional considerations impacted SLOs development. For example, the committee came to realize the implications of SLOs for instructors given the likely need to emphasize student-centered learning in addition to traditions of pedagogic practice that had been in place for some time. It was thought that there may be a mismatch between the current language teaching methods in the program and the potentially new and unfamiliar pedagogical demands of outcomes-oriented learning/teaching. This realization suggested a need to investigate current teaching methods. An additional concern was ensuring that new SLOs would articulate with subsequent course sequences (second and third year courses) later in the Arabic major.

Investigating students' perceptions of outcomes

After completing final drafts of the SLOs for first-year Arabic courses, the next goal was to ascertain students' perceptions of the outcomes with respect to clarity, comprehensibility, and meaningfulness. The committee's intent was to get at what might be called students' immediate reactions to the SLOs—a sense of whether the SLOs were understandable, or, if certain terminology and/or concepts hindered comprehension.

A second type of desired student feedback was the degree to which students who had completed MEAR 10001 and MEAR 10002 felt they had achieved the new

SLOs during the previous semester (even though the new SLOs had not yet been implemented). That is to say, the committee wanted a sense of first-year student learning as compared with the learning targets articulated in the new SLOs. Asking students to comment on the degree to which their previous courses had enabled them to attain the new SLOs was thought to provide insights into how courses were already addressing the new SLOs, or, where courses were failing to address the SLOs and what curricular modifications might be needed as a result.

Two data collection tools were used to capture the desired types of student feedback: (a) *focus group* sessions involving students who had completed first- and second-semester Arabic courses (conducted in early spring of 2011) and (b) an online *questionnaire* administered to students in three sections of MEAR 10002 who were close to completing the course (disseminated at the end of the spring semester of 2011).

Focus groups

Two focus groups were organized to generate student feedback on outcomes for first-year Arabic courses (MEAR 10001 and MEAR 10002). Focus group 1 (FG1) was formed to provide feedback on first-semester Arabic SLOs and was comprised of four students who had completed MEAR 10001 the prior semester and were enrolled, at the time, in MEAR 10002. Focus group 2 (FG2) was formed for students to comment on second-semester Arabic SLOs and was comprised of five second-year students (all having previously completed MEAR 10002). FG2 was a mix of sophomores and juniors, majors and non-majors, as well as one advanced freshman student who had placed into a second-year Arabic course.

While the number of participants in each focus group did not reach the ideal of 6–12 participants (as stipulated by Onwuegbuzie, Dickinson, Leech, & Zoran, 2009), 4–5 students was considered sufficient given the program size and the committee's course development needs. Moreover, the priority in forming the focus groups was to target participants who had similar characteristics and who would be most able to comment in an informed way on the SLOs statements (Krueger & Casey, 2008). Despite the size of the groups, both provided valuable data that proved especially useful in the committee's understanding of how students were interpreting and understanding the new first-year Arabic SLOs, as well as the extent of their perceived outcomes achievement.

Both focus groups met in early February of 2011, approximately one month after the beginning of the spring semester. A faculty member outside the Arabic Program acted as facilitator in order to avoid biasing participants' responses. The main objectives of the focus groups were to (a) to ascertain the extent to which students thought the outcomes clear and attainable and (b) to ascertain the degree to which students felt they had achieved the learning outcomes in the past course experiences (i.e., asking students, "How well do you think you did?"). Following data collection, the data were analyzing in detail to explore common themes and patterns in participants' comments, and then the entire committee met to discuss the focus group findings.

Focus group results

Inter-cultural competency outcomes

Focus group data indicated that aspects of outcomes related to inter-cultural competency were unclear to students in both FG1 and FG2. For example, one FG1 student pointed out a potential dual interpretation of "making one acceptable in some Arab societies," noting this could refer to making oneself acceptable in an Arab society or to the process of becoming accepted. In FG2, one student mentioned that the term "appreciate" in "be able to appreciate Arabic popular culture, especially films and song" was vague.

Again, students were asked to report on whether they felt they had attained the learning outcome benchmarks. Three students in FG2 noted the lack of emphasis on culture during the course: "very little done with regards to culture in classes;" "[we] never really got to the point where we 'compared culture' in class;" "[I] had a few cultural aspects in class;" "Islam is not very strongly addressed in class."

Listening outcomes

Listening SLOs were sufficiently clear for students in both focus groups. However, both groups thought the listening outcomes were the most difficult of all the outcomes, in terms of achievement. Students in FG1 characterized the listening outcomes as generally "hard" and "difficult." Comments from FG2 also referred to the perceived difficulty of the new listening SLOs: "I couldn't do all the goals;" "the stated goals may be too ambitious."

Both groups also felt that little class time was spent on listening activities per se. One student in FG1 said that he "didn't do much listening" and that there should be "more room for listening exercises and practice." Moreover, two FG1 students agreed that "writing from dictation is not so important." In general, there were indications of dissatisfaction with listening outcomes achievement, and a view that the listening SLOs were overly ambitious.

Speaking outcomes

Students in both focus groups described speaking as very important, the most important skill, in fact, among all the SLO skills. FG1 students found the speaking outcomes to be sufficiently clear. Moreover, FG1 students expressed general satisfaction with their speaking outcomes: "Speaking is ok. I can do simple sentences and respond." Furthermore, though speaking was considered "difficult," "speaking with the professor is easy."

Three students in FG2 pointed out that some of the terminology used for the speaking SLOs was vague or unclear (e.g., "familiar topics" and "sympathetic user"). In addition, when asked to comment on achievement—particularly the ability to "describe briefly places, actions, and situations…"—one FG2 student noted that the vocabulary learned during the course "wasn't particularly useful—no colors, clothing, food, practical stuff."

Writing outcomes

There were few comments from FG1 and FG2 students addressing writing SLOs. There were no indications of problems with comprehension of SLOs. Moreover, FG1 and FG2 students felt their achievement of the writing outcomes (as well as the reading outcomes) was the strongest of all their performances. Comments also suggested that most students considered writing less important than speaking and listening, and tended to diminish its value.

Reading outcomes

Clarity of the reading outcomes was an issue for FG1. Two FG1 students commented on the ability to "identify letters in signs written in different calligraphy styles." One did not understand the meaning of "calligraphy styles." The other pointed out that "different scripts are difficult in early Arabic, because we just learned the letters." No comments were made in FG2 about the reading SLOs, implying general agreement about clarity.

In FG1, students agreed that reading was their strongest outcome (together with writing). One FG1 student commented on the characteristics of the Arabic alphabet compared to his/her first language alphabet: "long vowels are difficult; it took a long time to understand their importance in words."

Summary of focus group findings

Focus group data provided useful insights into which outcomes seemed to be addressed, and unaddressed, in the Arabic courses at the time. A number of additional enlightening observations were also made regarding students' educational needs. First, the committee observed that the instructional emphasis in first-year courses was on reading and writing, and less so on listening. There was also insufficient focus on culture. Furthermore, attitudes towards the SLOs were mixed and at times contradictory: "I think some of these may be ambitious but it's good to set high goals because it's the foundation of Arabic learning, especially for majors;" and "it's important to be realistic about outcomes so that students don't feel cheated by outcomes/expectations; it takes more time than people initially realize."

Another issue that arose was the differences in student interests, backgrounds, and needs, which impacted opinions about learning outcomes. The new SLOs were written to encompass broad domains of Arabic language performance; they were not tailored to specific purposes. Since students expressed different learning preferences and needs, different SLOs were valued accordingly. For example, reading SLOs were most important for those who studied Arabic for academic purposes. By contrast, those intending to live in Arab countries prioritized speaking and listening outcomes. Some students were interested in contemporary issues of the Arab-speaking world—for them, reading and listening were the main goals. In general, however, almost all participants ranked speaking and listening as the most important outcomes among all SLOs.

The committee also noted two additionally salient issues arising in both focus groups. The first had to do with grammar instruction. Students viewed grammatical competency as an important component of Arabic language instruction, especially students in FG1 who thought an additional outcome statement was needed, dedicated exclusively to grammar learning. Second, students wanted SLOs to be available prior to registration. A suggestion was to post SLOs somewhere visible so that students would be informed about learning expectations prior to enrollment to help them understand what they would get out of taking particular courses.

Anonymous web-based survey

The second tool used to ascertain student perceptions of SLOs was an anonymous web-based questionnaire administered to three sections of MEAR 10002 toward the end of the 2011 spring semester. The total number of students who received the questionnaire was 36, with a very high response rate varying between 92% and 94% for particular questions. In order to elicit full and honest responses, the committee designed an anonymous web-based survey. The survey was administered during class by a facilitator from outside the Arabic program. The questionnaire results were analyzed by the entire committee, whose members reviewed all data and commented on their implications. One member of the committee was in charge of recording the analysis of the data.

The questionnaire was designed to evaluate the learning outcomes for MEAR 10002. Again, the survey was administered toward the end of the 2011 spring semester. Since students were very close to completing the course, they were able to report on a large proportion of their MEAR 10002 language learning experiences. The questionnaire consisted of 13 items. The first item solicited respondent consent. The next group of items asked students to respond to each learning outcome in two ways. First, students were asked to rate their ability to perform a given outcome at five levels of achievement: *not at all, somewhat, adequately, good,* or *very well* (see Appendix B for the survey). For example, in Speaking Proficiency, students were asked "To what extent are you able to articulate minimum courtesy norms and maintain simple face-to face conversations on familiar topics related to daily life with a clear pronunciation understandable by a sympathetic listener?" Second, respondents were prompted to explain their ratings to allow the Arabic faculty a better understanding of student learning. For each group of items, they were asked the following question: "If you have any explanation that will allow Arabic faculty to understand your ratings above, please explain below (e.g., Why do you think you were able/not able to achieve the outcomes?)."

Respondents were additionally asked if the scope of learning encompassed in the SLOs covered the range of learning students experienced during the second-semester Arabic course. The final item asked if there were any additional skills, domains of knowledge, or perspectives respondents felt they had gained from the course but were missing from the outcomes listed in the survey.

Anonymous web-based survey results

Thirty-six students were administered the questionnaire in the three sections of MEAR 10002. Thirty-two students completed the survey from start to finish, and two others completed most questions. Tables 1–5 show questionnaire results for self-rated proficiency of MEAR 10002 speaking, listening, writing, reading, and inter-cultural competence outcomes. Descriptive statistics were calculated for each SLO (mean ratings and standard deviations, each rating assigned a numerical value as follows: *not at all*=1, *somewhat*=2, *adequately* =3, *good*=4, *very well* =5). Values in **bold** indicate the maximum number and greatest proportion of ratings for a given SLO (i.e., the self-rating that the most respondents selected).

Table 1. Student self-rated performance of student learning outcomes: Speaking

To what extent are you able to…	N	M	SD	not at all	somewhat	adequately	good	very well
articulate minimum courtesy norms and maintain simple face-to face conversations on familiar topics related to daily life with a clear pronunciation understandable by a sympathetic listener?	34	3.4	0.6	1 (2.9%)	6 (17.6%)	9 (26.5%)	**14 (41.2%)**	4 (11.8%)
formulate and respond to longer questions with some justifications and background information?	33	3.2	0.6	1 (3.0%)	5 (15.2%)	**16 (48.5%)**	9 (27.3%)	2 (6.1%)
introduce elaborately oneself and others?	34	4.0	0.8	1 (2.9%)	3 (8.8%)	4 (11.8%)	**14 (41.2%)**	12 (35.3%)
describe briefly places, actions, and situations?	34	3.7	0.7	0 (0.0%)	2 (5.9%)	12 (35.3%)	**15 (44.1%)**	5 (14.7%)

Table 2. Student self-rated performance of student learning outcomes: Writing

To what extent are you able to…	N	M	SD	not at all	somewhat	adequately	good	very well
summarize, describe and analyze situations related to personal experiences with sufficient details?	34	3.3	0.8	0 (0.0%)	8 (23.5%)	8 (23.5%)	**17 (50.0%)**	1 (2.9%)
write social correspondences of an appropriate length (e.g., personal letters, invitations, and emails)?	34	3.1	0.6	2 (5.9%)	8 (23.5%)	9 (26.5%)	**14 (41.2%)**	1 (2.9%)
write short narratives and essays on familiar topics related to daily life using appropriate connectors and quantifiers?	34	3.4	0.5	0 (0.0%)	6 (17.6%)	**14 (41.2%)**	9 (26.5%)	5 (14.7%)
write with a good command of present tense verbs as well as gender, number and definiteness agreement, and basic command of past tense verbs?	34	3.8	0.6	0 (0.0%)	3 (8.8%)	10 (29.4%)	**12 (35.3%)**	9 (20.5%)

Table 3. Student self-rated performance of student learning outcomes: Reading

To what extent are you able to…	N	M	SD	not at all	somewhat	adequately	good	very well
read and understand headlines and short simple articles from Arabic media?	33	3.1	0.4	2 (6.1%)	9 (27.3%)	9 (27.3%)	9 (27.3%)	4 (12.1%)
understand the main ideas of simple verse and prose?	33	3.2	0.5	2 (6.1%)	7 (21.2%)	9 (27.3%)	12 (36.4%)	3 (9.1%)
demonstrate basic control using a dictionary?	32	3.7	0.6	0 (0.0%)	3 (9.4%)	10 (31.3%)	13 (40.6%)	6 (18.8%)

Table 4. Student self-rated performance of student learning outcomes: Listening

To what extent are you able to…	N	M	SD	not at all	somewhat	adequately	good	very well
understand some spoken Arabic when presented at a slow pace?	33	3.8	0.7	0 (0.0%)	3 (9.1%)	8 (24.2%)	15 (45.5%)	7 (21.2%)
understand and report the main ideas from simple Arabic news broadcast?	32	2.7	0.4	3 (9.4%)	12 (37.5%)	9 (28.1%)	7 (21.9%)	1 (3.1%)

As indicated in tables 1–5, few students felt they were "not at all" able to perform the new SLOs by the end of the second semester course. For most outcomes, only one or two students indicated a "not at all" rating, representing a low percentage of the total number of students. The exception, however, was for listening outcome ratings (table 4). Roughly 10% of students felt they were "not at all" able to perform listening outcome 2 ("understand and report the main ideas from a simple Arabic news broadcast"). Moreover, a large proportion of respondents (37.5%) indicated they were only "somewhat" able to perform this outcome. Roughly 50% of students, then, rated themselves as less than adequately able to perform this outcome as a result of instruction in MEAR 10002.

When students were asked if the scope of learning encompassed in the SLOs covered the range of language learning experienced during second semester Arabic courses, 97% of the students answered *yes* and 3% answered *no*. Finally, when respondents were asked if any skills, knowledge, and perspectives they gained from the course were missing from the outcomes listed in the questionnaire, two students mentioned their "ability to start recognizing differences between Arabic dialects," and one student noted the ability to "handle … past and future verbs."

Table 5. Student self-rated performance of student learning outcomes: Inter-cultural competence

To what extent are you…	N	M	SD	not at all	somewhat	adequately	good	very well
able to demonstrate understanding of Arab culture through comparison with students' own culture?	33	3.6	0.6	0 (0.0%)	8 (24.2%)	5 (15.2%)	**13 (39.4%)**	7 (21.2%)
familiar with some Arab language varieties, educational systems and religious institutions?	32	3.3	0.4	2 (6.3%)	7 (21.9%)	8 (25.0%)	**9 (28.1%)**	6 (18.8%)
able to locate and organize information about the Arab culture from the library, media and native people?	33	3.1	0.5	1 (3.0%)	9 (27.3%)	10 (30.3%)	**11 (33.3%)**	2 (6.1%)
able to appreciate Arabic popular culture, especially films and songs?	33	3.9	0.7	0 (0.0%)	3 (9.1%)	7 (21.1%)	**13 (39.4%)**	10 (30.3%)

Summary of anonymous web-based survey findings

The main finding gleaned from the questionnaire data was that respondents felt most SLOs had been attained sufficiently—if not at the highest level ("very well"), at least at "good" or "adequate" levels. Such a finding corresponds to FG2 focus group data indicating a general feeling that most outcomes had been met to some degree. On the other hand, a large proportion of students felt they had not achieved the new listening outcomes in MEAR 10002. Again, this finding also corresponds with focus group data in that listening outcomes were considered the most "unreachable." Finally, the committee was encouraged to see that most students felt the scope of learning encompassed in the new outcomes was also covered in the second semester Arabic course.

Using assessment: Insights and decision-making

Findings from the focus groups and online questionnaire were shared by the committee and discussed among all the Arabic faculty members. A key insight coming out of faculty discussions was the need for more cultural learning in first-year language classes. A number of steps were taken to redress this deficiency. First, the program adopted the newest version of *Al-Kitaab fii Taʿallum al-ʿArabiyya—A textbook for beginning Arabic* (Brustad, Al-Batal, & Tūnisī, 2011). The third and latest edition includes a broader spectrum of cultural knowledge and effectively integrates colloquial and formal written Arabic materials. Second, all instructors of first-year Arabic met and formulated a plan to increase cultural competency learning in their courses. Proposed course modifications included incorporating new audio, video, and print cultural materials into course content, as well as creating more cultural assignments and activities inside and outside the classroom.

A second insight to promote cultural learning was the decision to offer colloquial classes. Since the only native instructor in the program was of Lebanese descent, the department approved a proposal to offer for the first time a Lebanese colloquial course focusing exclusively on Levantine dialect speaking and listening. The course was offered in the Spring of 2012 to students who had completed first-year Arabic. The course provides a solid cultural and sociological background on the Levant, which helps interested students better understand and appreciate intercultural differences, as well as harness their speaking and conversational skills in at least one version of colloquial Arabic.

Finally, an important insight gained from the project was a critical shortage of the most important resource needed to ensure high-quality language learning: time. To address this issue, the committee put a recommendation to the Classics Department chair to increase the contact hours in first year Arabic language courses from 4 to 5 hours per week, and from 3 to 4 hours per week in the second year Arabic courses, trusting that the additional hour per week would give students a jumpstart on their language proficiency We believed that the extra contact hour would allow us to do more activities inside the classroom, mainly listening and speaking activities, hoping to improve in this way the low marks obtained for listening in the survey.

Next steps: Second-year SLOs, assessment of first-year SLOs

We have described the initial steps of an assessment project carried out in the PALC that involved developing—and seeking student feedback on—SLOs for first-year Arabic courses. These assessment efforts transpired up to the spring of 2012. In fall of 2012, based on perceived successes of our initial efforts, the committee began another assessment project, this time designing SLOS for second-year Arabic courses, a project the committee intends to finish at the end of this semester. Using current MEAR 10002 syllabi and MEAR 10001 Arabic SLOS as a starting point, the committee plans to develop second-year outcomes expectations as a continuation of the SLOS from first-year Arabic.

During the fall semester of 2012, the committee also began efforts to assess more directly one MEAR 10001 writing SLO: "writ[ing] notes and short essays about oneself on a familiar topic related to daily life." Students write several essays during the semester covering different personal topics such as their families and friends. The committee intends to collect a random sample of essays (roughly 30% of students) produced towards the end of the semester, and to develop and use a scoring rubric to ascertain outcome achievement. The rubric articulates four levels of performance: *not satisfactory*, *satisfactory*, *competent*, and *exemplary*. The committee will also assess one speaking SLO more directly, the ability "to talk about oneself, one's education, and family," again using a rubric to evaluate proficiency. Evidence of outcomes learning will be sought from a randomly selected sample of recorded student oral presentations at the end of the semester.

The committee also plans to administer another anonymous web-based survey at the end of the 2012 fall semester, this time to all students completing MEAR 10001. The questionnaire will be similar to the one administered to second semester Arabic students (at the end of the spring semester 2011), only it will address SLOs for MEAR 10001.

Finally, another major challenge to undertake in the near future is to further reflect on and develop our pedagogical practices to maintain and improve the academic excellence of our program. Members of the committee are already working on devising relevant assignments and assessment tools, such as rubrics, checklists, papers, projects, portfolios, interviews, tests, and ACTFL Oral Proficiency Interviews, all to be implemented in the fall of 2012 and the spring of 2013.

Conclusion

"As commonly used today, the term assessment can refer to two different activities: (a) the mere gathering of information (measurement) and (b) the use of that information for institutional and individual improvement (evaluation)" (Astin & Antonio, 2012, p. 3). The term "assessment" often connotes quantitative measures of student performance or representations of what students know at a specific point of time. This is not how the Arabic faculty at UND view assessment. Rather, the PALC has aimed to use assessment in the way Astin and Antonio describe: to better understand and improve Arabic curricula and teaching, and the effectiveness of what the Arabic program does as a whole. Put another way, the PALC uses assessment to ask important questions about the delivery of undergraduate Arabic language education at UND (see Norris, Davis, Sinicrope, & Watanabe, 2009). What are we teaching in the Arabic language courses? How well are we teaching? What changes will make our teaching more effective?

"Learning is a continuous process, not a product. However, because this process takes place in the mind, we can only infer that it has occurred from students' products or performances" (Ambrose, Bridges, DiPietro, Lovett, & Norman, 2010, p. 3). Assessment in the PALC is intended to be a living document referenced frequently and updated as necessary to guide the program's progress. Thus, an important goal for the PALC is to develop a sustainable infrastructure for ongoing evaluation and assessment procedures. As already mentioned, in the fall of 2012, the committee resumed their assessment work and started the process of drafting learning outcomes for second-year Arabic.

Rather than defining assessment as "testing" or the gathering of quantitative data on students learning at each stage of their learning journey, we now understand assessment as a continuous process of evaluation and improvement through systematic gathering of information (Norris, 2006). Therefore, the PALC is resolved to revisit course SLOs on an annual basis and to evaluate their continued relevancy. Surveys will also be conducted every year to benchmark and assess progress toward the stated objectives.

We would like to think that the beginning of the assessment journey for the Arabic program at Notre Dame has been successful thus far. Perhaps the most important factor that has shaped this initial success is the unified sense of direction of all members on the assessment committee who worked together closely with other faculty. Furthermore, while partnerships between faculty and administrators were crucial to achieving program reform and development goals, we believe that the future inclusion of our students in the committee will directly and positively result in more improvements in our curriculum and in our assessment work. The committee is thus planning to invite students to assist with drafting the second-year SLOs. We truly believe that our students are ready to take on this initiative, for they have a genuine interest in this type of work and are always eager to contribute to the advancement of our Arabic program.

References

Ambrose, S. A., Bridges, M. W., DiPietro, M., Lovett, M. C., & Norman, M. K. (2010). *How learning works: Seven research-based principles for smart teaching.* San Francisco, CA: Jossey Bass.

Astin, A. W., & Antonio, A. L. (2012). *Assessment for excellence: The philosophy and practice of assessment and evaluation in higher education* (2nd ed.). Lanham, MD: Rowman & Littlefield Publishers.

Brustad, K., Al-Batal, M., & Tūnisī, A. (2011). *Al-Kitaab fii Taʿallum al-ʿArabiyya: A textbook for beginning Arabic* (3rd ed.). Washington, DC: Georgetown University Press.

Krueger, R. A., & Casey M. A. (2008). *Focus groups: A practical guide for applied researchers* (4th ed.). Thousand Oaks, CA: Sage Editions.

Norris, J. M. (2006). The why (and how) of student learning outcomes assessment in college FL education. *Modern Language Journal, 90*(4), 576–583.

Norris, J. M., Davis, J. McE., Sinicrope, C., & Watanabe, Y. (2009). *Towards useful program evaluation in college foreign language education.* Honolulu: University of Hawaiʻi, National Foreign Language Resource Center.

Onwuegbuzie, A. J., Dickinson, W. B., Leech, N. L., & Zoran, A. G. (2009). Toward more rigor in focus group research: A new framework for collecting and analyzing focus group data. *International Journal of Qualitative Methods, 8*(3), 1–21.

Walsh, A., & Webb, M. (2009). *A guide to writing learning outcomes.* London, England: Academic Development Center, Kingston University. Retrieved from http://cdn.kingston.ac.uk/documents/services-for-business/staff-development/masters-awards-by-learning-agreement/documents/writing-learning-outcomes.pdf.

Appendix A. Student Learning Outcomes for MEAR 10001 and MEAR 10002

MEAR 10001 Learning Outcomes

At the conclusion of the first year Arabic I course, students will have proficiency in the following areas:

Speaking proficiency
1. Be able to distinguish and pronounce all phonemes of the Arabic sound system
2. Formulate and respond to simple questions
3. Initiate social interactions, exchange greetings, and ask for directions with understandable pronunciation
4. Talk about oneself, one's education, and family

Writing proficiency
1. Write scripts legibly
2. Write notes and short essays about oneself on a familiar topic related to daily life (e.g., family, friends, classes, weather, and state of being)

Reading proficiency
1. Identify letters in signs written in different calligraphy styles
2. Read simple authentic Arabic texts on topics related to daily life and comprehend the main idea

Listening proficiency
1. Write from dictation with some errors
2. Comprehend simple conversations and simple audio/video materials on familiar topics related to daily life (e.g., family, friends, classes, weather, and state of being)

Inter-cultural competency
1. Be familiar with some of the differences between formal and spoken Arabic
2. Identify and relate to some similar and dissimilar culture-specific practices of the various Arab societies and religious communities (e.g., holiday traditions, greetings, mealtime etiquette, dating conventions of young people)
3. Be able to describe an attitude important for making one acceptable in some Arab societies

MEAR 10002 Learning Outcomes

At the conclusion of the first year Arabic II course, students will build upon those skills outlined and described in first year Arabic I and will have additionally developed proficiency in the following areas:

Speaking proficiency
1. Articulate minimum courtesy norms and maintain simple face-to-face conversations on familiar topics related to daily life with a clear pronunciation understandable by a sympathetic listener
2. Formulate and respond to longer questions with some justifications and background information
3. Introduce elaborately oneself and others
4. Describe briefly places, actions, and situations

Writing proficiency
1. Summarize, describe and analyze situations related to personal experiences with sufficient details
2. Write social correspondences of an appropriate length (e.g., personal letters, invitations, and emails)
3. Write short narratives and essays on familiar topics related to daily life using appropriate connectors and quantifiers
4. Write with a good command of present tense verbs as well as gender, number and definiteness agreement, and basic command of past tense verbs

Reading proficiency
1. Read and understand headlines and short simple articles from Arabic media
2. Understand the main ideas of simple verse and prose
3. Demonstrate basic control using a dictionary

Listening proficiency
1. Understand some spoken Arabic when presented at a slow pace
2. Understand and report the main ideas from simple Arabic news broadcast

Inter-cultural competency
1. Be able to demonstrate understanding of Arab culture through comparison with students' own culture
2. Become familiar with some Arab language varieties, educational systems and religious institutions
3. Be able to locate and organize information about the Arab culture from the library, media and native people
4. Be able to appreciate Arabic popular culture, especially films and songs

Appendix B. Questionnaire

1. Survey consent

Your responses will be confidential and we do not collect identifying information such as your name, email address or IP address. All data is stored in a password protected electronic format. To help protect your confidentiality; the survey will not contain information that will personally identify you. The results of this study will be used for improving departmental effectiveness and for scholarly purposes only.

If you have any questions about the assessment project or survey, please contact Center for the Study of Languages and Cultures (CSLC) Assistant Director for Assessment & Testing, Stew Markel: smarkel@nd.edu.

ELECTRONIC CONSENT: Please select your choice below.

- Clicking on the "agree" button below indicates that:
- You have read the above information
- You voluntarily agree to participate
- You are at least 18 years of age.
- If you do not wish to participate in this survey for the Classics Department, please decline participation by clicking on the "disagree" button.
- Agree
- Disagree

2. To what extent are you able to perform the following outcomes?

	not at all	somewhat	adequately	good	very well
articulate minimum courtesy norms and maintain simple face-to face conversations on familiar topics related to daily life with a clear pronunciation understandable by a sympathetic listener?					
formulate and respond to longer questions with some justifications and background information?					
introduce elaborately oneself and others?					
describe briefly places, actions, and situations?					

3. If you have any explanation that will allow Arabic faculty to understand your ratings above, please explain below (e.g., Why do you think you were able/not able to achieve the outcomes?).

4. To what extent are you able to perform the following outcomes?

To what extent are you able to...	not at all	somewhat	adequately	good	very well
summarize, describe and analyze situations related to personal experiences with sufficient details?					
write social correspondences of an appropriate length (e.g., personal letters, invitations, and emails)?					
write short narratives and essays on familiar topics related to daily life using appropriate connectors and quantifiers?					
write with a good command of present tense verbs as well as gender, number and definiteness agreement, and basic command of past tense verbs?					

5. If you have any explanation that will allow Arabic faculty to understand your ratings above, please explain below (e.g., Why do you think you were able/not able to achieve the outcomes?).

6. To what extent are you able to perform the following outcomes?

To what extent are you able to...	not at all	somewhat	adequately	good	very well
read and understand headlines and short simple articles from Arabic media?					
understand the main ideas of simple verse and prose?					
demonstrate basic control using a dictionary?					

7. If you have any explanation that will allow Arabic faculty to understand your ratings above, please explain below (e.g., Why do you think you were able/not able to achieve the outcomes?).

8. To what extent are you able to perform the following outcomes?

To what extent are you able to…	not at all	somewhat	adequately	good	very well
understand some spoken Arabic when presented at a slow pace?					
understand and report the main ideas from simple Arabic news broadcast?					

9. If you have any explanation that will allow Arabic faculty to understand your ratings above, please explain below (e.g., Why do you think you were able/not able to achieve the outcomes?).

10. To what extent are you able to perform the following outcomes?

To what extent are you able to…	not at all	somewhat	adequately	good	very well
be able to demonstrate understanding of Arab culture through comparison with students' own culture?					
become familiar with some Arab language varieties, educational systems and religious institutions?					
be able to locate and organize information about the Arab culture from the library, media and native people?					
be able to appreciate Arabic popular culture, especially films and songs?					

11. If you have any explanation that will allow Arabic faculty to understand your ratings above, please explain below (e.g., Why do you think you were able/not able to achieve the outcomes?).

12. Do you think that the scope of learning outcomes listed below covers the variety of learning targets you learned through 2nd semester Arabic courses?

    Yes

    No

13. Are there any skills, knowledge, and perspectives you gained from these courses but are missing from the outcomes listed below? Please list them.

Assessing the Intermediate Level: A Critical Juncture in German Outcomes Assessment

Hannelore Weber
University of Notre Dame

In the spring of 2010, the German faculty at the University of Notre Dame embarked on an outcomes-focused assessment project. After preliminary discussions about the usefulness of assessing the four-year degree program in German, faculty members decided instead to concentrate on assessing the effectiveness and quality of the intermediate sequence of courses, considered a critical juncture prior to more advanced German study. In pursuit of this assessment project, the German section created student learning outcome statements for the major program, revised student learning outcome statements for the beginning and intermediate-level courses, conducted a focus group, undertook proficiency testing, and created and administered a student survey. After examining all the results gained by the use of these various instruments and procedures, the faculty identified critical aspects of the intermediate courses in need of review and planned to implement some changes to the intermediate courses. For the next step in the ongoing assessment process, and building on the experience gained from this initial project, the German section is now prepared to undertake the more comprehensive task of assessing the effectiveness of the German degree program as a whole.

Introduction and background

The University of Notre Dame is an independent national Catholic research university located near South Bend, Indiana. It is comprised of five colleges and a professional school and has approximately 8,000 undergraduates and 3,000 graduate students. The study of German has a long and rich tradition at Notre

Dame and is housed in the Department of German and Russian Languages and Literatures. Students can attain a major, secondary major, or minor in German. With nine faculty members in the German section, the department is able to offer a full range of German courses. Study abroad, formerly in Austria and now in Germany, is a firmly established tradition, which reaches back to 1964 and is considered integral to the program of studies for German students. Students with a second major in another field tend to be in associated disciplines in the humanities, but also come from business and the sciences. The Department has recently added the opportunity for a cross-disciplinary major in economics and German, the International Economics Major.

The decision by the German faculty at Notre Dame to undertake a utilization-focused outcomes assessment project was influenced by a number of factors. In 2007, 2008, and 2009, several German faculty members had attended presentations on assessment by various experts and were intrigued by the idea of assessing the effectiveness of our program of studies in German. At the same time, the director of Notre Dame's Center for the Study of Languages and Cultures (CSLC) decided that the CSLC would coordinate a longitudinal impact and research study on assessment in several foreign language departments at Notre Dame. All assessment projects were to be conducted with the expert assistance of Professor John Norris, of the University of Hawai'i at Mānoa (at the time), and Yukiko Watanabe, research associate at National Foreign Language Resource Center, University of Hawai'i at Mānoa. The chair of the Department of German and Russian proposed to the German faculty that the section undertake such an assessment project. Faculty agreed that the department would gain valuable information and insights on the effectiveness of the German curriculum and instruction, which could inform meaningful change. In addition, the project would serve the section well in the upcoming departmental review and reaccreditation process. Another factor in the decision was the pressure of the U.S. economic downturn (since 2008) and its impact on decreasing enrollments in the College of Arts and Letters. Added to this was the closing of the 46-year-old study abroad program in Innsbruck, Austria, and the subsequent commitment to The Berlin Consortium of German Studies program in Berlin, Germany. All of these factors spoke to the potential value of assessing our program in a new and meaningful way.

Assessment project

The German faculty—which at that time consisted of the department chair, four tenured faculty members, two assistant professors, and two associate teaching professors—agreed to take on the assessment project. The assessment initiative had the support of the Dean of the College of Arts Letters as well as the Provost's office, but the role of our chairperson as internal initiator of the project and consistent strong supporter of our efforts was crucial. It was important to show faculty that the project was not merely another bureaucratic assessment exercise but that it would instead provide the impetus for meaningful change in our program. The broad underlying and initial motivation, then, was a desire to provide the highest quality German education for our students.

Project planning

Putting a project leader in place was an important next step. The individual needed a strong interest and a background in assessment as well as genuine enthusiasm for the project. Committed leadership was needed since the process would be time consuming and would require sustained engagement over a period of perhaps two years. The role of the project leader would include proposing a design for the project, organizing, facilitating, and recording meetings with the faculty, and acting as a liaison with the project experts from the University of Hawai'i as well as the director of the CSLC who would coordinate the various projects on campus.

Another important factor for the success of the project was the emphasis on participation by all faculty members at all levels of instruction. Here again, our chair's role was crucial. He had the task of convincing the faculty that the success of the project would be worth our time, engagement, and work. Moreover, he had to reassure us that the project would tie in directly to accreditation and there would be no duplication of efforts. He also had to convince faculty that this project would result in meaningful information that could be used to implement change. It was thus important for all faculty members to feel they had a stake in this project and that their input would be valued.

After establishing the needed personnel for project success and with all members of the German faculty participating in the endeavor, departmental assessment work proceeded over a subsequent two-year period, during which time the project leader and the department chair kept in contact with John Norris and Yukiko Watanabe, who advised from afar and came to Notre Dame for a number of site visits. The project leader also availed herself of the experts and resources at the CSLC, where she was a member of a college-wide assessment committee and participated in some round-table discussions on assessment. Numerous useful resources were also made available on our Concourse website, such as a collection of relevant articles on assessment, and, after the German faculty had chosen the focus of the project, readings tailored to our specific assessment focus were added. One temporary complication during this time was the chairperson's leave of absence during the spring 2010 semester, but there was consistent communication as the project leader kept him apprised of our proceedings and progress by recording our meetings and sending him the digitized versions. He in turn provided feedback and support.

Focusing our assessment efforts

A key aspect of the project crucial to its success was choosing a feasible project which could be completed over a period of several semesters. Determining the scope of the project was the first decision, and we pondered several questions, such as "What should be assessed, the degree program, the beginning or intermediate level of courses, or a particular modality?" Whatever we chose for our focus, the specific assessment process to be implemented involved articulating student learning outcomes, choosing tools to gauge student achievement and proficiency, and using information on student learning to better understand and improve educational delivery—in keeping with clear accreditation and program review demands.

In our initial discussions, we considered assessing student learning across the entire degree program. We would ask whether graduating majors, supplementary majors, and minors had attained the learning outcomes we had set out for them and whether they had reached their own learning goals. In our discussions, though, we kept coming back to the 20000 course level, our intermediate sequence. The standard language requirement for the College of Arts and Letters is three courses. Our Intermediate German I (GE 20201) course is typically the last course of the requirement (unless an incoming student has placed into a higher course). This is the critical juncture at which many students decide if they are going to continue their study of German and move on to more advanced study. Thus, this intermediate course plays a crucial role in our curriculum. We asked ourselves a number of questions. Is this course stimulating and appealing enough to retain students and have them continue to take German courses, and perhaps commit to a major or minor in the language? Does the course respond to the linguistic and cultural needs and goals of the students? Is there consistency across the multiple sections of the course? Further, since we had just adopted a new textbook from Germany for Intermediate German I, we wondered if the "leap" from the beginning courses was too great. Did we need to adjust tasks and expectations?

We also asked ourselves many of the same questions about Intermediate German II (GE20202), a "language through content course." For instance, we were concerned about consistency. Since the particular content for this course is chosen by each instructor, could we ensure that we had consistency across the various iterations of the course in regard to course design and to giving students the appropriate opportunities to attain the stated SLOs for the course? Several additional important questions surfaced. After taking these two intermediate courses, did students have the necessary skills, knowledge, and dispositions for 30000 level courses, which lead to a major, supplementary major, or minor? Were we "hurrying" students through the language sequence (the first four courses) with the result that they lacked certain skills necessary for the 30000 level courses? Did we need better guidelines for expected proficiency levels and how to help students attain them?

Another important question arose in regard to study abroad. Did students have the necessary skills, knowledge, and dispositions for our new study abroad program? In January of 2010, the university had closed its study-abroad program in Innsbruck, Austria, the oldest study abroad program in Notre Dame's history. The program had offered a great deal of flexibility in that our students were able to study in Innsbruck after taking a minimum of two semesters of Intensive Beginning German. Many students had participated as sophomores and had come back to campus excited about continuing their study of German. Now we were participating in a program in Germany designed primarily for juniors. Our challenge, then, was to sustain the students' interest, motivate them, and keep them engaged in German until they could go abroad as juniors. The new program in Berlin, run by the Berlin Consortium for German Studies (BCGS), required a minimum of four semesters of college German or the equivalent (now five semesters) and that students take a combination of program courses as well as directly enroll in courses at the Freie Universität. It was crucial for the students' success that they be adequately prepared for this program. (If students started their study of German here at Notre Dame as first-year students, they would be in their fifth semester when they took the placement test for the Berlin program. They must have demonstrated at least intermediate proficiency by that time.)

All of these questions served the important purpose of raising our awareness as a department and program about what our priorities were at that time, and they allowed for the considered reflection on where assessment efforts might contribute the most. We ultimately chose to focus our efforts on student learning in intermediate-level courses because it is such a crucial juncture for our German Language and Literature program as a whole and for the German major in particular. In addition, this target was deemed a manageable project as our first foray into outcomes assessment at the programmatic level.

Developing student learning outcomes

Our initial task in the assessment process was to formulate student learning outcomes (SLOs) for the degree program. These outcome statements would provide the larger framework for determining and understanding outcomes at the intermediate level. What knowledge, skills, and dispositions should our graduating seniors in German possess and be able to demonstrate? What do the students know, what are they able to do with the language, and what do they value as a result of their study of German? Taking into account guidelines on developing SLOs for graduating majors (provided by John Norris), as well as already established course goals from various courses at 30000 and 40000 levels, and several sample sets of program SLOs from other institutions, we formulated the outcome statements for graduating seniors in German.

During these discussions, we also decided to use the Common European Frame of Reference[1] (CEFR) for benchmarks. We found the extremely detailed descriptors for every proficiency level and modality very useful. Since the outset, when the CEFR was introduced, German educators in Europe have developed a variety of materials for the application of the CEFR (e.g., *Profile Deutsch*; Glaboniat, Müller, Rusch, Schmitz, & Wertenschlag, 2005). Currently, textbooks and materials published in German-speaking countries for the teaching of German as a foreign language are also based on the CEFR levels. Some of these textbooks and materials are used in middle schools, high schools, and universities in the US, as well. At Notre Dame, for our first intermediate course, we use such a textbook published by Langenscheidt and designated as B1+ on the CEFR (*Aspekte I Mittelstufe Deutsch;* Koithan, Schmitz, Sieber, Sonntag, & Ochmann, 2007). In addition, our students who study abroad in Berlin and at various language institutes in Germany during the summer are tested and placed according to these levels. For graduating seniors, the German faculty set a B2.2 level as a minimum expectation and C1 as a target goal (see Appendix A for the German Degree Program SLOs).

Having drafted a set of initial degree-level SLOs, we also discussed whether we would seek input or review from other stakeholders and decided to send the SLOs to our graduating seniors and ask for their feedback. Were the statements clear and understandable? Were the expectations expressed in the outcome statements reasonable and realistic? Should there be additional outcomes or should some be eliminated? We collected the student responses and used them as input in revising the SLOs once more.

Overall, the responses were very positive. The only common concern centered on the wording of the first Student Learning Outcome: "Graduating German majors and supplementary majors can discuss the reciprocal bonds that connect German culture to the world at large and identify some of the ways by which cultural transfer

---

[1] For more information on the CEFR, see http://www.coe.int/t/dg4/education/elp/elp-reg/Source/Key_reference/Overview_CEFRscales_EN.pdf

occurs." Some of the respondents found the term "German culture" not inclusive enough and "cultural transfer" somewhat confusing. We reviewed the program SLOs once more and made minor revisions including the use of the phrase "German speaking communities" throughout. The first program SLO now reads, "Graduating German majors and supplementary majors can discuss the reciprocal bonds that connect the cultures of German-speaking communities to the world at large and identify some of the ways in which cultures influence each other."

Fortunately, the faculty had previously established learning outcomes for the two beginning and two intermediate courses, so these formed the basis for our next task, formulating student learning outcomes for the intermediate courses. We again used John Norris' guidelines and reviewed sample SLOs from various foreign language departments. After revising the SLOs for the 10000-level beginning courses, we concentrated on the intermediate courses. Our student learning outcomes focused on the four skills as well as reflectivity and cultural literacy. At the end of the Intermediate German I course, we expect the students to have reached the B1.1 level (on the CEFR) with a goal of B1.2. For Intermediate German II students, the minimum was set at B1.2 with a goal of B2.

In the intermediate-level courses, students expand their skills and move from a focus on everyday life and personal information to more complex topics of personal interest, to understanding, for instance, short lectures and longer authentic texts. They discern attitudes and viewpoints and describe their own reactions and views in response to issues and events related to the target country. In speech and writing, students express hopes, ambitions, and opinions. (See Appendix B for the full set of Beginning and Intermediate level SLOs.)

We had sent our SLOs to John Norris for review and he gave us substantive feedback which stimulated additional discussions and revisions of the degree program and intermediate level SLOs. He pointed out, for instance, that several of the statements were quite general and that we had not stipulated a language for each statement. Based on this input, we focused on refining the SLOs, making them as concrete as possible. He also posed questions on the use of the program statements. If they were to be used to convey the value of a degree for prospective students, would those students understand them as we intended, for example. If the statements would be used to guide degree-level assessment, would it be possible to assess them in their present form?

Assessment tools and levels

After we had established student learning outcomes, our next challenge was to find appropriate and effective methods and instruments for assessing these outcomes and the effectiveness of the curriculum and instruction at the intermediate level. In general, we were seeking an objective, external measurement; because we had established our SLOs and set our benchmarks largely in accordance with the CEFR, we needed an assessment instrument which would yield results based on CEFR levels.

Since our project was focused on the intermediate level, we decided to assess the language proficiency of our students on that level rather than on a more advanced level. We chose to carry out the assessment at the end of the intermediate sequence, in order to gather evidence that the students were linguistically prepared for participation in study abroad programs and in our higher level content courses.

We also sought to discover if the students' proficiency levels matched the SLOs we had put in place. We did not assess student proficiency at the end of the first intermediate course because many of the students enrolled in the course simply to fulfill the language requirement. Therefore, we were concerned that they would have little interest in or motivation for participating in assessment.

Proficiency testing

A possible starting point that we consider was the battery of DIALANG tests.[2] DIALANG would be easy to access and administer since it is a computerized test and available online without cost. All skills except speaking could be assessed (writing is assessed but not directly in the form of student-produced texts), and crucially, the DIALANG assessments are all anchored to the CEFR levels, with resulting scores presented on each skill in terms of the student's corresponding proficiency level. Beyond DIALANG, to assess speaking ability, we looked into the STAMP test, the German Speaking Test from the Center for Applied Linguistics, and others. The cost factor for these commercially available tests, and the fact that one or more of our faculty members would have to go through training as a rater, posed difficulties for us. In addition, these tests were all based on the ACTFL proficiency scale. (That may not be as much of a deterrent in the future, since others in the profession are developing correlations for levels on the ACTFL and CEFR scales.) We also investigated the possibility of having our students tested at the Goethe Institut in Chicago or having one of our faculty members trained as a rater by the Goethe Institut. The cost of the tests, as well as travel costs for the students, was again a negative factor, although it might have been possible to have a representative of the Goethe Institut come to Notre Dame and administer the test. One additional possibility we considered was to have faculty members gain insights on oral proficiency rating by utilizing the authentic samples and rating commentary in the print publication and accompanying DVD, *Mündlich, Mündliche Produktion und Interaktion Deutsch* (Bolton, Glaboniat, Lorenz, & Perlmann-Balme, 2008). To date, we have not found a practical and cost-effective instrument for assessing oral proficiency, although we plan to investigate some of the resources a second time and to look into possible ways of funding such an endeavor.

Additional sources of information about intermediate-level student performance existed in the German section already. John Norris suggested we might find it useful to gather all the data we have so far on the results of the study abroad online placement test which our students take before they are accepted for participation in the BCGS Berlin program. By reviewing results and sample performances in the various sections of the test, we could perhaps identify areas of weakness and/or strength, which might then prompt some alterations in the intermediate courses. We also considered having students use self-assessment checklists as both a learning and an assessment tool. The University of Salzburg website, for example, offers such checklists as well as specific descriptors for each level of the CEFR.[3]

---

[2] For more information on DIALANG tests see http://www.lancs.ac.uk/researchenterprise/dialang/about

[3] For more information on self-assessment, see http://www.uni-salzburg.at/portal/page?_pageid=144,607927&_dad=portal&_schema=PORTAL and http://europass.cedefop.europa.eu/LanguageSelfAssessmentGrid/en

One additional quick check for general proficiency considered by the section was a C-test, which would be relevant since this is the type of test administered by Berlin's Freie Universität to determine if students are linguistically prepared to study at the university (see also Norris, 2006). Although the faculty decided not to make use of a C-test at this time, we did not rule it out for the future.

An additional source for information on student perception of linguistic proficiency could be the utilization of the university-wide student evaluations, which are conducted at the end of every semester. In the section on questions added by the instructor, we could formulate and include questions based on the student learning outcomes for the individual course. Results are available only to the instructor but could be collected anonymously and over a period of time.

As noted above, we had decided to test only the students at the end of the second intermediate course. Ultimately, for the initial round of data collection, and in order to get a rough sense of the CEFR-based proficiency outcomes of our students at the end of the second intermediate course, we decided to administer the cost-free DIALANG assessments. After making the decision to use DIALANG, the project leader and a faculty member piloted the tests on their own computers, and then we tested students in Intermediate German II at the end of the fall semester, 2010. There were some unexpected technological problems which could not be overcome in the time available, so ultimately, only five students took the test in three skills areas. Nevertheless, the results gave us some interesting feedback, so we continued testing students at the same level over the course of several semesters. Finally, as seen in Table 1, with a total of 21 students tested, we have seen an overall quite broad range of CEFR scores: Listening, A2 to C1; Writing, A1 to C1; Reading, A1 to B2; Grammar, A2 to C1; Vocabulary, A2 to B2. In each area, A2 and B1 were the most common scores by far. (As noted, some students did not complete all parts of the test.)

Table 1. DIALANG Scores – German, University of Notre Dame (collected 12/2010, 5/2011, 5/2013)

CEFR level	listening	writing	reading	grammar	vocabulary
C1	1	1	0	1	0
B2	2	0	3	0	1
B1	9	9	8	5	8
A2	9	9	8	10	7
A1	0	2	2	0	0

We will continue to test students in Intermediate German II, but we will also continue to explore the possibility of finding a somewhat cost effective test which will assess the productive skills. (Although, DIALANG to a certain extent assesses writing, it does not assess an actual piece of writing produced by the student.) At this point, we do not feel that the DIALANG results have yielded sufficient valid evidence as a basis for curricular changes. To supplement these results, we are also gathering other placement test results from students who have studied abroad in Berlin or at various language institutes in Germany over several summers.

Student survey

Although linguistic proficiency can be assessed by utilizing instruments such as DIALANG, evaluating other aspects of educational delivery at the intermediate level would require totally different methods, especially where the intent is to elicit formative feedback for improvement of teaching and learning. Within the broad issue of whether the intermediate courses were functioning as intended and needed, we had raised questions regarding student interest, student perception of needs and outcomes, pace and consistency in courses, preparation for the next level of study and study abroad, among others. In order to gather some of the desired information, we chose to create and administer a survey to various groups of students who would have participated in one or both intermediate courses. For assistance in creating and administering the survey, we turned to the CSLC's assessment expert. During the entire process, which was surprisingly complex, we relied once again on the expert advice of our external consultants, John Norris and Yukiko Watanabe.[4]

To initiate the process, a subgroup of the German faculty generated the first draft of our survey questions, which we then revised and sent to our consultants for review. We also used these questions as the basis for a focus group which met in December 2010. John Norris had provided advice and documents on focus groups, and we had also found information on using a focus group to generate survey questions (Nassar-McMillan & Borders, 2002).[5] The purpose of the focus group was to gather student input for the final formulation of the set of survey questions. The group would be composed of current intermediate-level students as well as a few students from the next level. A common recommendation for conducting focus groups is that an external facilitator run the sessions, rather than someone inside the department, so that the students feel totally free to express their opinions. However, due to scheduling conflicts, we relied instead on a senior German major (i.e., a fellow undergraduate student) who had had previous training in running focus groups, and a student note-taker. We also briefly considered making an audio recording of the group's discussion, but felt that this would inhibit the students.

Prior to the focus group meeting, our project leader met with the focus group facilitator, explained what we hoped to gain from the focus group, and gave him the list of draft survey questions. Immediately after the focus group session, the group leader and the assessment project leader met for debriefing to review what had emerged from the session. Later, we received a detailed report on the discussions from the student note-taker. In the end, the results were somewhat more general than we had hoped, but they did provide pertinent and useful information, which was incorporated into the next draft of the survey questions.

Three issues came up repeatedly in the focus group: grammar instruction, speaking opportunities, and the value of study abroad. Students noted that in the first intermediate course, there was a strong emphasis on grammar instruction, but not in the second course. They felt it was important to continue grammar instruction even into the upper level courses. The students also expressed a wish for more opportunities for speaking in their classes on all levels. Several had felt at a loss when they had gone abroad but were very pleased with the improvement in

---

[4] For more information on using surveys in language program evaluation, see http://www.nflrc.hawaii.edu/evaluation/R_survey.htm

[5] For more information on using focus groups in language program evaluation, see http://www.nflrc.hawaii.edu/evaluation/R_interview.htm

their speaking skills by the time they had returned to campus. They were looking for opportunities to keep up their skills. A number of students mentioned the importance of study abroad opportunities during the academic year and in the summer. Some saw it as a great motivator for continuing with the language and others saw it as a way to interest students in studying German. Several mentioned the importance of having a study abroad option for those on the intermediate level, not just for more advanced students.

Over the course of the next year, we produced multiple drafts of the survey questions. We focused on making the questions specific to students who would not have had a great deal of experience in our courses (i.e., the intermediate-level students) rather than to juniors, seniors, or majors. We also tried to limit the number of open-ended questions, which would take a long time to answer and perhaps dissuade students from responding. Even though as a faculty we might have been interested in gaining more general insights into our program, we needed to keep the focus of our survey on the critical issues we had raised in regard to the intermediate level.

The process for generating questions and creating the final version of the survey proved to be more complicated than we had anticipated. The faculty began with the gist of the questions and then revised and refined them so that they would be effective and yield valid results. Again, we received extremely helpful input from our external consultants at this stage, in particular their advice and suggestions on format, question type, wording of questions, and general fine tuning for precision. Using the draft of the survey questions which the German faculty had created as a starting point, the German section's project leader and the assessment expert from the CSLC reviewed and revised the survey again, and we felt that it was ready for initial use (the survey can be seen in its entirety in Appendix C).

Survey description

In addition to background questions on previous knowledge of German, current enrollment in a German course or the most recent course taken, intent to major and/or study abroad, the survey focused on eliciting information which would give us insights into some of the issues we had identified, including student interest, perception of needs and outcomes, course pace, and transition from one course to another. Using 4- or 5-point Likert rating scales, we asked students for the following information:

- To what extent were their intermediate courses interesting?
- How difficult or easy was the transition from one level to another, including from high school German courses to one of our intermediate courses?
- How was the pace of the intermediate course(s)?
- How challenging was it to acquire each of the language skills?
- How did the students view the amount of focus on each of the language skills in the intermediate course(s)?
- What was the student's perception of his/her current German language skills?

- Did the student acquire language learning strategies in the intermediate course(s)?
- Which in-or out-of-class activities and experiences effectively advanced the student's learning of German on the intermediate level?

We also asked about the effectiveness of our advertising of German-related events and whether students would like to see some changes in these events. In addition, in the form of open-ended questions, we asked students to offer comments on their experiences learning German on the intermediate level, to describe their most memorable experiences related to learning German at Notre Dame, and to make one recommendation for improving the intermediate-level program.

The decision was made to deliver the survey on Survey Monkey (a web-based survey development application) and have it hosted by the CSLC. The CSLC's assessment specialist would make the survey available online, administer it, and collect the results. This would enable privacy and anonymity for the students so that they could freely and frankly express their thoughts and reactions. The CSLC assessment specialist also assisted in final revisions of the survey questions.

For the purpose of ensuring clarity, the survey was pilot-tested on five CSLC students and an administrator. The only issues the students had with clarity were, interestingly enough, a few terms typically used by FL professionals. The project leader and the department chair also accessed and completed the survey. After a few minor changes were made, the CSLC assessment specialist created a protocol (i.e., a set of survey instructions), which was sent to the faculty members whose students would be asked to take the survey.

We considered it very important to try to have personalized communications with students prior to the survey, in the hopes of stimulating interest: The goal was to reach out to individual students or small groups and to avoid mass e-mails. Relevant faculty were personally contacted and requested to encourage their students to participate in the survey. Faculty then sent their own students the protocol and a forwarded e-mail from the department chair which briefly described why the department was doing the survey and why it was important for students to respond. By having the e-mail originate with the department chair, we hoped to convey the importance of the survey. Template e-mails had been made available to the department chair as well as the faculty members for this purpose.

In early February 2012, the survey was sent to students in Intermediate German II (GE 20202) and in the first 30000-level course, as well as to students who had taken the first intermediate course in the fall of 2011 but were not taking a German course in the spring of 2012. In addition, we sent the survey to a student who had taken the second intermediate course in the fall of 2011 but was currently studying abroad in Berlin. No graduate students were asked to take the survey because their level and type of participation in the courses might vary and their reasons for continuing to pursue the study of German would be quite different from those of the undergraduates. There were also a few additional students in the second intermediate course and at the next level who were not asked to take the survey, because they had not taken one or both of the intermediate courses at our institution.

Student response was somewhat slow, so the survey administrator sent reminder e-mails. Again, for students in our courses, the e-mail came through the individual course instructors. The reminders proved to be somewhat effective. On February 19, 2012, we had 24 responses out of a possible 45, and after a reminder, the final number of responses was 29, or 64%, which was considered relatively high in light of typical response rates for anonymous surveys. (Similarly, in a later survey in April, we had 29 out of a possible 54 responses and the final count was 38, or 70% response rate; see below.) After the first survey results were collected, a member of the German faculty urged the project leader to enlarge the pool of survey takers so as to increase the number of responses. However, one concern raised about this suggestion was related to the possibility that we would probably conduct an assessment of the degree program in the near future. In that event, we could risk "survey fatigue" on the part of the students and we might jeopardize the response rate of the future survey. The determination was made that even if we were to undertake a degree program assessment in the future, we would probably be surveying a different group of students at that point.

Despite our initial reservations, we decided to go ahead and administer a second survey near the end of the semester in April 2012. This group included all students who were currently taking Intermediate German I, study-abroad students in Berlin, students who had taken Intermediate German II in the spring of 2011 but were currently not in a German course, the remaining upper-level students who had not taken the survey in February, as well as all majors, secondary majors, and minors. The protocol and the survey questions were adjusted slightly to make them appropriate for this group and we applied insights gained through the previous survey to make additional modifications. Most of the students received the invitations to participate from the department chair and through the course instructor. Those students who were no longer in a German course received an individual personalized e-mail from the project leader. We ran into one problem which had a minimal impact: The original version of the survey was still online in April during the second administration and several students completed it, but this issue was soon resolved. All participants took this survey outside of class.

Survey results

The results of both surveys were analyzed, and reports in several different formats were sent to us, by the survey administrator as well as one of the external consultants. In addition to data on responses from all survey takers, we were able to generate data for certain sub-groups, such as students in 20000 (intermediate) level courses versus students in more advanced courses, and students currently enrolled versus students not currently enrolled. Faculty received the complete survey results as well as a summary of items which seemed to warrant closer scrutiny. All told, data from 65 students was included in the analysis, but of course, not all students answered every question. Descriptive statistics and frequencies of responses on the rating scale items are reported in tables 1–6 below. Highlights of the most important patterns are discussed in turn.

One item which merited considerable discussion (and a possible review of course content and of the calibration of the placement test), asked students to rate their ease of transition from (a) high school to the two intermediate courses, (b) from our second beginning course to the first intermediate course, and (c) from our first intermediate course to our second intermediate course. Respondents rated their ease of transition on a four-point scale: 1=*Very difficult*, 2=*Somewhat difficult*, 3=*Somewhat easy*, 4=*Very easy*. If we add up the responses *Somewhat easy* and *Very easy*, for all transitions except from high school to the second intermediate course, 60% to 64% of respondents categorized these transitions as *Somewhat easy/Very easy*. In contrast, if we add up the responses *Very difficult* and *Somewhat difficult* for the transition from high school to the second intermediate course, we see that 65% of the students described this transition as *Very difficult/Somewhat difficult* (see Table 2).

Table 2. How would you describe your transition from one level to another?

transition	N	M	SD	very difficult (1)	somewhat difficult (2)	somewhat easy (3)	very easy (4)
from high school German to GE20201/20211:	27	2.74	0.86	7%	30%	44%	19%
from high school German to GE20202/20212	20	2.25	0.79	15%	50%	30%	5%
from GE 10102/10112 to GE20201/20211	33	2.61	0.75	9%	27%	58%	6%
from GE 20201/20211 to GE 20202/20212	20	2.70	0.66	0%	40%	50%	10%

The German faculty has not discussed this particular item in depth, but two measures could easily be taken. Before a student who is coming directly from high school is placed into this course, we should look at the types and frequency of errors made on the placement test. If the preponderance of errors is in grammar, and the score is in the lower half of the numbers for GE 20202, then a discussion with the student might be useful. The students who place into GE 20202 should also perhaps provide a writing sample in addition to taking the placement test, since the writing of compositions is a significant component of this course.

In questions related to language skills, we also found some noteworthy patterns, especially in regard to speaking. When students were asked their perceptions of their current speaking skills, 58% of respondents replied *Poor/Fair* (see Table 3). Of the currently enrolled students, the number was 49%, and of students at the intermediate level, it was 70%.

Table 3. What is your perception of your current German language skills, cultural competence, and ability to use vocabulary and grammar?

speaking	N	M	SD	poor (1)	fair (2)	good (3)	very good (4)
all respondents	64	2.39	0.79	11%	47%	34%	8%
currently enrolled respondents	35	2.54	0.74	6%	43%	43%	9%
respondents at the intermediate level	33	2.15	0.76	18%	52%	27%	3%

Similar results were recorded in response to the question on how challenging it was for the student to learn "Speaking" in the intermediate courses: 66% of respondents described the challenge as *A moderate challenge/A great challenge* (see Table 4).

Table 4. How challenging was it for you to learn the following in your intermediate German courses?

speaking	N	M	SD	no challenge at all (1)	a small challenge (2)	a moderate challenge (3)	a great challenge (4)
all respondents	66	2.76	0.93	12%	21%	45%	21%

Through ensuing discussion among the faculty, it became clear that the student concerns expressed in the survey in regard to speaking skills mirrored anecdotal feedback we had received from individual students over the years, from students who studied abroad during the academic year or the summer, as well as from students in our individual classes. The concern was also reflected in results from the online language test taken prior to admittance to the BCGS study abroad program in Berlin. This concern about competency in speaking prompted further faculty discussions, and we are currently collecting information on the frequency and types of opportunities for oral expression students have in our intermediate classes. We will discuss these findings and formulate a plan to increase a variety of speaking opportunities for our students in the intermediate courses.

Students also indicated a concern in regard to listening skills. In response to the question on the students' perceptions of their listening skills, overall 44% rated their abilities as *Poor/Fair*, but for students at the 20000 level, 63% rated their abilities as *Poor/Fair* (see Table 5). This is an issue we will also be discussing in the near future. Preliminarily, one possibility has been raised. Since audio materials in the first intermediate course are authentic materials from a "Deutsch als Fremdsprache" book on the B1 level, the students may have felt that this was very challenging compared to the materials in their more typical beginning level textbook which is published in the US. This topic merits some closer attention.

Table 5. What is your perception of your current German language skills, cultural competence, and ability to use vocabulary and grammar?

listening	N	M	SD	poor (1)	fair (2)	good (3)	very good (4)
all respondents	64	2.63	0.93	13%	31%	38%	19%
respondents at the intermediate level	33	2.30	0.92	18%	45%	24%	12%

The third area of concern, but to a lesser extent, was the ability to use grammar. Fifty-three percent of respondents indicated that learning grammar in the intermediate courses was a *moderate/great challenge* (see Table 6). Forty-one percent also stated that in the second intermediate course, the focus on grammar was *Far too little/Too little* (see Table 7). This result was reinforced by the student discussions in the focus group and by some of the open-ended comments on the surveys. The general request was to have more formal grammar instruction continue in the courses beyond the first intermediate course. This, then, is another issue slated to be discussed by the German faculty in the fall.

Table 6. How challenging was it for you to learn the following in your intermediate German courses?

grammar	N	M	SD	no challenge at all (1)	a small challenge (2)	a moderate challenge (3)	a great challenge (4)
all respondents	65	2.65	0.99	12%	35%	28%	25%
respondents at the intermediate level	34	2.65	1.07	18%	26%	29 %	26%

Table 7. What is your opinion on the amount of focus for each component in the GE 20202/20212 course?

grammar	N	M	SD	far too little (–2)	too little (–1)	about right (0)	too much (1)	far too much (2)
all respondents	37	2.54	0.73	14%	27%	59%	0%	0%

Based on feedback from the focus group, we also included two questions on the survey in regard to the advertising and structure of German activities and events. The responses to one of these questions indicated to us that we should advertise some of our German-related opportunities, such as Peer Tutoring, *Kaffeestunde* (a social coffee hour), and *Stammtisch* (a dinner and discussion opportunity) more effectively. Currently, our primary means of promoting events involves a general German listserv, a German Facebook page, and asking faculty to announce events. With the input of our students, we hope to put in place additional effective means of advertising our events. A surprising piece of information that came from the second question was the desire on the part of almost half of the respondents to sometimes have more structured, rather than just informal, learning opportunities at *Kaffeestunde* and *Stammtisch*. We will have to discuss this idea with the students in more detail and consider some appealing solutions.

Not surprisingly, a desire for more speaking opportunities in and out of the classroom was expressed often in the open-ended questions. Study abroad and summer opportunities abroad were cited as extremely valuable experiences. Students also promoted the use of peer tutors as a very beneficial and perhaps underutilized resource. Several students suggested that more emphasis be put on pronunciation and vocabulary acquisition. They also underlined the benefits of German films, *Deutsche Welle*, Wimba Voice Board, and pen pals as language learning tools. In the section on memorable experiences, students spoke very positively about a variety of outside of class activities such as the singing of *Weihnachtslieder* at a *Kaffeestunde*, having dinner at a professor's home, attending a lecture by a well-known German political figure, as well as German Club events such as visits to the *Christkindlmarkt* and the Art Museum in Chicago. Others recalled as very useful their presentation of skits and conversations with partners in their beginning classes. It was gratifying to see that students appreciated the various opportunities offered to them.

Project benefits

As a faculty, we have found the results of our proficiency assessments, surveys, and focus group very informative. In addition to the concrete information which the surveys and focus group have produced for us, an unexpected benefit has been the stimulus that the project has provided for us to have substantive discussions on curricular issues. For instance, we examined our first intermediate course closely and after soliciting input from faculty about the oral expression component and the number and type of writing assignments in the various sections of the course, we created a common plan for the course in regard to those skills. We will create a similar plan for the second intermediate course, based on expected student outcomes, despite the fact that the content and materials in that course vary from instructor to instructor. We will also discuss the introduction of more formal grammar instruction in the second intermediate course. Our goal is to ensure that all students have the opportunity to attain the student learning outcomes, irrespective of the section or individual instructor, while still respecting the instructor's academic freedom.

These discussions have offered us a rich opportunity to share ideas on pedagogy, curriculum, and materials. As an additional benefit, the project has provided multiple opportunities for the sharing of ideas and perspectives with faculty in other language departments. In the area of skills assessment, it was particularly helpful to draw on the experience of colleagues at this university and at other institutions. We sought input, for instance, on the interpretation of the survey results as well as perspectives on oral proficiency interviews (OPIs), from colleagues in the Department of Romance Languages, since they had been working on a skills assessment project for several years already. We also had the opportunity to get a first-hand look at a STAMP test through the kindness of colleagues at another institution.

We will continue to assess our intermediate level curriculum and will work toward finding more effective means of assessing language skills, but we have also determined that we will undertake an assessment of our degree program as a next major step in this line of work. Through this focused and limited initial project, we feel we have learned a great deal that we can apply in conducting the assessment of the degree program of studies in German Language and Literature at Notre Dame.

Acknowledgments

I would like to express my great appreciation to Dr. John Norris for his crucial support, advice, and input on our project as well as his editing of this chapter. I am also grateful to Yukiko Watanabe for her advice and technical assistance, especially in the creation of the survey and interpretation of the results. This assessment project was a collaborative venture, so my warmest thanks go to my colleagues on the German faculty for their engagement, positive ideas, and enthusiasm in our many discussions and to my former chairperson Dr. Robert Norton for his encouragement and support. I am also indebted to Prof. Stew Markel for his invaluable assistance in the creation of the survey and the collection of responses. Finally, I wish to thank our onsite organizer, Dr. Lance Askildson, and Dr. John Davis, co-editor of this volume.

References

Bolton, S., Glaboniat, M., Lorenz, H., & Perlmann-Balme, M. (2008). *Mündlich. Mündliche Produktion und Interaktion Deutsch: Illustration der Niveaustufen des Gemeinsamen europäischen Referenzrahmens* ["*Mündlich.*" *Oral Production and Interaction German: Illustration of the Levels of the Common European Framework of Reference*]. Berlin, Germany: Langenscheidt bei Klett.

Council of Europe. (2014). Common European Framework of Reference for Languages: Learning, teaching, assessment. Retrieved from http://www.coe.int/t/dg4/linguistic/Source/Framework_EN.pdf

Glaboniat, M., Müller, M., Rusch, P., Schmitz, H., & Wertenschlag, L. (2005). *Profile Deutsch*. Munich, Germany: Langenscheidt bei Klett.

Koithan, U., Schmitz, H., Sieber, T., Sonntag, R., & Ochmann, N. (2007). *Aspekte I Mittelstufe Deutsch* [*Aspekte I Intermediate German*]. Berlin, Germany: Langenscheidt bei Klett.

Nassar-McMillan, S. C., & Borders, L. D. (2002). Use of focus groups in survey item development. *The Qualitative Report*, *7*(1). Retrieved from http://www.nova.edu/ssss/QR/QR7-1/nassar.html

Norris, J. M. (2006). Development and evaluation of a curriculum-based German C-test for placement purposes. In R. Grotjahn & G. Sigott (Eds.), *The C-test: Theory, empirical research, applications* (pp. 45–83). Frankfurt, Germany: Peter Lang.

Appendix A. Degree program Student Learning Outcomes

Graduating German majors and supplementary majors can (in both German and English)

1. discuss the reciprocal bonds that connect the cultures of German-speaking communities to the world at large and identify some of the ways in which cultures influence each other.
2. identify, understand, and appreciate a variety of cultural differences which exist between their own culture and the cultures of the various German-speaking communities.
3. analyze and identify changes in their opinions and attitudes on a variety of topics over the course of their studies in German.
4. identify and discuss representative cultural works from various periods in the history of German- speaking communities, and relate them to a broader understanding of the context and events which gave rise to them.
5. relate their knowledge and experiences of the cultures of German-speaking communities to other intellectual pursuits.
6. identify a selection of major literary periods, authors, genres, and issues relevant to the cultures of German-speaking communities.
7. demonstrate familiarity with the vocabulary and concepts central to the analytical and critical discussion of primary texts within their social, historical, cultural, spiritual and intellectual contexts.
8. formulate, defend, and support their own interpretation of primary and secondary texts, in both oral and written form.

Graduating German majors and supplementary majors can (in German)

9. demonstrate linguistic proficiency at a minimum on the B2 level (Common European Frame of Reference) with a goal of the C1 level.

   B2: Can understand the main ideas of complex text on both concrete and abstract topics, including technical discussions in his /her field of specialization. Can interact with a degree of fluency and spontaneity that makes regular interaction with native speakers quite possible without strain for either party. Can produce clear, detailed text on a wide range of subjects and explain a viewpoint on a topical issue giving the advantages and disadvantages of various options.

   C1: Can understand a wide range of demanding longer texts, and recognize implicit meaning. Can express him/herself fluently and spontaneously without much obvious searching for expressions. Can use language flexibly and effectively for social, academic and professional purposes. Can produce clear, well-structured, detailed text on complex subjects, showing controlled use of organizational patterns, connectors and cohesive devices.[6]

---

[6] Wording for B2 and C1 descriptors comes from the Council of Europe's "Common European Framework of Reference for Languages: Learning, teaching, assessment" (2014, p. 24). See http://www.coe.int/t/dg4/linguistic/Source/Framework_EN.pdf

Appendix B. Beginning and intermediate level Student Learning Outcomes

10000 Level Student Learning Outcomes

Beginning German I

Comprehension

Listening: Students can understand familiar words and basic sentences about themselves as well as a variety of familiar topics (e.g., family, travel, food, entertainment and free time, shopping, etc.) when others speak slowly and clearly.

Reading: Students can read short, simple texts. Students can utilize reading strategies to find specific, predictable information in simple everyday materials such as advertisements, menus, directions, brief personal communications, and cultural information.

Production

Speaking: Students can use target language with a basic level of conversational accuracy on familiar topics with limited control of vocabulary, grammar, and memorized phrases. Students can ask and answer simple questions in areas of immediate need or on familiar topics. Students can use simple phrases and sentences to describe themselves and others.

Writing: Students can produce with limited accuracy short, simple pieces of writing dealing with everyday situations and tasks. Student can describe, in basic sentences, themselves, friends and family, immediate surroundings, and daily routines while maintaining some cultural awareness. Students can be understood with some effort by native speakers.

Culture

Students can identify some characteristics, events and places of importance in the German-speaking world. They can identify some similarities and differences between the US and German-speaking cultures.

Beginning German II

Comprehension

Listening: Students can understand phrases and high frequency vocabulary related to areas of personal relevance (i.e., basic personal and family information, shopping, travel, and employment) and identify the main points of simple descriptions, narrations, messages, and announcements when others speak slowly and clearly.

Reading: Students can read texts that consist mainly of high frequency everyday language; understand the description of events, feelings, and experiences; and understand, with some guidance, selected shorter texts, including prose and poetry

Production

Speaking: Students can communicate with a sympathetic listener in routine situations requiring a simple and direct exchange of information on familiar topics and activities. They can engage in short social exchanges and describe, in simple terms with some errors, family and other people, living conditions, educational background, present and past experiences as well as future plans.

Writing: Students can write notes, messages and letters describing their surroundings and daily routines. They can compose simple stories and relate present and past personal experiences, real or non-real.

Culture

Students can identify characteristics, events and places of importance in the German-speaking world. They can identify similarities and differences between the US and German-speaking cultures.

20000 Level Student Learning Outcomes

Intermediate German I

Comprehension

Listening: Students can understand the main points of clear standard speech on familiar matters regularly encountered. They can understand the main points of various media clips on topics of personal interest when the pace is slow and the delivery is clear.

Reading: Students can understand the main points of various texts that deal with familiar subjects and cultural topics. They can begin to understand authentic longer texts.

Production

Speaking: Students can converse on topics that are familiar, of personal interest, or pertinent to everyday life. They can connect phrases and sentences in order to describe experiences and to express hopes and ambitions. They can narrate a story in both the present and the past tenses.

Writing: Students can write a variety of texts on familiar topics with increasing attention to accuracy and coherence. They can describe experiences, express hopes, ambitions, opinions, and reactions. They can combine and link sentences into connected paragraphs.

Culture

Students can accurately describe various views that German speaking communities hold on a variety of issues and relate them to those held by their own culture. They can identify the significance of several individuals, organizations, and institutions that play an important role in the life of German speaking communities. They can identify the features of authentic texts and offer basic interpretations of them.

Reflectivity

Students can reflect on their personal learning styles and identify their strengths and weaknesses as language learners. They can articulate their own language learning goals, employ successful learning strategies, and analyze their progress towards meeting their goals. They can relate their study of German to their college education as a whole and describe potential benefits that foreign-language learning can have for both their personal and professional lives.

Intermediate German II

Comprehension

Listening: Students can understand the main points of extended speech and short lectures. They can generally follow an argument, provided the topic is familiar. They can understand standard speech from a variety of media.

Reading: Students can read and understand texts from a variety of sources and discern attitudes and viewpoints. They can understand texts written in a greater variety of styles and of a greater length and/or complexity.

Production

Speaking: Students can interact with some degree of fluency and spontaneity in most informal and classroom discussions on topics that are familiar, of personal interest, or pertinent to everyday life. They can combine and link sentences to describe experiences and express hopes and ambitions, and begin to give reasons and explanations for opinions and plans.

Writing: Students can write summaries and short compositions on a range of topics that are of general interest or that relate to the target language culture. They can combine and link sentences into connected, paragraph-length discourse, using several verb tenses and moods. They can demonstrate increased accuracy and organizational coherence.

Culture

Students can demonstrate a basic knowledge of a variety of issues drawn from the history, geography, culture, and social life of German speaking communities. They can begin to formulate arguments about the role that historical events have played in shaping these issues. They can identify ways in which cultures change over time and influence each other. They can understand the multicultural heterogeneous nature of German speaking communities.

Reflectivity

Students can articulate their own language learning goals and analyze their progress. They can describe course offerings and other resources for advancing in German and make informed choices from among them based on their own learning goals. They can demonstrate self-managed learning skills and strategies that will facilitate life-long learning.

Appendix C. University of Notre Dame Student Survey—The Intermediate Level in German (April 2012)

Intermediate Level German April 2012

As part of an ongoing assessment project, the German faculty in the Department of German and Russian is seeking information from students on their experience in our intermediate level program. The information you provide on this questionnaire will help us better understand the effectiveness of the intermediate curriculum and experience and help us identify possible areas that might be improved or enhanced for the benefit of current and future students in our program.

This survey is only seeking information on intermediate Notre Dame German courses in which you are currently enrolled or which you have completed. Please **do not** answer any questions that apply to a class you have *not taken*. Your responses will be confidential; the survey will not contain information that will personally identify you.

At the end of the questionnaire, you will have the opportunity to clarify any of your answers or to add other comments. Please provide us with as much information as you find pertinent, so that we can get an accurate and full picture of your experience.

*1. Survey Consent

Your responses will be confidential and we do not collect identifying information such as your name, email address or IP address. All data is stored in a password protected electronic format. To help protect your confidentiality; the survey will not contain information that will personally identify you. The results of this study will be used for improving departmental effectiveness and for scholarly purposes only.

If you have any questions about the assessment project or survey, please contact Center for the Study of Languages and Cultures (CSLC) Assistant Director for Assessment & Testing, Stew Markel: smarkel@nd.edu.

ELECTRONIC CONSENT: Please select your choice below.

Clicking on the "agree" button below indicates that:

- You have read the above information
- You voluntarily agree to participate
- You are at least 18 years of age

If you do not wish to participate in this survey for the German Department, please decline participation by clicking on the "disagree" button

- o Agree
- o Disagree

Background and Personal Information

2. What is your expected year of graduation?

- 2012
- 2013
- 2014
- 2015

Other (please specify)

[   ]

3. How many years of high school German did you have?

- None
- One
- Two
- Three
- Four

Other (please specify)

[   ]

4. Into which German course were you placed at Notre Dame?

- GE 10101/10111
- GE 10102/10112
- GE 20201/20211
- GE 20202/20212

Other (please specify)

[   ]

5. Was this placement accurate in your estimation?

- Yes
- No

If No, Please explain:

[   ]

* 6. Are you currently enrolled in a German course?

    o Yes

    o No

If not, please explain/give a reason:

[ ]

* 7. Please indicate in which course you are currently enrolled:

o GE 20201	o GE 20211	o GE 20202
o GE 20212	o GE 30104	

Other (please specify)

[ ]

* 8. What was your most recent German course at Notre Dame?

o GE 20201	o GE 20211	o GE 20202
o GE 20212	o GE 30104	

Other (please specify)

[ ]

9. Are you planning on a major, supplementary major, or minor in German?

o Yes	o No	o Undecided

Please explain your choice:

[ ]

10. Are you going to or hoping to study abroad?

o Yes	o No	o Undecided

Are there any issues which might lead to hesitation about studying abroad?

[ ]

Intermediate Level German

Please do not answer any questions that apply to a class you have not taken.

This survey is only seeking information on intermediate Notre Dame German courses in which you are currently enrolled or which you have completed.

11. To what extent were the following courses interesting?

	Not interesting at all	A little interesting	Interesting	Very interesting
GE 20201/20211	o	o	o	o
GE 20202/20212	o	o	o	o

12. How would you describe your transition from one level to another?

	Very difficult	Somewhat difficult	Somewhat easy	Very easy
From high school German to GE20201/20211:	o	o	o	o
From high school German to GE 20202/20212:	o	o	o	o
From GE 10102/GE 10112 to GE 20201/GE 20211:	o	o	o	o
From GE 20201/GE20211 to GE 20202/20212:	o	o	o	o

Please explain any difficulties you had in these transitions:

[   ]

13. How would you describe the pace of the intermediate course(s) you have taken.

	Too fast	Somewhat fast	About right	Somewhat slow	Too slow
GE 20201/20211	o	o	o	o	o
GE 20202/20212	o	o	o	o	o

Language Skills and Tools

Please do not answer any questions that apply to a class you have *not taken*.

This survey is only seeking information on intermediate Notre Dame German courses in which you are currently enrolled or which you have completed.

14. How challenging was it for you to learn the following in your intermediate German courses.

	No challenge at all	A small challenge	A moderate challenge	A great challenge
Speaking:	o	o	o	o
Reading:	o	o	o	o
Writing:	o	o	o	o
Listening:	o	o	o	o
Cultural knowledge:	o	o	o	o
Vocabulary:	o	o	o	o
Grammar:	o	o	o	o

15. What is your opinion on the amount of focus for each component in the GE 20201/20211 course?

	Far too little	Too little	About right	Too much	Far too much
Speaking:	o	o	o	o	o
Reading:	o	o	o	o	o
Writing:	o	o	o	o	o
Listening:	o	o	o	o	o
Cultural knowledge:	o	o	o	o	o
Vocabulary:	o	o	o	o	o
Grammar:	o	o	o	o	o

16. What is your opinion on the amount of focus for each component in the GE 20202/20212 course?

	Far too little	Too little	About right	Too much	Far too much
Speaking:	o	o	o	o	o
Reading:	o	o	o	o	o
Writing:	o	o	o	o	o
Listening:	o	o	o	o	o
Cultural knowledge:	o	o	o	o	o
Vocabulary:	o	o	o	o	o
Grammar:	o	o	o	o	o

17. What is your perception of your current German language skills, cultural competence, and ability to use vocabulary and grammar?

	Poor	Fair	Good	Very good
Speaking:	o	o	o	o
Reading:	o	o	o	o
Writing:	o	o	o	o
Listening:	o	o	o	o
Cultural competence:	o	o	o	o
Vocabulary:	o	o	o	o
Grammar:	o	o	o	o

18. In my intermediate German course(s), I have acquired strategies for learning which will be useful to me in continuing to improve my German skills.

o Strongly disagree   o Somewhat disagree   o Somewhat agree   o Strongly agree   o No opinion

Additional Comments:

Experiences and Activities

19. Please name in- or out-of-class activities and experiences that effectively advanced your learning of German on the intermediate level.

In class	
Out of class	

20. German-related events and opportunities are advertised effectively.

	Never	Sometimes	Usually	Always
German Club Activities	o	o	o	o
Kaffeestunde & Stammtisch	o	o	o	o
Tandem Group	o	o	o	o
Peer Tutoring	o	o	o	o
Internships, fellowships summer grants	o	o	o	o
Lectures	o	o	o	o

21. I would prefer that ONLY students participate at:

	Never	Sometimes	Usually	Always
Kaffeestunde	o	o	o	o
Stammtisch	o	o	o	o

Additional Comments:

22. I would prefer to have more structured learning opportunities/activities for:

	Never	Sometimes	Usually	Always
Kaffeestunde	o	o	o	o
Stammtisch	o	o	o	o

Additional Comments:

Comments and Recommendations

23. Please clarify any of your previous responses and/or add further comments about your experience learning German on the intermediate level at Notre Dame.

24. Please describe your most memorable experience inside or outside of class that is related to the study of German at Notre Dame.

25. If you had one recommendation for improving the intermediate level German program at Notre Dame what would it be?

Danke!

Journey Greater Than the Destination: A Department and Program Perspective on Utilization-Focused Assessment

Alessia Blad & Shauna Williams
University of Notre Dame

In this chapter, we reflect on our multi-year journey with outcomes assessment in the Department of Romance Languages and Literatures at the University of Notre Dame. This assessment journey set out with a primary focus on utilization of assessments for the overarching purpose of enhancing departmental and program understanding and enabling gradual yet persistent improvement in our practices. We present our reflections by highlighting overarching qualities of the assessment process that stand out, namely,
- *the creation and composition of an assessment working group,*
- *the reporting process, and*
- *faculty ownership of assessment.*

Part one of our chapter describes the participants in the process, our assessment enterprise and approach, methods pursued for collecting and reporting data, and project benefits at the department level. Part two then explores how our assessment practices shifted to include finer-grained, program-level assessment work, based on a case study in the Italian program.

Take flight

It started like a plane taking flight, with the slow roll of the airplane taxiing down the runway, not knowing for sure what lies ahead, but knowing you are going somewhere. Then before you know it, you are off, traveling fast and taken in by the view all around. From this new perspective, the journey begins to make sense,

---

Blad, A., & Williams, S. (2015) Journey greater than the destination: A department and program perspective on utilization-focused assessment. In J. M. Norris & J. McE. Davis (Eds.), *Student learning outcomes assessment in college foreign language programs* (pp. 173–197). Honolulu: University of Hawai'i, National Foreign Language Resource Center.

things begin to blend, merge, and piece together. We move from an initial ground-level perspective, where landscapes once appeared divided by a river, to a view from above where distinct domains become intricately connected by that same river, dependent on one another, going from multiple to singular, from isolated to connected. It was with this gradual yet inevitable movement and changing perspective that the assessment journey proceeded for the Department of Romance Languages and Literatures at Notre Dame.

At first, talking about "assessment and learning outcomes" was unfamiliar to many of us and generally interpreted as an intimidating concept associated with "accreditation." Sorting out words like *evaluation*, *assessment*, *learning outcomes*, and *goals*, was like the slow taxiing from the terminal to the runway, like the slow roll at take off when the weight of the plane is felt; the passengers are packed on-board, nervous and excited; the journey has started, but with a lot of territory yet to cover. Now, six years later, the same territory has become closely familiar, dare we say "comfortable," much like a plane well into its trip, moving calmly yet fast, soaring, indeed, flying. Our recommendation, based on this experience, from the outset is simple: Get started; start working; taxiing will lead to flight.

Journey unknown

In its ongoing commitment to undergraduate teaching and learning and in preparation for future accreditation, the Department of Romance Languages and Literatures initiated a project in 2006 that sought to establish student learning goals for all language learning sequences within the department, as well as an assessment plan to judge whether those goals are being met. Learning goals for beginning and intermediate language courses were completed in 2006–2007 (Appendix A). In 2007–2008, the department drafted learning goals for the upper-division French, Italian, and Iberian and Latin American programs.[1] These several years of activity, then, provided the starting point, establishing learning outcomes from beginning language and culture courses to upper-level, major requirement courses. It took 2 years to launch, but it was nevertheless a substantial accomplishment that enabled subsequent assessment-driven learning to occur.

In looking back to where it all began and seeing where we are now, a few key aspects of the journey stand out: (a) the creation and composition of an assessment working group (the Committee for the Study of Romance Languages and Cultures), (b) the reporting process, and (c) the fact that assessment is faculty owned. In part one, or Destination A, we will share our reflections about the participants, as well as our assessment enterprise and methods pursued for collecting and reporting assessment data, and we will highlight overarching assessment project benefits at the department level, in particular faculty-owned assessment. In part two, or Destination B, we will share how assessment shifted to include program (major) level assessment with a case study in Italian.

Destination A: The Department

The Department of Romance Languages and Literatures is a community of scholar-teachers located in the humanities division of the College of Arts and Letters, the oldest, and traditionally the largest, of the four undergraduate colleges of Notre

---

[1] Both sets of goals are in use and posted on-line on the department's homepage: http://romancelanguages.nd.edu/assessment/

Dame. As the largest of Notre Dame's foreign language and literature departments (2,100 students per semester; 500 majors), Romance Languages and Literatures offers majors and supplementary majors in French, Italian, and Spanish, as well as minors in Italian and Portuguese. Along with the Department of Economics, a major in International Economics Romance Languages is offered. Students may also study two languages through our Romance Languages major, or pursue an interdisciplinary Italian Studies concentration. The Department also offers the MA degree in French and Francophone Studies, Italian Studies, and Iberian and Latin American Studies. Of recent, Less Commonly Taught Languages (Catalan, Creole, Quechua) are offered at the beginning and intermediate levels. There are approximately 45 full-time faculty members: 25 tenure-track and 20 non-tenure track. Seventy-three percent of graduating seniors completing a major or minor in Romance Languages study abroad for a summer, semester, or year.

Reflecting on the early days of our assessment journey, it is important to describe the diverse make-up of our standing assessment committee, the Committee for the Study of Romance Languages and Cultures (CSRLC). In 2006, the CSRLC was initially formed to create learning outcomes for each major program in the department in preparation for future accreditation. At that time, only a handful of faculty (3–5) were involved from all languages, both tenure and non-tenure track faculty. These few key leaders were simultaneously learning about *assessment* and *evaluation* themselves, while drafting student learning outcomes across all levels of the curriculum for each major, and helping other interested faculty members become more familiar and "comfortable" with assessment. During this time, the small, somewhat informal committee sought advice from and consulted with key leaders in foreign-language assessment. Additionally, and in response to the need to reform as per the MLA reports *Foreign Languages and Higher Education: New Structures for a Changed World* (Modern Language Association, 2007) and *MLA report to the Teagle Foundation on the future of the undergraduate major in language and literature* (Modern Language Association, 2007), the CSRLC was more formally organized, intentionally including tenure and non-tenure track faculty as a means to bridge the two-tier structure commonly found in foreign language departments, and adopted utilization-focused assessment to address curriculum. Now, the CSRLC is comprised of an appointed group of 15 full-time faculty. Specifically, there is non-tenured and tenure-track representation from each program. The core group is made up of at least one lecturer and one teaching and research faculty member from French, Italian, and Iberian and Latin-American Studies. Because of their expertise and involvement with all foreign language Departments in our institution, we have also included a key faculty person from the Kaneb Center for Teaching and Learning, as well as other foreign language pedagogy specialists.

The committee seeks to approach assessment in a straightforward manner with comprehensive and open dialogue in our monthly (sometimes bi-monthly) meetings. The benefits of this approach are far reaching; there is a greater sense among all faculty of the need for a well-structured curriculum. Faculty members are now working together across rank, across curricular levels, and across programs. Since its formation, the CSRLC has emerged as the department's primary vehicle for pursuing its commitment to undergraduate teaching and learning.

Following the creation of student learning outcomes (SLOs), the next steps in assessment include implementing the goals: sharing them with faculty, including SLOs on all syllabi, making students aware of SLOs and referencing them periodically throughout the semester, deciding on direct and indirect measures to assess student learning, discussing the findings, and finally, adjusting the curriculum and/or pedagogy accordingly. We decided to focus first on oral proficiency, which for our department needed the most immediate attention, especially in terms of bridging curricular levels and including advanced courses where no focus was given to oral proficiency, formally. The CSRLC decided to implement the oral learning outcomes first, and then move to the writing learning outcomes. In both the oral and writing assessment projects, we started with internal benchmarking, finding out current practices in the department and reading scholarly articles from recent publications to be better informed on best practices in the field. For both the oral and the writing assessment, committee members created a list by level of instruction and by language of all the current practices in the department, such as how many times and when in the semester each instructor would administer oral exams, and written assignments. We also listed the different types of assessment for both skills and, following the guidance of our experts from the Kaneb Center and other foreign language specialists, we read several scholarly articles and learned about current practices in other universities.

Our initial oral proficiency project took 2 years to complete. For the project, students in fourth and fifth semester language courses and advanced literature courses were assessed by using WIMBA, a voice tool embedded in our campus course management system. Instructors assigned two or three activities to be completed via WIMBA in a semester. Students received feedback within a day or two and audio files were saved for future reference. Also, seniors, randomly selected, were directly assessed using the OPIc (oral proficiency interview by computer) for French and Spanish and OPI telephonic for Italian. Through assessment, we now have a better understanding of actual student learning outcomes in the area of oral skills. For example, the results of the external oral assessment surprisingly showed not only that students were meeting the SLO, but in some cases were scoring at a higher proficiency level than expected. In addition, we learned much about our own practices. In an effort to involve all Department faculty in this assessment project, the CSRLC created and distributed to every faculty member a simple survey asking questions about the nature and importance of oral proficiency in their courses and current practices. Many faculty members marked oral proficiency as important, but no formal assessment measures were in place, especially at advanced level. As a result of the project, oral assessment is now regularly included at all levels of the curriculum, course design and pedagogy have changed to include course-embedded informal and formal assessment, and common rubrics are used. Now, every two to three years, graduating seniors completing a major/minor in French, Italian, or Spanish are randomly selected and invited to complete an OPIc and OPI telephonic testing funded by the college. This format helps keeps oral proficiency assessment ongoing and is cost effective.

Once the oral assessment project was concluded, we moved to writing. To some degree, the writing project is still ongoing, but some best practices have already been established. Following the same process as oral proficiency, we first discussed as a department our current practices: types of writing, frequency of formal written assignments, how written work is corrected, how student feedback is given. Then, we collected student writing samples at the end of the term from third, fourth, and fifth semester language in French, Italian, and Spanish courses and advanced level literature courses. A faculty rating rubric was created and a select group of faculty, both non-tenure and tenure-track, assessed student work (Appendix B). Many questions arose from this project such as, "What is the best way to grade and give feedback on student writing?" and "What is an "A," "B," "C," "D," paper?" As a result, we invited an expert in the field of foreign language writing instruction and feedback to campus to meet with us and other languages and literatures departments, collected a large electronic file with scholarly articles on best practices in writing, and most recently created a department statement on writing including a department grading scale (see Appendix C).

In addition to the methods and approaches mentioned above, and as evidenced in the sample reports, a variety of methods and approaches are used to collect, analyze, distribute, and report assessment data (see Appendix D for executive summaries form 2010–2011 and 2011–2012 reports). At early and key stages of the project, outside consultants and experts in the field of foreign language pedagogy and assessment were regularly involved, providing constructive feedback and guidance. Support was also provided by other units on campus such as our Center for the Study of Languages and Cultures (e.g., for oral proficiency test administration).

In short, each year, the CSRLC sets an agenda, which includes at least one assessment project aimed at the development of best practices and assessing directly whether our learning goals are being met. For each project, specific goals are determined, and direct and indirect methods are used to gather information on student learning and gauge outcomes achievement. Faculty and program leaders, including members of the CSRLC, discuss the findings. Then a written report is created to summarize the process, assess the project goals, note recommendations, and list items requiring action. A final report is distributed to the faculty of the department, and shared with college officials and other interested groups as appropriate.

The approach of assessment being faculty owned and driven has positively impacted communication about curriculum and pedagogy among members in the department, between programs, and with other departments in the college and across the university. With assessment being faculty owned and driven, a new landscape has been formed. Where before there was a two-tiered structure divided by rank, now there is a single force or pilot in the cockpit: department faculty. Additionally, assessment is now driven by department need and interest and not by one language program or one faculty member or by administrators—another new landscape. Where before assessment was top-down in its genesis, those more directly responsible for teaching and learning, the department faculty, now guide the entire project.

Travel log: Tracking and reporting

Our assessment journey "travel log" is in the form of meeting minutes and annual reports. Aiming to keep faculty involved and informed about assessment and specific department projects and findings, meeting minutes are distributed to all department faculty and an annual report is submitted to the chair to be included in the annual department report. Reports include specific project goals, findings, methods and approaches used, suggested "next steps," and new assessment questions for future projects. Reporting has been especially beneficial when project goals were clearly articulated, processes and findings concisely summarized (with appendices as needed), and suggestions for improvement expressed in a non-threatening manner, all of this creating a source of trustworthy information for use by stakeholders and decision makers. By establishing a systemic and transparent reporting process, assessment efforts stay on course, are more effectively undertaken, allow for clearer reflection, and help guide where next to go. Reporting in this fashion helps track the flight and provides a record of accountability.

Having a regular tracking and reporting process has been beneficial in a number of ways. Specific benefits to note include maintaining open communication between students and faculty, faculty of varying rank and title, the department and university administrators—to audiences locally and more broadly defined. Each of these stakeholder groups are better able to communicate on matters of student learning and achievement, goals set and proficiencies gained (skills, knowledge, and dispositions at course, program, and department levels), potential areas of improvement relating to curriculum design, effective teaching, faculty development, and program and department needs such as funding for assessment and curricular design innovations, new faculty lines and searches, and professional development for faculty at all ranks.

Another effective reporting and sharing venue we recently discovered is holding an annual department mini-retreat (half-day) at the end of the fall semester. During the half-day activities, a portion of the time is given for language programs to meet and discuss relevant topics of interest among their faculty and to set 3–4 action items to address going forward. Then, all faculty/programs come together to summarize and share their goals going forward, followed by a general discussion of a larger, department project or topic. Benefits of having a more informed and involved faculty group and establishing departmental and programmatic accountability are far reaching. It is important that assessment be on-going in order to map progress over time, instead of single snapshot initiatives. By approaching assessment in this manner, faculty are more informed and better equipped to make clear, pro-active decisions instead of a disconnected group of faculty making uninformed, unfocused, reactionary decisions. In addition, accountability to students, the institution, and even to ourselves is a clear benefit of regular, useful, faculty-owned assessment. Taking the pulse of where we are in our educational endeavors, being open to hearing and seeing the truth reflected in data, and then having the courage to respond and adjust is empowering. We must be willing to check the gauges, read the instruments, recheck the map and reset course, if necessary, in order to keep us going towards our destination. Plan, record, take note. Track the journey for yourself and others.

Destination B: Italian Studies Program—A case study

We will now give specific examples of how the assessment and learning outcomes project at Notre Dame affected one of the departmental language programs, the Italian Studies program. Given the number of faculty members in Italian – 10 regular faculty members between tenure track faculty and lecturers – from the very beginning of our journey, the Italian section has been able to make substantial changes to the curriculum at all levels, changes that brought almost instantly visible results as well as long-lasting improvements in teaching and learning.

As one might guess, at the beginning it was very hard to see how we were supposed to go about achieving the very ambitious goal of creating learning goals and assessment methods/rubrics for each course in the program. In the local context of Italian Studies at Notre Dame, we felt very strongly the need to rethink our program. For us, the challenge was how to judiciously "inter-disciplinize" the Italian major, without giving up its traditional linguistic and literary character. Utilization-focused assessment[2] provided us with the theoretical and practical means to pursue the important project of redefining our program via assessment. We all understood the importance of engaging in assessment as a means of communicating more effectively, both to others and to ourselves, in empirical and meaningful terms. Engaging in this long-term assessment project has allowed us to assume a leading role in doing something that in our institution had not been done before. This journey has helped also in changing the perception of what it is we do from the outside of the program.

The assessment project started with analyzing and recognizing ourselves, through the exercise of defining our own goals. We methodically looked at each course we offer in the Italian section, in terms of which skills, knowledge, and dispositions we expected our students to achieve. We then did the same analysis vertically making sure there was continuity of expectations between, for example, the end of the learning goals of a 200-level course and the beginning of a 300-level course.

Embarking on the writing and oral assessment projects, the Italian faculty asked a number of questions. What strategies and methods can Italian Studies utilize to assess the acquisition of skills knowledge and dispositions by our students? Does the assessment of writing offer opportunities of assessing humanities dispositions and specialized knowledge from a perspective that is specific to writing? In addition to pursuing these kinds of queries was another concern: The assessment project involved having instructors disclose their materials, such as syllabi, prompts, students' written production, and the way instructors evaluate and grade assignments. Some instructors were enthusiastic about doing so, and immediately saw the assessment project as an opportunity to share ideas, practices, and materials with their colleagues; some were less open, and saw the assessment as an invasive process, perhaps fearing comparisons with their colleagues. We therefore asked ourselves if there was a way to make the assessment process psychologically more acceptable. How could we turn this effort into a sustainable practice?

Writing assessment project in Italian

The writing assessment project in the Italian program is part of a broader project undertaken by the Committee for the Study of Romance Languages and Cultures (CSRLC) at Notre Dame that started in AY 2010–2011. The main goals of the CSRLC assessment project were to establish writing pedagogy best practices, create learning goals and grading rubrics for all languages taught in the department for both the lower and upper division course sequences (Appendix E), and to

---

[2] Utilization-focused assessment refers to an approach to program inquiry and development in which assessment processes are guided by an initial specification of assessment uses (Watanabe, Davis, & Norris, 2012).

propose protocols for regular program-level assessment. A secondary aim of CSRLC department-wide projects was to also address specific programmatic issues though not that different from the department-wide issues alluded to earlier, such as improving communication between faculty teaching at different levels to ultimately achieve fluidity in the curriculum.

In the Italian section, we began the writing assessment project in Italian by examining the lower division courses—the first four semesters of Italian—and the gateway course entitled *Passage to Italy*, which is an introductory survey course on Italian literature, with a focus on grammar. The purpose of the writing assessment was twofold. On the one hand, we wanted to assess writing in each course and create a standard protocol (in terms of learning goals, writing assignment prompts, and criteria for evaluation) for each level. On the other hand, we wanted to assess writing focusing on the specific needs of the Italian section. In other words, we aimed at having instructional continuity throughout the program, as well as standardized teaching practices and procedures across both the lower and upper division in a coherent and recognizable flow.

To these ends, several subcommittees were formed from the original CSRLC committee with the addition of more Italian faculty members. We created the subcommittees by course levels (one subcommittee for the language courses at the 100 and 200-level and one subcommittee for the Gateway courses at the 300-level), and worked on the following six curricular, pedagogical, and assessment development tasks:

1. Defining the purpose of writing at each course level, in order to make explicit our learning goals at each curricular level. That is to say, the committees were asked to determine, and justify, what and how well students should be able to write at each course level.

2. Creating explicit learning goals and writing guidelines for all course syllabi. For example, the committees were to determine the number of writing assignments for each type of course in the curriculum in a semester; the length of writing assignments; the genres and content of writing assignments appropriate for each course; the desired grammar, syntax, vocabulary, structure, and organization of writing assignments; the criteria for evaluating writing assignments; and the percentage of the final grade for each writing assignment.

3. Creating grading rubrics specific to the writing assignments of each course offered, that break down the elements the Italian Studies section wanted to assess at each course level.

4. Collecting samples of graded and glossed writing assignments at each level, in order to have a practical example of what constituted an A paper, a B paper, and so on.

5. Collecting samples of the writing prompts at each course level to analyze their effectiveness. In order to define best practices for writing prompts the committees examined the context, purpose, and audience of a given assignment; the content of the assignment prompt; whether the assignment is an in-class or a take-home activity; the format requirements assignments

need to meet; and whether students are allowed to consult dictionaries, textbooks, or use the help of writing tutors.

6. Collecting and analyzing samples of the final writing assessment at crucial junctures of the program, for example, at the end of the language requirement and at the end of the gateway course. The purpose of this phase was to assess if the students' assignments reflected the conceptualization, and level, of language performance stated in our learning goals.

Writing assessment project impacts

The impact of the writing assessment project in the Italian section was significant, and immediately noticeable by each faculty member at each level, because it forced us to look closely and re-evaluate practices that had been in place for a very long time and that had never been questioned. For example, a significant pedagogical development resulting from these efforts was the classification of the different genres and writing task types used at different course levels. Thus, in the 100-level courses (first and second semester) our students write letters, emails, recipes, reflections, dialogues, skits, inquiries, and other forms of short communications based on personal preferences, daily routines, common events and other topics related to personal experiences and immediate surroundings. In the 200-level courses (third and fourth semester) our students write narrative compositions (stories, summaries, articles, investigative reports, Facebook updates), reflective compositions (journals, responses), persuasive/critical thinking compositions (essays, letters, book or movie reviews), descriptive compositions (essays, articles), and creative compositions (advertisements, screenplays, skits, dialogues, short stories, preparing an interview). At the 300 level (fifth semester) students write in order to respond to literary texts or other forms of art (mainly cinema) in a critical way. Student writing at this curricular level is constituted by mini-scholarly essays, in which they apply the different critical skills specific to literary criticism. A typical assignment is the analysis of a literary text of a specific genre (a lyric or epic poem, a short story, an excerpt from a drama or a novel, etc.) that should consider the historical/cultural context and literary tradition to which the text belongs, the poetics of its author, and the linguistic and rhetorical features of the text. Students are also encouraged to provide an original perspective on the text and to substantiate it through the analysis of the text itself.

From this brief description of the different types of writing assignments specific to different curricular levels, it is clear that there is a coherent and recognizable progression across the curriculum from a focus on the self to a focus on external objects, a performance trajectory that becomes progressively more authentic and sophisticated in terms of content and rhetoric. The writing assignments at the 200 level in fact still have a strong component embedded in the students' own, personal "cultures." If texts from the target culture often work as input meant to provide exposure to Italian culture, students nonetheless are asked to rhetorically imitate or describe rather than interpret. At the same time it is at the 200 level where instruction moves towards a hermeneutic approach to Italian culture via book and movie reviews (even at the 100 level students are encouraged to write movie reviews, which are often more descriptive of the plot rather than interpretive). At the 300 level, rounding out the expectations for development, the focus has shifted to the interpretation of the literary product, and writing seems to be the best way to construct meaning out of the encounter with Italian literature.

Of course, this progression from the self to the other, from description to interpretation, corresponds to a parallel progression in the command of linguistic abilities in terms of grammatical and syntactical structures, and discursive and strategic competence. This shift emerges also in the purpose of writing statements that our subcommittees created. At the 100—and 200-curricular levels the focus is on the acquisition of linguistic structures (writing is very much geared simply towards language acquisition) and on enabling students to write about themselves. In the 200 level statement of purpose for writing, the goal of approaching authentic texts in the Italian language is additionally stated. At the 300 level, on the other hand, the purpose of writing is articulated through the rationale that underlies the ACTFL Standards for Foreign Language Learning: Communication, Cultures, Connections, Comparisons, and Communities.

At this curricular level, it is precisely through writing that students carry out the maximum degree of critical thinking necessary in order to understand and interpret a sophisticated cultural product like a literary text. In other words, at this level and beyond, it is only through writing that students can get to the core of the texts they read. Moreover, writing about Italian literary texts provides students with the opportunity to explore how other scholars have done the same in Italian and to notice the differences between the way scholarly literature is written in English and Italian (in terms of style, rhetoric, organization of the discourse, etc.). Writing as a form of tangible expression of profound critical thinking also fosters an awareness of hermeneutical problems and skills that can be translated back to students' own culture and literary traditions, enabling them to draw comparisons between the two traditions (their own and the Italian tradition). Finally, developing communicative writing skills at the sophisticated level of the gateway course begins to enable students to pursue graduate studies in Italian, or in disciplines in which Italian is central, and to become part of a larger community of scholars and teachers who think and work in Italian.

Oral assessment project in Italian

As already mentioned above, during the 2008–2009 academic year, the Romance Languages and Literature Department undertook and completed a project to assess and improve oral proficiency of students in relation to the individual language and the department learning goals that were established in the previous academic year. Here we describe how the Italian section was able to modify the learning goals as a result of the oral assessment project, perhaps the main development that came about through this assessment focus.

The specific goals for this project were to

- establish pedagogical best practices and student performance criteria for oral proficiency;
- implement and test the effectiveness of technological tools such as WIMBA (an online voice recorder designed to support the collection, review, and storage of oral practices and assessment data across the curriculum); and
- propose protocols for regular program-level assessment of oral proficiency student learning outcomes.

In fall of 2008, faculty members in the department were trained in the use of WIMBA in order to help them understand how to use this technological tool in their courses. Using WIMBA made the best sense for us because, not only is it a very simple tool, but the university offers it as a free tool for every course. For these reasons, using WIMBA was both practical and economical. The aim of the CSRLC was to gather a sample of oral assessments for the assessment project. Students were initially randomly sampled in Italian, from beginning to intermediate courses. The CSRLC created and distributed grading rubrics to the students before they took the tests so that performance expectations were clear and known in advance. The first test was administered in early November and was a paired conversation recorded in response to a prompt recorded on WIMBA by the instructors. A second test was administered in early December; it was a response to a picture prompt with recorded instructions from the instructors.

During the spring term of 2009, as a continuation and extension of the oral assessment project started the previous semester, faculty in Italian also began sampling different types of students' speaking abilities via the WIMBA platform. Three to five formal oral assessments, depending on the course type and level, were included in the syllabi of the 100-, 200-, and 300-level Italian courses participating in the pilot project. The reason for this additional type of assessment was to go beyond the voice recording we had sampled with WIMBA the previous semester. We now wanted to assess other types of oral proficiency in our courses, more communicative and spontaneous ones, such as an in-class presentation followed by Q&A, in-class pair and group conversations, and so forth. The rationale for assessment was included in the syllabi at the beginning of the semester and specific rubrics were also created. Throughout this entire process, several anonymous surveys were given to students and faculty in order to constantly collect feedback we received from the surveys. Finally, at the end of the 2008–2009 academic year, a sample of 11 students of Italian took a computer-based OPI exam from which the CSRLC was able to gather a sample of their global oral proficiency as measured according to a program-external criterion (the ACTFL Proficiency Guidelines for Speaking). The reason behind the choice for the OPI test was to have an external, more objective and standardized test on which to base our interpretations of students' oral proficiency development.

At the same time, the CSRLC subcommittee met to discuss findings and create grading rubrics, and gave the following five recommendations:

1. Formal assessment of oral proficiency should take place every semester in all courses across the curriculum. Formal and informal oral assessment activities should be included in all course syllabi. The committee recommended three to six formal assessment activities be built in every course. Moreover, 20% to 30% of the final grade should be given to oral proficiency.

2. Oral practice can take place in or outside of the classroom. Voice tools such as WIMBA allow the instructor to collect, store, and review oral student data.

3. The performance rubrics developed by the CSRLC for all levels of the curriculum should be used regularly, first to provide students with a guideline of expectations, and then as a form of feedback from instructor to student.

4. Every other year, the oral proficiency of graduating majors and minors, and supplementary majors and minors, should be assessed in each program through the use of on-line tools that will allow for ACTFL-sponsored certification of levels.

5. Additional benchmarking should be considered at key points in each program such as after the completion of the language requirement, after the "Intro to literature" courses, and before and after study abroad.

It is also important to underline the substantial cultural benefits for faculty engaged in this project. The Italian faculty found that working together on the assessment project as a program, not in a two-tiered structure of language and literature, or tenure and non-tenure track faculty has helped to overcome some of the negative consequences of the traditional two-tier composition of the faculty in languages and literatures in our department. Our faculty composition, of course, reflects national trends, particularly in the larger programs. However, engaging the whole faculty in a holistically conceived collaborative approach to curriculum reform and assessment has been highly beneficial to faculty integration and the effectiveness of our programs in all languages. The assessment project has allowed non-tenure track faculty members in Italian, and later on in each language, to play a leading role so that our curricular reforms and innovations have been "bottom up" as much or more than "top down" from a curricular point of view.

Oral assessment project impacts

What did the assessment project mean for the Italian program? This year-long project addressing oral proficiency assessment led to the creation of a large number of best practices and recommendations, and it also contributed to greater awareness among all participating faculty of the importance of promoting oral proficiency at all levels, from lower to upper language and content courses.

First, the Italian section created detailed description of the different types of oral assessment across the program in order to cover the spectrum of genres that needed to be addressed. Next, the Italian section implemented the recommendations made by the CSRLC regarding the frequency of oral assessment and the grade distribution of the oral component within each Italian course at all levels. Finally, grading rubrics were created for each course and for each type of oral assessment (in class presentations, mini-dramas, skits, picture sequence description etc.), and starting in the fall of 2009, rubrics per genre and level have been available on our website to all faculty to use and share when needed during the course of each semester.

The Italian faculty is very satisfied with the impact the written and oral proficiency assessment project has had on our pedagogical practices. We can now say that the journey was as important, if not more important, than the outcome: All of us recognize that, by its very nature, the project promoted a culture of sharing ideas, materials, and methods, and this, along with the many discussions we have had, and the effort we put into defining common objectives and negotiating common standards, greatly helped us understand what our colleagues do and how they do it across our program.

Most importantly, this project brought us to reflect on our personal goals in the classes we teach from a new and broader perspective, and to be open to change.

There is an acknowledged need to follow up on more program-level outcomes assessment in the future. This may involve a regular review of oral and written proficiency, for instance, from random sampling of students' performances at critical junctures in our curriculum.

The Italian faculty has worked very closely on this project for several years and the result is a new level of communication, a clear understanding of what each one of us is doing in our classes and why, but most of all, an appreciation for each other's work. We now look at our Italian program at Notre Dame as a whole, not a series of levels, or individual courses, or individual faculty members, but as a holistic academic experience we can offer to our students.

Department reflection: Looking back

At the end of our journey, when we look back at all the work that has been done over the last few years, we realize how much we all have learned and gained, and we hope to have some advice to offer to other institutions that are embarking on a similar project. It is very important to start such a journey with a small group of key faculty willing to dedicate their time to such an extensive project as this. Not all faculty members will "buy in" at first, but slowly, over time, more may come on board. The creation of a core steering committee that represents all faculty types, meets regularly, has a consistent reporting mechanism (to committee, to department, to college, to university, to other departments, to other universities and national audiences) is essential. Established electronic storage that is well organized and regularly updated (where some information may be viewed publicly while other information may be password protected) is needed to track and report progress. Lead faculty need release time to focus on the important work at task, as it requires serious attention and on-going oversight. It is also important to choose and prioritize projects that are most needed/useful and feasible.

We have also learned to start projects by assessing internally, What are the current trends and practices of faculty in your department? Become informed about scholarly research and publications on the topic at hand, and if possible, invite experts to campus to teach and train your teams about theories and practices in the field. Create "best practices" summaries and guidelines in order to encourage faculty who are already engaged, and also to motivate faculty on the periphery to consider "trying" a new approach or engaging in the project. Suggest new approaches and changes in "bite size" amounts, so as to approach assessment and change as less scary, easily doable, welcomed, and not burdensome. Collaborate with others: other faculty members, other departments, other support units on campus, and leaders in the field.

The greatest gains are in reflection, as a department, program, and individual. If we say it is important, then we must do it. By practicing direct and indirect assessment, we assign value to what we do. Quality curriculum is important, therefore we assess our programs by implementing learning outcomes, establishing criteria and benchmarking for evaluating course goals, curricular mapping, and student achievement.

The challenges include the following: Maintaining on-going, regular assessment takes time; keeping faculty on board and up-to-date requires clear communication and commitment; having access to necessary technology and digital platforms for teaching and assessment can be an obstacle.

But the rewards far outweigh the challenges. For us, we are energized by the collaborative effort, even if it is a work in progress. We are struck by how similarly, yet differently, assessment is viewed, approached, and used in our programs and with faculty from other language departments. Seeing faculty engage in assessment continues to prove how important it is that projects be faculty led. And, of course, seeing students learn, excel, and go farther than ever before is rewarding. To obtain all these successes, we need each other. By working together we are better and stronger. Collaboration can and does make the journey more fulfilling.

Horizon: What lies ahead

So, what is next? Where do we go from here? Well, we stay the course. We keep flying. Through assessment we have learned a lot, yet there is more to learn, do, and understand. New topics to consider may include discussion of grade inflation, re-writing (adjusting) our learning outcomes based on what we are learning about actual student development, creating a centralized web space for storage and reporting of assessment data, more specified assessment and educational inquiry, exploring hybrid and blended language courses, and maybe even addressing the needs of less commonly taught languages, to name a few.

So, yes—maybe the journey is more important than the destination.

Anticipate the unknown. Look forward to what might lie ahead—a new place.

Acknowledgments

This work would not be possible without the contribution of others. We would like to thank Prof. Theodore Cachey for his vision and leadership during his terms as Department Chair (2004–2013) and for his continual dedication and support of assessment and curriculum. To John Norris and Yukiko Watanabe, we are truly indebted to you for your expertise in the field, counsel, guidance, and invaluable feedback you have provided through the years. This work has been a team effort at every point, and to the members of the CSRLC 2006 to present—thank you! Thank you, Dean John McGreevy, for your support of the study of languages and cultures in the College of Arts & Letters at the University of Notre Dame.

References

Modern Language Association. (2007). *Foreign languages and higher education: New structures for a changed world.* New York, NY: MLA. Retrieved from http://www.mla.org/flreport

Modern Language Association. (2008). *MLA report to the Teagle Foundation on the future of the undergraduate major in language and literature.* New York, NY: MLA. Retrieved from http://www.mla.org/teaglereport_page

Norris, J. M., Davis, J. McE., Sinicrope, C., & Watanabe, Y. (2009). *Toward useful program evaluation in college foreign language education.* Honolulu: University of Hawai'i, National Foreign Language Resource Center.

Appendix A. Department of Romance Languages and Literatures lower division learning goals

		Course Level			
		10101	10102	20201	20202
Comprehension	Listening	I will be able to understand familiar words and basic sentences, concerning myself and a variety of familiar topics (e.g. family, travel, food, some current events, technology, professions, etc.) when people speak slowly and clearly.	I will be able to understand phrases and high frequency vocabulary related to areas of immediate personal relevance (e.g. basic personal and family information, shopping, local area, employment) and identify the main points of simple descriptions, narrations, messages, and announcements.	I will be able to understand the main points of clear standard speech on familiar matters regularly encountered in school and leisure and understand the main points of selected clips from a variety of media on topics of personal interest when the delivery is slow and clear.	I will be able to understand the main points of extended speech and lectures and follow the general lines of more complex arguments, provided the topic is reasonably familiar. I will be able to understand standard speech from a variety of media.
	Reading	We aim for Novice High. The majority of students achieve at least Novice mid. I will be able to read short, simple texts. I will be able to utilize reading strategies to find specific, predict-able information in simple everyday materials such as advertisements, menus and brief personal communications.	I will be able to read texts that consist mainly of high frequency everyday language; understand the description of events, feelings, and wishes in personal communications; and understand, with some guidance, selected poems and shorter literary prose.	I will be able to read and understand the main points of texts from a variety of sources (articles, reports, literary excerpts, advertisements, song lyrics) that deal with familiar subjects and cultural topics. I will begin to understand longer literary excerpts from authentic texts of different genres.	I will be able to read and understand texts from a variety of sources and begin to discern writers' attitudes and viewpoints. I will be able to understand texts written in varying literary styles (colloquial, lyric, dramatic, comic, etc.) of greater length and/or complexity.
Production	Speaking	I will be able to use the target language with a basic level of conversational fluency and precision on familiar topics using limited	I will be able to communicate in routine situations requiring a simple and direct exchange of information on familiar topics and	I will be able to converse on topics that are familiar, of personal interest, or pertinent to everyday life. I will be able to connect phrases and sentences in	I will be able to interact with a greater degree of fluency and spontaneity in most informal and some formal discussions. I will be able to combine

	vocabulary, grammar, and memorized phrases. I will be able to ask and answer simple questions in areas of immediate need or on familiar topics and to use simple phrases and sentences to describe where I live and people I know	activities. I will be able to engage in short social exchanges; and describe, in simple terms, my family and other people, living conditions, educational background, present and past experiences as well as future plans.	order to describe experiences and to express hopes and ambitions . I will be able to give reasons and explanations for my opinions and plans. I will be able to narrate a story in the present, past, and future	and link sentences to describe experiences and express hopes and ambitions, and to give reasons and explanations for my opinions and plans.
Writing	We aim for Novice high. The majority of students achieve at least Novice mid. I will be able to write short, simple messages dealing with everyday issues. I will be able to describe, in basic sentences, myself, my friends and family, my immediate surroundings, and my daily routines.	I will be able to write notes, messages and letters describing my surroundings and daily routines. I will be able to narrate simple stories and personal experiences using the present, past and future tenses, and begin to formulate basic predictions and hypotheses	I will be able to write a variety of texts on topics that are familiar or of personal interest with increasing attention to accuracy and coherence. I will be able to describe experiences, express hopes and ambitions, and state and support basic arguments and opinions. I will begin to combine and link sentences into connected, paragraph-length discourse.	I will be able to write summaries and short compositions on a range of topics related to the target language culture and of general interest. I will improve my ability to combine and link sentences into connected, paragraph-length discourse, using a variety of verb tenses and moods and will further develop the accuracy and organizational coherence of my writing.
Cultural Awareness	I will be able to give examples of the relationship between language and culture. I will be able to identify some characteristics of the target culture and distinguish patterns from stereotypes. I will be able to note similarities and differences between home and target cultures.	I will further develop my understanding of the relationship between language and culture. I will be able to identify characteristics, events and places of importance in the target culture. I will be able to identify similarities and differences between home and target cultures, and give examples of one culture influencing	I will have gained good insights into many aspects of values, patterns, and institutions of the target language culture(s). I will be able to demonstrate a basic understanding of the impact of historical events, how cultures change over time, how they are transmitted, and how they influence each other. I will begin to recognize the depth and	I will be able to demonstrate knowledge of cultural topics introduced in class, including aspects of history, geography, literature, and popular culture. I will develop a better understanding of the target language and culture through authentic materials, and will gain more profound insight into the relationship

		another	complexity of cultural differences.	between the two.
Reflectivity	We aim for and typically achieve a common minimum of Stage 1 (AATF Culture Curriculum) I will be able to reflect, in English and, to a limited extent, in the target language, on personal experiences while learning a new language. I will begin to identify my personal learning style.	We aim for and typically achieve a common minimum of Stage 1 (AATF Culture Curriculum) I will be able to reflect, in English and, to a limited extent, in the target language, on personal experiences while learning a new language. I will be able to identify my personal learning style and recognize how this can be used to enhance my language-learning experience.	We aim for and typically achieve a common minimum of Stage 2 (AATF Culture Curriculum) I will be able to reflect, in English and, progressively, in the target language, on my progress and language-learning goals and objectives. I will understand the correlation between my personal learning style and the development of successful learning strategies and will be able to document progress and articulate goals.	We aim for and typically achieve a common minimum of Stage 2 (AATF Culture Curriculum) I will be able to reflect in the target language on my progress and language-learning goals and objectives. I will be able to define and refine my personal learning style and develop successful learning strategies. I will be more confident in my ability to document progress and articulate goals.

Appendix B. Faculty rating form—Writing Project, 20000-level and 30000-level

20000-level

Rubric-based questions

Please give an overall rating to the writing samples you reviewed, according to the following scale: strongly agree, agree, somewhat agree, disagree, strongly disagree. In addition, please write 3–5 sentences in the comment box to explain your rating.

1. Vocabulary is varied, accurate and level appropriate.

    strongly agree   5

    agree   5

    somewhat agree   5

    disagree   5

    strongly disagree 5

    Please write 3–5 sentences in the comment box to explain your rating. [comment box provided]

2. Grammar and spelling are correct and level appropriate.

    strongly agree 5…

    Please write 3–5 sentences…

3. Structure is well articulated and level appropriate.
4. Intellectual content is relevant and level appropriate.

Learning goals-based questions

Please consult the learning goals for writing at this level that were included in the packet you reviewed and rate whether the writing you reviewed corresponds to the stated goals for writing at this level according to the following scale: strongly agree, agree, somewhat agree, disagree, strongly disagree. Please write 3–5 sentences in the comment box to explain your rating.

5. The writing assignments and/or prompts for the samples reviewed were level appropriate according to the learning goals.
6. The majority of students were writing at the appropriate level as outlined in the learning goals.
7. The majority of students achieved an appropriate level of accuracy and coherence.
8. The majority of students were able to combine and link sentences in connected, paragraph-length discourse.

Feedback-based questions

Please give an overall rating to the instructors' written feedback on the samples you reviewed, according to the following scale: strongly agree, agree, somewhat agree, disagree, strongly disagree. In addition, please write 3–5 sentences in the comment box to explain your rating.

9. The quantity of feedback provided was appropriate.
10. The quality of feedback provided was high.
11. The feedback was communicated in a clear and efficient manner.

Draft best practices materials

Please consult the draft best practices materials for writing at this level that were included in the packet you received and rate them according to the following scale: strongly agree, agree, somewhat agree, disagree, strongly disagree. Please write 3–5 sentences in the comment box to explain your rating.

12. The purpose of writing statement articulates appropriately our curricular goals for this level.
13. The rubric effectively enables the efficient evaluation of the salient characteristics of writing at this curricular level.
14. The guidelines for the rubrics are clear and helpful.
15. Please share any concluding comments or reflections concerning the writing samples you reviewed, this survey and/or the writing assessment project.

Appendix C. Romance Languages and Literatures grading policy

The purpose of grading is to provide a fair assessment of student performance which can be useful in furthering a student's scholarly and professional development. Grades can have multiple functions, including evaluation, motivation, communication, encouragement of student reflectivity, and feedback to instructors. For grades to be useful to the student, it is important that they be determined according to principled criteria, established and clearly communicated by the instructors. Grades in the Department of Romance Languages and Literatures are earned according to the following guidelines, developed by the Academic Council:

A   Truly exceptional = work meets or exceeds the highest expectations for the course

A- Outstanding = superior work in all areas of the course

B+ Very good = superior work in most areas of the course

B   Good = solid work across the board

B- More than acceptable… = …but falls short of solid work

C+ Acceptable: meets all basic standards = all the basic requirements and standards for the course

C   Acceptable: meets most basic standards = basic requirements and standards in several areas

C- Acceptable: meets some basic standards = falls short of meeting basic standards in several areas

D   Minimally passing = work just over the threshold of acceptability

F   Failing = Unacceptable performance

All courses in the Department use the following grading scale, established by the Department:

```
96% to 100     = A
90% to 95.9%   = A-
87% to 89.9%   = B+
84% to 86.9%   = B
80% to 83.9%   = B-
77% to 79.9%   = C+
74% to 76.9%   = C
70% to 73.9%   = C-
60% to 69.9%   = D
59.9% or below = F
```

Appendix D. CSRLC Executive Summaries, AY 2010–2011, 2011–2012

Department of Romance Language and Literatures Annual Report 2010–2011

Assessment Report 2010–2011

The Committee for the Study of Romance Languages and Cultures (CSRLC), in support of the Department's ongoing commitment to undergraduate teaching and learning, continued the assessment project that began in AY 2006–07 with the establishment of student learning goals for all levels of the curriculum in each of the Department's major programs. Since that time the CSRLC has annually sought to support the development of best practices in pursuit of those goals and to assess whether the goals are being met.

Specifically in AY 2010–11, the CSRLC:

1. Implemented guidelines for fifth-semester culture courses (27500s) in all programs that were created in previous AY. http://romancelanguages.nd.edu/assets/112722/27500_guidelines_1_.pdf

    The guidelines provide faculty with a general framework for creating new culture courses at this upper intermediate level that are meant to "bridge" from language and culture courses to the gateway/advanced level courses. Additionally, the guidelines are intended to foster student success and to lead to increased enrollments at the advanced level. The guidelines will be re-evaluated after analysis of writing samples to be conducted during AY 11–12;

2. Continued the writing assessment initiative initiated in AY 2009–2010, including the establishment of best practices and assessment criteria for all programs, and for both the lower and upper divisions of the curriculum; the drafting of guidelines, best practices, rubrics, protocols for writing in beginning, intermediate and gateway courses in all programs; the collection of writing samples at benchmark levels in all programs, and started a review process of assessing writing samples at benchmark levels in all programs.

    In addition, subcommittees worked on:

    a. Defining the purpose of writing at each particular level, in order to make explicit our learning goals in writing/writing profiles at each curricular level (in other words in order to respond to the question: what should students be able to write at each level and why?);

b. Creating explicit writing guidelines for syllabi (how many writing assignments at each level in a semester? how long should writing assignments be? what genres and contents of writing assignments are most appropriate at each level? What language (grammar, syntax, and vocabulary) and writing features (structure and organization of the writing assignments) should students use? What are the criteria followed for the evaluation of the writing assignments? What percentage of the total final grade is each writing going to represent?);

c. Creating rubrics that break down the elements we want to assess in writing assignments at each particular level (for instance: vocabulary and style; grammar and syntax, organization of the composition; creativity; coherence of the ideas etc.). The rubrics are meant to be shared with students at the beginning of the semester as an explicit statement of what their writing assignments will be evaluated for and what type of feedback they should expect from their instructor;

d. Collecting samples of graded and glossed writing assignments at each level, in order to have a practical example of what we consider an A paper, a B paper etc.;

e. Collecting samples of writing prompts we currently use at each course level, in order to assess their effectiveness (in terms of providing clear instructions about what a given writing assignment should contain: what are the context, purpose and audience of a given assignment? What content should be included? Is the writing an in-class or a take-home assignment? Is there a conventional format assignments need to meet? Are students allowed to consult dictionaries, textbooks, or to use the help of writing tutors?). On the other hand we want to assess if the prompts reflect the learning goals/writing profiles we have been defining so far, and to define best practices for writing prompts;

f. Collecting samples of the final writing assessment at crucial junctures of the program (at the end of the language requirement, which is the end of third semester; and at the end of the gateway course): this stage will be completed at the end of the current semester, of course, and its purpose is to assess if the students' assignments reflect the level of language/content we state as our learning goals for the language requirement/end of the gateway courses.

Members of the CSRLC and other select faculty using an on-line rating survey in summer 2011 will review writing samples. Observations and findings will be shared with the department and programs in fall 2011 for further discussion and formal recommendations by end of AY 11–12;

3. Continued participation and collaboration on Utilization-focused outcomes assessment with University of Hawai'i and consortium on assessment in the humanities with Georgetown, Emory and Rice;

4. Generated on-line senior surveys (see attached appendix II);

5. Distributed online alumni surveys in April 2011 and will be collected in early August and will report findings next year.

This report is to be provided to the faculty of the Department, and shared with the College administration, and with other interested groups as appropriate. It will be used by the CSRLC to make recommendations to the Department that will lead to improvements in the curriculum and teaching practices.

Department of Romance Language and Literatures

Assessment Report 2011–2012

Specifically in AY 2011–12, The CSRLC

Created guidelines for fifth-semester conversation courses in all programs and for the new Community-Based Learning course in Spanish to be offered fall 2012:

http://romancelanguages.nd.edu/assessment/

The guidelines provide faculty members with a general framework for creating new courses at this upper intermediate level that are meant to "bridge" from language and culture courses to the gateway/advanced level courses. Additionally, the guidelines are intended to foster student success and to lead to increased enrollments at the advanced level. The guidelines will be re-evaluated after implementation during AY 12–13;

The CSRLC writing assessment initiative initiated in AY 2009–2010 was continued.

Samples of graded and glossed writing assignments at each level were collected, in order to have a practical example of what we consider an A paper, a B paper etc.;

Samples of writing prompts we currently use at each course level were collected, in order to assess their effectiveness (in terms of providing clear instructions about what a given writing assignment should contain: what are the context, purpose and audience of a given assignment? What content should be included? Is the writing an in-class or a take-home assignment? Is there a conventional format assignments need to meet? Are students allowed to consult dictionaries, textbooks, or to use the help of writing tutors?). On the other hand we want to assess if the prompts reflect the learning goals/writing profiles we have been defining so far, and to define best practices for writing prompts;

Samples of the final writing assessment at crucial junctures of the program were collected (at the end of the language requirement, which is the end of third semester; and at the end of the gateway course to the major). Its purpose is to assess if the students' assignments reflect the level of language/content we state as our learning goals for the language requirement/end of the gateway courses;

Members of the CSRLC and other select faculty using an on-line rating survey reviewed writing samples. Observations and findings were shared with the department and programs in fall 2011 for further discussion.

The CSRLC arranged a half-day retreat during exam week (Mid-December).

The goal was to involve all faculty members in the Department in the important conversation about writing that started in the CSRLC. All faculty members were provided, before the retreat, necessary materials that had been reviewed by the committee. Faculty members were asked to review the materials and identify strengths and areas of opportunity for improvement for discussion. Additionally, each program sent out a set of questions a head of time to help guide the discussion concerning writing assessment. The afternoon was organized into two sessions with a break between sessions and ending with a reception. (Each session lasted one hour, thirty minutes) Program Liaisons and members of the CSRLC lead the discussions.

In part one, following a brief introduction, respective programs met separately to discuss writing assessment rating surveys and senior survey responses. Each program was asked to come up with 3–5 action items to move forward with and to share in the second session.

In part two, each program reported their findings. From the general discussion recommendations of next steps for respective Programs and the Department were made.

This was found to be such a valuable way to talk about assessment and curricular issues as a Department that it is now an annual event. On our agenda for next year is "grade inflation."

Additionally, as a result of the half-day retreat in mid-December, the CSRLC arranged and co-sponsored with the CSLC on Error Correction in Foreign Language and to provide consultation in regards to our writing assessment project.

The CSRLC created an on-line survey to collect feedback from faculty members in order to continue the discussions in fall 2012 that started with Lourdes' visit.

The CSRLC continued participation and collaboration on Utilization-focused outcomes assessment with University of Hawai'i and consortium on assessment in the humanities with Georgetown, Emory and Rice;

The CSRLC distributed revised online senior surveys in April 2012 to all graduating seniors completing a major/minor in our programs. For student response trends see attached appendix II;

The CSRLC ran a second round of OPI testing with a randomly selected group of graduating seniors in each of our programs. Staff in the Center for the Study of Languages and Cultures (CSLC) helped facilitate testing. Thirteen students in French were tested, fifteen in Italian and 16 in Spanish. Romance Language majors were included with individual programs.

The CSRLC revised observation forms used for formative reviews of lecturer faculty.

Senior survey questionnaire

Background questions

1. What is your expected year of graduation?
2. What is/are your major(s) at ND?
3. What is/are your minor(s) at ND?
4. What was your first Romance Language course taken at ND?
5. How many Italian courses have you taken at ND, including courses taken abroad and during this semester?
6. How many years of high school Italian did you have?

7. What is your native language?
8. Which other language(s) do you know? Indicate language and estimated level of ability: near native, very high, high, intermediate, low.
9. List three most significant experiences you have had in the Italian speaking world. Indicate (1) age when there; (2) length of stay (in weeks) and (3) nature of experience (e.g.,16–17 years old; 40 weeks; high school year abroad in X country)

Appendix E. Italian Studies learning goals for upper division courses

30310 Textual analysis and advanced grammar review

Skills

Most students will achieve at least Intermediate High in reading and listening comprehension; the course aims for Advanced. Students will be able to understand most points of extended speech and lectures (with some rephrasing and repetition) on cultural/literary topics, begin to follow more complex arguments, begin to understand standard speech from various media, and begin to recognize nuances of meaning. Students will be able to read and understand a variety of short literary texts (with some time and effort), expand their vocabulary, and begin to recognize nuances of meaning.

Most students will achieve at least Intermediate High in speaking and writing; the course aims for Advanced Low. Students will be able to interact in informal discussions on cultural/literary topics, combine and link sentences into paragraph-length discourse, using various tenses, and be able to make arguments related to course content. They will be able to write short academic essays (1–3 pages) on literary/cultural topics (for example, summarizing the analysis of a text or artifact done collectively in class) with increasing accuracy and coherence, and begin to apply the analytic techniques and terms presented in class to new texts and artifacts. Students will have substantial control of simple target-language sentence structures, begin to demonstrate control of more complex structures, and be able to revise and edit their writing to improve its clarity, coherence, and correctness.

Students will be able to do a basic formal analysis of short but authentic texts in different genres (lyric poetry, novella, drama). For poetry this means being able to do a metrical and structural analysis of varied lyric forms (canzone, sonetto, ballata), including verse scansion, rhyme types, stanza types, formal structure. For the novella or short excerpts from novels, this means being able to apply the basic categories of narrative technique: space, time, narrative voice, point of view, character type, etc...). Students will be able to recognize basic rhetorical tropes and figures. They will begin to relate the analysis of texts to their cultural, social, and historical contexts.

Knowledge

Students will gain a more analytical knowledge of grammatical structures and terms, fill in the gaps in their previous study of grammar (e.g., *passato remoto*), and begin to have a more unified, comprehensive, and systematic grasp of the grammar as a whole.

Students will expand their vocabulary, through careful attention to the meaning of words as they function in texts. This course in part teaches the language through texts, while also teaching texts through the language.

Students will be familiar with the basic genres of literature (drama, short story, lyric poetry, novel, epic, etc...), with the key periods and movements of Italian history (*medioevo, umane-simo, romanticismo*, etc...) and some of the key authors and figures of Italian literature and culture.

Students will be exposed to a variety of cultural forms and artifacts within this course, including film, art, architecture, music, and media, as a complement to the analysis of literary texts, and to give a sense of the integral unity of culture,. They will gain a first introduction to some basic terms and techniques in the analysis of film, opera, and media.

The basic texts for the course are: *Mezzadri, Grammatica essenziale della lingua italiana con esercizi* (Guerra) for grammar; *Balboni and Cardona, Storia e testi di letteratura italiana per stranieri* (Guerra) for literary texts and basic historical/cultural context. These textbooks could well be supplemented: for example, by a short history of Italy, perhaps a short guide to Italian film and media, and perhaps a guide to grammatical terms and structures in English.

Dispositions

Students should develop excitement as they begin to discover the keys to how literature works and conveys meaning, as they become sensitive to music and rhythm in poetry, as they begin to grasp the profundity and complexity of allusion and meaning in film and other cultural artifacts. They should begin to feel literature, and each of the forms of culture (art, music, architecture, media, etc..) as part of an integral cultural context.

Students should begin to respond to beauty in literature and the other arts, and feel the power of literature and the arts to reveal deeper dimensions of life and experience, to make us more conscious of ourselves and our experience.

Students should feel that they are beginning to have ownership of a few literary text and cultural artifacts. They should begin to feel how language and literature and culture are one (for example, how literary techniques and tropes pervade all our language and thought).

Students should fall more deeply in love with Italy, with the Italian language, and with Italian culture.

Assessing Student Perceptions of Writing and Culture in an Italian Curriculum

Anna De Fina
Donatella Melucci
Georgetown University

This chapter reports on an assessment project in which the Department of Italian at Georgetown University investigated student perspectives on the department's student learning outcomes. The focus of the project was on writing and cultural learning, areas at the center of a previous curriculum renewal and development effort. The project involved the creation of a survey to shed light on student perceptions about their writing achievement and cultural learning, as well as on student opinions about aspects of the writing and culture curriculum and instruction more generally. The chapter describes the design and implementation of the survey and reports on main findings and implications for instructional practice and curricular design. The chapter also stresses the importance of outcomes assessment as a tool to evaluate the effectiveness of curricula and provide insights into potential adaptations necessary to enhance educational quality of language programs.

Introduction

The usefulness of outcomes assessment in language instruction has recently been emphasized in the applied linguistics literature and evidenced by assessment practice in foreign language departments across the country (see, among others, Byrnes, 2002; Dassier & Powell, 2001; Grau Sempere, Mohn, & Pieroni, 2009; Pfeiffer & Byrnes, 2009). Indeed, assessing student learning outcomes is an important part of foreign language educational delivery, since learning outcomes represent a realistic and tangible picture of a program's value. As stated by

Norris (2006), "[student learning outcomes] serve as a touchstone for curriculum development, instructional practice, learner advancement and achievement, and to be sure, program evaluation and improvement" (p. 577).

Ideally, outcomes assessment should be an ongoing, collaborative process through which educators systematically collect, analyze, and interpret evidence of student learning in order to determine how well student performance matches program expectations and standards. The resulting information on student learning is useful for documenting, understanding, explaining, and improving performance, and also for identifying pedagogical strategies and other program reforms that take into consideration changes in educational environments and student needs (Angelo, 1995). In response to recent trends and developments in language program assessment practice, the Italian Department at Georgetown University (GU), in collaboration with researchers from the National Foreign Language Resource Center at the University of Hawai'i at Mānoa, embarked on a project to assess student learning outcomes within the context of a curriculum renewal project implemented in 2010.

Curriculum renewal project

A curriculum renewal project was initiated by the Italian Department in 2005. The project was developed under the leadership/supervision of both the Language Coordinator and the Head of Department and involved collaboration of all the staff, including tenure and non-tenure track members. Its objective was to develop greater curricular coherence between beginning-level language courses with an emphasis on language instruction, and upper-level courses emphasizing literary and cultural studies. The department had perceived a gap between the achievement of students completing the lower-level, language-learning component of the curriculum and the expected abilities for students in upper-level courses. Faculty thus felt that greater instructional continuity was needed between these two components of the Italian curriculum.

In order to achieve greater coherence, faculty decided to focus on developing two aspects of the lower-level curriculum. The first was the integration of cultural content into language courses, focusing in particular on increasing students' general knowledge of basic cultural issues and social movements in Italy. The second was the development of writing ability and critical thinking skills from the first semester of instruction. The department agreed that a focus on writing skills, within culturally meaningful tasks, could be a way to develop not only writing ability but students' critical thinking skills as well. A number of curricular revisions resulted from these initial reflections and decisions, including (a) the creation and implementation of a gateway and a capstone course in Italian literature; (b) a restructuring of the Senior Seminar; (c) the creation of a set of specific writing tasks centered on culturally salient topics reflective of expected learner development at distinct levels of the language curriculum; (d) the design of sample writing tasks for some of the upper level courses; (e) the implementation of process writing throughout the curriculum including upper level courses; (f) the articulation of specific student learning outcomes for writing for the Language Program; and (g) the rewriting of the general learning outcomes for the major and the minor with a specification of outcomes for writing.

Italian curriculum at Georgetown University

Students learning Italian at Georgetown University initially enroll in four semesters of intensive language instruction; Basic Italian (the first semester course), Intermediate Italian (second semester), Advanced I Italian (third semester), and Advanced II Italian (fourth semester). Completing this sequence satisfies requirements for pursuing a minor or a major in Italian. Italian minors are required to take two additional courses taught in Italian at the 200 or 300 level. Italian majors, instead, continue on to the upper-level sequence, enrolling in six to eight courses on Italian society, linguistics, literature, art, film, history, and business, and one gateway course in English taken in the second semester of the first year. This course satisfies one of the two literature and writing requirements of the college. Majors are also required to spend a semester or an academic year in Italy studying at an Italian university. Both majors and minors are required to take Writing and Culture, a three-credit course at the 200-level, after they have completed four semesters of intensive language study. The course is articulated around the production of writing tasks representing different genres, from academic essays to application letters to film reviews.

The department defines student achievement in writing in terms of the writing outcomes derived from the curriculum renewal project. Outcomes for the cycle Intensive Basic through Intensive Advanced II (4 semesters) are expressed in terms of *language foci* and *writing performance*. Language foci include the lexico-grammatical structures that students are supposed to be able to manage at a particular level. Writing performance includes linguistic functions, level of textual cohesion, textual genres that students are expected to produce at that level, and topics on which they are expected to write. Outcomes for the minor include the incorporation of a greater variety of writing tasks (as reflected in the Writing and Culture course), production of work on a wide spectrum of culturally salient topics, as well as production of academic writing with respect to the basic language cycle. Achievement is defined also in terms of greater accuracy in grammar, spelling, punctuation, and vocabulary with respect to students having completed only the 4 semesters of language study. Majors are expected to write more complex texts demonstrating ability to produce argumentation and critical analysis in various genres, and likewise displaying accurate grammar, spelling, punctuation, and varied use of vocabulary (see Table 3 for examples of textual genres and topics for majors). The Italian program's focus on writing exposes students at all levels to a wide variety of literary and non-literary texts, and requires that they produce different types of writing every week. Student writing is assessed through rubrics that evaluate language accuracy, coherence, pragmatic adequacy, and (in the case of advanced students) the ability to connect specific ideas to more general cultural issues. Tables 2, 3, and 4 show the revised outcomes in these areas.

Assessment project

The assessment project undertaken between 2011 and 2012 was part of an ongoing effort initiated by the Italian Department to evaluate the effectiveness of the curriculum renewal described above. In particular, the faculty wanted to understand current levels of student achievement and the perceived value of learning outcomes for writing from the students' point of view. To these ends, the department decided to develop assessment tools that would shed light on student perceptions, as well as suggest potential pedagogic strategies to help students reach stated outcomes.

Faculty had already initiated a periodic revision of the writing tasks in the lower-level language courses and had carried out an informal assessment of student writing in May of 2010. The assessment involved language teachers rating student writing samples according to rubrics based on the newly-developed learning outcomes. The findings from this process led to a number of changes in the writing tasks and modifications in the learning outcome statements. The department was thus interested in knowing what impacts these changes had on student learning and the opinions of students on the curricular changes. A subsequent assessment project—the project described herein—was conceived to address these concerns.

The first phase of the assessment project—initiated in Fall 2010 in collaboration with John Norris and Yukiko Watanabe from the University of Hawai'i at Mānoa (both experts in foreign language outcomes assessment)—involved a revision and reconsideration of the learning outcomes for the major and minor. In particular, the department decided to focus on writing outcomes and how well they expressed appropriate and valued targets for Italian language studies at GU. Following suggestions by John Norris, faculty rewrote the learning outcomes for the minor and the major, revising them based on a clearer differentiation between programmatic goals and specific learning outcomes, spelling out expected outcomes for the language component, and better expressing the departmental mission statement (see Appendix). The writing outcomes for all language levels were also revised, including a clearer statement of the relationships between pedagogic activities, language foci, and expected performance. Reviewing and rewriting learning outcomes was a reflective practice that led to important insights into the curriculum design of the Italian language program. Indeed, discussing and rewriting learning outcomes was a way of reflecting on the coherence among the specific objectives of courses, the developmental stages of the curriculum, and the department's general educational mission and educational priorities. Having revised the writing outcomes, the department felt that it had established a firm foundation from which it could start designing meaningful and useful assessment tools.

Assessment project focus and survey development

The assessment project involved the creation of a survey to be administered to students at different stages in the Italian curriculum. In particular, the survey was administered to students enrolled in intermediate and advanced levels. Students at the intermediate level were those enrolled in an intermediate Italian course in the spring of 2012. Advanced-level students consisted of (a) students enrolled in the Writing and Culture course (during the fall of 2011 and the spring of 2012) and (b) graduating majors enrolled in a course on Dante (enrolled in spring 2012). The questions on the survey would specifically address students' perceptions about the department's focus on writing and culture, and about their ability to reach expected outcomes at different levels. As mentioned above, writing and cultural learning had been the primary foci of the curriculum renewal project, and the department felt it was important to shed light on students' perspectives on these recent curriculum changes.

Survey development and administration involved collaboration with John Norris and Yukiko Watanabe and the Georgetown Center for New Design in Learning and Scholarship, which provided assistance in disseminating the survey online. The survey was designed to provide maximally useful data in response to specific, well-established intended uses. As mentioned, the focus was on students' opinions about the emphasis on writing and culture in the curriculum and on how they view their performance and learning within the program. In particular, the questions that the faculty wanted to answer via the assessment project were as follows:

What are students' perceptions regarding whether they are able to perform the writing outcomes at the targeted ability levels the program expects students to achieve?

- What are students' perceptions regarding the value of this emphasis?
- What do students think about the program's emphasis on culture?
- What do they feel that they are learning with respect to cultural issues?

Within these broad categories of interest, the faculty further identified a number of narrower concerns. More specifically, the department wanted to know

- whether students feel that they learn how to perform the different types of writing tasks that are specified in the writing outcomes and how well they think they perform in them;
- whether students understand that writing has a central place in the Italian curriculum (and why);
- whether students think there is a connection between writing and the development of cultural awareness and critical skills (a link which motivated the whole curriculum renewal);
- whether students agree on the importance of writing in the Italian curriculum;
- whether students feel that a focus on writing conflicts with the development of oral abilities;
- what specific pedagogical tools and strategies have helped students (or not) in developing writing abilities; and
- how students rate their cultural literacy in Italian.

In the fall of 2011, a draft of the student survey was created by the Language Program Coordinator. The draft was then reviewed by the rest of the faculty, both individually and collaboratively, and by John Norris and Yukiko Watanabe. Two versions of the survey were created: one to be administered to students at the intermediate level and one to be administered to students at the advanced level, with survey questions referring to writing tasks, pedagogical writing strategies and techniques, and learning outcomes specific to those students at those levels.

Survey

The survey consisted of a total of 32 questions. Some questions were open ended (i.e., open response allowing comments); others were based on a 4-point Likert scale. The survey was divided into five sections, each focusing on a specific area of interest:

Section I: Academic, linguistic, and cultural background questions

Section II: Self-assessment of performance on cultural and writing outcomes

Section III: Students' perceptions of department's cultural and writing outcomes

Section IV: Students' perceptions on writing tasks and their usefulness

Section V: Students' perceptions about the usefulness of pedagogical strategies

The first section of the survey consisted of 11 background questions focused on academic, linguistic, and cultural information. For example, students were to indicate the year they enrolled at Georgetown; if they were an Italian major, minor, or undeclared; whether they had studied Italian before; if they were enrolled in an Italian course at the time of the survey; whether they had experienced study-abroad in Italy; and if they had an Italian heritage.

The second section of the survey (Section II) contained questions, based on a Likert scale, on students' self-rated learning and was meant to investigate if students felt they had achieved some of the new learning outcomes set by the Italian department (e.g., *To what extent can you...write texts in Italian with correct grammar? Not at all, A little, Adequately, Very well, Not sure*). Students had to rate their ability to write an essay in Italian expressing personal opinions, or using correct syntax, grammar, and spelling (see Tables 2 and 3 for examples of outcomes statements). Students were also asked to indicate the extent to which they gained knowledge and understanding of Italian culture (e.g., *To what extent do you feel that studying Italian you have gained knowledge and understanding of...[the] organization of social life in Italy: Not at all, A little, Adequately, Very well, Not sure*). In addition, some open-ended questions asked students if there were certain cultural aspects of the curriculum they wanted to study more deeply, such as Italian history, Italian social issues, Italian interaction and communication patterns, or Italian literary and artistic traditions.

The third section of the survey (Section III) contained some general questions, based on a Likert scale (*Very dissatisfied, Somewhat dissatisfied, Somewhat satisfied, Very satisfied*) about students' satisfaction with the department's instructional emphasis on writing and culture (e.g., *Please rate your overall satisfaction with the instructional emphasis on writing/culture in the Italian program.*). In addition, students were asked to express their opinions on whether the emphasis on writing helped or hindered the development of other skills such as speaking or reading in Italian, and also if the emphasis on culture helped them think critically about social and academic issues, generally, as well as stimulate thinking about their own culture.

The fourth section (Section IV) focused on the usefulness of specific tasks used in the teaching of writing (e.g., *How useful are the following tasks for helping you learn to write in Italian?*). Using a Likert scale (*Not at all, A little, Somewhat, A lot, Not sure, N/A*) students were asked about specific writing assignments such as personal descriptions, discussion forum posts, diaries, personal narratives, expository texts, film reviews, creative fiction, summaries, critical interpretation, and academic papers. In this section, students had to also indicate whether writing tasks were appropriate for learners at their proficiency level and if these tasks helped them to think critically and to understand Italian cultural issues.

The fifth and last section of the survey (Section V) included specific questions about pedagogical techniques used by students and instructors to improve the learning process of writing (e.g., *How useful are the following strategies for helping you learn to write in Italian?*). Using a Likert scale (*Not useful at all, A little useful, Somewhat useful, Very useful, Not sure*) students had to express their opinions on the usefulness of particular student learning strategies (e.g., writing multiple drafts, outlines, discussing a paper with peers or teachers), as well as strategies used by teachers (e.g., providing example models of genres of texts, providing written comments or corrections, using grading rubrics, identifying resources, working with students in class, reviewing common writing problems and errors).

In order to elicit honest and rich responses, an anonymous web-based version of the questionnaire was created with the help of Georgetown CNDLS. This allowed the department to obtain detailed information from students regarding their perceptions and opinions, and also provided students an opportunity to express their opinions frankly. Moreover, the anonymity of the survey helped reassure instructors that the survey was not intended to assess the quality of individual courses or the performance of individual instructors and was only a tool for improving the curriculum.

As mentioned before, the assessment project followed a pre-post curricular design (using a cross-sectional rather than longitudinal sample) in that the survey was distributed to students at different points in the curriculum. Again, the survey was administered to intermediate students enrolled in Intermediate Italian, and to advanced students enrolled in Writing and Culture as well as graduating majors enrolled in a literature course on Dante. Indeed, although the department introduces writing instruction at the beginning, lower-level courses of the language curriculum, students at the intermediate level are just starting to be exposed to aspects of "process" writing (such as peer review) as compared with the more advanced students and majors who had encountered many process-writing tasks throughout their advanced-level courses. That is to say, the further a student progresses in the curriculum, the more the student will have experienced process writing and different types of writing task. Thus, the survey was supposed to provide some sense of whether increased exposure to process writing and more complex writing tasks leads to change in students' language proficiency and cultural content knowledge. In addition to gathering important baseline data on students' perceptions regarding learning development at key points in the curriculum, faculty expected the survey results to help determine the effectiveness of teaching strategies, thus allowing adjustments to be made if necessary.

When a final version of the survey was ready, a pilot was conducted in fall 2011 with a small number of intermediate and advanced students, to ensure that both the instrument and the administration procedures were meaningful and feasible. The survey was distributed in written form to two students from Intensive Intermediate Italian I and two students from Italian Writing and Culture. The students were given a tape recorder and asked to record their observations on the survey. Based on the pilot, some further small changes were introduced to the survey by the Language Coordinator. As mentioned above, the survey was then distributed to students who were enrolled in either intermediate- or advanced-level courses. A total of 32 participants were enrolled in Intensive Intermediate Italian. Advanced-level participants came from three groups: two groups (26 participants) enrolled in two Writing and Culture courses (in Fall 2011 and Spring 2012), and one group enrolled in a course on Dante (8 participants). In total, 34 advanced-level participants responded to the survey, for a total of 66 respondents altogether.

Data collection, analysis, and findings

Raw survey response data were provided by GU CNDLS, the hosts of the online survey. Data were initially analyzed by the University of Hawai'i team who sent a summary to the Language Coordinator. Then, they were discussed in a committee composed of the Language Coordinator and a colleague from the Language Program. Finally, they were presented to the whole department for discussion and interpretation. Analysis of results for sections II through V involved comparing responses between intermediate and advanced level-students in order to gauge differences in (a) perceptions of student learning achievement, (b) opinions about the department's cultural and writing outcomes, and (c) the usefulness of curricular writing tasks and pedagogical strategies. In the following, findings are summarized for each section of the survey.

Participants' backgrounds

The department was interested in knowing students' background information, particularly whether participants were pursuing a major or minor in Italian, or if they were undeclared. In addition, the department wanted to know if students identified themselves as having Italian cultural heritage or Italian linguistic heritage. Finally, faculty were interested in knowing which students had attended a study–abroad program (through Georgetown or another institution). Table 1 shows survey results for intermediate-level and advanced-level participants' academic, linguistic, and cultural backgrounds.

Table 1. Comparisons on academic, linguistic, and heritage background across groups

group	total	major	minor	cultural heritage	linguistic heritage	study abroad
intermediate	32	1	5	24	7	1
advanced	34	10	18	20	12	14

As shown in Table 1, the backgrounds of intermediate students were similar. One student was pursuing a major in Italian, five students were pursuing a minor, and the majority of respondents had an Italian cultural or linguistic heritage background (only one student had experienced study-abroad). Given the background similarities between intermediate respondents, these variables were not taken into account in subsequent analyses for the intermediate-level groups.

By contrast, background data for advanced-level students showed more variation. Faculty were thus interested in conducting analyses across the different background categories to see whether such variables play a role in advanced-level student perceptions of writing/cultural learning, or opinions on the writing curriculum. Hence, advanced-level participants were divided into the following subgroups:

Major/minor/undeclared: Students pursuing a major in Italian (MJ), a minor (MN), or no major/minor (No MJ/MN) declared

Study abroad: Students who experienced a study abroad program (SA) with Georgetown University or another institution; students with no study abroad experience (No SA)

Heritage learners: Students identifying an Italian linguistic heritage (LH); students with no Italian language heritage (No LH)

Cultural heritage: Students identifying an Italian cultural heritage (CH); students with no Italian cultural heritage (No CH)

Analysis: Sections II–V

Again, respondents in sections II through V were asked to self-assess their level of writing learning or achievement, their degree of satisfaction with various program elements, and the usefulness of various teaching and learning strategies. In addition, each section provided an open response item giving respondents an opportunity to comment and elaborate on their ratings responses. A mean rating was calculated for each group on each survey item to indicate aggregate levels of satisfaction, learning, or helpfulness for a given group as a whole.[1] Moreover, the committee/faculty defined "positive" results from sections II through V in terms of mean values of three (3) or above. That is to say, mean ratings of 3 or above were regarded as indicating sufficient levels of (perceived) student achievement, satisfaction, or instructional helpfulness. Mean values below 3 were regarded as indicating areas for concern and in need of attention.

Results: Section II–V

Overall, responses to the survey from intermediate and the advanced–level students revealed that respondents were generally optimistic about their learning achievement, confident about their writing abilities, and satisfied with the quality of instruction within the Department of Italian. Moreover, students found the Italian curriculum to be useful for their performance and learning in other non-Italian courses. The results were informative since students' perceptions of the Italian curriculum, especially the emphasis on writing and culture, helped identify the strengths and weaknesses of Italian department program. Student feedback also provided insights into the usefulness of certain writing tasks and pedagogical strategies. In the next section, results for each of the remaining survey sections (II, III, IV, and V) will be presented.

Section II—Self perceptions of cultural and writing learning

In Section II, the majority of participants at the intermediate level responded positively with regard to their self-assessed competence in performing certain writing outcomes (see Table 2). For example, respondents felt able to produce writing texts with correct grammar ($M=3.00$) and correct spelling and punctuation ($M=3.13$). Respondents also felt able to write paragraphs with connectors and free of isolated sentences ($M=3.16$). However, as shown in Table 2, some concerns emerged that respondents were less able to write with sufficiently varied vocabulary ($M=2.97$) and express a personal point of view on issues and texts ($M=2.91$).

---

[1] Each point on the Likert scale was assigned a value (not at all=1; a little=2; adequately=3; very well=4). All ratings were summed and divided by the number of respondents, producing a mean value for each survey rating item.

Table 2. Self-assessment of performance in cultural and writing learning outcomes (intermediate)

Q1. To what extent can you do the following?	N	M	SD	not at all	a little	adequate	very well	not sure
(a) Write texts in Italian with correct grammar	32	3.00	0.62	0%	19%	63%	19%	0%
(b) Write texts in Italian with correct spelling and punctuation	32	3.13	0.66	0%	16%	56%	28%	0%
(c) Write texts in Italian with sufficient vocabulary	32	2.97	0.65	0%	22%	59%	19%	0%
(d) Write in paragraphs with connectors and not in isolated sentences	32	3.16	0.68	0%	16%	53%	31%	0%
(e) Express my personal point of view on issues and texts in writing	32	2.91	0.64	0%	25%	59%	16%	0%

These concerns were also expressed in comments written by respondents elaborating on their self-ratings:

> "I still lack the vocab to cohesively and elegantly express my own opinions."

> "I know what I want to say in English but I have trouble thinking of the right Italian words without simplifying my ideas too much."

A concern with lacking vocabulary is understandable at the intermediate level since students are eager to express themselves as they do in their first language, though their competence in the target language is still limited.

Responses from advanced-level participants showed that students have positive perceptions of their ability to write texts in Italian with correct grammar, spelling, and pronunciation (see Table 3). Moreover, their confidence on the use of vocabulary is greater ($M=3.55$) compared to the intermediate level ($M=2.97$). Advanced-level students' perceptions about their ability to write on works of art ($M=2.93$) were the lowest of all ratings in this section of the survey. This is likely due to the fact that such tasks are not given frequently in any of the courses of the curriculum. If comparisons are made between each advanced-level subgroup, we observe that the majors expressed slightly more positive responses overall compared to the other subgroups.

Table 3. Mean self-assessment of performance on cultural and writing learning outcomes (advanced and subgroups)*

Q1. To what extent can you do the following?	all	advanced subgroups								
		MJ	MN	no MJ/MN	SA	no SA	CH	no CH	LH	no LH
(a) Write texts in Italian with mostly correct grammar	3.53	3.80	3.33	3.67	3.64	3.45	3.64	3.44	3.70	3.46
(b) Write texts in Italian with correct spelling and punctuation	3.65	3.80	3.61	3.50	3.79	3.55	3.64	3.67	3.70	3.63
(c) Write texts in Italian using the vocabulary that you have learned	3.55	3.56	3.56	3.50	3.57	3.53	3.60	3.56	3.44	3.58
(d) Write a critical analysis of Italian literary texts	3.50	3.70	3.39	3.50	3.57	3.45	3.64	3.22	3.60	3.46
(e) Write a critical analysis of non-literary texts	3.53	3.60	3.56	3.33	3.57	3.50	3.64	3.33	3.60	3.50
(f) Write a critical analysis of films	3.33	3.22	3.38	3.40	3.17	3.44	3.30	3.17	3.33	3.33
(g) Write a critical analysis of works of art	2.93	3.10	2.80	3.00	2.58	3.18	3.00	2.57	3.10	2.84
(h) Write argumentative texts about academic and social issues	3.48	3.70	3.35	3.50	3.62	3.40	3.55	3.13	3.60	3.43
(i) Connect Italian texts to their contexts (historical, literary and cultural contexts)	3.39	3.60	3.24	3.50	3.57	3.26	3.55	3.00	3.50	3.35

* Italian major (MJ), minor (MN), undeclared (No MJ/MN), study abroad (SA), no study abroad (No SA), Italian cultural heritage (CH), non-Italian cultural heritage (No CH), Italian linguistic heritage (LH), non-Italian language heritage (No LH)

Table 4. Mean student perception ratings of cultural understanding (intermediate and advanced groups)*

Q2. To what extent do you feel that studying Italian you have gained knowledge and understanding of the following topics	int.	adv.	advanced subgroups								
			MJ	MN	no MJ/MN	SA	no SA	CH	no CH	LH	no LH
(a) The organization of social life in Italy (family, education, entertainment, etc.)	3.63	3.86	3.70	3.83	3.83	3.86	3.75	3.64	3.89	3.70	3.83
(b) The geography of Italy	3.59	3.14	3.30	3.44	3.17	3.64	3.15	3.55	3.44	3.50	3.29

continued...

Table 4. Mean student perception ratings of cultural understanding (intermediate and advanced groups)* *(cont.)*

Q2. To what extent do you feel that studying Italian you have gained knowledge and understanding of the following topics	int.	adv.	advanced subgroups								
			MJ	MN	no MJ/MN	SA	no SA	CH	no CH	LH	no LH
(c) Social issues such as youth, migration, and unemployment	3.19	3.86	3.70	3.78	3.83	3.93	3.65	3.55	3.89	3.70	3.79
(d) Communication patterns (such as politeness, gesture, pragmatics) in Italy	3.06	3.36	3.50	3.39	3.33	3.50	3.35	3.45	3.44	3.60	3.33
(e) The linguistic situation of Italy	N/A**	3.64	3.40	3.67	3.50	3.57	3.55	3.45	3.56	3.60	3.54
(f) Major artistic traditions of Italy	N/A	3.21	3.00	3.33	3.17	2.93	3.40	3.00	3.44	2.90	3.33
(g) Major literary authors in Italy	N/A	3.36	3.60	3.33	3.00	3.21	3.45	3.27	3.44	3.40	3.33
(h) Major events in the history of Italy	N/A	3.57	3.50	3.78	3.33	3.64	3.60	3.55	3.78	3.50	3.67
(i) Italian culture in general	3.44	3.93	3.78	3.94	4.00	3.93	3.89	3.80	4.00	3.78	3.96

* Intermediate (INT), advanced (ADV), Italian major (MJ), minor (MN), undeclared (No MJ/MN), study abroad (SA), no study abroad (No SA), Italian cultural heritage (CH), non-Italian cultural heritage (No CH), Italian linguistic heritage (LH), non-Italian language heritage (No LH)

** Items (e), (f), (g), and (h) were not included in the survey for the intermediate level.

Table 5. Mean student satisfaction ratings with writing and culture curriculum (intermediate and advanced groups)*

	int.	adv.	advanced subgroups								
			MJ	MN	no MJ/MN	SA	no SA	CH	no CH	LH	no LH
Q1. Please rate your overall satisfaction with the instructional emphasis on writing in the Italian program.	3.19	3.45	3.44	3.33	3.83	3.64	3.89	3.40	3.11	3.33	3.50
Q4. Please rate your overall satisfaction with the instructional emphasis on culture in the Italian program.	3.44	3.56	3.30	3.72	3.50	3.50	3.60	3.36	3.67	3.30	3.67

* Intermediate (INT), advanced (ADV), Italian major (MJ), minor (MN), undeclared (No MJ/MN), study abroad (SA), no study abroad (No SA), Italian cultural heritage (CH), non-Italian cultural heritage (No CH), Italian linguistic heritage (LH), non-Italian language heritage (No LH)

Students at both levels expressed positive perceptions of their gained knowledge and understanding of certain culturally salient topics. As shown in Table 4, intermediate-level students indicated high ratings for learning about the organization of social life in Italy (M=3.63), the geography of Italy (M=3.59) and Italian culture in general (M=3.44). At the advanced level, all mean ratings increased, except for the topic Geography in Italy (M=3.14), demonstrating a gain in knowledge and understanding on these topics. The only topic rated by the advanced levels lower than our expectation (M=3.21), compared to other categories, is that of major artistic traditions of Italy, a result that the department needs to address through adjustments in the program at all levels. Minor differences are noticed in the mean values across the subgroups of the advanced-level students.

In the open-ended question, students in both intermediate—and advanced-level courses had the opportunity to elaborate on topics they would like to study more in Italian classes. Responses varied and included broad domains such as history, social and political issues, economy, art, poetry, music, and food.

Section III—Opinions of cultural and writing outcomes; satisfaction with the writing and culture curriculum

Table 5 shows that students have high levels of satisfaction with the instructional emphasis on writing and culture in the Italian program, as evidenced by increases in agreement ratings from the intermediate level (writing, M=3.19; culture, M=3.44) to the advanced level (writing, M=3.45; culture, M=3.56). However, when observing responses by subgroups within the advanced level, students not pursuing a major or a minor, along with students with no experience in a study-abroad program, showed a more positive perception of the instructional emphasis on writing than the other subgroups. Also, students pursuing a minor in Italian, along with students with no cultural or language heritage, express a more positive perception about the instructional emphasis on culture than the other subgroups.

It was also interesting to discover that both intermediate and advanced students felt the emphasis on culture in the Italian program helps them think critically about domains not necessarily related to the Italian courses, such as social issues, academic issues, and their own culture (see Table 6). Furthermore, in regards to social and academic issues, we notice that ratings increased for students at the advanced level, with some minor differences across the subgroups. A possible explanation for this increase has to do with the exposure to these issues or topics that occurs at a higher level of language competence, as well as with the level of awareness of Italian culture acquired with longer periods of study. Students at the intermediate level, by contrast, expressed a higher rating in regards to whether emphasis on Italian culture helps them think critically about their own culture. This could be due to the fact that students who come to Italian with little or no previous experience with the language could value their learning in general and the learning of culture more highly than other students precisely because, having had little contact with Italian, they better appreciate the opportunity to discover new things and make comparisons between cultures. These students are important to the department because they may become majors and in any case they may decide to pursue Italian language study further.

Table 6. Mean ratings on general questions about Italian courses with emphasis on writing and culture (intermediate and advanced groups)*

Q5. To what extent does the emphasis on <u>culture</u> in the Italian program help you to think critically about the following?	int.	adv.	advanced subgroups								
			MJ	MN	no MJ/ MN	SA	no SA	CH	no CH	LH	no LH
(a) social issues	3.31	3.65	3.50	3.71	3.67	3.64	3.65	3.45	3.67	3.50	3.71
(b) academic issues	3.03	3.29	3.00	3.33	3.00	3.14	3.30	3.09	3.33	3.10	3.29
(c) your own culture	3.47	3.44	3.50	3.42	3.33	3.50	3.40	3.55	3.44	3.50	3.42

* Intermediate (INT), advanced (ADV), Italian major (MJ), minor (MN), undeclared (No MJ/MN), study abroad (SA), no study abroad (No SA), Italian cultural heritage (CH), non-Italian cultural heritage (No CH), Italian linguistic heritage (LH), non-Italian language heritage (No LH)

Some of the comments that intermediate and advanced students provided about how writing in Italian improved their skills in other domains are listed below. A main theme that arose relates to a connection between Italian and other languages.

Intermediate-level student comments

"It taught me the proper way to start writing in another language, relying on dictionaries and translators as little as possible."

"Learning Italian grammar has helped me better understand both English and Spanish grammar, which has significantly improved my writing level in all 3 languages."

"Learning proper grammar and writing styles in one language always helps to reinforce the rules of the other language simply through contrast."

"Through Italian I have gained a better understanding of English grammar and syntax. My study of Italian has improved my writing."

Advanced-level student comments

"As an economics major, writing is not an activity I do often. The emphasis on writing in my Italian courses gives me that creative writing outlet and allows for right-brain cultivation."

"I also take numerous science courses. I am very satisfied with the emphasis the Italian department has placed on writing because I am more accustomed to writing/formulating arguments/communicating ideas in science courses, as well—perhaps more than the other science-only students."

In regards to the open-ended question whether the emphasis on writing helped or hindered the development of other skills such as speaking and reading in Italian, the majority of the students at all levels found the emphasis on writing helpful because it is related to the other skills. Some comments are listed below.

"The emphasis on writing improves all such skills by expanding vocabulary and syntactic understanding."

"Writing has definitely improved, or at least drawn my attention more to, my spoken grammar."

"I think that the writing instruction helps the development of speaking, listening and reading skills. In terms of speaking skills, you understand how to express correctly what you wish to say; listening skills improve because you are familiar with the structure the speaker is using; and you read at a faster pace and have a more comprehensive understanding of what you read once you understand how Italian grammar works, too."

Section IV—Perceptions on writing task usefulness

In section IV students expressed their opinions on the usefulness of a variety of writing tasks. The list of writing tasks was slightly different between the intermediate and the advanced levels. Critical interpretations of texts (i) and academic term paper (j) were not in the list for the intermediate level because they are not genres whose production is required at that level of language competence. Table 7 shows how students' opinions vary across groups. Students at the intermediate level point to diaries ($M=3.50$), creative pieces of work ($M=3.44$), personal descriptions ($M=3.41$), and personal narratives ($M=3.42$) as helpful for learning to write in Italian. Students at the advanced level seem to find more useful the most complex tasks such as creative pieces of work ($M=3.83$), academic term papers ($M=3.70$) and critical interpretations of texts ($M=3.78$), the latter probably due to their significance as tasks in advanced levels of study in the Italian curriculum. There are minor differences in the opinions across the advanced subgroups (see Table 7).

Table 7. Mean ratings on usefulness of writing tasks (intermediate and advanced groups)*

Q1. How useful are the following tasks for helping you learn to write in Italian?	int.	adv.	advanced subgroups								
			MJ	MN	no MJ/MN	SA	no SA	CH	no CH	LH	no LH
(a) personal descriptions	3.41	3.37	3.11	3.44	3.60	3.45	3.32	3.11	3.71	3.22	3.43
(b) discussion forum posts	3.20	2.92	3.00	2.83	3.00	3.00	2.88	3.13	3.00	3.00	2.88
(c) diaries	3.50	2.96	2.88	2.73	3.60	2.75	3.06	2.71	2.80	2.88	3.00
(d) personal narratives	3.42	3.59	3.44	3.67	3.60	3.55	3.61	3.40	3.67	3.44	3.65
(e) expository texts	3.18	3.53	3.50	3.56	3.50	3.50	3.56	3.56	3.14	3.50	3.55
(f) film reviews	3.34	3.62	3.56	3.60	3.80	3.45	3.72	3.33	3.67	3.56	3.65
(g) a creative piece of work	3.44	3.83	3.78	3.80	4.00	3.64	3.94	3.70	3.83	3.78	3.85
(h) textual summary	3.28	3.55	3.70	3.41	3.67	3.36	3.68	3.73	3.63	3.70	3.48
(i) critical interpretations of texts (such as poems, novels, etc.)	N/A**	3.78	3.67	3.76	4.00	3.77	3.79	3.70	3.75	3.67	3.83
(j) an academic term paper	N/A	3.70	3.70	3.65	3.83	3.71	3.68	3.64	3.63	3.70	3.70

* Intermediate (INT), advanced (ADV), Italian major (MJ), minor (MN), undeclared (No MJ/MN), study abroad (SA), no study abroad (No SA), Italian cultural heritage (CH), non-Italian cultural heritage (No CH), Italian linguistic heritage (LH), non-Italian language heritage (No LH)

** Items (i) and (j) were not included in the survey for the intermediate level.

In the open-ended item, a theme that arose for students from both levels was the mismatch between student proficiency and the level of proficiency required to complete a given task.

Intermediate-level student comments

"Expository texts often use vocabulary outside the intermediate level making it very hard to learn from them."

"I feel like expository texts and summaries are pretty boring and repetitive so I don't get as much out of them."

"With expository writing I think the emphasis would be taken off of Italian and onto the paper. Maybe in upper level classes this would be useful, but for the lower level classes where we are trying to learn how to communicate in Italian in a functional way and not necessarily in a formal and scholarly way through writing analytical papers it would be better to stick to descriptions and reviews and personal narratives. I think those are easier to write about in the thought process and they offer good practice for different verb tenses and vocab in Italian keeping the emphasis on language learning."

Advanced-level student comments

"Diaries always end up being busy work. Personal descriptions are useless at this level of the language. Forum posts never seem to catch."

"Discussion forum posts are hard because if they are on sites outside Georgetown (real Italian forums) the post often include shorthand abbreviations (like k for che) which are hard to figure out. They are very informal, and the rest of the writing we do is very formal, so it is doesn't teach you how to do academic writing."

Section IV of the survey included three additional open-ended questions in which students could express their opinions on (a) whether the writing tasks develop critical thinking, (b) whether the writing tasks are appropriate at their level of Italian study, and (c) whether the tasks are helpful for understanding cultural issues.

Despite comments in the previous section to the contrary, students at the intermediate level unanimously indicated that the writing tasks were appropriate to their level of Italian study and developing critical thinking. Moreover, intermediate respondents identified writing film reviews as among the most useful writing tasks for understanding cultural issues.

"Film reviews because they show entertainment for people in Italy, it helps us relate to them. Having to watch Italian films provides a lens through which we can view Italian cultural norms and understand their entertainment in contrast to our own."

"The textual summaries and film reviews are particularly helpful because you can analyze a reflection of a specific aspect of Italian culture during a time period, such as class consciousness or social protocol."

"Having to summarize anything-be it a film or text-always advances the ability to think critically because it forces the student to examine what they have just taken in, pick out the key points, and then concisely rewrite them in his or her own words."

Students in advanced-level courses indicated that writing tasks develop critical thinking and that film reviews and critical interpretation of texts are helpful for understanding cultural issues. It also emerged from some comments that there is a need to incorporate more culture into the advanced courses:

> "Critical interpretations of texts, expository texts, and academic term papers are the kinds of assignments that develop critical thinking skills and thus help develop the way you write critically in Italian. Summaries or reviews do not help develop critical thinking because they do not demand critical thinking."

> "Film reviews, critical interpretation of texts and academic term papers tend to do this. In order to write, we must first read, understand and analyze the text and then develop an argument all of which expand our abilities to think and write in the language we are learning."

> "Film reviews, textual summaries and critical interpretations are helpful for understanding cultural issues. However, when you surpass the course 'Contemporary Italy,' there is not much a focus on Italian culture and its societal issues. I think there needs to be more of a focus on this because the students find it very interesting and there isn't much offered."

However some mixed opinions emerged from advanced-level students about the appropriateness of writing tasks given their proficiency level, another issue that needs addressing in the future.

> "I think the reading comprehension questions required during the reading of *Io non ho paura*[2] became repetitive e.g., character descriptions and plot summaries do not develop critical thinking nor do they seem like worthwhile assignments because of that reason."

> "Some of the reading comprehension questions are inappropriate because they are just used as a tool to show that we have done the reading and not necessarily test us on our understanding, as well as just adding to the already lengthy work of the student to not only read the assignment but then go through and answer many questions that are uninspiring and then having to answer longer, more thematic based questions."

> "I think the many summaries I had to write for certain courses (some of which were assigned once or twice a week) were busy work for me. I guess they could help with grammar in lower level courses but were probably unnecessary for upper level students."

Section V—Perceptions about pedagogical strategies

In Section V participants had to indicate which strategies used by students and teachers are more useful for learning Italian (see Tables 8 and 9). According to the intermediate group, the most helpful strategies students use for learning how to write Italian (Table 8) are discussion of papers with a teacher ($M=3.74$) and preparing a written outline for an oral presentation ($M=3.60$). The least useful strategy is preparing an outline of a paper ($M=2.96$). The strategies used by teachers that intermediate students found the most useful (Table 9) are going over common writing problems and errors ($M=3.81$) and providing written comments and corrections ($M=3.74$).

---

[2] Title of a novel that is read in the Writing and Culture course.

Table 8. Mean ratings on usefulness of writing strategies (intermediate and advanced groups)*

Q1. How useful are the following strategies for helping you learn to write in Italian?	int.	adv.	advanced subgroups								
			MJ	MN	no MJ/ MN	SA	no SA	CH	no CH	LH	no LH
(a) Writing multiple drafts of your paper	3.16	3.63	3.50	3.65	4.00	3.62	3.63	3.55	3.50	3.40	3.73
(b) Discussing your paper with peers	3.09	3.03	2.70	3.12	4.00	2.79	3.21	2.91	3.11	2.60	3.22
(c) Preparing an outline of a paper	2.96	3.26	3.20	3.17	4.00	3.21	3.30	3.18	3.11	3.20	3.29
(d) Preparing a written outline for an oral presentation	3.60	3.56	3.70	3.50	4.00	3.71	3.45	3.82	3.44	3.70	3.50
(e) Discussing your paper one-to-one with your teacher	3.74	3.77	4.00	3.63	4.00	3.92	3.67	3.89	3.38	4.00	3.68

* Italian cultural heritage (CH), non-Italian cultural heritage (No CH), Italian linguistic heritage (LH), non-Italian language heritage (No LH)

Table 9. Mean ratings on usefulness of instructional writing strategies (intermediate and advanced groups)*

Q2. How useful are the following strategies that teachers use for helping you to write in Italian?	int.	adv.	advanced subgroups								
			MJ	MN	no MJ/ MN	SA	no SA	CH	no CH	LH	no LH
(a) Give models of genres or parts of texts that you may follow	3.44	3.45	3.50	3.47	4.00	3.42	3.47	3.33	3.50	3.67	3.48
(b) Provide you with written comments	3.74	3.91	3.80	3.94	4.00	3.93	3.90	3.91	3.89	3.67	3.96
(c) Provide you with corrections on your paper	3.74	3.91	3.90	3.89	4.00	3.86	3.95	3.91	3.89	3.67	3.92
(d) Use grading rubrics to evaluate your writing	3.37	3.47	3.20	3.67	4.00	3.57	3.40	3.45	3.56	3.67	3.58
(e) Pointing to resources and working with them in class (Orthographic correctors, dictionaries, etc.)	3.35	3.60	3.40	3.86	4.00	3.46	3.71	3.60	3.67	3.67	3.70
(f) Going over common writing problems and errors found in students' papers in class	3.81	3.88	3.80	3.89	4.00	3.86	3.90	3.82	3.89	3.67	3.92

* Italian cultural heritage (CH), non-Italian cultural heritage (No CH), Italian linguistic heritage (LH), non-Italian language heritage (No LH)

According to advanced-level students, the most useful student strategies for learning Italian (Table 8) were discussing a paper with a teacher ($M=3.77$) and writing multiple drafts ($M=3.63$). The least useful strategies appeared to be discussing a paper with peers ($M=3.03$), especially in some advanced-level subgroups. The most useful strategies used by teachers (Table 9) were providing students with written comments ($M=3.91$) and corrections on a paper ($M=3.91$). None of the teachers' strategies ratings fell below a mean value of 3.00 for both the intermediate and the advanced groups. This suggests that all writing strategies are considered useful by students. However some variations occur in the advanced subgroups.

In the open-ended question, students elaborated on the ratings reported in Tables 8 and Table 9. Students at all levels found detailed feedback on grammar mistakes very useful. Reported here are some of the answers given on the kind of feedback students prefer.

Intermediate-level student comments

"Corrections and then explanations based on what Italians use more often or why a certain grammar rule is being violated in the sentence are the most helpful."

"Explaining my most common mistakes is the most helpful, as well as elaborating on the correct ordering and forming of various phrases and sentences, which can sometimes get mixed up in translation."

"When your peers are on the same level as you it does not really help much because you both just don't know what is going on or how to fix it."

Advanced-level student comments

"Discussing papers with peers is not really useful, other students are sometimes too harsh or too timid to actually be honest. Preparing an outline is a waste of time. Every student has their own way of organizing their thoughts and writing."

"It becomes difficult to discuss paper topics with peers because they do not possess the background information necessary to give critical feedback."

"Peer reviews are generally useless because they come in unprepared or unable to critique your work. Multiple drafts is just a waste of time. Write it well the first time."

Section V ended with two open-ended questions in which students were asked to provide suggestions for improving the Italian program generally, and then specifically in terms of instructional emphasis on writing and culture. This kind of feedback was very helpful for understanding the strengths and weaknesses of the program and will lead to constructive discussions in our department to address all areas of concern expressed by our students.

Intermediate-level student comments

"Basic Italian is so easy and then there is a HUGE jump in difficulty level to Italian Intermediate. The difficulty should be more spread out so the transition is not so difficult for everyone!"

"I wish there were more cultural opportunities outside of the classroom to attend as a class, rather than simply reading from the textbook all of the time. I like the emphasis on writing because I feel like I excel most in that area."

"Focus more on speaking because I really believe that to be able to write well and to understand the culture better it is important to first be able to speak the language and understand the language and just really think in that language first. I really enjoy Italian it just gets really hard to stay caught up and learn when I cannot speak it very well and can't really think in the language yet."

"I think the Italian program should offer a non-intensive track because although I love studying Italian, the intensive courses are demanding and I feel as if they deter other students from potentially learning Italian. Also, taking Intensive Basic & Intermediate as a freshman puts me at a disadvantage because I cannot fit Advanced into my schedule next year and therefore will have to take a year off before I want to study abroad junior year, as opposed to spreading out Basic I/II and Intermediate I/II over two years."

Advanced-level student comments

"As I have seen in my past four years, culture is not emphasized after a certain point. We dive into literary works and focus on critical analysis. This is a great tool to help me improve my writing abilities, but I feel as though I am missing important information on what is going on in Italy."

"I do think, particularly in comparison with my experiences with the Spanish department that the general level of speaking ability among people in high-level Italian classes is pretty low, and that's probably because the emphasis in grading etc. is on writing rather than verbal production. Past the Writing & Culture class, there doesn't seem to be any focus on bettering anyone's Italian ability; students are just taking random electives and not necessarily improving at all. I'm not entirely sure how to fix this, although for me the big change was going abroad—after all, in our classes at the University of Florence, our grades were entirely determined by oral final exams. At the same time, most people don't take the study part of study abroad all that seriously. I also didn't get much formation in the study of Italian culture before I went abroad, but I imagine for most people that's taken care of in the early classes."

"There should be more emphasis on culture. In the upper level Italian, there is not much offered even though the catalogue of courses lists a TON of culture courses I've never seen being offered."

Reflections and implications

The experience of developing the survey and reviewing student responses was positive both as a collective exercise in assessment and because of the insights the survey provided on the various questions that we were asking. With respect to the first point, the department as a whole had an opportunity to discuss and reflect on the curriculum, which was important not only for its practical effects but also to foster a productive dialogue between colleagues working on the language curriculum and colleagues working mostly on upper-level courses. Having to design survey questions also led us to reformulate and better understand our own goals and outcomes across the different levels of the program.

In general terms, the survey constituted a strong endorsement of our curriculum renewal, an extremely important result, as we could not have continued with such an endeavor without student involvement and appreciation. Moreover, the analysis of responses was also useful in providing insights on possible changes in pedagogical strategies and in the formulation of outcomes. For example, responses led us to assess possible gaps in the cultural content presented to students at different levels, and to recognize the need to explain specific choices in terms of content or pedagogy. We have been reassessing, for example, the need to introduce activities including writing on topics that the students regard as important and that they feel have been neglected such as the history of art in Italy. We have also reflected on the student responses regarding teaching strategies that they consider successful or not appropriate. Thus, we realized that peer review has little acceptance among students and that for intermediate students the disadvantages of such a technique may outweigh the advantages. In this regard, we have eliminated peer review for the lower levels. We have decided to maintain it at the advanced levels, but we have also discussed ways to communicate its importance to students more clearly.

Among other changes that the survey's results have spurred is a heightened consciousness of the need to tailor the tasks more closely to students' levels of writing ability. Thus, we have been more careful in guiding students towards the performance of more complex writing tasks such as academic essays through provision of models and vocabulary that will help them perform adequately.

In general, the analysis of students' responses has lead to changes in content, teacher strategies, and tasks that we would not have foreseen had we not embarked on the survey project. Such changes will no doubt contribute to the success of the Italian curriculum at Georgetown University. However, the survey has also shown to us that there are no easy formulas to reach our objectives and may be the most important point that has become clear is that the department needs now to go beyond a general assessment of students' perceptions and initiate an assessment of students' performance which can provide information on whether students actually reach the goals expressed in our statement of outcomes.

Acknowledgments

We want to thank John Norris and Yukiko Watanabe for the assistance with the implementation of the Writing and Culture Assessment Plan, and John Davis for his careful review of a first draft of this chapter.

References

Angelo, T. (1995). Reassessing (and defining) assessment. *The AAHE Bulletin, 48*(2), 7–9.

Byrnes, H. (2002). The role of task and task-based assessment in a content-oriented collegiate FL curriculum. *Language Testing, 19,* 419–437.

Dassier, J., & Powell, W. (2001). Formative FL program evaluation: Dare to find out how good you really are. In C. M. Cherry (Ed.), *Dimensions: The odyssey continues. Selected proceedings of the 2001 conference on language teaching* (pp. 15–30). Valdosta, GA: Southern Conference on Language Teaching.

Grau Sempere, A., Mohn, M. C., & Pieroni, R. (2009). Improving educational effectiveness and promoting internal and external information-sharing through student learning outcomes assessment. In J. M. Norris, J. McE. Davis, C. Sinicrope, & Y. Watanabe (Eds.), *Toward useful program evaluation in college foreign language education* (pp. 139–162). Honolulu: University of Hawai'i, National Foreign Language Resource Center.

Norris, J. M. (2006). Assessing FL learning and learners: From measurement constructs to educational uses. In H. Byrnes, H. Weger-Guntharp, & K. Sprang (Eds.), *GURT 2005: Educating for advanced FL capacities: Constructs, curriculum, instruction, assessment* (pp. 167–187). Washington, DC: Georgetown University Press.

Pfeiffer, P., & Byrnes, H. (2009). Curriculum, learning, and the identity of majors: A case study of program outcomes evaluation. In J. M. Norris, J. McE. Davis, C. Sinicrope, & Y. Watanabe (Eds.), *Toward useful program evaluation in college foreign language education* (pp. 183–208). Honolulu: University of Hawai'i, National Foreign Language Resource Center.

Appendix: Georgetown University Italian Department mission statement

Today's interconnected and interdependent world requires a deep understanding of cultures other than one's own. The Italian Department's goal is to prepare future scholars and informed leaders, knowledgeable about the enduring power of Italian Culture—Italy's greatest natural resource. Building upon Georgetown's strong tradition of international understanding and ethos of intercultural education, our curriculum integrates language studies with knowledge of Italian, literature, history, politics, and the arts.

The Italian Department's integrative approach prepares students to explore connections and understand the literary and cultural tradition from past to present. From the Gateway course to the Senior Seminar, all our courses are designed to introduce students to Italian culture in all its manifestations, to develop critical and analytical skills through intellectual dialogue in small class settings, and to provide an integrated overseas study experience that will give students new perspectives on world issues.

Foreign Language Curriculum as a Means of Achieving Humanities Learning Goals: Assessment of Materials, Pedagogy, and Learner Texts

Marianna Ryshina-Pankova
Georgetown University

Recently, there have been urgent calls (e.g., MLA, 2007) to explicitly conceptualize the goals of FL study beyond proficiency in a foreign language and in line with a more comprehensive humanistic learning framework characteristic of collegiate education in general. In view of this need to draw transparent connections between FL study and humanistic inquiry, we conducted a project that aimed to establish a framework for understanding and assessing the nature of "humanities learning" in the German Department at Georgetown University. This chapter describes the stages of the assessment initiative in its first cycle by (a) outlining the goals and intended uses of the assessment project, (b) reporting on the process of formulating the learning outcomes, and (c) describing an investigation of student writing performance that sought to determine whether students are achieving the specified outcomes. The chapter demonstrates the transformative impact of the program-internal and curriculum-based approach to assessment on the understanding of humanities learning as well as on tasks and pedagogical practices that can foster humanistic inquiry.

Introduction

Of the many disciplines in the humanities, foreign language (FL) programs are perhaps the most experienced in undertaking curricular improvement through

---

Ryshina-Pankova, M. (2015) Foreign language curriculum as a means of achieving humanities learning goals: Assessment of materials, pedagogy, and learner texts. In J. M. Norris & J. McE. Davis (Eds.), *Student learning outcomes assessment in college foreign language programs* (pp. 221–246). Honolulu: University of Hawaiʻi, National Foreign Language Resource Center.

development of assessment frameworks that help enhance the learning outcomes of their students. And yet, it is precisely FL departments that more and more often find themselves in crisis, with some programs being closed and others split into language centers and English-based literature and culture studies programs. In view of this crisis, there is an urgent need to answer a central question of what FL study offers learners as an endeavor of humanistic inquiry and how FL study fits into the framework of collegiate education in general. To address the central aspects of liberal arts education—as spelled out, for example, in the global learning outcomes of the Liberal Education and America's Promise (LEAP) initiative (American Association of Colleges and Universities, 2007)—FL programs need to reformulate their learning goals in terms that go beyond mere language acquisition. As suggested by the MLA 2007 Report and other advocates of text-based, literacy-oriented, and content-oriented FL curricula (e.g., Byrnes, Maxim, & Norris, 2010; Kern, 2000, 2004, 2008), post-secondary language learning can link up with current conceptualizations of liberal arts education if it is conceived within a more comprehensive humanistic learning framework that combines a focus on language, content, and development of cognition.

Recently, various attempts have been made to answer the question about what constitutes the essence and significance of humanistic learning (e.g., Harpham, 2005; Heiland & Rosenthal, 2011; Stewart, 2005; public debate about the role of humanities in the *Chronicle of Higher Education* at http://chronicle.com/article/Harvard-Mounts-Campaign-to/139687 and on the MLA website at http://mlaresearch.commons.mla.org/). Geoffrey Harpham (2005) offers a particularly illuminating definition of humanistic inquiry that not only helps one understand what humanities have in common, regardless of disciplinary distinctions, but also see how FL study fits within a larger project of humanistic scholarship. Harpham defines humanistic inquiry in terms of three major aspects (p. 23). The object of such inquiry is texts and artifacts created by human beings; its subject is human experience; and its purpose is the development of self-understanding indispensable for living in the present and building the future. All three elements can be readily identified as significant constituents of FL learning. FL study can be conceptualized as engagement with textual language that requires comprehension, interpretation, and creation of new texts. These texts (understood in the broad sense as including oral and multimedia genres, as well as written texts) enable exploration of human action, intention, and reflection in a particular cultural realm. Importantly, they potentially reveal to the learner a multiplicity of human voices, as well as the various complexities and forces shaping human experience, personal and public, conscious and unconscious, in a world geographically and culturally different from one's own. And finally, FL study fosters a shift in the understanding of self that almost inevitably ensues as a result of contact with the other. Harpham's eloquent articulation in reference to the texts from the past applies just as much to foreign language texts: Engagement with these "involves a provisional suspension of identity, and even, in certain cases, puts that identity at risk by subjecting it to new information, new stimuli, new questions, new stresses" (p. 25). For Harpham, who is a literary scholar, this engagement with interpretation and representation of human experience is primarily along the time axis: He emphasizes a historical outlook, a turn to the past as distinctive of the humanities. Those in FL study undertake a journey into a different space, signification, and often a different time.

Given a university FL curriculum oriented towards humanistic inquiry as sketched above, how would one know whether learning conceived in these terms is occurring? In this paper, I report on an assessment project conducted in the context of a well-articulated, content-based, and literacy-oriented German program at Georgetown University. In contrast to previous assessment initiatives concentrating on the language development dimension (Byrnes, 2002, 2009; Byrnes, Maxim, & Norris, 2010, especially Chapters 8 and 9; Byrnes & Sinicrope, 2008; Norris & Pfeiffer, 2003; Ryshina-Pankova, 2010, 2011), the project described here aimed to establish a framework for assessing the nature of humanities learning in the German curriculum. The chapter presents an entire cycle in the assessment initiative. It starts by outlining the goals and intended uses of the humanities learning assessment project. Following is a description of how the humanities learning outcomes at a particular curricular level were reformulated as a result of exploring links between curricular materials, pedagogical practices, an assessment task, and student performance. The next section reports on an investigation of writing performance to gauge whether students are achieving the specified humanities learning outcomes. Discussed next is the transformative impact of assessment on the understanding of humanities learning, tasks, and pedagogical practices. The chapter concludes with a discussion of the transformative impact of assessment on the understanding of humanities learning, tasks, and pedagogical practices, and a brief outline of some further steps in the project.

Goals and intended uses of the assessment project

The humanities learning assessment project currently underway in the Georgetown University German Department (GUGD) can be seen as a second phase of inquiry following a prior investigation of curricular effectiveness that initially took place between 1997 and 2000 (but extended well beyond in terms of ongoing program evaluation and student learning assessment efforts). The prior curriculum development project resulted in a highly articulated, language- and content-integrated undergraduate program of German study. While initial assessment information demonstrated promising results in terms of the ability of the program to enhance L2 language development (Byrnes, Maxim, & Norris, 2010; Norris & Pfeiffer, 2003), the value of the integrated curriculum in terms of fostering humanistic learning has not yet been examined. Thus, the goal of the new assessment project was to address our assumptions about the role of humanistic and cultural learning as a central educational goal of the GUGD curriculum. Conceptualizing language learning as a fundamentally humanistic enterprise is, indeed, the foundation of FL programs in various educational settings. However, the challenge of delivering language education conceived in these terms—either through educational practices that instantiate humanistic learning via principled integration of content and culture, or through assessment procedures that capture the interrelatedness of these two aspects of FL study—has been mostly unmet (MLA, 2007). Rather, humanistic learning that involves exploration of human experience in a different culture has often been conceptualized (and assessed) as discreet domains of content knowledge (e.g., food, art, music) to be acquired by students as largely separate from the linguistic system of the target language or from the textual and contextual "situatedness" of certain cultural phenomena. Indeed, this conceptualization often finds its expression in the commonplace practice of teaching FL culture using English as the medium of instruction, thus undermining the very connection between language and human cultural experience assumed by many in FL education to be a fundamental aspect of language and communication.[1]

The overarching purpose of the project was to determine what humanistic learning in our FL program really means. The participants in the project, a curriculum development group of self-selected graduate students and faculty interested in the issue, sought to devise ways of defining the meaning of humanistic learning in the specific context of our curriculum. Thus, the assessment working group avoided generic and program-external approaches to assessing humanities inquiry, for example in terms of cultural learning or cultural competence (for an overview of various approaches see Sinicrope, Norris, & Watanabe, 2007). In keeping with a "use-focused"[2] approach to language program assessment and evaluation (adopted by the German department since the beginning of curriculum development efforts), the assessment working group first identified the primary intended uses (i.e., specific actions or desired understandings) for the assessment project. There were three important intended uses for this investigation. First, we hoped to enable the faculty to create a shared vision and shared way of understanding learning in the humanities, and help faculty align their educational actions with this vision. The second use of the project was to demonstrate program effectiveness with regard to student achievement of the humanities learning outcomes. And finally, we hoped to translate the results of the assessment project into renewing and improving the curriculum, materials, pedagogies, and assessment practices of the program.

Specifying humanities learning outcomes

The first aim of the assessment project was to establish learning criteria—or statements of student learning outcomes—capturing the qualities of learning in the humanities that were valued by the department. To do so, we initially turned to the overall educational goals of the program, which had been formulated at the beginning of the curricular reform:

> The curriculum aims to enable students to become competent and culturally literate users of German by combining a focus on content with carefully conceived pedagogical interventions that reflect the best available knowledge in classroom-based second language acquisition research. Students gain a rich understanding of the German-speaking world through a variety of content areas and their topical emphases and range of texts, through the medium of the German language itself, and through a process of learning German that attends to accuracy, fluency, and complexity of language use and development. They will critically explore their own assumptions in terms of that world, and learn to value the multiple perspectives learning German and engaging the German language opens up. In short, the curriculum is conceptualized to allow learners to become competent and literate nonnative users of German who can employ the language in a range of intellectual and professional contexts and who can also draw from it personal enrichment and enjoyment.

Taking this overarching statement as an initial conceptual basis for outcomes development, the assessment working group specified a set of broad provisional

---

[1] See Scarino (2009) and Hammer and Swaffar (2012) for some language-based approaches to assessing cultural knowledge.

[2] See Norris (2008) and Patton (1997, 2008).

humanities learning goals (or goal categories), which would be an organizing framework for the development of outcomes at different levels of the curriculum. The goals were expressed in terms of three interrelated facets of content learning: (a) the learning of cultural content, (b) understanding of cultural content through multiple perspectives within the German speaking area, and (c) reflective stance towards various viewpoints on content including students' own perspectives as learners at an American university (many of whom have multilingual backgrounds).

Next, the assessment working group used the humanities learning goals to create a template (see Figure 1), which could be used to guide development of outcomes statements on the basis of reviews of existing course content, texts, materials, and pedagogical practices. The template links content and language through the concept of *genre* understood as a staged verbal action aimed at achieving specific communicative goals in particular social contexts (Martin, 1984, 1997). The template also presents the development of critical thinking as contingent on the learning of language, as well as exploration of and reflection on cultural content areas. Instructors were asked to supply the relevant information in each category so that outcomes statements could be developed within the pedagogical approach of the department (privileging text, genre, and content) and guided by the department's newly devised conceptualizations of humanities learning.

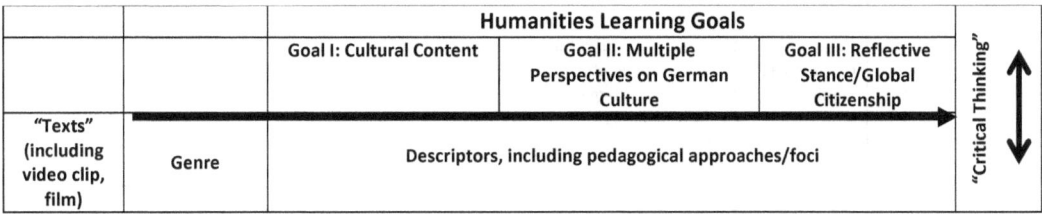

Figure 1. Template for specifying humanities learning goals in relation to texts, genre, and pedagogy.

Given that humanistic inquiry characterizes the entire GUGD curriculum, we selected three focal points in the program for the assessment project: (1) end-of-program (i.e., major), (2) the end of the language requirement (Level II, second year), and (3) the end of the third year (Level III) early-advanced course taken by minors, majors, and other interested students, as well as the minimum curriculum level required of students before they sit for the proficiency exam (a requirement of the School of Foreign Service, from which many of our students come). Most of the procedures related to the assessment project (and reported on in this chapter) have been so far conducted at Level III. This level is represented by the specific course "German Stories, German Histories," which introduces students to historical and social issues in Germany from 1945 to the present through a variety of genres, such as personal narratives, historical chronicles, essays, journalistic articles, films, and literary works. Completing the course means that students have had 255 hours of instruction.

Developing humanities learning outcomes at this curricular level took place in three stages. In the first stage, existing course materials were analyzed by instructors who collaboratively reinterpreted course content in terms of the three humanities learning goal categories. Figure 2 provides an example of such an analysis for two texts used in the final unit of the Level III course, both of which focus on the topic of migration.

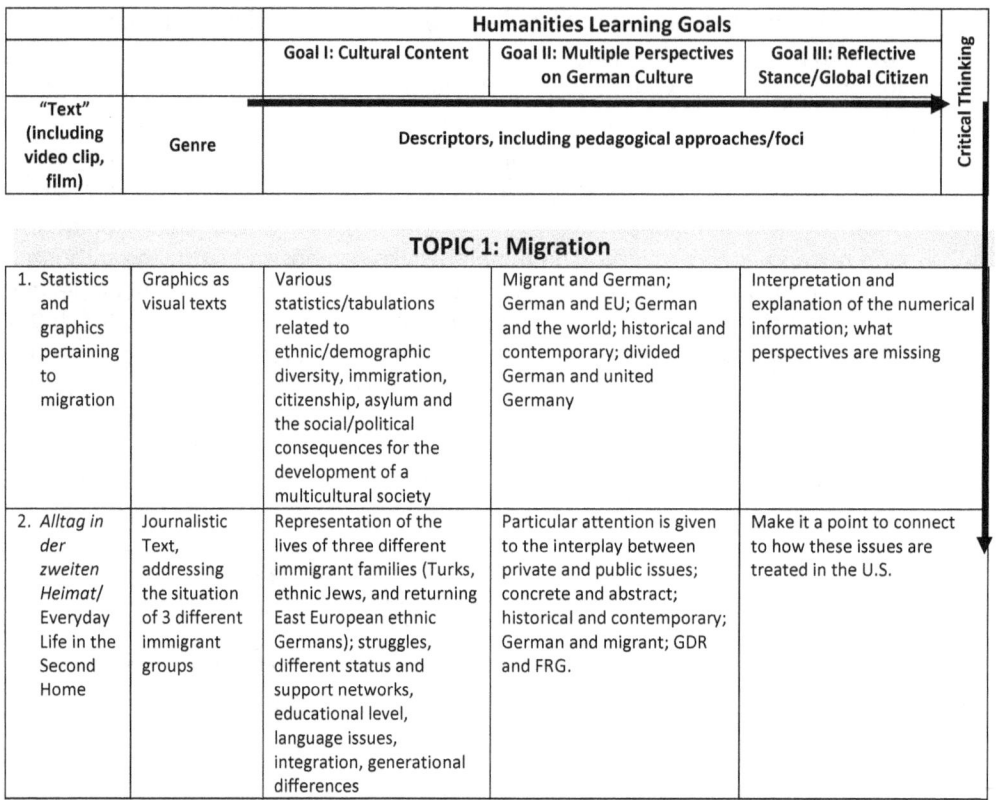

Figure 2. Description of materials for the topic "On the way to multicultural society."

In Figure 2, the *cultural content* goal category lists information about specific thematic areas under focus during instruction on a particular text (e.g., the lives of three different immigrant groups). The *multiple perspectives* category lists the types of "voices" present in the texts (e.g., private, public, German, migrant). The reflective stance column points to the cognitive actions and pedagogies intended to foster student reflection (e.g., interpretation and explanation).

Once this process had been completed, the initial descriptors provided by instructors in the template (see Figure 2) formed the basis for consolidated statements on GUGD humanities learning outcomes for Level III. That is to say, instructors elaborated on the information collected in the template to craft general articulations of desired knowledge and cognitive skills in each of the three humanities learning goals categories for Level III students. For example, *cultural content* learning outcomes for Level III students were stated as follows:

> At the end of the level, learners have developed a good understanding of the contemporary scene in the Federal Republic of Germany (FRG) in light of major political and social developments since World War II and will have become

familiar with some major players, particularly cultural actors who contributed to the possibility of unification.

Moreover, the domains of knowledge delineated in the cultural content outcome were further elaborated into a number of content sub-topics.

The thematic foci through which students have expanded their insight of the German world include:

- political and economic situation in Germany after World War II
- emotional, physical, and economic hardships in post-war Germany
- the question of guilt and responsibility as a result of the Nazi past
- gradual shift in relationship between former war time allies and the divided Germany, particularly the US and the Soviet Union in relation to the FRG and GDR
- political, social, and personal impact of the building of the Berlin wall
- daily life in the divided Germany, with emphasis on German Democratic Republic (GDR)
- political and economic aspects of GDR (and a number of others)

The learning outcome capturing *multiple perspectives* was expressed as follows:

> At the end of this level, learners continue to move beyond viewing cultural historical content as uniform and typified and have developed an ability to see it as constructed from a variety of points of view. Specifically, students are able to differentiate between the following often contrastive standpoints [see below]. Thus, learners are able to identify various facets of the content and understand how the context of meaning-making about particular issues, which includes the deeper assumptions, emotions, interests, and ideologies as well as means of expression (e.g., music vs. lexicogrammar of emotion) that lie behind them, actively shapes our knowledge of the German past and present.

As with the cultural content outcome statement, the multiple perspectives outcome was elaborated into greater detail specifying the precise "contrastive standpoints" students were to differentiate. These included East (GDR) and West (FRG), divided Germany versus unified Germany, German versus American/international, German versus migrant, personal versus public, abstract versus concrete, contemporary versus historical (e.g., directly after World War II), narrative versus interpretative/argumentative, literary versus "factual," and multimedia/visual versus verbal.

Finally, the assessment working group created the following statements to capture desired *reflective stance* learning for Level III students.

Students take a reflective stance on the thematic issues that are foregrounded in the course:

- Students recognize the contextual dependency and inherent ideological underpinnings of knowledge construction and knowledge constructors.

- Students are able to contextualize, compare, contrast, interpret, and evaluate the content and develop their own opinion on the issues.
- As learners express their own voice, they actively engage with the perspectives of others in such a way that the process of negotiation between their own ideas and those of others becomes evident.

The first draft of the outcomes statements was prepared by the Curriculum Director and circulated among the entire assessment working group. As a result of ensuing whole-group discussion, some points were revised and additional details were added. Unlike content and multiple perspective outcomes, the assessment working group did not further specify and define reflective stance at finer, subordinate levels of detail. Clearly, the reflective stance rubric is the least factual and the most interpretative. Its illustration would have required citing and interpreting whole passages from student work; however, a close textual reading of the learner essays was not part of this step in the assessment process.

Creating a prototypical writing task and rating criteria

In the next stage of the assessment project, two new assessment tools were created to gauge the degree to which students were able to achieve the new humanities learning outcomes: a "prototypical writing task" eliciting relevant outcomes performances and a rating criteria/rubric for which the newly developed Level III outcomes statements served as a frame of reference. A prototypical writing task (in the parlance of the GUGD) is an assessment task assigned at the end of each curricular level to elicit performances that reflect the content and language learning expected to take place throughout the level.[3] Whereas in the original assessment project, writing tasks were used primarily to assess writing and language development, in the current study we used the Level III prototypical writing task to provide insights into humanities learning as conceived and articulated by the department via the process described above.

A written task was deemed an appropriate procedure for the purpose of the assessment project since it was thought to provide insight into a learner's ability to select appropriate cultural content, consider it from multiple perspectives, and reflect on both. Written assignments, depending on how they are designed, function effectively as a "window" into such abilities and have been commonly used in other academic subjects to assess learning, be it through a reflective essay, as typical in the humanities, or via a lab report, as in the natural sciences. Indeed, the link between writing and educational knowledge construction has long been established in various literacy studies and investigations of scientific discourse (e.g., Berkenkotter & Huckin, 1995; Halliday, 1994, 2004; Halliday & Martin, 1993; Hood, 2010, 2011; Swales, 1990). Particularly relevant for our project was Carter's (2007) theorization of the role of writing in the assessment of disciplinary knowledge. Carter argues for understanding writing in particular genres as reflective of the unique ways of doing and knowing that are characteristic of different academic disciplines.

---

[3] See Byrnes, Maxim, and Norris (2010) for a discussion of prototypical writing tasks (especially Chapter 9, pp. 152–153).

outcome	rating meets (3) does not meet (0) in the middle (1, 2)	justifications Why or why not? Explain your rating with regard to both positive and negative aspects
content Students have a good understanding of the following issues: • Increasingly multicultural society in Germany as a result of an opening toward Eastern Europe, the influence of the European Union, and changing labor market • Social, cultural, economic, educational, and linguistic challenges in the life of immigrants of various descent in Germany (e.g., Turks, Jews, Vietnamese, East European ethnic Germans) • Problems of integration • German citizenship law and procedures for applying for citizenship		
multiple perspectives Students are able to identify various facets of the content and differentiate between contrastive standpoints, viewing cultural historic content as constructed from a variety of points of view: • German, American/international; • German, migrants; • Personal, public; • Abstract, concrete; • Contemporary, historical		
reflective stance Students take a reflective stance on the thematic issues that are foregrounded in the course: • Students are able to contextualize, compare, contrast, interpret, and evaluate the content. • Students develop their own opinion on the issues. • As learners express their own voice, they actively engage with the perspectives of others in such a way that the process of negotiation between their own ideas and those of others becomes evident.		

Figure 3. Holistic rating sheet for humanities learning outcomes: Level III prototypical writing task.

The prototypical writing task that we designed to capture the humanities learning outcomes was a part of the final instructional unit from the Level III course that centers on the issue of multiculturalism in Germany. Learners were asked to write a journalistic article describing the lives of Vietnamese migrants in Germany by connecting concrete private stories of Vietnamese individuals with the public voices and opinions about these migrants. This comparison would then have to be related to more general phenomena within the broad topic of migration to Germany (see the original writing task in Appendix A). Learners had to read two additional articles on the topic independently and incorporate this information into their compositions.

In addition to creating the prototypical writing task, a rating rubric and set of criteria were developed to enable judgment, in a holistic way, of the extent of a student learning and knowledge construction within prototypical writing task performances. The rating rubric and a corresponding four-point Likert scale (from 0, does not meet expectations, to 3, fully meets expectations) was designed to shed light on the degree to which students were attaining the new outcomes of humanistic learning conceived by the department in terms of cultural content knowledge, multiple perspectives, and reflective stance. An example of the rating rubric is presented in Figure 3. These rating criteria, particularly the points that illustrate the content and multiple perspectives outcomes, were developed by the assessment working group in line with the specific instructions on the writing task sheet and as a result of examining the texts that served as sources for learners' own writing tasks.

Capturing humanities learning outcomes through holistic ratings: Focusing on reflective stance

Assessment of student performance using the rating rubric presented above (Figure 3) was conducted for 28 essays collected after the Level III course had been completed (the grades received for the essays were not considered). Four instructors were involved in the rating process: two who had previously taught the Level III course and two who had not taught at this level. Holistic ratings of the compositions involved assigning a score for each of the three outcome categories on a scale from 0 to 3, and explaining the ratings by providing comments in the right-most column ("justifications"). Prior to assessing performances, raters met for a training session to familiarize themselves with the rating sheet, rate one practice essay, and jointly discuss rating justifications. Following the familiarization session, raters assessed the entire set of essays independently, with every essay rated by each of the four raters. Each rater assigned one rating per each outcome rubric for each student paper. Then, raters met to discuss any rating differences. Discrepancies in ratings were defined as a difference in ratings at the outcome category level (e.g., different ratings for the "cultural content" outcome). Discrepancies were resolved through discussion so that each category was assigned one final score the group of four raters decided on (e.g., everyone agreed that the score for cultural content on a given essay would be 2). Then, the three final scores were summed up for the three outcomes goals to provide a total rating score (the maximum score an essay could receive was a 9, and the minimum, 0). Table 1 presents the results of the rating procedure. All student essays were grouped into three categories: high-rated essays (a score of 8 or 9, $n=11$), mid-rated (a score of 6 or 5, $n=13$; no essay had a 7 score), and low-rated essays (a score of 3 or 4, $n=4$; no essay had a score lower than 3). For the subsequent analysis of discrepancies and justifications (see below), only essays with scores at the upper end of each holistic rating range were chosen (i.e., 9, 6, 4), with one essay with an overall score of 3 also included to enhance the analysis of low-performance data by increasing the low number of essays in this category (20 essays in total).

Table 1. Holistic ratings by four raters (maximum score=9)

	total essays rated (N=28)	essays retained for analysis (N=20)
high rated score: 8–9	11	6[a]
mid rated score: 5–7	13	11[b]
low rated score: 0–4	4	3[c]

[a] essays receiving a score of 9
[b] score=6
[c] score=4, plus one essay that received a score of 3

The results of the ratings enabled the pursuit of two key assessment uses mentioned in Section II. First, rating results demonstrated that the majority of the essays were judged as meeting the Level III humanities learning outcomes. Eighty-six percent (24 essays) received high- or mid-range ratings, and 39% (6 essays) received the highest rating of 9. This is a noteworthy finding interpreted by the department as demonstrating program effectiveness. That is to say, results indicated that the humanities learning outcomes specified for this level, and targeted via the prototypical writing task, were being achieved by most learners.

Second, with regard to developing a shared vision and expectations for humanistic learning, the rating process itself, including discussion and resolution of discrepancies, played an important role in achieving this common understanding of the humanities learning outcomes within the educational mission of the department. Despite the fact that the four raters contributed to the creation of the assessment sheets and were familiar with the content- and language-integrated approach of the program, the discrepancies in their individual ratings comprised 40.4% (see Table 2) of the total ratings assigned. While the high discrepancy rate could be partly attributed to the high number of raters as well as the high number of potential ratings across three rating rubrics, we decided to conduct a more detailed investigation of the discrepancies that would help us understand their nature better. As shown in Table 2, the highest percentage of rating discrepancies was found in mid-rated essays (25%), while low- and high-rated essays involved far fewer disagreements (8.75% and 6.7%, respectively). This outcome could be expected as it is easier to rate essays at the two opposing ends of a continuum rather than the "grey" area in between.

Table 2. Rating discrepancies by high-, mid-, and low-essay scores (total ratings=240)

	discrepancies
high score (n=6)	16 (6.7%)
mid score (n=11)	60 (25%)
low score (n=3)	21 (8.75%)
total	97 (40.4%)

note. Each essay had 3 ratings assigned by 4 raters per each of 20 essays retained from the original analysis of 28 essays for subsequent qualitative analysis of justifications.

Furthermore, in terms of rating disagreements across the humanities learning outcomes categories, Table 3 shows that discrepancies were greatest in the reflective stance category. Of the total number of discrepancies, 38.2% were in the reflective stance category; 34% were for multiple perspectives; and 27.8% occurred for cultural content ratings.

Table 3. Discrepancies by outcome category in high-, mid-, and low-rated essays (frequency and percentages)

	cultural content	multiple perspectives	reflective stance
high	4	5	7
mid	17	21	22
low	6	7	8
total (%)	27 (27.8%)	33 (34%)	37 (38.2%)

These results were perhaps unsurprising given the abstract and general nature of the reflective stance learning outcome. Whereas the other two categories included specifications for each general description, it was difficult to create specific examples for the reflective stance outcome. Discussions during the follow-up sessions indicated that reflective stance was understood by the raters differently and in terms of a broad spectrum of abilities. Hence, this rating process enabled a deeper, considered discussion and development of what exactly "reflective stance" should look like in student writing.

Understanding reflective stance

Since the examination of the nature of discrepancies revealed most disagreements in the reflective stance rubric, we decided to explore this category further through the analysis of raters' written justifications for the reflective stance—usually the longest comments on the rating sheets—in order to find out how raters understood and conceptualized this outcome. Three main themes seemed to motivate rater comments. First, raters emphasized the importance of the author's voice expressed through evaluative statements, which, however, needed to be contextualized within the complexity of other positions on the issue, as stated on the writing task sheet. The following quotes illustrate this point:

"[the] author's voice is clear through evaluative constructions"

"[the] author's opinion should shine through the quotes or synthesis: your opinion against other people's"

"statements are commented upon, contextualized and relativized vis-à-vis other statements"

"clear statement of opinion at the end"

"[the] author's voice is clear"

"prognosis and recommendations are given"

"mediation by the author between opposing viewpoints"

The second important theme was the realization that an author's reflective stance was not a discrete set of skills and often involved incorporating skills or knowledge from the other two outcomes: the ability to present cultural content and to take multiple perspectives on it. In the comments quoted above, raters referenced the overlap of multiple perspectives and a reflective stance by pointing out how authors tie in the views of others to their own position on an issue (e.g., "mediation by the author between opposing viewpoints"). Furthermore, in the raters' comments, contextualization and differentiation between perspectives were often mentioned when commenting in the multiple perspectives category *and* in the reflective stance category. Moreover, comments on content learning demonstrate that a high score was contingent not only on what specific content was discussed (e.g., historical aspects, comparisons with other immigrant groups) but also on how the content was configured by the writer as a result of reflection on the issue (elaborated, contextualized, etc.). The following quotes from the comments on content illustrate this juncture between content and reflection:

"doesn't explore content or contextualize sufficiently"

"problems in organizing content"

"doesn't elaborate on content"

Finally, raters' comments suggested that successful performance of reflective stance was necessarily connected to a notion of coherence, which had not been addressed by any of the rating criteria. Whereas traditionally coherence has been seen as a marker of writing quality, here it was explicitly linked to reflective stance as an indication of conceptual quality. Coherence was subsequently defined by the assessment working group as an ability to create unifying concepts derived from content under focus and to develop these concepts textually. The following quotes from the raters' justifications provide examples for this theme:

"coherent stance on the issue"

"good framing of the issue"

"good line of argument"

"the author takes pains to frame and explore this as a complex theme"

"effective rhetorical structure"

"presence of transitions associated with effective presentation of multiple perspectives"

The importance of an overarching and coherently developed conceptualization of the material seemed to emerge as a significant factor in differentiating the performance outcomes between successful and less successful ratings of the compositions. The raters' comments on some mid- and low-rated essays revealed that merely including one's opinion on the issue and/or discussing comparisons and contrasts were insufficient for earning a high score. Even when some of the evaluative features mentioned above were present, the lack of an overarching rhetorical structure led to the "reproduction of content," a phrase that raters often used to justify a lower rating for reflective stance performances.

Transformative impact of the assessment project: Changes in pedagogy and assessment

The insights gained as a result of the assessment cycle, particularly the rating process described above, were not only helpful for specifying the nature of reflective stance as a central goal of humanistic learning, but also led to a number of curriculum revisions as specified in our initial list of intended project uses. Reforms were introduced across three dimensions of curricular practice: (a) modifications in the outcomes statement for reflective stance for Level III in general, and for the prototypical writing task in particular; (b) changes in the formulation of the prototypical writing task; and (c) transformations in pedagogical practices preparing students to complete the writing task.

Modifications in outcomes statements: Reflective stance

Starting with the changes to the outcomes statements, it became clear that the task students were asked to produce did not really require active and textually explicit negotiation with the perspectives of others since the task instructions did not explicitly elicit an argumentative essay. Raters came to realize that within the context of the writing task at Level III, reflection had more to do with contextualizing, comparing, and contrasting the discrete experiences of others (i.e., immigrants) in terms of some overarching concept or phenomenon. Thus, a change in the description of the outcomes was made to reflect a shift from the understanding of reflection as expression of opinion and clear argumentative voice, to an ability to present an issue evaluatively through synthesis of disparate information in terms of various facets and drawing connections between these facets. Table 4 presents the old and new description of the reflective stance outcomes.

Table 4. Humanities learning outcome for reflective stance: Revised and original

reflective stance (revised)	reflective stance (original)
Students take a reflective stance on the thematic issues that are foregrounded in the course:	Students take a reflective stance on the thematic issues that are foregrounded in the course:
Students can reconfigure information • by construing various phenomena in terms of abstract rubrics and • by elaborating on these rubrics in a coherent way Students are able to contextualize, compare, contrast, interpret, and evaluate the content and thus develop their own opinion on the issues.	Students are able to contextualize, compare, contrast, interpret, and evaluate the content. Students develop their own opinion on the issues. As learners express their own voice, they actively engage with the perspectives of others in such a way that the process of negotiation between their own ideas and those of others becomes evident.

In line with this new conceptualization, the goals for teaching reflective stance in the context of particular texts have also changed. For example, the reflective stance outcome for the text *Everyday Life in the Second Home* (*Alltag in der zweiten Heimat*; see Figure 2) is now expanded to include the following statement: "Identification and evaluation of phenomena that are characteristic of the situation of a particular immigrant group in Germany."

Changes in the prototypical writing task

Reproduction of information and lack of coherence noted in some mid- and low-rated compositions led raters to question the instructions for the task. It appeared to the raters that essays were rated higher where writers treated the task as expository and provided a thesis and supporting evidence. This raised a question about the genre students could be expected to produce at the end of Level III: Should it be a report, exposition, or argumentation? Given the progression from narrative to argumentative genres that characterizes the shift from Level III to the higher curricular levels, it was decided that the prototypical task for Level III would need to be formulated as a type of *explanation* that can be located between *narration* and *argumentation* (for a discussion of the similarities and differences between these genres see Coffin, 2006, Chapter 4). With these considerations, the task was modified accordingly (see the revised writing task in Appendix A).

Two major aspects distinguish the new task. First, the task steers students in a much more explicit way towards synthesizing the discrete experiences of Vietnamese immigrants in Germany and helps them reach a more abstract interpretative level in presenting these experiences. Second, the task provides a clear structure of how to elaborate on an essay topic within the parameters of the explanation genre. In line with Coffin's (2006) analysis of the moves or stages in explanation genres, the new task instructions ask students to (a) first present a characteristic aspect of Vietnamese life from personal and public perspectives; (b) present and illustrate the historical and cultural causes of the issue of interest (e.g., child labor or generational conflicts or integration readiness); (c) identify the consequences of this issue for contemporary Vietnamese life in Germany; and (d) evaluate the consequences and/or impacts of this issue for Vietnamese people. Equipping learners with these structural stages, which can be seen as "abstracted content," helps move students away from reproducing information they read about in the source texts towards configuring it in a particular way. The structure guides the learners to know where and how certain types of content can be positioned in the discourse structure of a particular text. For example, the historical background of Vietnamese immigration, often missing from lower-ranked compositions, can be successfully incorporated by a student into an essay specifically with instructions asking for elaboration on the causes of a particular political or social issue within Vietnamese communities (assuming students are capable of doing that).

Significantly, the writing task sheet does not include a separate reflective stance rating criteria. Instead, the understanding of the specific realization of the abstract and hard-to-pinpoint notion of reflective stance at this stage of the curriculum is incorporated in the formulations of the three rubrics of genre, content, and language that characterize all speaking and writing tasks in the curriculum.

Transformations in pedagogical practice

Modifications in the outcomes description and writing task subsequently led to a number of changes in pedagogical practice. In order to scaffold learning and enable students to achieve the specified humanities learning outcomes, class instruction had to include a particular approach to the texts that function as sources of information for the assessment task. While the original worksheets for the readings asked students to identify and describe the private and public perspectives on the issue, as well as select the most representative quotes from the source texts, the new worksheets aim to demonstrate how the presentation of perspectives function within the textual whole (see Appendix B for an example of a worksheet). In particular, the new worksheets ask students to first identify the textual structure, which contains some or all stages of the explanation genre as listed in the task sheet, and then demonstrate how the private and public voices are used by the author to realize this structure. Moreover, the linguistic construal of the voices of others, as well as generalization of specific experiences, now form a more prominent language focus of the lessons, these including the grammar of indirect speech, verbs of diction and other constructions (e.g., *according to*), as well as formulation of causes and consequences through nominalizations, nominal clauses, and causative verbs. After analyzing the uses of different voices in the various structural parts of the text, students are further attuned to the evaluative and partial nature of the explanation genre by questions that ask them to reflect on which voices are used or not used in the article, whether they judge the situation positively or negatively, and how inclusion and exclusion of voices affect the overall stance of the text.

To summarize the discussion in this section, engagement in the assessment project allowed us to clarify the nature of humanities learning implicit in the minds of department educators and jointly articulate what this learning means in the context of our curriculum at a particular point in learner development (the early-advanced level). Such insights also had a transformative impact on assessment practices, whereby the learning outcomes and the assessment task have been modified. Furthermore, the washback effect involved changes in instruction within a particular unit and beyond, as it led to modifications within the entire Level III course. For example, instruction on the thematic units preceding the unit on migration now includes more emphasis on the functions of indirect speech and nominalizations in conceptual construal of various genres learners encounter at this level (e.g., public speeches, chronicles). Moreover, changes to the writing task and instruction could also be regarded as improving the curricular articulation of the entire program since the requirement to produce a more interpretative rather than narrative or descriptive prototypical task at the end of Level III potentially contributes to a smoother transition to the higher curricular levels that focus more on argumentation.

Expanding the project

An important extension of the assessment initiative involved a discourse-semantic and linguistic analysis of the rated essays that aimed to determine the nature of the language resources necessary for successful knowledge construction and expression of reflective stance in Level III essays (Ryshina-Pankova & Byrnes, 2013). This study identified *grammatical metaphor* as realized through nominalizations as one such feature. It revealed how grammatical metaphor functions in learner texts to "distill" experience into general and abstract categories, an understanding of which further enables students to elaborate on and evaluate on those experiences. The study further demonstrated the crucial role of nominalized concepts for creating well-structured and coherent learner compositions. This research has already had important implications for pedagogical practice at Level III. A training workshop has been developed to make instructors aware of the role of grammatical metaphor for construal and evaluation of experience and for presenting it in coherent texts. Furthermore, as already indicated in the previous section, instruction on various forms and functions of nominalizations now forms an important focus at the advanced level.

The next logical step in the project will be assessing whether modifications in pedagogical practice and the writing task at Level III result in better achievement of humanities learning outcomes. We will be collecting new data from the students who will have worked with the new materials and the new task, rating in accordance with the revised rating sheet, and conducting a linguistic analysis of the compositions. Another goal is to continue with the identified assessment procedures at other focal points in the curriculum (e.g., end of the language requirement sequence) to be able to clarify outcomes for these points and determine various continua in humanities learning across the curricular progression.

Conclusion

This chapter has described a locally developed approach to assessment that aimed to clarify the nature of humanistic inquiry as it relates to FL study within undergraduate liberal arts education. The focus on the humanities learning outcomes in the project was instrumental for articulating our understanding of the elusive notion of reflective stance. In the end we realized that reflective stance encompassed two humanities learning components: cultural content knowledge and the consideration of multiple perspectives. This understanding was first spelled out in holistic terms but also ultimately tied to the linguistic and textual resources that are necessary for realizing humanistic inquiry and enabling a reflective stance. Thus, as a result of research inspired by the project, crucial connections between language, writing, and humanistic knowledge construction have been made explicit (see Ryshina-Pankova & Byrnes, 2013). Furthermore, an important feature of these efforts is the developmental perspective within which the outcomes were considered. Not only are these outcomes defined in close alignment with the curriculum and its goals as a whole, but also in accordance with a specific level in the major program. Naturally, a definition of reflective stance will be different for other curricular levels, and further assessment and curriculum development efforts will ultimately enable us to formulate a developmental continuum for this type of learning outcome.

Another significant consequence of the project is in its contribution to faculty and graduate student professional development. The project created opportunities for educators to revisit and negotiate the ultimate goals of FL instruction in the department and learn about aligning these with their educational actions.

The project also demonstrated well how "useful" outcomes assessment, as a deliberate inquiry into the value of FL education, is an effective vehicle for curricular innovation. In our project, assessment functioned as an inseparable part of the curriculum development cycle: At the start, existing curricular goals, materials, and pedagogies served as the point of departure for the formulation of the outcomes; at the end, insights gained as a result of assessment procedures formed the basis for reformulating learning outcomes and renovating curricular materials and pedagogies.

To conclude, the official title of our curriculum is "Developing Multiple Literacies." The "developing" part of the title has to be understood not only in terms of fostering student learning but also as the continuous curriculum work of the department's faculty and graduate students which is never fully complete. The humanities learning assessment project is a fair illustration of these efforts that are necessary for establishing the value of FL education as well as enhancing it.

Acknowlegments

This project would not have been possible without the collaborative work among the faculty and graduate students in the Georgetown University German Department. I would like to thank my colleagues for their contribution to the project. I would also like to express my gratitude to John Norris and Yukiko Watanabe for their guidance and valuable suggestions on this initiative.

References

American Association of Colleges and Universities. (2007). *College learning for the new global century. A report from the National Council for Liberal Educaiton and America's Promise.* Washington, DC: AAC&U.

Berkenkotter, C., & Huckin, T. N. (1995). *Genre knowledge in disciplinary communication: Cognition/ culture/ power.* Hillsdale, NJ: Erlbaum Associates.

Byrnes, H. (2002). The role of task and task-based assessment in a content-oriented collegiate foreign language curriculum. *Language Testing, 19*(4), 419–437.

Byrnes, H. (2009). Emergent L2 German writing ability in a curricular context: A longitudinal study of grammatical metaphor. *Linguistics and Education, 20*, 50–66.

Byrnes, H., Maxim, H. H., & Norris, J. M. (2010). Realizing advanced foreign language writing development in collegiate education: Curricular design, pedagogy, assessment [Monograph]. *Modern Language Journal, 94* (supplement s–1).

Byrnes, H., & Sinicrope, C. (2008). Advancedness and the development of relativization in L2 German: A curriculum-based longitudinal study. In L. Ortega & H. Byrnes (Eds.), *The longitudinal study of advanced L2 capacities* (pp. 109–138). Mahwah, NJ: Erlbaum.

Carter, M. (2007). Ways of knowing, doing, and writing in the disciplines. *College Composition and Communication, 58*(3), 385–418.

Coffin, C. (2006). *Historical discourse: The language of time, cause and evaluation.* London, England: Continuum.

Halliday, M. A. K. (1994). The construction of knowledge and value in the grammar of scientific discourse: With reference to Charles Darwin's *The Origin of Species.* In M. Coulthard (Ed.), *Advances in written text analysis* (pp. 136–156). London, England: Routledge.

Halliday, M. A. K. (2004). On the grammar of scientific English (1997). In J. J. Webster (Ed.), *The language of science* (pp. 181–198). London, England: Continuum.

Halliday, M. A. K., & Martin, J. R. (1993). *Writing science: Literacy and discursive power.* Washington, DC: The Falmer Press.

Hammer, J., & Swaffar, J. (2012). Assessing strategic cultural competency: Holistic approaches to student learning through media. *Modern Language Journal, 96*(2), 209–233.

Harpham, G. (2005). Beneath and beyond the "Crisis in the humanities." *New Literary History, 36*(1), 21–36.

Heiland, D., & Rosenthal, L. J. (2011). *Literary study, measurement, and the sublime: Disciplinary assessment.* New York, NY: The Teagle Foundation.

Hood, S. (2010). *Appraising research: Evaluation in academic writing.* London, England: Palgrave Macmillan.

Hood, S. (2011). Writing discipline: Comparing inscriptions of knowledge and knowers in academic writing. In F. Christie & K. Maton (Eds.), *Disciplinarity: Functional linguistic and sociological perspectives* (pp. 106–128). London, England: Continuum.

Kern, R. (2000). *Literacy and language teaching.* Oxford, England: Oxford University Press.

Kern, R. (2004). Literacy and advanced foreign language learning: Rethinking the curriculum. In H. Byrnes & H. H. Maxim (Eds.), *Advanced foreign language learning: A challenge to college programs* (pp. 2–18). Boston, MA: Heinle & Heinle.

Kern, R. (2008). Making connections through texts in language teaching. *Language Teaching, 41(3),* 367–387.

Martin, J. R. (1984). Language, register and genre. In F. Christie (Ed.), *Children writing: Reader* (pp. 21–30). Geelong, Australia: Deakin University Press.

Martin, J. R. (1997). Analysing genre: Functional parameters. In F. Christie & J. R. Martin (Eds.), *Genre and institutions: Social processes in the workplace and school* (pp. 3–39). London, England: Cassell.

MLA Ad Hoc Committee on Foreign Languages. (2007). Foreign languages and higher education: New structures for a changed world. *Profession 2007,* 234–245.

Norris, J. M. (2008). *Validity evaluation in language assessment.* Frankfurt-am-Main, Germany: Peter Lang.

Norris, J. M., & Pfeiffer, P. C. (2003). Exploring the use and usefulness of ACTFL oral proficiency ratings and standards in college foreign language departments. *Foreign Language Annals, 36,* 572–581.

Patton, M. Q. (1997). *Utilization-focused evaluation: The new century text* (3rd ed.). Thousand Oaks, CA: Sage.

Patton, M. Q. (2008). *Utilization-focused evaluation: The new century text* (4th ed.). Thousand Oaks, CA: Sage.

Ryshina–Pankova, M. (2010). Towards mastering the discourses of reasoning: Use of grammatical metaphor at advanced levels of foreign language acquisition. *Modern Language Journal, 92,* 181–197.

Ryshina-Pankova, M. (2011). Developmental changes in the use of interactional resources: Persuading the reader in FL book reviews. *Journal of Second Language Writing, 20(4),* 243–256.

Ryshina-Pankova, M., & Byrnes, H. (2013). Writing as learning to know: Tracing knowledge construction in L2 German compositions. *Journal of Second Language Writing, 22(2),* 179–197.

Scarino, A. (2009). Assessing intercultural capability in learning languages: Some issues and considerations. *Language Teaching, 42(1),* 67–80.

Sinicrope, C., Norris, J., & Watanabe, Y. (2007). Understanding and assessing intercultural competence: A summary of theory, research and practice

[Technical report for the Foreign Language Program Evaluation Project, University of Hawai'i at Mānoa]. *Second Language Studies, 26*(1), 1–58.

Stewart, S. (2005). Thoughts on the role of the humanities in contemporary life. *New Literary History, 36*(1), 97–103.

Swales, J. (1990). *Genre analysis: English in academic and research settings.* Cambridge, England: Cambridge University Press.

Appendix A. Prototypical writing tasks: Original and revised

Translation from German of Level III prototypical writing task (original)

Level III.2: German stories, German histories

Unit IV: Germany: On the way to a multicultural society

At home in Germany? A portrait of a Vietnamese family

Genre: Journalistic portrait

The magazine *Deutschland* is currently planning a new series of articles on different immigrant groups in Germany. Because you have dealt with this topic in the past several weeks, you have been asked by the magazine's editors to research and then write an article about the lives of Vietnamese in Germany. Your research is based on the three articles about the situation of the Vietnamese that you read in class.

The editors have also asked that you follow the structure of the first series of articles on this topic in the magazine by including the following sections:

- First describe the personal situation of one of the Vietnamese (for example, Huyen from Text 2).
- Then compare this situation with those of two other young Vietnamese. Here you can use information from Texts 2 and 3.
- Then explain the situation of the Vietnamese in Germany in general, from the public perspective. Here you can also use the official documents about the migrants in Germany, specifically the Vietnamese (Text 1).
- End the article with concluding comments about the Vietnamese in Germany.

Content:

- The materials that your instructor made available to you about Vietnamese in Germany serve as the basis for this assignment.
- Read through the materials and look for relevant information that you can include in your portrait.
- Pay attention to the following issues for both the personal and the public portrayal:
    a. reasons for immigrating or emigrating; time frame for immigration; length of stay
    b. experiences upon arrival; steps taken toward integration (e.g., language courses, help with the authorities, professional training, social support)
    c. activities the everyday experiences (e.g., housing, language ability, professional, education, free time activities, citizenship, activities of young people)
    d. cultural differences between the Vietnamese and German youth; communication with Germans; communication with one's own family and other Vietnamese

Language focus:

At the discourse level
- Establish chronology via temporal adverbs
- Draw comparisons between private and public situations
- Establish links between different parts of the text (e.g., through inversion, discourse markers)

At the sentence level
- Complex syntax (focus: position of the verb): subordinate clauses
- Indirect speech
- Hypothetical formulations (*what would be, if...?*)

At the word level
- Vocabulary from the texts and various semantic fields, e.g., citizenship, bureaucracy
- Evaluative adjectives for describing the situation
- Spelling

Writing process:

Preparation worksheet: due on _____.

First version: due on _____.

Revision: due on _____.

Length: 3–4 pages, double-spaced, with typed Umlauts

Evaluation criteria:

The categories of task, content and language are weighted equally (33% each rubric).

Translation from German of Level III prototypical writing task (revised)

Level III.2: German stories, German histories

Unit IV: Germany: On the way to a multicultural society

At home in Germany? A portrait of a Vietnamese family Task:

Genre: Explanation of a particular aspect in the situation of Vietnamese migrants in Germany

The magazine *Deutschland* is currently planning a new series of articles on different immigrant groups in Germany. Because you have dealt with this topic in the past several weeks, you have been asked by the magazine's editors to research and then write an article about the lives of Vietnamese in Germany. Your research is based on the three articles about the situation of the Vietnamese that you read in class.

From these texs you learned about particular characteristics of the life of the Vietnamese in Germany. Choose one aspect of the situation of the Vietnamese as migrants for your article in order to describe and explain their experiences in Germany (for example, child labor, generataional conflicts, readiness for integration, etc.). The choice and formulation of this aspect presupposes that you have informed yourself about the topic, reflected on the important aspects of the life of the Vietnamese migrants, and can now generalize and summarize these experiences abstractly as well as illustrate them with various examples that reflect the personal public perspectives on the issue.

Focus on the selected aspect/phenomenon in such a way that you present its causes and consequences from the personal (on the basis of specific stories of the Vietntamese from the texts) and public perspectives (on the basis of the opinions of the experts from the texts). End your article with a differentiated evaluation of the situation, whereby you point out the positive and negative sides of the phenomenon, as well as suggest strategies for dealing with it in the future.

Content:
- **Title** that reflects your interpretation
- **Introduce a particular aspect** as a concrete story/stories
- **Illustrate this aspect** by turning to the public perspective
- **Present the causes of the aspect**: e.g., historical background, cultural peculiarities
- **Illustrate the causes of the aspect**: from the personal and public perspectives
- Identify consequences of the aspect: from the public and private perspectives
- Evaluate the aspect/suggest a strategy of dealing with it in the future
- *Optional*: **End with an opinion/quote from a particular inviduum** to form a circle with the beginning of the article

Language Focus:

At the discourse level
- Establish chronology via temporal adverbs
- Establish causes and consequences via nominalizations, causative verbs
- Draw comparisons between private and public situations
- Establish links between different parts of the text (e.g., through inversion, discourse markers, nominalizations and nominal clauses, rhetorical questions)

At the sentence level
- Complex syntax (focus: position of the verb): subordinate clauses
- Indirect speech
- Hypothetical formulations (*what would be, if...?*)

At the word level
- Vocabulary from the texts and various semantic fields, e.g., citizenship, bureaucracy
- Evaluative adjectives for describing the situation
- Spelling

Writing process:

Preparation worksheet: due on _____.

First version: due on _____.

Revision: due on _____.

Length: 3–4 pages, double-spaced, with typed Umlauts

Evaluation criteria:

The categories of task, content and language are weighted equally (33% each rubric).

Appendix B. Translation from German of the worksheet for the text "Das vietnamesische Wunder" [The Vietnamese Wonder], by Martin Spiewak, *Zeit*, 03/08/2009

I. How is the article structured? Fill out the table.

part	notes with information and expressions from the text
1, 2 paragraphs: Presentation of the phenomenon as a specific example	*Die besten Schüler an dem Gymnasium sind oft die Vietnamesen. Besonders in Mathematik und in den Naturwissenschaften sind sie stark.*
3 paragraph: Presentation of the phenomenon in general	
4, 5 paragraphs: Evaluation of the phenomenon by the author	
6–12 paragraphs: Explanation of the phenomenon, Reason 1 Reason 2:	
13—15 paragraphs: Reason 3	
16 paragraph: Reason 4: 17, 18 paragraphs: Illustration	
19—21 paragraphs: Consequences of this mentality	
22 paragraph: Evaluation of the phenomenon by the author	

II. How do the quotes function? Fill out the table.

who speaks: name, position	quote	verb of diction (or another structure)	function (connect the quote with the communicative purpose of the textual part in which it appears)
Detlef Schmidt-Ihnen, Rektor am Ostberliner Barnim-Gymnasium	Hiess die Gewinnerin in der Klassenstufe sieben nun Tran Phuon Duyen oder Duyen Tran Phuon? Und wie war es mit Duc Dao Mohn aus der Zehn?	kein Verb	*die Stimme des Rektors hören zu lassen, der es schwierig findet, die Namen der vietnamesischen Migranten auszusprechen. Er muss das aber tun, weil die Vietnamesen oft unter den besten Schülern sind.*
	„Gerade in den Naturwissenschaften und in Mathematik sind viele von ihnen stark."		
	„Die Leistungen vietnamesischer Schüler stehen in einem eklatanten Gegensatz zum Bild, das wir sonst von Kindern mit Migrationshintergrund haben."		
	„Kokosmilchsuppe scharf", „Bandnudeln mit Hühnerbrust knusprig"		
	Wie ist das möglich, Herr Nguyen?		
	„Weil alle vietnamesischen Eltern wollen, dass ihre Kinder gut sind in der Schule."		
	„Bildung ist für vietnamesische Familien das höchste Gut."		
	„Sogar bei Fragen, die ein tieferes mathematisches Verständnis erfordern, schnitten die Vietnamesen besser ab."		
	„Von nichts kommt nichts", „Die Kinder sollen es einmal besser haben."		
	„Meine Eltern haben mir laufend vorgehalten, dass andere Schüler bessere Zeugnisse haben als ich."		
	„Die vietnamesischen Schüler gleichen sich den einheimischen an."		
	„Die Jugendlichen leben in zwei Kulturen."		
	„Wir wollen lernen und vorankommen. So können wir vielleicht einmal zur Elite dieses Landes gehören."		

III. How are the statistics used? Fill out the table. Does the author indicate sources of the statistics? How do the statistics evaluate the phenomenon, positively or negatively?

statistics	function in this part of the text
17 Prozent der Schüler an dem Gymnasium im Stadtteil Lichtenberg stammen aus einer vietnamesischen Familie, in den unteren Klassen sind es mehr als 30 Prozent.	*Die Statistik stützt mit den Zahlen die Aussagen über den Erfolg der Vietnamesen in einem konkreten Gymnasium*
Über 50 Prozent ihrer Schüler schaffen den Sprung aufs Gymnasium. Damit streben mehr vietnamesische Jugendliche zum Abitur als deutsche. Im Vergleich zu ihren Alterskollegen aus türkischen oder italienischen Familien liegt die Gymnasialquote fünfmal so hoch.	
Rund 30 Prozent der Auserwählten in Ostdeutschland sind Vietnamesen.	

IV. From what perspective is the article written? Which voices are included, which are not? How do these voices evaluate the situation? How do these voices contribute to the overall authorial stance in the article? Justify your opinion with examples.

About the Contributors

Lance R. Askildson, an interdisciplinary scholar of second language acquisition and international studies, is Vice-Provost and an associate professor of English Language and Linguistics at Kennesaw State University. Previously, he was the founding director of the Center for the Study of Languages & Cultures at the University of Notre Dame, where he also served as the founding assistant provost for Internationalization and associate professor of Second Language Education.

Alessia Blad, a PhD candidate in Italian and French at Middlebury College, is an associate lecturer and coordinator of Italian language courses at the University of Notre Dame. She also teaches the Second Language Acquisition and Teaching Methods course to the Department of Romance Languages and Literatures graduate students. As part of the Committee for the Study of Romance Languages and Cultures, she was involved in a department-wide project that sought to establish student learning goals for all levels of the curriculum, as well as an assessment plan to measure whether those goals are being met. Her interests include new media literacy and assessment, hybrid and online learning, and curriculum design and assessment. She is the AAUSC Italian section head (2014–2017).

Ghada Nemr Bualuan is an assistant teaching professor of Arabic and Director of Undergraduate Studies in Arabic and Mediterranean Middle Eastern Studies at the University of Notre Dame. She received her bachelor's degree from the American University of Beirut in Business Administration with a minor in Arabic and Islamic Studies and her master's degree from the Lebanese American University in Business Administration. She is currently an MA candidate in Arabic Language and Literature at Middlebury College, Vermont (expected August 2015).

Theodore J. Cachey, Jr. is the inaugural academic director of the University of Notre Dame's Rome Global Gateway in Rome, Italy. A professor of Italian Studies, he specializes in Medieval and Renaissance literature, in particular Dante and Petrarch, the history of the Italian language, and travel literature.

He is the founder and co-editor of the Devers Series in Dante and Medieval Italian Literature and serves on the editorial boards of the *Nuova Rivista di Letteratura Italiana*, *Italica: Journal of the American Association of Italian Studies*, and *Italian Culture: The Journal of the American Association for Italian Studies*.

John McE. Davis is a visiting assistant professor of Linguistics at Georgetown University and co-director of the Assessment and Evaluation Language Resource Center. He conducts research on educational accountability, language program evaluation, and classroom-based assessment. His most recent publications have focused on the impacts of accreditation-mandated assessment on college language programs. He has also worked as an assessment and evaluation consultant/coordinator with the National Foreign Language Resource Center, the National Middle Eastern Language Resource Center, and the College of Languages, Linguistics, and Literatures at the University of Hawai'i at Mānoa.

Anna De Fina is a professor of Italian Language and Linguistics in the Italian Department at Georgetown University where she is also the language program coordinator. Her interests and publications focus on migrant communities, discourse, identity, and narrative. She has authored numerous articles in internationally renowned journals and edited special issues on these topics. Her books include *Analyzing Narratives* (2011, co-authored with Alexandra Georgakopoulou), *Identity in Narrative: A Study of Immigrant Discourse* (2003), and the co-edited volumes *Dislocations, Relocations, Narratives of Migration* (2005, with M. Baynham), *Discourse and Identity* (2006, with D. Schiffrin and M. Bamberg), and *Italiano e italani fuori d'Italia* (2005, with F. Bizzoni).

Amaya Martin is an assistant teaching professor in the Arabic Language and Culture program at the University of Notre Dame, Indiana. She earned her PhD in Arabic in the Department of Arabic and Islamic Studies at Georgetown University, Washington, DC, where she taught until 2011. Her academic specialization is Arabic linguistic analysis, especially of works by or about minorities to discern the subtleties of their social status.

Hiram H. Maxim is a professor of German Studies at Emory University. His research focuses on instructed adult second language acquisition with specific interest in the relationship between reading and writing and curricular approaches that facilitate that intersection. His work has appeared in *Modern Language Journal*, *Foreign Language Annals*, *Die Unterrichtspraxis*, *ADFL Bulletin*, and various edited volumes. Recent work includes a volume co-edited with Heather Allen on foreign language graduate student education (Cengage, 2013) and the monograph *Realizing Advanced Foreign Language Writing Development in Collegiate Education: Curricular Design, Pedagogy, Assessment* (Wiley-Blackwell, 2010), jointly authored with Heidi Byrnes and John Norris.

Donatella Melucci is an associate teaching professor of Italian at Georgetown University. Her background and research interests focus on applied linguistics with particular emphasis on the Communicative Language Teaching (CLT) approach. She is currently working on integrating new technologies with traditional classroom instruction to enhance language teaching and learning.

She has also co-authored two Italian language textbooks, *Da capo* (2009) for the intermediate level and *Piazza* (2014) for the beginning level. These publications represent her linguistic and pedagogical principles which embrace teaching language in a cultural context.

John Norris is an associate professor in the Linguistics Department at Georgetown University. His research and teaching interests include educational assessment, program evaluation, language pedagogy (task-based language teaching in particular), and research methods. His publications have appeared in journals such as *Applied Linguistics*, *Foreign Language Annals*, *Language Learning*, *Language Learning & Technology*, *Language Teaching Research*, *Language Testing*, *Modern Language Journal*, *TESOL Quarterly*, and *Die Unterrichtspraxis*. He has served as chair of the TOEFL Committee of Examiners and the International Consortium on Task-Based Language Teaching. He speaks German, Spanish, and Portuguese.

Peter C. Pfeiffer is a professor of German at Georgetown University. His academic interests are divided between his love of literature, especially of the 19th and early 20th centuries, and his deep involvement with curricular innovation, academic administrative action, and learning assessment. He served as chair and in other administrative functions for many years. He has published widely on his interests and is currently completing a study of representations of work in literary texts of the 19th century.

Amanda Randall is a PhD candidate in Germanic Studies at The University of Texas at Austin specializing in 20th century comparative cultural studies. Her dissertation, a case study of "institutional memory," examines the symbiosis of disciplinary historiography and structural reform of German *Volkskunde / europäische Ethnologie*, 1945 to present. Other research interests include film studies and translation studies. Her article "Austrian *Trümmerfilm*? What a Genre's Absence Reveals about National Postwar Cinema and Film Studies" won the 2014 German Studies Association Prize for Best Graduate Student Essay and will appear in *German Studies Review 38.3* (2015).

Marianna Ryshina-Pankova is an assistant professor of German at Georgetown University. As director of curriculum, she is actively involved in the maintenance, revision, and evaluation of the undergraduate curriculum and in mentoring graduate students teaching in the program. Her research interests include content- and language-integrated curriculum design, language teacher education, second-language writing development, and student learning outcomes assessment. She has published in *Modern Language Journal, Journal of Second Language Writing, Die Unterrichtspraxis,* and in various edited volumes on genre-based pedagogy and development of advanced foreign language literacy.

Shoko Sasayama is a PhD candidate in Linguistics at Georgetown University. Her academic interests include language pedagogy (Task-Based Language Teaching in particular), program evaluation, and second language testing and assessment. She is especially interested in language teacher training as a foundation for improvement of and innovation in language programs. Prior to moving to Georgetown, she was a Fulbright scholar at the University of Hawai'i, and she also has experience teaching Japanese and English to learners of various age groups. Currently, she works as a teaching associate in the Department of Linguistics at Georgetown University.

Janet Swaffar is a professor emerita who has taught German for over 50 years at levels from grade school to graduate programs. She has published books and articles on 19th and 20th century German literature and language studies. Her most recent publication is a chapter that assesses the history of FL instruction in the United States since 1945 in her edited volume (with co-editor Per Urlaub) *Transforming Postsecondary Foreign Language Teaching in the United States* (2014).

Hannelore Weber is a teaching professor in the Department of German and Russian at the University of Notre Dame. She is the director of the German Language Program and teaches language courses at the beginning and intermediate levels, as well as Business German. She is active in the Indiana chapter of AATG and a member of the Goethe Institute's trainer network. Her interests lie in pedagogy and language acquisition, especially in the use of the use of technology enhanced learning.

Shauna Williams is an associate special professional faculty in Spanish and the director of undergraduate studies for the Department of Romance Languages and Literatures at the University of Notre Dame. She also serves as chair of the Department's committee for curriculum and assessment. Recent projects and presentations include department-wide utilization-focused evaluation, program specific learning outcomes and assessment, course embedded oral and written assessments, and, most recently, hybrid models in beginning language courses. In addition, she teaches Spanish language courses.

ordering information at nflrc.hawaii.edu

Pragmatics & Interaction
Gabriele Kasper, series editor

Pragmatics & Interaction ("P&I"), a refereed series sponsored by the University of Hawai'i National Foreign Language Resource Center, publishes research on topics in pragmatics and discourse as social interaction from a wide variety of theoretical and methodological perspectives. P&I welcomes particularly studies on languages spoken in the Asia-Pacific region.

PRAGMATICS OF VIETNAMESE AS NATIVE AND TARGET LANGUAGE
CARSTEN ROEVER & HANH THI NGUYEN (EDITORS), 2013

The volume offers a wealth of new information about the forms of several speech acts and their social distribution in Vietnamese as L1 and L2, complemented by a chapter on address forms and listener responses. As the first of its kind, the book makes a valuable contribution to the research literature on pragmatics, sociolinguistics, and language and social interaction in an under-researched and less commonly taught Asian language.

282pp., ISBN 978-0-9835816-2-8 $30.

L2 LEARNING AS SOCIAL PRACTICE: CONVERSATION-ANALYTIC PERSPECTIVES
GABRIELE PALLOTTI & JOHANNES WAGNER (EDITORS), 2011

This volume collects empirical studies applying Conversation Analysis to situations where second, third, and other additional languages are used. A number of different aspects are considered, including how linguistic systems develop over time through social interaction, how participants 'do' language learning and teaching in classroom and everyday settings, how they select languages and manage identities in multilingual contexts, and how the linguistic-interactional divide can be bridged with studies combining Conversation Analysis and Functional Linguistics. This variety of issues and approaches clearly shows the fruitfulness of a socio-interactional perspective on second language learning.

380pp., ISBN 978-0-9800459-7-0 $30.

TALK-IN-INTERACTION: MULTILINGUAL PERSPECTIVES
HANH THI NGUYEN & GABRIELE KASPER (EDITORS), 2009

This volume offers original studies of interaction in a range of languages and language varieties, including Chinese, English, Japanese, Korean, Spanish, Swahili, Thai, and Vietnamese; monolingual and bilingual interactions; and activities designed for second or foreign language learning. Conducted from the perspectives of conversation analysis and membership categorization analysis, the chapters examine ordinary conversation and institutional activities in face-to-face, telephone, and computer-mediated environments.

420pp., ISBN 978–09800459–1–8 $30.

Pragmatics & Language Learning
Gabriele Kasper, series editor

Pragmatics & Language Learning ("PLL"), a refereed series sponsored by the National Foreign Language Resource Center, publishes selected papers from the International Pragmatics & Language Learning conference under the editorship of the conference hosts and the series editor. Check the NFLRC website for upcoming PLL conferences and PLL volumes.

PRAGMATICS AND LANGUAGE LEARNING VOLUME 13
Tim Greer, Donna Tatsuki, & Carsten Roever (Editors), 2013

Pragmatics & Language Learning Volume 13 examines the organization of second language and multilingual speakers' talk and pragmatic knowledge across a range of naturalistic and experimental activities. Based on data collected among ESL and EFL learners from a variety of backgrounds, the contributions explore the nexus of pragmatic knowledge, interaction, and L2 learning outside and inside of educational settings.

292pp., ISBN 978–0–9835816–4–2 $30.

PRAGMATICS AND LANGUAGE LEARNING VOLUME 12
Gabriele Kasper, Hanh thi Nguyen, Dina R. Yoshimi, & Jim K. Yoshioka (Editors), 2010

This volume examines the organization of second language and multilingual speakers' talk and pragmatic knowledge across a range of naturalistic and experimental activities. Based on data collected on Danish, English, Hawai'i Creole, Indonesian, and Japanese as target languages, the contributions explore the nexus of pragmatic knowledge, interaction, and L2 learning outside and inside of educational settings.

364pp., ISBN 978–09800459–6–3 $30.

PRAGMATICS AND LANGUAGE LEARNING VOLUME 11
Kathleen Bardovi-Harlig, César Félix-Brasdefer, & Alwiya S. Omar (Editors), 2006

This volume features cutting-edge theoretical and empirical research on pragmatics and language learning among a wide variety of learners in diverse learning contexts from a variety of language backgrounds and target languages (English, German, Japanese, Kiswahili, Persian, and Spanish). This collection of papers from researchers around the world includes critical appraisals on the role of formulas in interlanguage pragmatics, and speech-act research from a conversation analytic perspective. Empirical studies examine learner data using innovative methods of analysis and investigate issues in pragmatic development and the instruction of pragmatics.

430pp., ISBN 978–0–8248–3137–0 $30.

NFLRC Monographs
Julio C Rodriguez, series editor

Monographs of the National Foreign Language Resource Center present the findings of recent work in applied linguistics that is of relevance to language teaching and learning (with a focus on the less commonly taught languages of Asia and the Pacific) and are of particular interest to foreign language educators, applied linguists, and researchers. Prior to 2006, these monographs were published as "SLTCC Technical Reports."

CULTURA-INSPIRED INTERCULTURAL EXCHANGES: FOCUS ON ASIAN AND PACIFIC LANGUAGES
Dorothy M. Chun (Editor), 2014

Although many online intercultural exchanges have been conducted based on the *Cultura* model, most to date have been between and among European languages. This volume presents several chapters with a focus on exchanges involving Asian and Pacific languages. Many of the benefits and challenges of these exchanges are similar to those reported for European languages; however, some of the difficulties reported in the Chinese and Japanese exchanges might be due to the significant linguistic differences between English and East Asian languages. This volume adds to the body of emerging studies of telecollaboration among learners of Asian and Pacific languages.

183pp., ISBN 978–0–9835816–7–3 (paperback) $25.
      ISBN 978–1–63443–578–9 (eBook) $10.

NOTICING AND SECOND LANGUAGE ACQUISITION: STUDIES IN HONOR OF RICHARD SCHMIDT
Joara Martin Bergsleithner, Sylvia Nagem Frota, & Jim Kei Yoshioka (Editors), 2013

This volume celebrates the life and groundbreaking work of Richard Schmidt, the developer of the influential Noticing Hypothesis in the field of second language acquisition. The 19 chapters encompass a compelling collection of cuttingedge research studies exploring such constructs as noticing, attention, and awareness from multiple perspectives, which expand, fine tune, sometimes support, and sometimes challenge Schmidt's seminal ideas and take research on noticing in exciting new directions.

374pp., ISBN 978–0–9835816–6–6 $25.

NEW PERSPECTIVES ON JAPANESE LANGUAGE LEARNING, LINGUISTICS, AND CULTURE
Kimi Kondo-Brown, Yoshiko Saito-Abbott, Shingo Satsutani, Michio Tsutsui, & Ann Wehmeyer (Editors), 2013

This volume is a collection of selected refereed papers presented at the Association of Teachers of Japanese Annual Spring Conference held at the University of Hawaiʻi at Mānoa in March of 2011. It not only covers several important topics on teaching and learning spoken and written Japanese and culture in and beyond classroom settings but also includes research investigating certain linguistics items from new perspectives.

208pp., ISBN 978–0–9835816–3–5 $25.

DEVELOPING, USING, AND ANALYZING RUBRICS IN LANGUAGE ASSESSMENT WITH CASE STUDIES IN ASIAN AND PACIFIC LANGUAGES
JAMES DEAN BROWN (EDITOR), 2012

Rubrics are essential tools for all language teachers in this age of communicative and task-based teaching and assessment—tools that allow us to efficiently communicate to our students what we are looking for in the productive language abilities of speaking and writing and then effectively assess those abilities when the time comes for grading students, giving them feedback, placing them into new courses, and so forth. This book provides a wide array of ideas, suggestions, and examples (mostly from Māori, Hawaiian, and Japanese language assessment projects) to help language educators effectively develop, use, revise, analyze, and report on rubric-based assessments.

212pp., ISBN 978–0–9835816–1–1 $25.

RESEARCH AMONG LEARNERS OF CHINESE AS A FOREIGN LANGUAGE
MICHAEL E. EVERSON & HELEN H. SHEN (EDITORS), 2010

Cutting-edge in its approach and international in its authorship, this fourth monograph in a series sponsored by the Chinese Language Teachers Association features eight research studies that explore a variety of themes, topics, and perspectives important to a variety of stakeholders in the Chinese language learning community. Employing a wide range of research methodologies, the volume provides data from actual Chinese language learners and will be of value to both theoreticians and practitioners alike. *[in English & Chinese]*

180pp., ISBN 978–0–9800459–4–9 $20.

MANCHU: A TEXTBOOK FOR READING DOCUMENTS (SECOND EDITION)
GERTRAUDE ROTH LI, 2010

This book offers students a tool to gain a basic grounding in the Manchu language. The reading selections provided in this volume represent various types of documents, ranging from examples of the very earliest Manchu writing (17th century) to samples of contemporary Sibe (Xibo), a language that may be considered a modern version of Manchu. Since Manchu courses are only rarely taught at universities anywhere, this second edition includes audio recordings to assist students with the pronunciation of the texts.

418pp., ISBN 978–0–9800459–5–6 $36.

TOWARD USEFUL PROGRAM EVALUATION IN COLLEGE FOREIGN LANGUAGE EDUCATION
JOHN M. NORRIS, JOHN MCE. DAVIS, CASTLE SINICROPE, & YUKIKO WATANABE (EDITORS), 2009

This volume reports on innovative, useful evaluation work conducted within U.S. college foreign language programs. An introductory chapter scopes out the territory, reporting key findings from research into the concerns, impetuses, and uses for evaluation that FL educators identify. Seven chapters then highlight examples of evaluations conducted in diverse language programs and institutional contexts. Each case is reported by program-internal educators, who walk readers through critical steps, from identifying evaluation uses, users, and questions, to designing methods, interpreting findings, and taking actions. A concluding chapter reflects on the emerging roles for FL program evaluation and articulates an agenda for integrating evaluation into language education practice.

240pp., ISBN 978–0–9800459–3–2 $30.

SECOND LANGUAGE TEACHING AND LEARNING IN THE NET GENERATION
Raquel Oxford & Jeffrey Oxford (Editors), 2009

Today's young people—the Net Generation—have grown up with technology all around them. However, teachers cannot assume that students' familiarity with technology in general transfers successfully to pedagogical settings. This volume examines various technologies and offers concrete advice on how each can be successfully implemented in the second language curriculum.

240pp., ISBN 978–0–9800459–2–5 $30.

CASE STUDIES IN FOREIGN LANGUAGE PLACEMENT: PRACTICES AND POSSIBILITIES
Thom Hudson & Martyn Clark (Editors), 2008

Although most language programs make placement decisions on the basis of placement tests, there is surprisingly little published about different contexts and systems of placement testing. The present volume contains case studies of placement programs in foreign language programs at the tertiary level across the United States. The different programs span the spectrum from large programs servicing hundreds of students annually to small language programs with very few students. The contributions to this volume address such issues as how the size of the program, presence or absence of heritage learners, and population changes affect language placement decisions.

201pp., ISBN 0–9800459–0–8 $20.

CHINESE AS A HERITAGE LANGUAGE: FOSTERING ROOTED WORLD CITIZENRY
Agnes Weiyun He & Yun Xiao (Editors), 2008

Thirty-two scholars examine the sociocultural, cognitive-linguistic, and educational-institutional trajectories along which Chinese as a Heritage Language may be acquired, maintained, and developed. They draw upon developmental psychology, functional linguistics, linguistic and cultural anthropology, discourse analysis, orthography analysis, reading research, second language acquisition, and bilingualism. This volume aims to lay a foundation for theories, models, and master scripts to be discussed, debated, and developed, and to stimulate research and enhance teaching both within and beyond Chinese language education.

280pp., ISBN 978–0–8248–3286–5 $20.

PERSPECTIVES ON TEACHING CONNECTED SPEECH TO SECOND LANGUAGE SPEAKERS
James Dean Brown & Kimi Kondo-Brown (Editors), 2006

This book is a collection of fourteen articles on connected speech of interest to teachers, researchers, and materials developers in both ESL/EFL (ten chapters focus on connected speech in English) and Japanese (four chapters focus on Japanese connected speech). The fourteen chapters are divided up into five sections:

- What do we know so far about teaching connected speech?
- Does connected speech instruction work?
- How should connected speech be taught in English?
- How should connected speech be taught in Japanese?
- How should connected speech be tested?

290pp., ISBN 978–0–8248–3136–3 $20.

CORPUS LINGUISTICS FOR KOREAN LANGUAGE LEARNING AND TEACHING
Robert Bley-Vroman & Hyunsook Ko (Editors), 2006

Dramatic advances in personal-computer technology have given language teachers access to vast quantities of machine-readable text, which can be analyzed with a view toward improving the basis of language instruction. Corpus linguistics provides analytic techniques and practical tools for studying language in use. This volume provides both an introductory framework for the use of corpus linguistics for language teaching and examples of its application for Korean teaching and learning. The collected papers cover topics in Korean syntax, lexicon, and discourse, and second language acquisition research, always with a focus on application in the classroom. An overview of Korean corpus linguistics tools and available Korean corpora are also included.

265pp., ISBN 0-8248-3062-8 $25.

NEW TECHNOLOGIES AND LANGUAGE LEARNING: CASES IN THE LESS COMMONLY TAUGHT LANGUAGES
Carol Anne Spreen (Editor), 2002

In recent years, the National Security Education Program (NSEP) has supported an increasing number of programs for teaching languages using different technological media. This compilation of case study initiatives funded through the NSEP Institutional Grants Program presents a range of technology-based options for language programming that will help universities make more informed decisions about teaching less commonly taught languages. The eight chapters describe how different types of technologies are used to support language programs (i.e., web, ITV, and audio- or video-based materials), discuss identifiable trends in e-language learning, and explore how technology addresses issues of equity, diversity, and opportunity. This book offers many lessons learned and decisions made as technology changes and learning needs become more complex.

188pp., ISBN 0-8248-2634-5 $25.

AN INVESTIGATION OF SECOND LANGUAGE TASK-BASED PERFORMANCE ASSESSMENTS
James Dean Brown, Thom Hudson, John M. Norris, & William Bonk, 2002

This volume describes the creation of performance assessment instruments and their validation (based on work started in a previous monograph). It begins by explaining the test and rating scale development processes and the administration of the resulting three seven-task tests to 90 university-level EFL and ESL students. The results are examined in terms of (a) the effects of test revision; (b) comparisons among the task-dependent, task-independent, and self-rating scales; and (c) reliability and validity issues.

240pp., ISBN 0-8248-2633-7 $25.

MOTIVATION AND SECOND LANGUAGE ACQUISITION
Zoltán Dörnyei & Richard Schmidt (Editors), 2001

This volume—the second in this series concerned with motivation and foreign language learning—includes papers presented in a state-of-the-art colloquium on L2 motivation at the American Association for Applied Linguistics (Vancouver, 2000) and a number of specially commissioned studies. The 20 chapters, written by some of the best known researchers in the field, cover a wide range of theoretical and research methodological issues, and also offer empirical results (both qualitative and quantitative) concerning the learning of many different languages (Arabic, Chinese, English, Filipino, French, German, Hindi, Italian, Japanese,

Russian, and Spanish) in a broad range of learning contexts (Bahrain, Brazil, Canada, Egypt, Finland, Hungary, Ireland, Israel, Japan, Spain, and the US.).

520pp., ISBN 0–8248–2458–X $30.

A FOCUS ON LANGUAGE TEST DEVELOPMENT: EXPANDING THE LANGUAGE PROFICIENCY CONSTRUCT ACROSS A VARIETY OF TESTS
THOM HUDSON & JAMES DEAN BROWN (EDITORS), 2001

This volume presents eight research studies that introduce a variety of novel, nontraditional forms of second and foreign language assessment. To the extent possible, the studies also show the entire test development process, warts and all. These language testing projects not only demonstrate many of the types of problems that test developers run into in the real world but also afford the reader unique insights into the language test development process.

230pp., ISBN 0–8248–2351–6 $20.

STUDIES ON KOREAN IN COMMUNITY SCHOOLS
DONG-JAE LEE, SOOKEUN CHO, MISEON LEE, MINSUN SONG, & WILLIAM O'GRADY (EDITORS), 2000

The papers in this volume focus on language teaching and learning in Korean community schools. Drawing on innovative experimental work and research in linguistics, education, and psychology, the contributors address issues of importance to teachers, administrators, and parents. Topics covered include childhood bilingualism, Korean grammar, language acquisition, children's literature, and language teaching methodology. [in Korean]

256pp., ISBN 0–8248–2352–4 $20.

A COMMUNICATIVE FRAMEWORK FOR INTRODUCTORY JAPANESE LANGUAGE CURRICULA
WASHINGTON STATE JAPANESE LANGUAGE CURRICULUM GUIDELINES COMMITTEE, 2000

In recent years, the number of schools offering Japanese nationwide has increased dramatically. Because of the tremendous popularity of the Japanese language and the shortage of teachers, quite a few untrained, nonnative and native teachers are in the classrooms and are expected to teach several levels of Japanese. These guidelines are intended to assist individual teachers and professional associations throughout the United States in designing Japanese language curricula. They are meant to serve as a framework from which language teaching can be expanded and are intended to allow teachers to enhance and strengthen the quality of Japanese language instruction.

168pp., ISBN 0–8248–2350–8 $20.

FOREIGN LANGUAGE TEACHING AND MINORITY LANGUAGE EDUCATION
KATHRYN A. DAVIS (EDITOR), 1999

This volume seeks to examine the potential for building relationships among foreign language, bilingual, and ESL programs towards fostering bilingualism. Part I of the volume examines the sociopolitical contexts for language partnerships, including:

- obstacles to developing bilingualism;
- implications of acculturation, identity, and language issues for linguistic minorities; and
- the potential for developing partnerships across primary, secondary, and tertiary institutions.

Part II of the volume provides research findings on the Foreign Language Partnership Project, designed to capitalize on the resources of immigrant students to enhance foreign language learning.

152pp., ISBN 0–8248–2067–3 $20.

DESIGNING SECOND LANGUAGE PERFORMANCE ASSESSMENTS
John M. Norris, James Dean Brown, Thom Hudson, & Jim Yoshioka, 1998, 2000

This technical report focuses on the decision-making potential provided by second language performance assessments. The authors first situate performance assessment within a broader discussion of alternatives in language assessment and in educational assessment in general. They then discuss issues in performance assessment design, implementation, reliability, and validity. Finally, they present a prototype framework for second language performance assessment based on the integration of theoretical underpinnings and research findings from the task-based language teaching literature, the language testing literature, and the educational measurement literature. The authors outline test and item specifications, and they present numerous examples of prototypical language tasks. They also propose a research agenda focusing on the operationalization of second language performance assessments.

248pp., ISBN 0-8248-2109-2 $20.

SECOND LANGUAGE DEVELOPMENT IN WRITING: MEASURES OF FLUENCY, ACCURACY, AND COMPLEXITY
Kate Wolfe-Quintero, Shunji Inagaki, & Hae-Young Kim, 1998, 2002

In this book, the authors analyze and compare the ways that fluency, accuracy, grammatical complexity, and lexical complexity have been measured in studies of language development in second language writing. More than 100 developmental measures are examined, with detailed comparisons of the results across the studies that have used each measure. The authors discuss the theoretical foundations for each type of developmental measure, and they consider the relationship between developmental measures and various types of proficiency measures. They also examine criteria for determining which developmental measures are the most successful and suggest which measures are the most promising for continuing work on language development.

208pp., ISBN 0-8248-2069-X $20.

THE DEVELOPMENT OF A LEXICAL TONE PHONOLOGY IN AMERICAN ADULT LEARNERS OF STANDARD MANDARIN CHINESE
Sylvia Henel Sun, 1998

The study reported is based on an assessment of three decades of research on the SLA of Mandarin tone. It investigates whether differences in learners' tone perception and production are related to differences in the effects of certain linguistic, task, and learner factors. The learners of focus are American students of Mandarin in Beijing, China. Their performances on two perception and three production tasks are analyzed through a host of variables and methods of quantification.

328pp., ISBN 0-8248-2068-1 $20.

NEW TRENDS AND ISSUES IN TEACHING JAPANESE LANGUAGE AND CULTURE
Haruko M. Cook, Kyoko Hijirida, & Mildred Tahara (Editors), 1997

In recent years, Japanese has become the fourth most commonly taught foreign language at the college level in the United States. As the number of students who study Japanese has increased, the teaching of Japanese as a foreign language has been established as an important academic field of study. This technical report includes nine contributions to the advancement of this field, encompassing the following five important issues:

- Literature and literature teaching
- Technology in the language classroom

- Orthography
- Testing
- Grammatical versus pragmatic approaches to language teaching

164pp., ISBN 0-8248-2067-3 $20.

SIX MEASURES OF JSL PRAGMATICS
Sayoko Okada Yamashita, 1996

This book investigates differences among tests that can be used to measure the cross-cultural pragmatic ability of English-speaking learners of Japanese. Building on the work of Hudson, Detmer, and Brown (Technical Reports #2 and #7 in this series), the author modified six test types that she used to gather data from North American learners of Japanese. She found numerous problems with the multiple-choice discourse completion test but reported that the other five tests all proved highly reliable and reasonably valid. Practical issues involved in creating and using such language tests are discussed from a variety of perspectives.

213pp., ISBN 0-8248-1914-4 $15.

LANGUAGE LEARNING STRATEGIES AROUND THE WORLD: CROSS-CULTURAL PERSPECTIVES
Rebecca L. Oxford (Editor), 1996, 1997, 2002

Language learning strategies are the specific steps students take to improve their progress in learning a second or foreign language. Optimizing learning strategies improves language performance. This groundbreaking book presents new information about cultural influences on the use of language learning strategies. It also shows innovative ways to assess students' strategy use and remarkable techniques for helping students improve their choice of strategies, with the goal of peak language learning.

166pp., ISBN 0-8248-1910-1 $20.

TELECOLLABORATION IN FOREIGN LANGUAGE LEARNING: PROCEEDINGS OF THE HAWAI'I SYMPOSIUM
Mark Warschauer (Editor), 1996

The Symposium on Local & Global Electronic Networking in Foreign Language Learning & Research, part of the National Foreign Language Resource Center's 1995 Summer Institute on Technology & the Human Factor in Foreign Language Education, included presentations of papers and hands-on workshops conducted by Symposium participants to facilitate the sharing of resources, ideas, and information about all aspects of electronic networking for foreign language teaching and research, including electronic discussion and conferencing, international cultural exchanges, real-time communication and simulations, research and resource retrieval via the Internet, and research using networks. This collection presents a sampling of those presentations.

252pp., ISBN 0-8248-1867-9 $20.

LANGUAGE LEARNING MOTIVATION: PATHWAYS TO THE NEW CENTURY
Rebecca L. Oxford (Editor), 1996

This volume chronicles a revolution in our thinking about what makes students want to learn languages and what causes them to persist in that difficult and rewarding adventure. Topics in this book include the internal structures of and external connections with foreign language motivation; exploring adult language learning motivation, self-efficacy, and anxiety; comparing the motivations and learning strategies of students of Japanese and Spanish; and enhancing the theory of language learning motivation from many psychological and social perspectives.

218pp., ISBN 0-8248-1849-0 $20.

LINGUISTICS & LANGUAGE TEACHING: PROCEEDINGS OF THE SIXTH JOINT LSH-HATESL CONFERENCE
Cynthia Reves, Caroline Steele, & Cathy S. P. Wong (Editors), 1996

Technical Report #10 contains 18 articles revolving around the following three topics:
- Linguistic issues—These six papers discuss various linguistic issues: ideophones, syllabic nasals, linguistic areas, computation, tonal melody classification, and wh-words.
- Sociolinguistics—Sociolinguistic phenomena in Swahili, signing, Hawaiian, and Japanese are discussed in four of the papers.
- Language teaching and learning—These eight papers cover prosodic modification, note taking, planning in oral production, oral testing, language policy, L2 essay organization, access to dative alternation rules, and child noun phrase structure development.

364pp., ISBN 0–8248–1851–2 $20.

ATTENTION & AWARENESS IN FOREIGN LANGUAGE LEARNING
Richard Schmidt (Editor), 1995

Issues related to the role of attention and awareness in learning lie at the heart of many theoretical and practical controversies in the foreign language field. This collection of papers presents research into the learning of Spanish, Japanese, Finnish, Hawaiian, and English as a second language (with additional comments and examples from French, German, and miniature artificial languages) that bear on these crucial questions for foreign language pedagogy.

394pp., ISBN 0–8248–1794–X $20.

VIRTUAL CONNECTIONS: ONLINE ACTIVITIES AND PROJECTS FOR NETWORKING LANGUAGE LEARNERS
Mark Warschauer (Editor), 1995, 1996

Computer networking has created dramatic new possibilities for connecting language learners in a single classroom or across the globe. This collection of activities and projects makes use of email, the Internet, computer conferencing, and other forms of computer-mediated communication for the foreign and second language classroom at any level of instruction. Teachers from around the world submitted the activities compiled in this volume—activities that they have used successfully in their own classrooms.

417pp., ISBN 0–8248–1793–1 $30.

DEVELOPING PROTOTYPIC MEASURES OF CROSS-CULTURAL PRAGMATICS
Thom Hudson, Emily Detmer, & J. D. Brown, 1995

Although the study of cross-cultural pragmatics has gained importance in applied linguistics, there are no standard forms of assessment that might make research comparable across studies and languages. The present volume describes the process through which six forms of cross-cultural assessment were developed for second language learners of English. The models may be used for second language learners of other languages. The six forms of assessment involve two forms each of indirect discourse completion tests, oral language production, and self-assessment. The procedures involve the assessment of requests, apologies, and refusals.

198pp., ISBN 0–8248–1763–X $15.

THE ROLE OF PHONOLOGICAL CODING IN READING KANJI
Sachiko Matsunaga, 1995

In this technical report, the author reports the results of a study that she conducted on phonological coding in reading kanji using an eye-movement monitor, and draws some pedagogical implications.

In addition, she reviews current literature on the different schools of thought regarding instruction in reading kanji and its role in the teaching of nonalphabetic written languages like Japanese.

64pp., ISBN 0-8248-1734-6 $10.

PRAGMATICS OF CHINESE AS NATIVE AND TARGET LANGUAGE
GABRIELE KASPER (EDITOR), 1995

This technical report includes six contributions to the study of the pragmatics of Mandarin Chinese:

- A report of an interview study conducted with nonnative speakers of Chinese; and
- five data-based studies on the performance of different speech acts by native speakers of Mandarin—requesting, refusing, complaining, giving bad news, disagreeing, and complimenting.

312pp., ISBN 0-8248-1733-8 $20.

A BIBLIOGRAPHY OF PEDAGOGY AND RESEARCH IN INTERPRETATION AND TRANSLATION
ETILVIA ARJONA, 1993

This technical report includes four types of bibliographic information on translation and interpretation studies:

- Research efforts across disciplinary boundaries—cognitive psychology, neurolinguistics, psycholinguistics, sociolinguistics, computational linguistics, measurement, aptitude testing, language policy, decision-making, theses, and dissertations;
- training information covering program design, curriculum studies, instruction, and school administration;
- instructional information detailing course syllabi, methodology, models, available textbooks; and
- testing information about aptitude, selection, and diagnostic tests.

115pp., ISBN 0-8248-1572-6 $10.

PRAGMATICS OF JAPANESE AS NATIVE AND TARGET LANGUAGE
GABRIELE KASPER (EDITOR), 1992, 1996

This technical report includes three contributions to the study of the pragmatics of Japanese:

- A bibliography on speech-act performance, discourse management, and other pragmatic and sociolinguistic features of Japanese;
- a study on introspective methods in examining Japanese learners' performance of refusals; and
- a longitudinal investigation of the acquisition of the particle *ne* by nonnative speakers of Japanese.

125pp., ISBN 0-8248-1462-2 $10.

A FRAMEWORK FOR TESTING CROSS-CULTURAL PRAGMATICS
THOM HUDSON, EMILY DETMER, & J. D. BROWN, 1992

This technical report presents a framework for developing methods that assess cross-cultural pragmatic ability. Although the framework has been designed for Japanese and American cross-cultural contrasts, it can serve as a generic approach that can be applied to other language contrasts. The focus is on the variables of social distance, relative power, and the degree of imposition within the speech acts of requests, refusals, and apologies. Evaluation of performance is based on recognition of the speech act, amount of speech, forms or formulae used, directness, formality, and politeness.

51pp., ISBN 0-8248-1463-0 $10.

RESEARCH METHODS IN INTERLANGUAGE PRAGMATICS
Gabriele Kasper & Merete Dahl, 1991

This technical report reviews the methods of data collection employed in 39 studies of interlanguage pragmatics, defined narrowly as the investigation of nonnative speakers' comprehension and production of speech acts, and the acquisition of L2-related speech-act knowledge. Data collection instruments are distinguished according to the degree to which they constrain informants' responses, and whether they tap speech-act perception/comprehension or production. A main focus of discussion is the validity of different types of data, in particular their adequacy to approximate authentic performance of linguistic action.

51pp., ISBN 0-8248-1419-3 $10.

www.ingramcontent.com/pod-product-compliance
Lightning Source LLC
Chambersburg PA
CBHW081203170426
43197CB00018B/2907